Series Editors: B. Guy P

Political science today is a dynamic discipline. Its substance, theory and methods have all changed radically in recent decades. It is much expanded in range and scope and in the variety of new perspectives – and new variants of old ones – that it encompasses. The sheer volume of work being published, and the increasing degree of its specialization, however, make it difficult for political scientists to maintain a clear grasp of the state of debate beyond their own particular subdisciplines.

The *Political Analysis* series is intended to provide a channel for different parts of the discipline to talk to one another and to new generations of students. Our aim is to publish books that provide introductions to, and exemplars of, the best work in various areas of the discipline. Written in an accessible style, they provide a 'launching-pad' for students and others seeking a clear grasp of the key methodological, theoretical and empirical issues, and the main areas of debate, in the complex and fragmented world of political science.

A particular priority is to facilitate intellectual exchange between academic communities in different parts of the world. Although frequently addressing the same intellectual issues, research agendas and literatures in North America, Europe and elsewhere have often tended to develop in relative isolation from one another. This series is designed to provide a framework for dialogue and debate which, rather than advocacy of one regional approach or another, is the key to progress.

The series reflects our view that the core values of political science should be coherent and logically constructed theory, matched by carefully constructed and exhaustive empirical investigation. The key challenge is to ensure quality and integrity in what is produced rather than to constrain diversity in methods and approaches. The series is intended as a showcase for the best of political science in all its variety, and demonstrates how nurturing that variety can further improve the discipline.

Political Analysis Series
Series Standing Order ISBN 978–0–333–78694–9 hardback
Series Standing Order ISBN 978–0–333–94506–3 paperback
(*outside North America only*)

You can receive future titles in this series as they are published by placing a standing order. Please contact your bookseller or, in the case of difficulty, write to us at the address below with your name and address, the title of the series and one of the ISBNs quoted above. Customer Services Department, Macmillan Distribution Ltd, Houndmills, Basingstoke, Hampshire, RG21 6XS, UK

Political Analysis

Series Editors: B. Guy Peters, Jon Pierre and Gerry Stoker
Editorial Advisory Group: Frank R. Baumgartner, Donatella Della Porta, Scott Fritzen, Robert E. Goodin, Colin Hay, Alan M. Jacobs, Eliza W. Y. Lee, Jonathon W. Moses, Craig Parsons, Mitchell A. Seligson and Margit Tavits.

Research Design in Political Science

Dimiter Toshkov

First published 2016 by
PALGRAVE

Palgrave in the UK is an imprint of Macmillan Publishers Limited, registered in England, company number 785998, of 4 Crinan Street, London N1 9XW.

Palgrave Macmillan in the US is a division of St Martin's Press LLC, 175 Fifth Avenue, New York, NY 10010.

Palgrave is a global imprint of the above companies and is represented throughout the world.

Palgrave® and Macmillan® are registered trademarks in the United States, the United Kingdom, Europe and other countries.

ISBN 978-1-137-34283-6 hardback

ISBN 978-1-137-34282-9   ISBN 978-1-137-34284-3 (eBook)
DOI 10.1007/978-1-137-34284-3

A catalogue record for this book is available from the British Library.

A catalog record for this book is available from the Library of Congress.

Brief Contents

Contents

List of Figures, Tables and Boxes

Figures

Tables

Boxes

Preface

Research, to me, is freedom and fun. It is the freedom to challenge authority with carefully selected evidence and well-crafted arguments. It is the fun of looking things up for yourself and playing around with data to disclose the truth behind. Unfortunately, for many students (and some professionals) of political science, research is anything but freedom and fun. It is mostly anxiety and boredom.

Learning about research methods and design needs to take a large share of the blame for why, to many, research incites boredom and anxiety. With all the '*do this*' and '*don't do that*', '*can't say this*' and '*must say that*', with all its formulas, checkboxes, and lists of best practices, research design seems to be about the exact opposite of freedom. It seems to be about rigour, discipline and rules, strictness and constraints. And, yet, the rigour imposed by research design *is* liberating; it is what makes a study powerful and an argument persuasive.

Of the many textbooks on research design and methods in the social sciences, few convey the power and intellectual liberty research can bring. To me, the great books by King, Keohane, & Verba (1994); Pearl (2000); Ragin (2000); Brady & Collier (2004); Goertz (2006); Elster (2007); Gelman & Hill (2007); Morgan & Winship (2007); Gerring (2012b); and some older classics, do. But, in my experience, many political science students are challenged by trying to learn from these books and fail to appreciate their insights. It is the first major motivation of the current text to make these insights more accessible, while retaining a sufficient degree of rigour.

The second major motivation is to integrate in a balanced way the many valuable lessons dispersed in the existing methodological literature. Some available textbooks are great for learning one kind or aspect of research design, but less so for others. Those that try to be comprehensive often either implicitly privilege one type of research or present a picture that is not entirely coherent. To students, this is confusing. Their reactions from reading the great debates in the methodological literature often remind me of the old joke about the rabbi who had to settle a dispute between two people. The rabbi listened to the first man and said, '*You're right*'. After that, he listened to the second man and said, '*You're right*'. Then the rabbi's wife exclaimed, '*But they cannot both be right!*', to which the rabbi replied after some thought, '*You know, you are right, too!*'

In my view, as reflected in this text, many of the various research designs in political science are in fact compatible as long as their different goals are made clear. Accordingly, my approach is ecumenical and the chapters of this text present, in good faith, descriptive and explanatory, experimental and observational research, large- and small-N, cross- and within-case designs. At the same time, I have tried to delineate where research approaches disagree to avoid the situation the old rabbi got himself into.

* * *

This text has its origin in a course on Research Design that I put together and taught at Leiden University for several years. One learns best by teaching. I certainly did, and these chapters are an effort to partly repay my debt to the students. Many of the ideas introduced in the pages to follow are the direct offspring from my highly rewarding, although never easy, experience in teaching the class and indirect responses to my frustrations from trying to communicate, not always successfully, some of the more involved issues. It is in dialogue with the students that my thinking about research design developed, and the students deserve to receive a big part of the compliments for anything that is good in this text and none of the responsibility for its mistakes.

For several years Brendan Carroll shared with me the experience of teaching the course, and our reflections on how to improve it have left a clear imprint on the text. Discussions with Markus Haverland on various issues of research design were another powerful source of inspiration.

Many colleagues were kind enough to read parts of the book and provide encouragement, as well as comments and constructive criticism. I offer my gratitude to Brendan Carroll, Toon Kerkhoff, Patrick Overeem, Frank Häge, Ellen Mastenbroek, Markus Haverland, Antoaneta Dimitrova, Sandra Groeneveld, Elitsa Kortenska, and Maarja Berkens. Over the years, I have learned a lot about the practice of political science research from my co-authors and research collaborators. From the ones who have not been mentioned yet, I would like to thank in particular Bernard Steunenberg, Anne Rasmussen, and Dave Lowery. My gratitude is further extended to the anonymous reviewers who read and commented on the manuscript prior to publication.

I would also like to thank the Palgrave's editors for political science. Steven Kennedy prompted me to start working on a research design textbook and offered plenty of valuable guidance along the way. Steven retired before the text was complete, and Stephen Wenham oversaw the final revisions and the publication.

Finally, I would like to express my gratitude to my family. Without the support of my wife, Radostina, I would not have been able to complete this project at all, and without her love it would not have been worth it. Our two daughters, Julia and Natialia, who were born while I was busy with the text, provided me with the best of motivations to work and write. To you three I dedicate this book.

Chapter 1

Introduction

This is a guide to designing and evaluating scientific research in the field of political science, broadly defined to include the study of public administration and international relations in addition to the core domains of national and comparative politics.

Research is about providing answers to questions. Political science deals with some of the most pressing questions related to our shared human experience; for example: *How can we devise just and effective political institutions? How can we avoid war between states and among communities within states? What are the intended and unintended effects of public and social policies?*

Research *design* ensures that the answers we provide are as valid as possible and are discovered as efficiently as possible. By studying this text you will learn to devise effective and efficient research plans that can deliver valid inferences and new insight. Moreover, you will become proficient in assessing the research plans and results of others. Being able to develop an informed opinion about the merits and shortcomings of social and political science research is important for every enlightened citizen and even more so for aspiring policy makers, public officials, diplomats, and political commentators. There is much to gain from mastering research design.

Research design is *not* a settled body of abstract theory but an evolving set of rules, recommendations, some theoretical starting points, and many practical considerations. These inform the main steps of the research process: problem definition, theory development, conceptualization, operationalization, variable selection, and case selection. Some of the material discussed in the chapters to follow, such as the problem of causal inference and the rules about case selection, is simply an extension of general logic. Other parts, like the advice on choosing a research question or selecting the right level of analysis, stem mostly from received wisdom and experience.

Research design is a *craft* as much as it is a science. As with any craft, one learns it better from apprenticeship under a master's supervision than from books alone. Nevertheless, this text can help you get started and serve as a reference along the way.

1

What Is Research?

Scientific, or academic, research is about providing answers to questions we do not know the answers to. It would not be re*search* if we already knew the answers. This should be obvious, but I can tell you from experience that it is not. Too often, students, and some scholars as well, want to do research only to show what they think they already know – newspapers have undue influence on what people think, states only care about their geopolitical interests, politicians are corrupt, and so on. These might be the right conclusions, but it is the wrong attitude. Research is about seeking answers with an open mind, not about pursuing confirmation for a pre-existing belief, conviction, or prejudice. In rhetoric you search for the best facts and arguments to support your position; in science you search for the position that can be best supported by the available facts and arguments.

Sometimes we can find the answers we are looking for in an encyclopedia, in other published works, or on the internet. But more often than not available research would not provide satisfactory answers and solutions to our problems, questions, and puzzles. Then we need to complement the existing scholarship by bringing in new observations, evidence, and/or theoretical ideas. This text is not about the first type of research, which can be referred to as a literature review, but about the second type, which not only summarizes what is already known but ventures into the uncharted in order to provide new, more valid and precise answers. Naturally, literature review remains an indispensable step to be performed before original research.

Successful research is as much about asking good questions as it is about providing good answers. We review what can be said about the latter in Chapter 2.

The product of research is often in the form of a written report. Especially in the social sciences it is generally assumed that an academic publication, such as a book, a journal article, or a thesis, is the only possible output of a research project. This need not be the case. For example, the product of research can be a predictive model, which might be described in a paper but could also just reside as a software implementation. Alternatively, it could be an interactive web-based visualization that efficiently describes and explores an original dataset. The product of research could also be a policy evaluation and advice – analysis that directly feeds into the selection of public policies or informs a decision about some political choice. In any case, research output needs to be communicated effectively, and this is one of the issues that Chapter 12 deals with.

What Is Science?

Scientific research is most often conducted in the world of academia, but there are other contexts where research is done. A journalist investigating a case has similar objectives – reconstructing a process or explaining an outcome – to those of a political scientist, although their tools might differ in important respects (see Chapter 10). A political party office that builds a model of electoral behaviour to help increase its vote share would use many of the same techniques that a scientist would use to build a causal model. Political marketing companies rely on the same principles of research design to evaluate the effectiveness of political messages that an academic would use, and pollsters rely on the same theorems that would allow a scientist to estimate public opinion with minimum costs and maximum precision. Policy impact evaluations conducted by a consultancy firm are subject to the same challenges and limitations that an academic study would need to address. A crime detective analysing evidence works in a very similar way to a scientist evaluating competing hypotheses. We can continue adding examples – think about medical doctors, judges, and so on – but the point is clear: the academic world has no monopoly on research.

But if academic scientific research shares so much with other human endeavours, what are the features that distinguish it from journalism, criminal investigations, consultancy, and marketing? It is hard to define science. Scholars have compiled long lists of its essential features (for example, Gerring, 2012b), but the philosophical debates about the nature of science rage on (for a gentle introduction, see Chalmers, 1999). Nevertheless, a minimal definition of science need only highlight two crucial aspects: publicness and adherence to the scientific method.

Publicness

First, academic scientific research is public and open to scrutiny. It is not only that it is almost always, directly or indirectly, funded by the public and that it contributes to the common good rather than to private gain. The requirement of publicness goes to the very heart of what academic science is and how it differs from other applications of the human spirit and intelligence. While a private consultancy would jealously protect the details of its predictive models and algorithms, scientists must always disclose the methods they work with. While political party offices are free to keep any data they use undisclosed, any data employed in an academic project should be made freely accessible. While governments or pharmaceutical companies are not required to publicize any of the prospective evaluations of policies or drugs that they commission (although they should be), scientists have an obligation not to withhold findings based on whether they suit or not their favoured hypotheses or ideological predispositions.

Publicness and transparency of methods, data, and results are indispensable, because science is a community affair. A scientist's work is scrutinized by other academics (his or her peers) and made open to critique by any valid argument. It is the way science proceeds: by collective scrutiny and criticism that allow for gradual improvements and the correction of mistakes; by replicating, adjusting, and, occasionally, overturning what others have done before.

The scientific method

Second, scientific research is subject to the scientific method. Consultancies and political parties are free to use whatever method they choose, including asking oracles and tossing sheep bones, to come up with their models and predictions; scientists are constrained to follow the rules of the scientific method. That would be fine, if all people who would describe themselves as social or political scientists (or even the subset who get paid by a university or a public research institute) would agree as to what these rules are.

A popular account of the scientific method follows the normative ideal put forward by logical positivists. In short, according to this view, scientists start with a theoretically motivated hypothesis, test the hypothesis with data, and proceed to conclusions rejecting the hypothesis that fail the empirical tests (see Popper, 1959; Hempel, 1965; and Chapter 3 of this text for details). This view is seductively clear and simple, but it has been disqualified both as a descriptive (how science works) and as a prescriptive (how science should work) model (Kuhn, 1962; Lakatos & Musgrave, 1970).

In contrast to the views of logical positivists, in contemporary political science most would agree with three major points. First, empirical puzzles and substantive problems are as common starting points for research work as theories. Second, theory testing is not the only and perhaps not the most important goal of science. Third, ideas are not simply tossed in the garbage bin of history at the first sign of empirical inadequacy. But beyond this consensus, there are a wide variety of ways of doing what goes under the label 'political science' research. This pluralism makes it hard to define a version of the scientific method that would satisfy all political scientists. Yet, we need such a definition to complement publicness as the second criterion delineating science from other human activities.

Instead of aiming for a single, all-encompassing definition, let us explore the main disagreements about how to do science within the field of political science. This should give us a sense of the most important issues involved and should also serve to position the current text in these debates.

Currently, the major dividing lines are three: between subjectivists and positivists (in a broad sense, not in the narrow sense of logical positivism); between empiricists and scientific realists; and between qualitative and quantitative researchers.

Subjectivism and positivism (in a broad sense) The most fundamental faultline is the one between subjectivists and positivists. According to subjectivism as a philosophical position, 'the essential, unique characteristic of human behavior is its subjective meaningfulness' (Diesing, 1966, p. 124). Hence, social science cannot be construed as a value-free pursuit of objective truths about the social and political worlds. In fact, the mere possibility of social *science* becomes highly suspect due to the irreducibly subjective nature of human perception and experience. According to subjectivists, research should be concerned with interpreting the meaning of and reflecting on the reasons for human action. Searching for, and even speaking of, social *mechanisms* and *causal* factors is not only futile, it is misguided and offensive. Under this strong subjectivist view – a view that critical theorists, post-modernist philosophers, and many interpretivists, reflectivists, and feminist scholars tend to espouse – social science can only function as radical *social critique*. Blurring the distinction between scientific research and advocacy/social action is detrimental to the practice of both. For an extensive overview of interpretivist political science, see the four volumes edited by Mark Bevir (2000).

In contemporary political science the opponents of radical subjectivists are not objectivists, as you might have expected, but a diverse group of scholars who would agree with many of the basic tenets of subjectivism but would resist taking them too far. For a lack of a better term, we refer to this group as positivists, although they are very different both from the often naive positivism of nineteenth-century social theorists and from twentieth-century logical positivism. In the aftermath of the seminal contributions of philosophers such as W. V. O. Quine (1951) and Thomas Kuhn (1962), cultural anthropologists such as Clifford Geertz (1973), and sociologists such as Peter Berger and Thomas Luckmann (1966), few if any social scientists would defend a completely objectivist worldview. Contemporary positivists – who include among their ranks the majority of political scientists around the world – would, for the most part, accept that social reality is not set in stone, objectively given, and directly accessible to human perception, but constructed and reconstructed through a variety of social processes. In other words, social reality is to a large degree *inter-subjective*. However, and here is the crucial difference from radical subjectivism, social *science* remains possible. Moreover, social science is conceived as a quest for the discovery and explanation of the causes and mechanisms of social phenomena, including individual events as well as broader regularities and patterns. And it is subject to transparent rules, standards, and procedures that ensure reproducibility, reliability, and validity of the results.

Subjectivists would object that one cannot entirely separate the observation of social facts from values and theoretical notions (see Chapter 3). This might be true, but only in an abstract and purely formal philosophical sense. Even if there is no completely objective, value-free point of view, we can still do much to acknowledge and limit the influence of our particular values in doing research on politics and governance. While there may be no final truths, some inferences are still less valid than others (given a context), and the task of research is to discover the 'more' valid ones.

The position taken in this text is pragmatic. That is, we concede the philosophical upper hand to subjectivists but endorse a positivist outlook when it comes to the practice of research in political science. It remains important to be aware of the inherent limitations of social science highlighted by subjectivism, but within the territory outlined by these limitations, there is plenty of scope for scientific research subject to rigorous procedures and explicit standards. The rest of this text is devoted to presenting and explaining the logic of these standards and procedures in the context of research design in political science. For the most part, we will not engage with research in the radical subjectivist tradition (with the exception of one section of Chapter 2). But many of the lessons and insights subjectivists have to offer are implicitly integrated in the text, most notably in Chapters 2 and 4, which deal with, respectively, the status of theory and the process of conceptualization.

Empiricism and scientific realism   The second divide in contemporary political science is less fundamental. While subjectivists and positivists disagree whether social reality can be studied scientifically in the first place, empiricists and scientific realists (who would both be positioned within the positivist camp) disagree about the ways to conduct the study. At a deeper philosophical level, empiricism and realism imply different ontological views (what is reality), but in practice these are only manifested as differences in epistemology (how to know reality). Empiricists deny reality to unobservable entities such as theoretical concepts and causal structures and usually adopt an instrumentalist view of theoretical assumptions. The latter means that the assumptions of our theories and models do not need to be realistic as long as they work; that is, as long as they prove useful for prediction and manipulation. A famous proponent of the instrumentalist view was the economist Milton Friedman, who argued in a much-cited passage (1953, p. 14) that

> the relevant question to ask about the 'assumptions' of a theory is not whether they are descriptively 'realistic,' for they never are, but whether they are sufficiently good approximations for the purpose in hand. And this question can be answered only by seeing whether the theory works, which means whether it yields sufficiently accurate predictions.

Empiricists are interested in successful prediction and intervention and care little about *understanding* the underlying structure of the world that generates the outcomes we observe. Even the mere concepts of 'causes' and 'effects' are suspect, as they cannot be directly observed. By contrast, scientific realists strive for a 'deep understanding' that goes beyond the instrumental uses of scientific results (see Chapter 6).

In contemporary political science it is hard to find 'pure' empiricists, but there are two popular styles of research that are closer to its tenets than to those of scientific realism. First, there is a strong line of theoretical work, very much inspired by economics and game theory, that develops models of political processes (legislative decision-making, for example) on the basis of extremely simplified (hence, instrumental) assumptions about human rationality and the nature of social interactions. But such work is often deployed to provide understanding rather than prediction only, in contrast to the goals of pure empiricism. Second, a lot of research in empirical political science, both in its quantitative and qualitative modes (see below), operates at a level very close to empirical reality, making only modest attempts to link explicitly to theory. Such research can be highly rigorous, but it is primarily interested in describing and exploring political phenomena, such as public opinion, electoral campaigns, or policy implementation, rather than building and testing abstract theoretical models. This second form of empiricism common in political science is content with systematic description and avoids even prediction, let alone deep theoretical understanding of reality, as a scientific goal.

In this text, the focus is on explanation and the discovery of causal structures. Causal structures and concepts, although not directly observable, are considered to be the primary targets of scientific inference. The endorsement of scientific realism is reflected heavily in the structure of this text, which deals extensively with the role of theory development (Chapter 3), operationalization of theoretical concepts into observable variables (Chapter 4), and causal explanations (Chapters 6–11).

Quantitative and qualitative   The third major dividing line in contemporary political science concerns the mode of research. It runs between those who are more quantitatively oriented (that is, they use numbers and statistics) and those who do qualitative research (that is, they do dense case studies) (Goertz & Mahoney, 2012). This rift is largely artificial and receding. According to the approach taken in this text, quantitative and qualitative research are both subject to the same rules and challenges of inference. In short, there is a place for and value in both. Chapter 11 will also explain how they can be fruitfully complemented.

While there need not be *fundamental* (ontological and epistemological) differences between quantitative research, qualitative comparative research, and case studies, there are important differences in what each can achieve. Under such a pragmatic understanding of science, there is a place under the scientific sun for a multitude of research approaches, designs, methodologies, and techniques. Some make heavy use of numbers, others rely exclusively on words to advance an argument; some would trade detail for generality, others would rather have precision rather than a broad scope. These are no reasons to conclude, however, that researchers who use numbers are subject to different rules of logic from those who do not. Many things go, but that does not mean that anything goes.

A minimal definition   In view of the distinctions made above, is there after all *some* way left to define the scientific method that is logically sound and at the same time fair to the actual diversity of practice of scientific research? Instead of looking for a single definition, we are better off considering the various activities that make up the scientific process separately and putting forward some requirements for each step of the way. For example, theoretical ideas should be internally consistent and have clear and precise observable implications that lay the theories open to refutation. Measurement should be done in a replicable way that achieves valid representations of the underlying concepts. Inference from data should respect the rules of logic. Theoretical and empirical work, discovery and testing, exploration and confirmation, description and explanation might be related in more complex ways than suggested by logical positivism, but there are still some rules that govern each of these activities, that, taken together, make up the method of science.

To some, this discussion might appear unsatisfactory – after all, it seems that we have just kicked the bucket down the road by raising new questions, such as 'What is validity?' and 'What are the rules of inference from data?' These further questions, and more, will be dealt with in much greater detail in the chapters to follow.

In sum, science is characterized by (1) being public and transparent and (2) adherence to certain rules regarding theory development, measurement, inference from data, and other aspects of the research process. So, going back to the examples raised earlier in the chapter, how is the work of a political scientist different from that of a journalist? Well, apart from the fact that a journalist usually works under stricter deadlines and has access to different sources of evidence, as long as he or she derives conclusions in a transparent and rigorous way that respects the rules of inference, there need not be a real difference. Similarly, somebody developing an election prognosis model for a private company is doing scientific research, as long as the details of the model can be made public and open to scrutiny.

Why Research Design?

Few would disagree that science and research are important, but do we really need lessons in research design as such? After all, humans have been able to get by just fine without it for many centuries, and progress in some of the sciences pre-dates any focused concern about method and design. Isn't the innate human problem-solving capacity sufficient to guide substantive research? Don't we all just have the rules of inference encoded in our brains, so that an external guide is redundant?

Humans have been shaped by evolution to be excellent problem solvers, indeed. Faced with new information, we are quick to find similarities and differences and to build implicit causal models of how things are connected to each other (Sloman, 2005). People are very good at finding patterns. In fact, we are too good. This section of the chapter will argue, based on a wide selection of evidence, that there are significant biases to human judgement and problem-solving capacity which require us to pay close attention to how we plan and execute research projects, especially in a domain as emotionally and ideologically charged as politics.

Consider the famous Rorschach psychological tests. They involve showing people inkblots and asking them what they represent. Look at Figure 1.1, which shows one example. What do you see? People have little problem projecting all kinds of images onto the *random* spills of

Figure 1.1 *An example of a Rorschach inkblot (Number 1)*

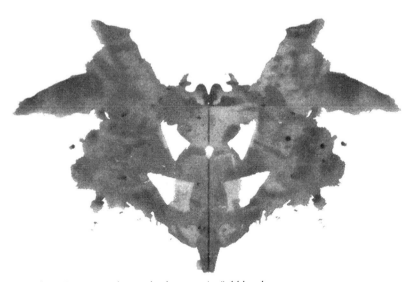

Source: http://www.test-de-rorschach.com.ar/en/inkblots.htm.

ink on paper – bats, butterflies, moths, humans, and so on. It is *too* easy to find patterns in randomness. But what makes the Rorschach test a particularly good example of this tendency is that not only laymen have been fooled into seeing images in inkblots. Psychologists themselves have been fooled into thinking that the types of images people see in the inkblots are predictive of personality traits, sexual orientation, and emotional functioning. The test has been in use since the 1920s, but at the moment there is very little and much contested evidence that any correlations between what people tend to see in the inkblots and the features of their personalities exist (Chapman & Chapman, 1969). What irony! Not only can regular people see patterns in randomness, but trained professionals and scientists can be just as good (or, rather, just as bad).

For a different example of the human tendency to over-interpret randomness and sustain belief in the utility of their efforts even in the face of recurrent evidence to the contrary, consider the following facts about 'expert' judgements in different domains. On average and over a sufficiently long period, the return to investment of a financial portfolio managed by professional fund managers does not beat a simple index that tracks the average performance of the stock exchange (Fama & French, 2010). And this one: predictions made by political scientists, economists, journalists, and other experts about future political events were only a little better than random guessing (or a dart-throwing chimpanzee, if you prefer the image) (Tetlock, 2006). In general, research has concluded that in

> nearly every study of experts carried out within the judgment and decision-making approach, experience has been shown to be unrelated to the empirical accuracy of expert judgments. (Hammond, 1996, p. 278)

On a sidenote, while an individual expert's judgement is often no better than a random guess, averaging expert opinions seems to provide some predictive leverage. And predictive markets have shown how powerful the wisdom of crowds can be in predicting election winners, even if each individual has very limited and biased information.

The examples above are not mere anecdotes. We actually know quite a lot about how human judgement and inference from data systematically deviate from normative models. Over the past few decades, social psychologists and cognitive scientists have catalogued a large number of biases in and limitations to human decision-making, many of which would directly impair the scientific process. The literature on biases and heuristics is enormous and cannot be summarized here – see Kahneman & Tversky (2000) for an introduction or Kahneman (2011) for a popular account – but we can mention just a few examples to give some illustrations of the problems involved.

The *confirmation bias* is perhaps the most relevant for the context of research design. It relates to the human tendency to seek only information that would confirm a guess or a hypothesis but no information that would contradict it. For example, in a famous experiment conducted first by Peter Wason in 1960, people (students actually) were given a short sequence of numbers, 2, 4, and 6, and asked to discover the rule generating the sequence. They were also given the opportunity to test whether any other sequence of numbers fits the rule or not. Most people would quickly recognize a pattern and form the conjecture that the numbers are generated by the rule 'increasing even numbers', and they would ask whether 8, 10, 12, and so on, fit the rule. Crucially, having formed this conjecture, people would *not* test whether sequences of numbers that *would not pass the test if their initial guess is correct* actually do pass the test. So most people would not even ask whether the sequences 1, 2, 7, or 23, 24, 25, or −2.5, 0, 134 fit the rule. But the sequence *could* as well have been generated by the rule 'Any increasing number', or 'Any integer', or even 'Any real number'. By seeking only information that would confirm their pre-established beliefs, people tend to miss alternative explanations that might just as well account for the patterns.

It is a hallmark of the scientific method in contrast to casual human thinking to search for *disconfirmatory* evidence and properly test intuitions and ideas. This attitude needs some reinforcement, since apparently it does not come to us all that naturally, and our innate tendency to quickly find patterns needs to be disciplined. A good research design fulfils these purposes.

There are further limitations to human decision-making – among others, the *hindsight bias* that makes us believe that events have been more foreseeable than they actually were; *framing effects* that lead people to make different inferences from the same information with only some innocuous-looking change of words; the *availability bias* that makes us take into account only the most salient information that comes first to mind; and so on (Kahneman, Slovic, & Tversky, 1982). People have been discovered to be particularly challenged in mentally manipulating probabilities (especially when they are not expressed as natural frequencies), which is of course an essential skill for drawing correct inferences from observations. For example, people would often judge the event 'dying from a heart attack' as less probable than 'being obese *and* dying from a heart attack', although obesity is clearly just one of the possible causes of heart attack, so the first probability cannot *logically* be smaller than the second. This is the so-called *conjunctional fallacy*, studied by Kahneman and Tversky (as discussed in Sloman, 2005, p. 105).

Moreover, even our direct perceptions – of pain, for example (Quattrone & Tversky, 1984) – and memories (Tversky & Marsh, 2000) can be subject to biases and self-deceptions. But if human cognition can be so easily manipulated, scientific measurement and observation surely need to be subject to some rules and standards. Research design helps discipline the process of data collection – what kind of evidence should be sought and how – to overcome the limitations of informal human cognition that have been shown to affect laymen and experts alike.

Importantly for students of political science, human reasoning is subject to specific biases related to the political and ideological predispositions people hold. In one study Brendan Nyhan and Jason Reifler (2010) made people read a misleading claim in a news article and a correction afterwards. When the correction contradicted the ideological beliefs of the subjects, they failed to take it into account, and in some cases the level of misperceptions actually increased in response to the provision of the correct information (the so-called *backfire effect*). And just being smart does not always protect against ideological cognitive biases. As Dan Kahan and colleagues showed (2013), people with higher than average numeracy skills were just as likely to fail to draw the correct inferences from factual data, *when* the inferences would conflict with their prior political ideological beliefs. Political scientists cannot be assumed to be exempt from these common fallacies of human reasoning, which is yet another argument for the importance of research design and rigorous data analysis.

While humans can be too quick to find patterns in random data and to seek confirmatory evidence only, the opposite problem also exists. There are many famous examples where people have failed to recognize real connections in the world despite centuries of experience and observation. Just consider that the modern theory of *plate tectonics* (Oreskes, 2003) was only developed during the 1960s, although it has been possible to observe that the shapes of Africa and South America fit together like two pieces from a puzzle ever since the first good maps of the two regions became available (roughly, since the late sixteenth century). The discovery that *scurvy* – a disease that decimated the crews of thousands of ships for many centuries – is a result of vitamin C deficiency and can be prevented simply by eating fruit came only in the twenty-first century despite several occasions of accidental 'near discoveries' and extremely high pay-offs to finding a cure (see Brown, 2003 for a popular historical account). Even though *cholera* has been with humans since ancient times, it was only in 1854 that a careful data analysis by Dr John Snow revealed that the disease is transmitted by infected water (and it took a few more years to persuade the medical establishment of this fact; see Johnson, 2006).

Medical examples are not the only ones demonstrating our limited capacity to uncover 'real' patterns in observational data, but they are often well-documented. The social sciences as well abound with instances of false findings and real associations that remained hidden and, doubtlessly, there are many still remaining that we have not noticed yet. That is why, in addition to helping the production of *valid* inferences rather than chasing randomness, research design ensures that the process of discovery is as *efficient* as possible, for example by directing focus on theoretically anomalous cases.

As valuable as it is, research design is no substitute for substantive knowledge. It is a framework for the organization of substantive knowledge in the most efficient and effective way to provide novel, valid, and reliable inferences. But no clever design gimmick can salvage a research project that is insufficiently embedded in the substantive problems that animate a research field and that ignores the state of the art of existing scholarship. There are no tips or tricks on offer for choosing a research question, measuring and operationalizing concepts, or developing explanations that can *make up* for a lack of substance. In fact, you can only make full use of the advice offered in this text if you already have enough substantive knowledge to identify, for example, a credible instrumental variable for causal inference (Chapter 8), know which factors to control for (Chapter 9), and know what indicators to use to measure your concepts (Chapter 4). In short, proper research design is a necessary but not a sufficient condition for successful research projects.

But perhaps the importance of research design is a thing of the past, now that we live in an age of big data? Don't the already massive and growing amounts of social, political, and economic data available speak for themselves? Do we still need rules about case selection and sampling now that there are millions of observations at our fingertips? In 2015, the academic journal *PS: Political Science and Politics* ran a symposium addressing precisely these questions (Clark & Golder, 2015). The conclusion was that attention to theory, research design, and the rules of causal inference are even more important in the age of big data. Data are not the same as creative insight, and big data plus computer algorithms cannot substitute for sound thinking, good research design, and careful data analysis. But the *combination* of big data and rigorous social-scientific methods can make a strong contribution to science (Monroe et al., 2015). Current students of political science are well placed to benefit from the synergy between the two.

What Is Political Science?

Little of the discussion so far is specific to the field of *political* science. The limitations to informal human reasoning have general validity, the challenges to define the scientific method concern all social and human sciences, and the value of design to the research process transcends any particular field. So what is it that makes this text one about *political* science, as the title announces?

In fact, not much, apart from the selective emphasis on certain topics (observational designs for causal inference, comparative, and within-case analysis), the relative neglect of others (prediction, machine learning for theory generation), and the choice of most (though not all) examples in the chapters to follow. There is a methodological unity to the social sciences and beyond. Whether one wants to understand the impact of electoral institutions on political polarization, of early childhood education on learning outcomes later in life, of social programs on future employment, or even of exercise on health, the challenges involved and the potential solutions are very similar. This methodological unity is good news, because it means that learning research design in the context of political science gives lessons with a wider field of application (see below). That being said, there are certain peculiarities to research in politics that make some issues more salient than for, say, educational science or economics. But let us first see what *is* political science.

Clearly, political science is the study of politics – voting, elections, and political parties probably first come to mind, especially if you live in a democracy – but it is also more than that. A useful scheme for organizing things is given by the triad *polity, politics, policy*. Political science is about all three and about their connections as well. The *polity* part of the triad concerns the political organization of nations, the fundamental set-up of the state, the forms of government, and the division of power within societies. It is about themes such as federalism, separation of powers, democracy, and so on. International relations focuses on the relationships *between* polities, and studies conflict and cooperation among the nation states and different forms of international governance. The *politics* part of the triad concerns the political process: the way power is exercised within states and societies. It is about decision-making within political institutions, such as legislatures, and the links between institutions, such as those between the president and the parliament; it is also about political competition, citizen representation, and interest mobilization. Finally, the *policy* part of the triad is focused on the making, implementation, and evaluation of public policies – the products of the political process – in various domains, such as the economy, foreign affairs, or the environment.

To see for yourself what contemporary political scientists actually study, have a look at Figure 1.2. The figure shows the 60 most popular keywords of more than 10,000 academic articles published in the top 20 journals in the field of political science between 2003 and 2013. In this word cloud, the size of each word is proportional to its popularity. Clearly, modern political science is mostly concerned with problems of globalization, democracy, conflict, regulation, development, and more – themes that cut through the division between domestic and international politics, and between politics and administration.

In some countries, the study of public policy and administration is institutionalized as a separate discipline, rather than as a subfield of political science. But it makes a lot of sense to consider the study of

Figure 1.2   *A word cloud of the 60 most popular keywords in political science, based on 10,000 articles published in the top 20 journals over the last ten years*

policy, politics, and polity together, not only because of the important substantive linkages and feedbacks between the parts of the triad and the overlap of issues they focus on, but also to highlight the common methodological ground that these academic (sub)fields share. Therefore, this text adopts a rather encompassing view of political science to include not only the 'core' areas of electoral, legislative, and comparative politics but also international relations and public policy and administration.

Such an encompassing view reflects to heart one of the most influential perspectives on politics conceived a system that translates inputs from society into outputs in the form of policies (Easton, 1965). While a narrow view of political science focuses predominantly on the input side and policy analysis on the output side, a comprehensive view needs to encompass the entire process. Take Easton's own famous definition of politics as 'the authoritative allocation of value' for society, which echoes Lasswell's earlier view that politics is about who gets what, when, and how (1936). The societal allocation of value is not completed when an election is held, or when a government is formed, and not even when a law is passed. To understand the real impact of politics on our lives, an integrated perspective is needed that pays attention to the entire cycle from the formulation of social demands to policy implementation.

To reflect an integrated perspective, the substantive themes and examples used to illustrate the problems of research design in this text are balanced between the different subfields of political science.

The study of politics is a science, but also a vocation. In the words of Aaron Wildavsky (1979), political and policy analysis should be about 'speaking truth to power'. It is important to keep this in mind while learning about research design. Unlike politicians, activists, policy entrepreneurs, civil servants, diplomats, or lobbyists, political scientists have an obligation only to truth and not to a particular group, cause, or ideology – this is, after all, what makes their work distinctive and valuable. Each of us harbours some political preferences and predispositions of different colours; the scientific method ensures that these are not allowed to play a role in the process of research other than in motivating the choice of problems to study.

Moreover, science has the obligation to report how much uncertainty surrounds what we take for established truths in politics, governance, and international relations. In the public sphere, it is frequently taken for granted that the experts with the sharper predictions, broader generalizations, louder advice, and more self-assured conclusions are the ones who benefit society the most. Not so. Often, the major contribution of a scientific analysis would be to point out how little we know about the likely effects of a certain policy change, how unpredictable the course of a political event is, or how uncertain the future impact of some new institution could be. Research design and the rules of inference help delineate what can be known from what we can only speculate about, and thus provide a much greater service to society than the illusory confidence of clairvoyants, political pundits, and other 'experts'. The concluding chapter will return to these issues, but now it is time to reveal what the chapters in between are all about.

The Purposes of This Text

The purposes and motivation of this text were already touched upon in the Preface and at the beginning of this chapter, but they require some more explication.

The main purpose is to provide students of political science with the knowledge and tools to develop ideas for original research, and to translate these ideas into potent and workable research designs. By studying this text, you can learn how the research process works, from the initial idea to the final communication of the results. You can also get a comprehensive understanding of the menu of available research design options, as well as the ability to assess their major strengths and shortcomings. Taken together, detailed knowledge of the research process and the skills to make the right design choices are powerful assets.

The practical utility of these assets depends on the personal and professional interests of the reader. At the very least, it includes the preparation of research proposals for student papers and graduate theses; for academic articles and scientific reports; for grants, tenders, and project applications.

Knowing how to design research implies that you will have the knowledge and tools to assess the research results and plans of others. We are all much more often consumers than producers of research. The ability to evaluate claims and inferences made in academic publications or the press is an important ability to have. By studying the material in these chapters, you can learn which claims to trust and which to ignore, and how to assess the real rather than the reported uncertainty of scientific and other conclusions. Altogether, this amounts to a significant upgrade of general critical thinking skills.

There are three main distinctive features of this book. First, the book provides a balanced coverage of descriptive and explanatory, experimental and observational, large-N (statistical) and small-N (comparative), cross-case and within-case (single case) research in a single text.

Second, the book delivers an integrated and consistent picture that not only catalogues different ways of doing research but puts the various designs into a coherent framework. Many edited volumes on research design have excellent individual chapters, but which, however, do not always easily fit well together.

Third, the book makes the lessons of research design as accessible as possible without sacrificing too much of the depth and subtlety of the arguments. To this end, I have avoided any specialized notation, formalizations, equations, and even footnotes and endnotes. I have also used plenty of examples throughout the chapters. The examples are of two types. The first consists of short, 'toy' examples about very general problems that most people can relate to without having a specialized background, such as the links between wealth and voting. The purpose of these is to quickly illustrate a point or add some substantive 'meat' to an abstract discussion. The second type consists of examples from actual published research, introduced in more depth and at a greater resolution. These serve to show how research design problems are tackled in a real-life setting and to give a taste of how various modes of research in political science work. The book is also complemented by an extensive index that can help orientation in the material and that showcases the cross-links among the various topics and issues throughout the chapters.

Of course, no single text on research design and methodology can present a detailed and comprehensive picture of the variety of research in contemporary political sciences. The major limitations of the current one are related to the level of operation, the relative neglect of philosophical issues in favour of more applied ones, and the lack of coverage of techniques for data analysis.

It is customary in military theory to divide the planning of a military campaign into strategic, operational, and tactical issues. Using this analogy, this text is positioned at the level of grand research design *strategy* and at the intermediate *operational* level that connects strategy and tactics. But the minute *tactical* choices involved in implementing any single research strategy and operation are outside our scope. There is a simple reason for that – the details of *any* particular design could easily fill up not a chapter but a book of their own.

The focus on strategy is appropriate because strategy has primacy over tactical issues. The choice of research question, goal, approach, and design (which are all covered in the following chapters) are all made before the choice of data collection and analysis technique, which is also more easy to adapt in the course of a project.

Often, asking a sharp question and linking it with an appropriate research design will make data analysis a breeze. When data analysis is difficult, it is frequently because the design and its implementation have been weak (resulting in noncompliance, missing observations, unbalanced comparisons, wrong level of analysis, noisy measures, selection bias, and so on). While you can always master a specific data-analytic technique once you have collected the data, learning the lessons of research design at that stage would often mean having to start all over again.

Who is this text for?

The primary audience for this text is *students* of political science. As noted, political science is broadly conceived to include the study of public policy and administration, as well as international relations.

The second target group is *professionals* who need to use or commission new research in their daily line of work. For example, policy makers might need an impact assessment of a proposed regulation, government officials might need to know what the public thinks about a social problem, party functionaries might need advice on campaign strategies, and political commentators might need an election forecast. Of course, all these assessments, surveys, advice, and models would be products of research and as such subject to the same requirements, challenges, and limitations as an academic research article or a graduate student paper. Studying this text one can learn why randomized controlled trials would usually provide a better impact assessment than ex post observations of an enacted regulation (Chapter 7), why convenience samples might provide a distorted view of what the public thinks (Chapter 5), how theoretical modelling can inform strategic choices (Chapter 3), and how a forecast is different from an explanation (Chapter 6).

But making decisions informed by scientific research is not a privilege and a requirement for public officials only. I like to think that all citizens, no matter what their educational background or profession, can benefit from some knowledge of the way (social) science works, if only to appreciate its limitations. Those of us lucky enough to live in liberal democratic societies can freely debate and make proposals for the improvement of our political institutions and public policies. A lot of these ideas, debates, and proposals could, and should, be informed by results of scientific research to a much greater degree than is currently the case. The increasing availability of free open political data and the spread of the internet mean that even citizens in non-democratic states can consult, make use of, and build informed opinions on the basis of facts and scientific evidence.

Political science is no rocket science. Its results, when properly communicated, should be accessible to any intelligent citizen with a minimum of substantive background in the social sciences and some awareness of the design issues involved in the practice of research.

Moreover, as people living in the information society, we are all bombarded with journalistic interpretations of scientific results about the effects of new drugs, cosmetics, health regimes, and exercise routines; of educational interventions, parenting styles, and student evaluations; of macroeconomic policies, gun control laws, and foreign policy interventions; of genes, history, and culture. Often, the journalistic interpretations exaggerate, misrepresent, or fail to point to critical assumptions of the underlying studies. Although this is a text about political science research, one can take many valuable lessons about how to critically evaluate scientific claims coming from a wide range of disciplines. The fundamental problem of causal inference and the more specific issues of random variation, unrepresentative samples, underpowered studies, confounding, self-selection, reversed causality, measurement validity, generalization, and more, are similar no matter whether the context is research on voting, international conflict, and bureaucratic delegation, or epidemiology, social psychology, and economics. The critical thinking skills that this text is designed to sharpen have wider applicability than political science research proper.

There is very little prior background assumed for understanding this text. If you have had a basic course in research methods that introduced concepts such as variable, sample, population, and the like, you will probably find it somewhat easier to think about research design in these terms than if you encounter them for the first time here. And some familiarity with philosophy would certainly ease comprehending a few themes (such as the nature of causality or counterfactual reasoning). But none of this is strictly speaking required, because I try to explain potentially unfamiliar concepts and ideas along the way.

Though the chapters link the foundations of research design to broader philosophical concerns about how we can know anything and what it means to explain, our aim always remains pragmatic: to derive useful lessons and clear some ground for the applied political scientist, rather than to resolve or even comprehensively present the inevitably knotty philosophical debates involved.

This text stops where the collection and analysis of data begin (and picks up again when the results from the analysis are clear and need to be communicated). One cannot learn how to chart a plot, run a logistic regression, perform a qualitative comparative analysis, or conduct an effective elite interview from these chapters. Again, the reason is that each data collection and analysis technique deserves a book of its own.

Nevertheless, it is quite impossible to understand the rationale of different research designs unless one has at least a rough idea of the subsequent step of data analysis. Many research design decisions are taken in view of the requirements, limitations, or assumptions of different data-analytic techniques. You need to be aware that certain problems of design, such as missing data or censored observations, can be addressed during the stage of data analysis and do not have to mean the end of a project. For these reasons and more, I introduce in very broad strokes how analysis of experimental, large-N, comparative, and within-case data proceeds in the respective chapters. In sum, this is not a text about research *methods* as such, but about research *design* proper.

The Way Ahead

There are two different ways to work with this text. One is to first read the general chapters (1–4, 6, and 12) and then, if you know what you need, focus on a specific class of designs (see below). The other is to follow the order of the chapters to get acquainted with all the options before you settle for one, and then go back to study it in detail. In any case, here is a brief summary of what each chapter deals with.

This chapter explained what research design is and argued for its importance. Chapter 2 delves further into the differences between normative and positive; theoretical and empirical; descriptive, predictive, and explanatory; and theory-building, theory-applying, and theory-testing research. These distinctions are fundamental, as all other decisions about design are guided and constrained by the type and objective of the research project. The chapter also looks into the more practical side of choosing and sharpening a research question once the overall topic, type, and objective of the research have been settled.

Whatever the type of research, theory has a role to play. Chapter 3 deals with the place and functions of theory in the research process. It clarifies the structure of explanatory theories and presents a few different ways in which theory can be developed deductively. The chapter discusses the criteria that good theories should meet and offers some practical considerations about choosing, developing, and using theory in political science research.

Chapter 4 explains how you get from theoretical ideas to empirical observations. It introduces the idea of a 'concept' and shows how to translate abstract concepts into observable and measurable factors and variables via the processes of conceptualization and operationalization. Various criteria and challenges for fruitful conceptualization and valid operationalization are introduced and critically discussed.

Chapter 5 focuses on measurement and descriptive research. Description exists in various modes, and the chapter presents in some detail several quite different ways of doing descriptive research in political science. First, quantitative description via surveys is discussed. Since surveys and other sources of quantitative data play an important role in contemporary political science research, the chapter outlines some common methods and tools for the efficient analysis and presentation of quantitative empirical data. Second, ethnographic thick description via participant observation is presented. Third, the peculiarities of historical description based on archival and other documentary sources are noted.

While description is indispensable, explanation remains a primary goal of scientific research. Therefore, the focus of the remaining chapters is on explanatory theoretically informed empirical research. Chapter 6 prepares the ground for understanding the various research designs for causal inference presented in Chapters 7–11. It introduces the notions of mechanistic causal explanation and counterfactual causality. These allow us to express clearly the fundamental challenge of causal inference and to outline some potential solutions pursued in the remainder of the text.

The first class of designs for causal inference, presented in Chapter 7, are experimental designs, not only because of their growing importance for political science but also because they show very clearly what the problems of making causal claims are. The chapter introduces the logic of experimental research and explains why random assignment is so powerful. The basic design elements of experiments are also covered, including choosing the level of analysis and the sample size. Furthermore, various complications that arise in practice are introduced together with some ways of dealing with them. The chapter presents in detail several real applications of (different types of) experiments in political science research and concludes by discussing the limitations of the experimental approach.

Chapter 8 is the first of several to deal with observational designs and discusses large-N quantitative research for causal inference. Four distinct approaches to identifying causality in large-N research are presented – natural experiments, instrumental variables, mediation, and conditioning. In addition, the chapter deals with the issue of estimating causal effects (and the related problem of statistical significance) and goes on to discuss design questions such as choosing the level of analysis and case selection.

Chapter 9 considers comparative research approaches when only a few cases are available for observation. It argues that comparative designs are a hybrid, mixing cross-case logic and within-case analysis. The most prominent strategies for case selection in comparative designs are discussed and the extension to qualitative comparative analysis and fuzzy sets is made.

Chapter 10 is about single-case studies. Within-case analysis relies on a different rationale to derive proper explanatory accounts, and the chapter deals with its logic, strengths, and limitations. It focuses in particular on the various types of evidence that assist making causal claims about single cases.

Chapter 11 shows how different designs and research methods can be combined to improve inference. Furthermore, the chapter considers how political science proceeds in the long term with a focus on the connections between theory and empirical analysis in the framework of research programs.

Finally, Chapter 12 focuses on how to effectively communicate results from scientific research in the field of political science. The questions of structuring research reports and academic writing style are considered. This is the place where special attention is paid to ethical issues of research, and where we look back to reflect on the dialectical relationship between normative questions and the answers empirical political science research can provide.

Chapter 2

Types of Research and Research Questions

What is good governance? How can the functioning of democracy in Africa be improved? Is supporting democracy in foreign countries just and justifiable? What is the impact of foreign aid on democratic consolidation? Will India remain a democracy 20 years from now? Is South Africa a democracy? Is an ethnically diverse country more likely to have a weak government than an ethnically homogeneous one?

It is questions like these that motivate people to study politics, international relations, and public administration. We all want political science to provide us with knowledge about how the political world works and how to improve it. But there are important differences between the various questions one can pose: while some ask for descriptions, factual statements, or predictions, others focus on possible causes and effects, and yet others deal with what is considered good, moral, and just. Different types of research are appropriate for answering these different types of questions.

The first part of this chapter provides a general, low-resolution, analytic map of the terrain of contemporary political science in order to present the major research types and goals. It explains what makes normative questions fundamentally different from positive ones, and goes on to clarify that the latter can be addressed with purely theoretical analysis or with research that engages with the empirical world. Empirical research itself can have various goals: description, prediction, and explanation are currently considered the three most important ones. Explanatory research in its turn brings together projects that aim to generate, to test, or to apply theories.

Knowing the various options in the menu of political science research types and goals is important, but it is only the first step in the process of selecting a research question. The second part of this chapter provides some advice, rules, tricks, and tips on choosing and sharpening an appropriate research question. Well-thought out and well-formed questions can guide effective research projects that can contribute to our principal goals of understanding and improving the social and political worlds.

Normative and Positive Research

The most fundamental distinction related to the types of research questions one can pose is that between normative and positive research. Normative, or ethical, questions deal with what *ought to be*, while positive questions deal with what *is* (or used to be, or will be). Normative issues are those examining the moral order of the world, and normative research seeks to find answers to what is good, appropriate, just, fair, or otherwise desirable. Normative statements claim that some political system (say, direct democracy) is better than another (say, representative democracy), that some course of action (say, economic sanctions) is more justified than another (say, military intervention), that one behaviour (say, taking a bribe for delivering a public service) is less appropriate than another (say, taking a salary for working in a public office). In other words, normative questions are those about ethics, values, and value judgements. Normative research is prescriptive, while positive research is descriptive (or predictive, or explanatory).

Positive questions focus on describing, understanding, explaining, or predicting reality *as it is*. Value judgements are suspended. The focus is squarely on empirical phenomena, on the links between them, and on the links between empirical phenomena and theoretical concepts. Relationships between abstract concepts can also be studied positively, if no ethical judgements are implied. Our focus in the remaining chapters is on positive rather than on normative research. You might feel disappointed, if the reason you got into studying politics was to learn how to improve governance and accountability in your country or some other highly noble goal. But there is no reason to despair. Although normative and positive objectives should be kept separate in the process of research, they remain intrinsically connected. In particular, normative concerns inevitably drive the selection of the research question, and the conclusions from positive research have normative implications as well. In short, results from positive scientific research bear on normative issues. (Do not confuse *positive* research, which is all research that is not normative, irrespective of the specific form or method, with *logical positivism*. The latter is a particular philosophy of science emphasizing the testing of deductively derived hypotheses and associated with the names of Karl Popper and Carl Hempel. We briefly mentioned logical positivism in Chapter 1 and shall discuss it in more depth in Chapter 3.)

At this point an example might help you grasp the relationship between normative and positive research. Imagine that you study politics with the primary motivation to make the political system of your own country better. Normative research, on the one hand, can clarify what 'better' means, single out characteristics necessary for a 'good' political system (equality, efficiency, responsiveness, accountability, and so on), illuminate trade-offs between some of these (for example, accountability versus efficiency), or possible contradictions within any ideal of a 'good' polity. Positive research, on the other hand, can show how certain elements of a political system (say, the electoral system or the rules for party financing) influence other elements of the system and bear on normative notions like equality or accountability. A purely positive empirical study of the impact of majoritarian versus proportional electoral systems on the representation of national minorities has huge normative implications about the design of 'good' political systems, *provided* we agree that minority representation is a characteristic of any 'good' political system. Positive research cannot contribute to the question whether minority representation is indispensable for a just polity, but it can show that a proportional electoral system increases the chances of minorities being represented at the highest political level. (For actual empirical studies of the link between electoral systems and representation, see Lijphart, 1994; Canon, 1999; Karp & Banducci, 2008. For normative ones, see Guinier, 1994; Reilly, 2001; Anderson et al., 2005.)

Figure 2.1 represents visually the relationships between normative values, theoretical concepts, empirical facts, and the types of research that connect them. Research focused on relationships between values or between values and theoretical concepts is normative. Research that studies relationships between theoretical concepts (but without reference to values), that explores links between empirical facts, or that analyses the interconnections between both facts and concepts is positive in nature. As we will see shortly, at a deeper philosophical level the ontological distinctions between values and facts and between theory

Figure 2.1 *Research and the normative, theoretical, and empirical domains*

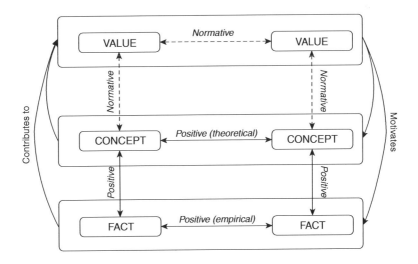

and facts are not always absolute. Yet, for the practice of political science research, it remains important to hold the distinctions illustrated in Figure 2.1 in mind – both when positioning your own research and when evaluating the research of others. The figure also reminds us that normative issues motivate positive research, the results from which in their turn contribute to normative discussions.

Why is the distinction between normative and positive research so important? In a nutshell, because it helps separate subjective value judgements ('democracy is good') from objective statements about facts ('voter turnout at the 2012 US presidential elections was 57.5 percent') or concepts ('majoritarian electoral systems increase turnout'). Keeping normative and positive elements of a research question separate ensures that we leave our subjective value-ridden judgements and opinions at the door and enter the research process with an open mind. Scientific research relies on objectivity, impartiality, and an open mind in order to produce valuable results. The best way to ensure that research results will contribute to normatively important social problems is to leave your own conceptions of what is right and what is wrong for society out of the research process. We can never completely transcend our own subjectivity, since part of the normative fabric of society is encoded in the language we use and the mental constructs we employ. Nevertheless, social researchers should make a conscious effort to prevent normative elements from creeping into positive research questions. Otherwise, the line between advocacy and analysis becomes blurred, with negative consequences for both. Even the most devoted advocate of, say, guaranteed minimum income for the poor would benefit from a neutral, positive, scientific study of the impact of such a social intervention on, say, work motivation, whatever the outcome of the research turns out to be.

Normative political science is closer to philosophy, while positive political science emphasizes its affinities with the other social sciences, such as economics and sociology. Normative political science is much older, with its roots stretching back into antiquity and beyond. Moreover, normative political analysis often proceeds as a commentary on the classic texts of Plato and Aristotle, Hume and Lock, Rousseau and Montesquieu, Kant and Hegel. The systematic positive, and especially empirical, study of political and administrative affairs must be considered much younger, if one discounts the occasional reference to purported empirical patterns and regularities in the classic texts and the astute observations of authors such as Alexis de Tocqueville.

In summary, positive research is usually motivated by normative concerns and its results contribute to ethical discussions, but in itself it is (or at least should be) free from subjective, value-ridden judgements and biases. Sometimes it can be quite tricky to uncover the normative cloak of positive research questions. For example, the question '*What is the optimal level of taxation?*' is a normative one, despite the disguise of the phrasing ('*what is*'). Words like 'optimal', 'appropriate', 'rational', 'normal', and 'natural' often signal hidden normative assumptions that should be closely scrutinized, and frequently the research question would need to be rephrased to fit a positive research project. For example, the question above can be reformulated as '*What level of taxation minimizes social inequality?*', which would make a positive research project (either empirical or theoretical, see below) possible. Importantly, the revised question leaves it to the reader to decide whether social equality as such is valuable or not.

The fundamental distinction between normative and positive social science is rooted in the value/fact dichotomy – the gulf that separates a statement like '*Wealth is bad*' from a statement like '*John is wealthy*'. Positive social and political sciences strive for an objective and disinterested point of view. Although the value/fact dichotomy has been challenged by modern philosophers (Putnam, 2002) and anthropologists (for example, Fabian, 2002), who claim that in some cases the difference is not clear-cut, the point remains that positive science should strive to eliminate value judgements in the course of research. At the very least, researchers should try to disentangle the normative (prescriptive) and positive elements of their research plans and ideas.

Positive scientists in their turn have challenged the claim of normative research to scientific status. Since any ethical system is anchored by some fundamental premises (whether God-given or not) that are beyond scientific reasoning and empirical verification, does it follow that normative work falls outside the realm of science? My position is that, although the first principles of any ethical system cannot be proven, the exploration and analysis of the ethical system itself can be a valuable and useful academic endeavour, and the question whether it is a science or part of philosophy need not concern us too much.

All *recommendations* for adopting certain policies, making some decisions, or taking particular actions inevitably have implicit or explicit normative components. Political scientists frequently engage in providing recommendations and other forms of policy-relevant advice. It is critical to be clear about what part of the advice is based on positive, scientific knowledge about relationships between facts and concepts and what part is based on the belief that some values are worth striving for.

To avoid any confusion, we should note that values and norms can be studied in a positive research framework. On can ask, for example, what are the prevalent values of public officials working in contemporary Western governments (for example, Andersen et al., 2013), or what accounts for the shifting conceptions of corruption during the early modern period (Kerkhoff, Kroeze, & Wagenaar, 2013). Although the object of inquiry is *values*, the research itself remains positive, so long as it does not take sides in the debate as to which values are better or worse.

Little can be said about research design in the context of normative research. Normative work proceeds mostly as philosophizing and, as mentioned already, commentary on the canon of great political thinkers. Although thought experiments and other rhetorical devices are regularly used, there is no design template apart from the general application of logic and rhetoric. Nevertheless, Chapter 3 on (explanatory) theory development and Chapter 4 on concepts and operationalization might prove useful to those embarking on normative research projects. Anthony Weston's book (2008) is an accessible introduction to building (normative) arguments, and the chapters in Leopold & Stears (2008) provide further guidance to the field. (See also the suggestions for further reading at the end of this chapter.)

Reading political science books and scientific journals, it is easy to get confused about what is normative and what is positive, yet theoretical, research (more on positive theoretical research below and in Chapter 3). Under the heading of 'political theory' we find, more often than not, *normative* political theory: theory that discusses what is good and just but that does not provide any hypotheses, explanations, or predictions about political phenomena. Normative and positive theoretical research share a lot, but the difference in their goals renders them distinct. While all normative research is necessarily theoretical, the reverse is not true: theory can attempt to reconstruct the world as it is, not as it ought to be. Having clarified the nature of normative research, we are now ready to exit the realm of normative inquiry and enter the huge and varied domain of positive research.

Theoretical and Empirical Research

In the context of political science, positive research engages with the empirical world most of the time. Nevertheless, it is important to clarify that positive political theory exists as a distinct type of research. It deals with the rigorous analysis of the properties of abstract concepts, such as democracy, governance, and power, and the relationships between them. It starts and ends in the world of abstractions. But, unlike normative research, it does not attach any moral values to the abstract concepts it analyses nor does it automatically endorse ethical implications of the analytical results. For example, positive theoretical research can clarify that no voting rule can satisfy a certain number of requirements for aggregating individual preferences (Arrow, 1951), but it would not argue which voting rule is 'best' in a normative sense.

Positive theoretical research can be conducted for its own sake, as in the example above, or as a component in broader research projects and programs that engage with the empirical world. In the latter case, it is a phase of the research process with the primary aim of deriving

Figure 2.2 *Theory development and the research process*

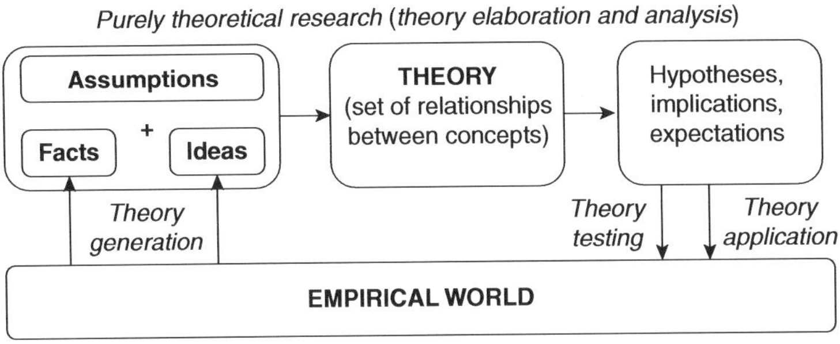

empirical implications from initial, often vaguely expressed, theoretical ideas. This sort of theory development will be discussed at length in Chapter 3, and several different tools for theoretical analysis will be illustrated with examples from real-world research in political science. Theory development is indispensable for explanatory research, which, as we shall see shortly, is one major type of empirical research, next to descriptive and predictive. As Figure 2.2 shows, in the context of explanatory empirical research, theory development is a stage that sits between (1) the inductive generation of initial theoretical ideas from empirical patterns and (2) the deployment of theoretical propositions to test the theory against new data and to apply the theory to explain individual cases and discover novel patterns in the empirical world. But remember that purely theoretical analysis can be conducted in its own right, outside the context of larger empirical projects, as well.

In essence, theoretical analysis pursues the implications of a number of premises to their logical end. The logic is deductive. The aim is to derive a set of statements (also called propositions) that are internally consistent and logically related with each other. Every theory is based on premises, which might come from established facts or from assumptions. Analysing the premises, theoretical analysis identifies all the propositions that can be deduced from them. Some of these propositions may provide implications about the empirical world. In this case they will be regarded as hypotheses, which can be empirically tested.

There is one major reason why it is important to distinguish between purely theoretical research and analysis, and empirical research in its many manifestations. Namely, the truth of theoretical statements is of a different nature from the truth of statements with empirical content. The former has been designated as analytic, and the latter as synthetic. The truth of analytic statements is derived only and entirely from their premises and the rules of logic. If the premises are true, the conclusions are true, provided that the rules of logic are respected when deriving the conclusions from the premises. In this sense, all truthful theoretical statements are either definitions or tautologies. Importantly, their truth value is bound to the specific framework of assumptions on which the theory is built. That is, starting with different assumptions, different conclusions might be declared true. (The distinction between analytic and synthetic propositions is mostly associated with the philosophical school of logical positivism. For a powerful critique, see Quine, 1951.)

Once acquainted with theoretical research in its normative and positive guises, it is easy to define empirical research: it is any research that makes reference to real-life phenomena and empirical facts. Theory still plays a role, but the research goes beyond the world of abstractions. Clearly, reference to reality may take many forms – description, interpretation, exploration, explanation, prediction, or theory generation, to name but a few. The commonality is the idea that *some* form of knowable 'reality' exists out there beyond the world of abstract mental constructs. And this reality can be, and indeed needs to be, described, interpreted, and explained. While Chapter 3 deals with the place of *theory* in the research process, the bulk of this text (Chapters 4–11) presents in depth the varieties of theoretically informed *empirical* research. But before we get into a detailed exploration of specific research designs, let us get a bird's eye view of the terrain of empirical research.

Descriptive, Predictive, and Explanatory Research

Figure 2.3 presents the various empirical research types as branches of a tree (formally, this classification is called a taxonomy; see Chapter 3). The figure shows only the big branches (for now); individual research designs are still out of sight. As you can see, descriptive, predictive, and

Figure 2.3   *A taxonomy of major types of research in political science research*

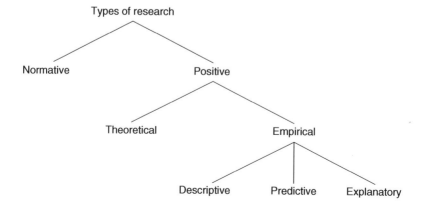

explanatory research get their own branches (exploration is not mentioned separately, because it can be considered an advanced form of description).

Once the mode of research (purely theoretical or empirically informed) is set, the research objective becomes key once more. Once the objective is specified, the appropriate research design follows, given the practical constraints of available resources and the state of prior knowledge. The main objectives positive empirical research might have are description, prediction, and explanation. All of them bring insight into a topic, but they have different emphases defined by the goal of the researcher. All shed light on a problem, but the focus varies. While description and prediction are content with collecting patterns of empirical facts and projecting these patterns into the future, explanatory research seeks for a deeper structure connecting the facts. Clearly, explanation is impossible without prior description, prediction is doomed without some understanding of the underlying causality, and description is of little use if it cannot provide insights about the deeper casual structure of the social world. In practice, real-life research projects combine elements of these three modes of inquiry. But usually one ambition dominates. And it is still useful to consider description, prediction, and explanation first in isolation before you get proficient enough to juggle them in your own work.

Description

Let us start with description, which deceivingly appears to be the simplest form of empirical inquiry. Description attempts to describe the world as it is, but *scientific* description goes beyond simple fact collecting. When describing, one not only lists the attributes of an item (India has competitive elections; the Ministry of Defence has six directorates), but also assigns facts into classes or categories (India is in the category 'democracies'; the Ministry of Defence is in the category 'bureaucracies'). And description does not collect just *any* facts but those that are relevant for interpreting a case and that can be used as evidence in subsequent theory building or hypothesis testing. It is easy to see that description is not completely removed from theory and normative concerns: the categories that we use are theory-given and laden with values, and what could constitute relevant facts and evidence is informed by existing theories as well.

As do explanation and prediction, description also relies on *inference* – making valid statements about the whole from observing only a part. For example, in survey research we want to make inferences about a population (for example, of France), but we can only observe a limited number of (French) people. Similarly, in historical research we want to draw conclusions about a long time period by studying a limited number of archival documents. Even in anthropological work – the academic discipline most exclusively associated with description – we can only observe a local neighbourhood or a remote tribe for a limited amount of time, but we want to generalize about their *typical* patterns of life and conflict. Inference from a sample of people or documents to a population or something more abstract such as a time period is necessary not only because of the limited resources available for research but also because of diminishing returns to describing ever more subjects and items in ever greater detail. After a while, each additional person we interview, document we consult, or week we spend with the natives provides for only a small marginal improvement of the descriptive knowledge we have already accumulated. Hence, inference is indispensable. How to provide valid and reliable descriptive inferences has been a subject of intense scholarship and will be extensively discussed in Chapter 5.

Descriptive research can have various goals and is performed in practice in very different modes – from historical archive work to ethnographic participant observation to standardized large-N surveying of populations. It can be focused on the comprehensive description of a single case in great detail and along many dimensions. But it can also deal with the description of a collection of cases for a small number of variables; with classifying, sorting, ranking, and exploring in more complex ways the distributions of a small number of traits in a population.

Scientific description is not confined to analysing individual facts and processes in isolation. It can study how different aspects or dimensions of a phenomenon tend to go together or cluster in a population of cases (description as data reduction). It can compare the distribution of some variable across different populations of interest. And the discovery of *associations* between social phenomena and events is also part of description. Consider the statement: 'Democracies tend *not* to go to war with each other.' Expressed as it is, the statement is purely descriptive: it points to the association between one type of political system and the (non-) occurrence of wars. No causality is implied (see Chapter 6). Of course, the statement contains the seeds of a causal story – the association invites hypotheses about why democracies happen to stage wars with each other less often. Perhaps democratic leaders are more accountable to the generally peace-loving ordinary citizens, or maybe the experience of past wars makes countries both less likely to be democracies and more likely to be belligerent in the future, or perhaps nature plays tricks on us by throwing in a random association without any causal story behind it. (For an overview of the literature on democratic peace, see Gartzke & Weisiger, 2013.) Descriptive work cannot distinguish among these possibilities. But, as in this example, good descriptive research contains the seeds of something more and inspires theories and the search for explanations.

Unlike other books on research methods and design in political science, this text does not consider *exploration* as a distinct research goal because there is a great overlap between exploration and description. Exploration can be regarded as an advanced form of description, which probes for possible explanatory hypotheses, but in a more unstructured (playful, if you will) way than explanatory theory-building or theory-testing empirical research. The importance of this *play* with data and ideas for generating discoveries and explanations is severely underestimated in the methodological literature.

Prediction

What description does for the present, prediction does for the future. Prediction has close affinity with description, because the extrapolation of information from the present to the future has much in common with the extrapolation from a sample to a population. Prediction involves projections about empirical phenomena and processes in the future. Forecasting is a near synonym. As defined here, prediction can be conducted without explicit understanding of the causal data-generating process. In other words, prediction is distinct and rather different from explanation (Toulmin, 1961). For example, we can make predictions about the likely winner of the next presidential election on the basis of current public opinion polls and without any clue about the possible determinants of individual votes. In principle, all we need to make the forecast is some method of combining current opinion polls and perhaps the historical movements of public opinion. (See, for example, the site of data scientist and forecaster Nate Silver 'FiveThirtyEight' http://fivethirtyeight.com/.)

It is unlikely that such naive data extrapolations would make, for very good predictions, but the point remains – prediction is qualitatively different from causal explanation. Note the asymmetry: while casual explanations normally entail predictions, the reverse is not true – predictions can be entirely data-driven and need not be based on a causal model. (In some cases, explanatory models can suggest that prediction is not possible; see below.) In reality, one needs at least a rudimentary understanding of the causal process in order to make even remotely successful predictions. To continue the presidential election forecast example, we could adjust our current opinion poll-based projection by including information on the likely future state of the economy, if we suspect that the state of the economy has something to do with the voting decisions people make.

We mentioned above that in principle all causal explanations imply predictions. This stems from the fact that explanatory theories identify the relevant causal factors and mechanisms that produce outcomes and, if theories are successful, by plugging in new values for the explanatory factors, we can derive relevant predictions. But sometimes, even if we have reasonably good explanatory theories, prediction remains outside our reach. This can be due to several reasons.

First, some scholars posit an irreducible indeterminacy at the fundamental level of physical reality. At the quantum level, outcomes are only probabilistic (see Omnes, 1999). Using the quantum indeterminacy as an analogy, we can argue that, even if we understand the reasons for individual and social action, we can only arrive at probabilistic predictions.

Second, sometimes we can understand the causal mechanisms relatively well but still remain impotent to predict due to the nature of the process producing the events. Think about the prediction of earthquakes: we have a rather good understanding of the mechanisms and processes that produce earthquakes – the movement of tectonic plates, the accumulation of pressure, and the release of energy. Nevertheless, the only thing we can predict, or forecast, is that some areas are more prone to earthquakes than others and that in the very long term the distribution of earthquakes of different sizes might follow a certain pattern (Schorlemmer, Wiemer, & Wyss, 2005). But successful prediction of when and where an earthquake of a certain size will strike remains as elusive as ever. (For a popular account of earthquake prediction, see Shuker, 2000, or Hough, 2010.) Interestingly, one approach that might have merit is based on the detection of elevated levels of the gas radon. This does not actually require that we have a good theory of how earthquakes occur, but just that we establish an empirical regularity between an indicator – radon – and the event (earthquakes). Clearly, *to predict* and *to explain* are separate activities.

Consider this additional example. Everyone knows that as we keep adding sand to a sandpile, the pile will eventually crumble down. But which grain of sand will produce the collapse and where the rupture will occur are questions beyond anyone's power to predict (see Buchanan, 2000). Similarly, with the onset of political revolutions and repression, for example, we can posit that the accumulation of political tension (repression of conflict and so on) makes the system more likely to crumble in the long term, but when and where the revolution will start remains beyond prediction. (For actual studies of the link between political revolutions and repression, see Almeida, 2003; Moore, 2000.)

Third, and more trivially, we might be unable to predict events in the future, even armed with a good explanatory model, if the values of the predictive factors are themselves not predictable or possible to measure. For example, we might believe that aggregate levels of public support for the EU are causally explained by levels of trust in the EU institutions, current evaluations of the economic situation, and attachment to post-materialist values (see, for example, Hooghe & Marks, 2005). So to predict the levels of EU public support, say, two years from now, one would need to ascertain what the values of these three factors would be – a task that is close to impossible.

It is useful to distinguish between predictions that can be applied to the future with information available now and predictions that cannot be projected onto the future since they require contemporaneous information to be performed. For example, scholars have developed models predicting the votes of US Supreme Court judges on the basis of the votes of the other judges (and other factors) (Guimera & Sales-Pardo, 2011). Obviously, even if the model is correct, the predictions can be made only once information about the votes of the other members of the Court is available, which is generally not the case before the actual decision we wish to predict has been taken.

Despite these complications, we have to insist that, in general, causal theories entail predictions – otherwise it is difficult to see how they differ from description. If the post-hoc explanations we offer are supposed to work only backwards, we need at the very least to identify the conditions that make the explanation work in one case but not in general and why it is unlikely to hold in the future.

What really makes the distinction between prediction and explanation important is the explosion of available data on politics and governance over the last few years (the age of big data). The more data we have, the clearer our goals need to be: are we interested in providing the best possible prediction or are we interested in getting at the deep causal structure. These two goals need not lead to the same research design or to the same choice about the selection of variables to measure and analyse.

Explanation

While description and prediction remain worthy scientific goals, **explanation gets the bulk of attention in political science.** Because it is so important, explanation gets its own chapter (Chapter 6), in which we discuss at length the various notions of explanation and causality. Explanations are also closely linked with theories, which is the topic of the next chapter (Chapter 3). Here we only need to outline some of the various goals that explanatory research might have and, on a sidenote, to discuss how it relates to the notion of 'interpretation'.

Explanations point to the causes of events, identify general causal effects, and reveal the causal mechanisms that produce them. Explaining means to uncover the causal process – the chain of causally relevant events that lead to an outcome – in general and for particular cases. Explanations answer 'Why?' questions about causal effects, but also 'How?' questions about causal mechanisms.

The goals of explanatory research can be to explain a particular case, to build a comprehensive causal account of a general phenomenon, or to establish a general causal relationship that holds for a population of cases.

Explanations can be about *specific* events (for example, the onset of World War II) or about *general* phenomena (for example, the onset of wars). In both cases, they can be *complete* – building a comprehensive causal model of how a phenomenon is produced – or *partial* – focused on a single possible causal relationship. Complete explanatory theories attempt to provide a complete account of how and why certain events (for example, transitions to democracy) happen. Partial explanations focus on the relationships between two phenomena without the ambition to explain in full any of them. For example, a partial causal theory can study the relationship between democracy and economic development; even if democracy is somehow causally important for economic development and/or the other way round, everyone would agree that both democracy and economic development as such are subject to a much wider set of influences. (For a much-cited empirical study of the impact of democracy on economic development, see Burkhart & Lewis-Beck, 1994.)

Explanations can build a retrospective account of why and how a particular event occurred, and they can prospectively evaluate the likely effects of a new policy or other intervention in the social world. For example, we can ask: what would be the effect of lowering the minimum voting age on the electoral outcomes of conservative parties? It might seem that we are asking for a prediction rather than an explanatory account, but this is not the case. Even though the question is about the future, so long as the focus is on what would happen if we were to *change* something in the world (in this case, the minimum voting age requirement), we need a causal explanatory account, and not a mere prediction. Purely predictive questions would be: Will the voting age requirement be lowered five years from now? Or what will be the electoral outcome for the Conservative party in the next election in Britain? Questions about impact and effects are always explanatory, even when they refer to the future and even when the cause being evaluated is not under human control.

It is important to specify in advance whether one is interested in prospective or retrospective explanation, in explaining a particular case or in accounting for a general phenomenon, and whether the research goal is to provide a full or a partial explanation. These different goals call for different research modes and designs.

In some corners of the social sciences (cultural anthropology in particular) people shy away from 'explanation' as their goal and prefer to talk about 'interpretation'. Interpretation is a process of inference, which *'begins with a set of (presumptive) signifiers and attempts to place them within an intelligible frame'* (Geertz, 1973, p. 26). It is not meant to be predictive, but a sort of *'thick description'*. Its task is to uncover the

> *'conceptual structures that inform our subjects' acts ... and to construct a system of analysis in whose terms what is generic to those structures, what belongs to them because they are what they are, will stand out against the other determinants of human behavior'* (p. 27).

In essence, interpretation can be regarded as a specific form of explanation; one that deals with the application of theory and careful observation to particular cases with the aim of *understanding*. But interpretation cannot be excluded from the rules of inference and research design discussed in this book. (Note that Jon Elster similarly posits that 'to interpret *is* to explain', 2007, p. 52). Just because one wishes to 'interpret' rather than 'explain' does not mean that concerns about operationalization, or the selection of observations, or the use of evidence do not apply. The basic rules of inference are essentially an extension of general logic and are not bounded by the particular social-scientific field of application.

To conclude for the moment the discussion of the goals of explanatory research, let us sum up what makes explanation different from description and prediction. Most importantly, causal explanations offer 'deep' understanding and the possibility for manipulation and control. Explaining means understanding the causal structure, which in its turn implies the ability to manipulate this structure to change the outcomes. If the explanatory mechanisms we identify are truly causal, they provide us with a means to control. If the relationships we discover are truly causal and not merely associational, they provide us with levers to change the social reality we study. The promise of manipulation and control is what elevates explanatory research goals above purely descriptive and predictive ones.

If taken seriously, social scientific explanations provide policy makers and society at large with tools for social change. As a consequence, the scientific requirements for causal inferences are more stringent, and the responsibility of researchers offering explanatory accounts is greater. While many would object to social engineering on moral grounds, at the same time, the difficulties and moral dilemmas of causal explanation in the social and political worlds should not discourage researchers from trying to explain and provide causal models. Politicians, policy makers, business and social leaders will not stop making myriads of decisions every single day because of the doubts and objections of social scientists. Researchers should try to bring some rigorous knowledge and insights that can influence public decisions, but it is also their responsibility to make clear the limitations and uncertainty of their explanations and predictions. At the very least, social research can illuminate the inherently uncertain and often perverse effects of public policies and social action. We will have more to say on the ethics of research in politics and public administration in the final chapter. For now, let us return to the discussion of explanation as a scientific goal.

Theory Generation, Theory Testing, and Theory Application

Explanations are intrinsically related to theory, because it is theory that supports explanatory accounts, no matter whether we are interested in causal effects or causal mechanisms; general relationships or individual cases; partial or complete, retrospective or prospective explanations.

We posited that purely theoretical work is fundamentally different from research that engages with empirical reality (Section 2 of this chapter). But empirical research is intimately related to theory. While deductive theoretical work operates at the level of concepts and can exist without reference to real-world phenomena – think about pure mathematics as the archetypal example – empirical work, and explanatory research in particular, cannot exist in a theoryless vacuum. But the terms of engagement can be quite different. First, empirical research can be used to *generate* a theory; second, it can *test* a theory; third, it can be used to *apply* an existing theory. To recap, once we decide that we have a positive, empirical, and explanatory research goal, we need to specify whether we want to generate, test, or apply a theory. This section provides more details about each of the three options.

Theory generation

Theory generation is a natural outgrowth of descriptive research. Once a series of events is traced and meticulously documented, it is easy to propose conjectures about how the events are causally related. Once a phenomenon is described in detail for a set of cases, it is a small step to propose ideas about how the phenomenon comes about and develops. Once the variation of some trait across populations is systematically explored, we cannot avoid forming hypotheses about causal relationships. The source of initial theoretical insight is very often descriptive research (indeed, one of the hallmarks of excellent descriptive research is the theory-building insight it brings). Note that our notion of theory is very broad and covers proposed explanations (interpretations) of individual cases, complete causal models of a phenomenon, and individual hypotheses about causal links between two variables.

Theory-generating research can build on existing and published descriptive accounts, but it can also be designed with such a goal in mind. This would be appropriate when there is no explanatory theory for the case or general phenomena we are interested in, or when existing theory is unsatisfactory. The design of empirical projects for theory generation follows different logic from the design of projects testing existing theoretical propositions (for details, see Chapter 9). Different methods can help generate theoretical ideas. An in-depth study of a single case, a small-N comparison of several carefully selected cases, but also statistical analyses of large datasets can be used to come up with novel hypotheses.

The process of theory generation is inductive. It starts with empirical facts and builds its way up to abstract theoretical propositions. It is important to note how this empirically informed theory building is different from the mode of theoretical research outlined in Section 2 of this chapter (see also Figure 2.2). While empirical theory generation develops propositions and ideas that stem from and are consistent with some data, purely theoretical analysis works with these propositions by extending them, probing their assumptions, trying to bring them together in a consistent framework, exploring their implications, deriving empirically verifiable expectations, and so on. Empirical theory-building research generates ideas; theoretical analysis stretches and folds, pulls and pushes these ideas to uncover their logical foundations, structure, and consequences. The result of this process is a clarified and hopefully coherent set of ideas about relationships among concepts. This refined theory can in turn be tested and applied to new cases. It is crucial to realize that until an inductively generated explanatory theory has been matched against new data – be that new data about the same cases that were used to generated the theory or new data about new cases – it remains nothing more than an intriguing idea; a conjecture that needs further probing to determine its validity and relevance.

Theory testing

Once a theory has been generated and analytically developed, it needs to be tested to prove its worth. When testing, we do not necessarily aim to confirm a theory; on the contrary, refutation might be more informative (and, unlike confirmation, logically possible with empirical data). In political science there is no lack of theories. Quite the opposite – there is usually an overwhelming amount of theoretical arguments proposed for any topic and question, and one of the main aims of research projects is to test these theoretical arguments. Theory testing can be accomplished using a variety of methods that will be covered in Chapters 7–11, but, in short, they include experimental and observational, within-case analysis, quantitative large-N and comparative small-N approaches, and any mixture of these (the 'N' stands for the number of cases in the study). Different research strategies can be appropriate for theory testing depending on the 'maturity' of a theory. A novel theory can be tested with a small number of case studies to establish its basic credibility. Preliminary case studies can also serve to illuminate the workings and logic of the theory. Once a theory gains some acceptance, more comprehensive and rigorous tests are required to delineate the domain of the theory (the cases for which it works successfully) and its limitations and to calibrate the effects of specific variables suggested by the theory. And when a theory becomes accepted as the received wisdom in the field, it becomes vulnerable to discreditation by a few but carefully selected case studies.

Theory testing follows a deductive logic: we start with abstract propositions and put them to the test of empirical reality; the ones that are not disconfirmed survive (at least for another round), and the ones that do not match the patterns in the real world get discarded. This sketch does not really do justice to the general way scientific research works in reality, but it is still useful as an illustration of the logic of theory testing. The logic and importance of theory testing are grounded in *falsification-ism* and logical positivism as scientific philosophies and the work of Karl Popper, in particular. Despite refinements and extensions, falsification-ism remains a major mode and part of scientific research.

There is a variant of theory testing that is interested in the fate of a single proposition (hypothesis) rather than a bigger theory. This single proposition might have great substantive importance, so we would want to test it directly, irrespective of whether and how it is connected to broader theories. For example, we might be interested in the effect of supplying free insecticide-treated bed nets to families in malaria-infected regions on infant mortality (Cohen & Dupas, 2010). For another example, we might want to estimate the effect of providing free bikes to girls in poor Indian villages on their school attendance (Muralidharan & Prakash, 2013). These hypothesized relationships can be construed as propositions to be tested with empirical data, and we might want to quantify the average causal effects that the bed nets and the free bikes would have for a certain population. The logic of these tests would resemble the logic of theory testing sketched above. The difference is that with the tests we would not aim to bring evidence in favour of or against a bigger theory, but solely for the propositions that motivate the research. That being said, to truly understand the causal mechanisms behind the effects of the provision of bed nets and bikes on, respectively, life expectancy and school attendance, we would need to eventually embed these relationships in broader theories. These theories would be expressed in more abstract concepts, such as risk attitudes and material incentives rather than bed nets and bikes, and would require additional testing, but, if successful, would allow for more general insights that can transcend the immediate empirical contexts of the initial hypothesis-testing research.

Theory application

In the simplest and least ambitious case, we can apply a theory to an empirical case with the aim of explaining it. For example, we might use the spatial theory of government coalition formation (for an introduction, see Shepsle, 2010) to try explain why Germany ended up with a government composed of Socialists and Conservatives after the 2005 elections. The intent would be to interpret the case in light of the theory, and the hope would be that the theory will shed light on the causal mechanisms and factors that produced this particular coalition and not any other. Importantly, our goal with this project would not be to contribute in any way to the theory itself, but just to use its propositions to account for the particular case. To take a different example, we can try to apply the theory of democracy consolidation (for an overview, see Diamond, 1999) to explain why Georgia (the country, not the US state of the same name) stumbles on the way to functioning democracy, or we can apply some of the many flavours of institutional theory to explain the survival of the Dutch waterboards (communal organizations governing water management) over the last seven hundred years (see Toonen, Dijkstra, & Van Der Meer, 2006). The crucial difference between theory application and theory testing/theory generating is one of ambition: applying a theory to explain a case has a very narrow ambition and little care is given to the question of how the findings from the research relate to the body of existing theory. As a result, theory application is often more suited to private and not to academic purposes. In the collective academic enterprise, each research project aims to contribute to the collective goal of advancement of scientific knowledge, which usually requires explicit consideration of what the case contributes to theory.

At the same time, routine successful application of theory to explain individual cases and guide effective social interventions can be seen as the ultimate success of the scientific process. In political science, very few areas would claim to have reached this stage. In most, there are numerous competing theories but no single one that can adequately account for all cases and empirical patterns.

Each research goal – theory generation, theory testing, and theory application – can be based on many particular forms of research designs, and the rest of this text goes on to discuss in detail many of the possibilities. But remember that the choices of design and method are secondary: the choice of research goal comes first.

* * *

We have covered a good deal of ground already in this chapter, so let's recap. The choice of research type is guided by the research goals and objectives. The most fundamental distinction is between normative and positive research goals. While normative research asks questions about values and what ought to be, positive research asks questions about facts and what is. Within positive research, the main separation is the one between purely theoretical research and research that engages with the empirical world in one way or another. Within the big house of empirically informed research, three broad families coexist, which have either descriptive, predictive, or explanatory goals. Zooming in on explanatory research, the differences between theory generation, theory testing, and theory application become visible. Following this route, we choose the main goal of our research project, and this choice leads to a range of options for research designs appropriate for the goal. Importantly, the choice of a research goal also *precludes* the use of certain designs. Experiments are not the most efficient tool for theory generation, and individual case studies are usually not the best tool for theory testing. Depending on the goal, different ways of case selection and different selections of variables to analyse become appropriate.

Theory can be sidelined if one is interested mostly in predictions, but it is essential if one wants to develop an explanation.

In principle, all research goals are appropriate and valuable, but some fit the existing state of the art in a research field better than others. It makes little sense to add inductively generated hypotheses to a field overcrowded with existing theories, and it makes even less sense to design a theory-testing project for a problem that has not even been described sufficiently well yet. The remainder of the chapters provide more details about how the research goal limits and enables certain designs, which parts of the research design are crucial for fulfilling the research goal, and how to assess the strengths and weaknesses of different research strategies. But do come back to this chapter when you need a low-resolution map providing a general orientation into the many possibilities.

Alternative Approaches

The range of possible research we discussed is vast and encompassing, but nevertheless some forms of social research are left out. Notably, these are forms of research that blur the boundaries between facts and values, analysis and social critique, research and social action. Grounded theory, for example, is an approach that does not fit into the world of social scientific research mapped above (see Charmaz, 2006). Grounded theory mixes inductive and deductive reasoning to produce a theory that is supposed to stay very close to the described reality. In our opinion, one is better off analytically separating the inductive and deductive parts of the research process and clearly labelling which conclusions are based on data aggregation (inductive) and which on purely theoretical reasoning (deductive). This allows for more clarity about which parts of our theory we should have more confidence in and which parts are just compact descriptions of particular cases.

A more radical departure from the modes of social scientific research outlined in this chapter is social action research (see Greenwood & Levin, 1998) for whose practitioners research is useless if it does not lead immediately to action for improving the social world. While the goal of engagement with the real world and the call for social relevance are to be welcomed, in my opinion both are served better if we keep for the *duration of the analysis* the normative and the positive elements of research separate. We first need to have confidence in the findings from the research, before we (or someone else) decide to act on them, and rigorous research is best achieved when you leave your own preferences and prejudices at the door of the research laboratory: it just makes for more reliable research, no matter how high your moral aspirations are.

Somewhat relatedly, critical theorists (for an introduction, see Bronner, 2011) would find it hard to place themselves in the picture we sketched in this chapter, because for them the goal of the social sciences is to unmask the power implications of various social relations and to expose the corrupting role of the state in all its manifestations. Deconstructing social reality rather than naive attempts at positive explanation and prediction is the ultimate, and only possible, objective for critical theory. Starting from a platform of radical subjectivity, critical theorists consider positive social science impossible, and any attempt to 'sell' results of positive research projects dangerous. Critical theory has produced important insights into social reality, and while we share the concerns about the objectivity of scientists and endorse the call for critical analysis of the state, we do not believe that one needs to go as far as rejecting the possibility of positive social science as such. Within the limits on objectivity set by our personal histories, education, language, conceptual frames, and dominant academic discourses, there is enough space to conduct research into politics and administration that has positive goals of descriptive and causal inference and, however modest, empirical and theoretical generalizations.

Another approach to social science that does not fit easily into our organizing scheme of research types is *applied phronesis* (Flyvbjerg, 2001; Schram & Caterino, 2006; Flyvbjerg, Landman, & Schram, 2012). The starting point of phronesis is that 'context and judgement are irreducibly central to understanding human action' (Flyvbjerg 2001, p. 4), which is taken to imply that explanatory and predictive theory is not possible, or at least not probable for the foreseeable future, in the social sciences (Flyvbjerg, 2004). The proponents of this approach trace their intellectual lineage to Aristotle, but in practice there are as yet very few applications to political science problems (but see Flyvbjerg, Landman, & Scram, 2012). Practical wisdom is what phronesis aims for, and in the process of research sensitivity to issues of ethics and power play central roles. Such an approach obviously challenges the distinctions between research and action, between theory and empirics, and between facts and values on which we relied. Instead of an alternative to positive political science, however, phronesis can be considered as an attempt to integrate results and insights from positive research, conducted in various modes, into a process that helps uncover power relations, provides relevant input for policy deliberation, and supports social change.

To conclude, alternative forms of research in the social sciences exist, and you are welcome to explore them, but in these chapters we are going to focus on positive research, because the differences with grounded theory, social action research, critical theory, phronesis, and the like are too fundamental to bridge in a single volume on research design.

So far we have introduced the various goals and modes of research one can follow, but the discussion has remained pretty abstract. If it is so crucial to be clear about one's objectives before the research is conducted, formulating a good research question obviously becomes a task of prime importance. But how does one practically choose a research question? How does one transform a vaguely defined interest in a topic into a sharp question that can be answered using theoretical and/or empirical research? The remainder of this chapter will leave the abstract world of research taxonomies and delve into the messy reality of formulating research questions. While we cannot offer anything as clear as the roadmap presented above, there are several tips and best practices you can follow to produce a research question that will make a successful research project possible. Read on!

Choosing a Topic

Research projects answer questions. Hence, the quality of the answer is constrained by the quality of the question. Research projects that address irrelevant, vague, or otherwise poorly specified questions are doomed from the start. Sometimes interesting ideas can be stumbled upon while playing around in a laboratory, fooling around with a dataset, random reading, or casually browsing the Internet. All these activities are to be encouraged, but more often than not research requires a more focused and structured effort that has a research question at its heart. Note that we are not saying that research starts with a question, because arriving at the right question takes time, effort, and, yes, research, itself.

The task of formulating your research question can be separated into two components: selecting a topic and shaping the topic into a well-defined question. Both steps have to ensure that once the research is actually complete, and irrespective of the way the findings turn out, you will have made a contribution to scientific knowledge. But how do you settle on a topic? Obviously your interests, ideas, and inclinations should play a leading role, but in case you find yourself short of inspiration, here are some standard routes you can follow.

Everyone interested in politics and governance is fascinated by the 'big' questions in the field: how can the world achieve lasting peace, how to govern a just society, how to manage an increasingly globalized world, perhaps how to alleviate poverty if you are more economically minded. There is nothing wrong in being motivated by these big societal problems, but they do not necessarily make the best topics for low-scale, short, individual research projects – exactly the type students are most likely to conduct. The reasons are the following. First, the big questions have been attracting the greatest amount of attention and funding for many, many years, and many of the greatest minds have contributed at one time or another to their analysis. Automatically, that makes it less likely that a short, individual research project can make a real contribution. That being said, you should not be discouraged from researching the big questions society faces, but you need to find your own angle to attack the problem. Which leads us to the second reason why the big problems are not always the best choice for research questions: they are multifaceted with implications often spanning different academic disciplines. For example, researching how to govern societies in a just way involves legal, administrative, political, philosophical, and technological aspects. Third, the big problems evoke strong emotions and people tend to have very strong prior opinions about the possible solutions. Emotional attachment makes it difficult to separate the normative from the empirical in the analysis, which we agreed is crucial for a good research project. In summary, addressing the big problems facing contemporary society is an obvious way to go about selecting a research topic, but be aware that these problems are complex, have already been extensively researched, and have strong normative connotations. So unless you are familiar with the state of the art of existing research on the problem, it will be hard to offer an original and innovative perspective that can make the eventual research project worthwhile.

Another obvious source of inspiration for research topics and questions is the front (web)pages of the newspapers. A financial crisis focuses attention on banking regulation. A terrorist attack spurs interest in security management. A refugee crises directs attention towards migration policies. Journalistic reports on the horse-trading involved in the passage of the annual national budget raises questions about political bargaining more generally. The latest scandal about a corrupt public official exposed in the news leads to interest in the ethics of the public service. There is nothing wrong with research projects being inspired by current events. On the contrary: to be relevant, scientific research needs to address the issues that currently animate the public sphere. But keep in mind two words of warning. First, an academic research project requires sustained attention for a longer period of time than the typical life cycle of news stories. Simply put, long after the newspapers have moved to another topic you would still be busy with your research project. So your interest might be spurred by the current news, but needs to be genuine in order to motivate you sufficiently to complete the research. Second, 'hot' issues are often difficult to gather information about. Twenty-first-century piracy in the Red Sea is a fascinating story that regularly makes it to the papers, but it is not a very likely (or desirable) candidate for a 'participant observation' kind of study; yet, without additional information it is impossible to produce an academic analysis that goes beyond the journalistic accounts. (You can try getting access to and interviewing high-level officials making anti-piracy policy at international organizations, but the chances of this happenings are only slightly higher than getting embedded in a Somali pirate gang).

By their nature, 'hot' issues are very new. This implies that there is rarely archival material you can use for research and that the people involved will be unable and unwilling to talk to you. You might be successful in interviewing the finance minister about the current budget negotiations a few years *after* he has retired, but you are guaranteed not to get any access to him at the height of the negotiations, which is when the issue hits the news. In sum, be inspired by the news of the day, but be careful in selecting an issue you truly care about and one that does not create insurmountable problems for academic research. And research inspired by current events still needs to contribute to an identifiable body of academic literature.

Suspected empirical patterns and regularities often make for interesting research questions. The human mind is programmed to search for and recognize patterns in its natural and social surroundings. This type of research question starts with an observation. The Eastern coast of South America and the Western coast of Africa seem to fit together: could it be that they were once part of the same continent? There are very few examples of democracies fighting wars with each other: could it be that there is something that makes democracies less likely to engage in armed hostilities? Transitions to democracy seem to come in waves (Latin America in the 1980s, Eastern Europe in the 1990s, Northern Africa in the 2010s): is there something contagious in the onset of democracy in one country that makes the whole region susceptible to democratization? More often than not these patterns will turn out to be illusionary, but occasionally their pursuit will turn up important systematic features of the social world. And disconfirming a suspected empirical pattern or regularity is important in its own right. The key to successful research projects pursuing a suspected empirical pattern is to retain an open mind about the end result of the project and accept it if the pattern turns out to be nothing more than a statistical fluke or a spurious correlation. Even if that's the case, we would still have learned something useful about the world.

Actually, one of the best ways to choose a research question is to focus on a puzzle. A puzzle is a real-world event, or pattern of events, that 'doesn't make sense' in light of intuitions, accepted wisdom, or a dominant theoretical perspective on the problem. A puzzle is something that doesn't fit with our current state of understanding, so it automatically satisfies the condition of linking to an existing body of knowledge. Moreover, puzzles are fun and itch the brain until they are solved. A puzzle can be an unsual period of policy stability as well as a rapid policy change. In 2002 no European country had a policy restricting smoking in bars and restaurants, and in 2010 they all did; yet, no new scientific evidence about the effects of second-hand smoking had appeared during this period (Toshkov, 2013). How come? What triggered this transformation? Or consider the regulation of gun use and possession in the US: despite massive social and technological transformations and repeated calls for reform, the core principles of the policy have survived intact for more than a century. What makes this policy so stable (Godwin & Schroedel, 2000)? Unexpected similarities as well as differences can be similarly puzzling. Why did Singapore and Azerbaijan end up with winner-take-all electoral systems? Why did West European countries, which share so much in political and economic terms, end up with rather different welfare regimes? Why does the Belgian region Flanders have a popular extreme right-wing party, while the other Belgian region of Wallonia has none (Coffe, 2005)? (Belgian regions have their own party political systems; it's complicated.) Why did the Arab Spring of 2011 succeed in overthrowing the regimes in Egypt and Libya, but not in Syria? Why is Sweden part of the EU, but Norway is not? (Well, Norway is still part of the European Economic Community; it's complicated.) Once you start looking for puzzles in social and political life, you will find them everywhere. But a puzzle is only a puzzle with reference to some pre-existing body of knowledge, which can be more or less formalized as a scientific theory.

Consider cooperation. To a layman, there could be nothing more natural than the fact that humans cooperate to achieve political and other goals. After all, cooperation happens at all levels all the time. So there is no puzzle there, time to move on. Not so fast. Cooperation often works seemingly effortlessly, but sometimes it doesn't, as everyone who has tried to muster support for a public cause such as cleaning the local beach would testify. Trying to analyse cooperation, social scientists have realized that not only does cooperation not arise naturally, but it is in fact rather difficult to sustain. Theoretical models such as the Prisoner's Dilemma and the Tragedy of the Commons have put human cooperation in such a different light that observing successful cooperation in the real world, and not its absence, becomes puzzling and requires explanation (Hardin, 1968; Axelrod, 1984; Ostrom, 1999). Similarly for voting: to a naive observer, the fact that people turn up at the voting stations might seem trivial, but in light of utilitarian cost–benefit theories of voting it can be pretty puzzling why people vote, given the very slim chances that *their* vote will be decisive (for a discussion, see Feddersen, 2004). So puzzles are always relative to what we (think we) know.

The big problems facing society, current news, empirical patterns, and puzzles are all different avenues to arrive at a research topic. What is common to them is that they are rooted, although to different degrees, in the real-world. Alternatively, one might seek inspiration for research entirely in the realm of theory and published research. Normally, social science proceeds incrementally, and one of the safest ways to make a contribution is to replicate, extend, or adapt an existing project. Although such projects might appear modest at first, they can often produce important results. Replication projects (too) often discover imperfections and even mistakes in existing studies that can lead to reconsideration of their results. To take an example from the field of political economy, a highly influential paper on the links between government debt and economic growth published in one of the flagship economics journals (Reinhart & Rogoff, 2010) was discovered to suffer from data processing errors and questionable statistical modelling decisions which, once corrected, significantly altered the conclusions and implicit policy recommendations of the paper. The discovery of these deficiencies started with an effort of a graduate student to replicate the published paper for a class assignment (Herndon, Ash, & Pollin, 2013).

And the value of replication is certainly not confined to the study of economics. In 2015, two political science graduate students attempted to replicate and extend a high-profile study of public opinion on gay equality (LaCour & Green, 2014). Their failure to do so (Broockman, Kalla, & Aronow, 2015) uncovered a likely case of academic fraud and led to the retraction of the original article.

Applying an existing research approach in a new setting is an entirely legitimate and valuable exercise as well. The theories, methods, and techniques of successful projects inspire application in different empirical settings and extension of the ideas to new contexts. Good ideas are, and should be, replicated. For example, the empirical study of policy agendas originated in the US, but once the first studies were published, people quickly realized that the approach could be adapted and could lead to important insights about other countries and political systems as well, so the project was extended to cover almost all European and a number of other countries as well (See Baumgartner et al., 2009 and http://www.comparativeagendas.info/.) To take a different example, formal models first designed to explain legislative decision-making have been adapted for use in studying executive and judicial politics as well (see McCarty & Meirowitz, 2014). (And the legislative decision-making models were inspired by models of economic decision-making in their turn).

The transfer of research ideas and approaches should not stop at disciplinary borders. In fact, some of the most interesting research in political science and public administration has drawn inspiration from fields such as history, ethnology, economics, biology, ecology, ethology, and even physics. For example, models of lobbying and interest group mobilization have been adapted from population ecology (Gray & Lowery, 2000; Lowery & Brasher, 2004). The study of bee colonies has provided important insights about collective decision-making in humans (List, Elsholtz, & Seeley, 2009). Concepts from chaos theory have been used to study the distribution of wars, social networks, and so on (Kiel & Elliott, 1996). Academic fields cross-fertilize. To be a successful political scientist one needs to venture well beyond the '*pol sci*'-labelled library shelves. Reading outside your narrow academic field is essential not only for pushing the horizon of your substantive knowledge but also for collecting ideas, analogies, and inspiration that you can use for research in your own discipline.

The lesson of all this is that picking an appropriate research topic and question is hard work. Given that books and advice on research design usually assume that one already has a question to research, the importance of this work tends to be forgotten. In some sense, selecting the topic and the question is the more difficult part of the process – designing and conducting the actual study are more straightforward than the selection of a research question that can advance the state of the art. Much of the reading for academic research goes into getting familiar with what is already well established by previous research, where the current boundaries of existing knowledge lie, and what are feasible directions to push these boundaries further. Because of that, do not underestimate how much time selecting a good research problem takes.

The number of academic papers on any given topic increases every month, and keeping track with what is the state of the art even in a relatively small academic domain is a daunting task. But there are several tools and tips that can help. First, there are databases of academic research you can use to get a quick overview of the existing studies on a topic. Both the freely available Google Scholar (http://scholar.google .com) and the proprietary Web of Science database can lead you to most, and the most recent, scholarship on any topic. Other services, such as JSTOR, provide alternative ways to quickly get to know a field. An additional advantage of these databases is that you can see which are the most highly cited articles in the field, and trace arguments and academic debates by following citation chains. Second, visiting a bricks-and-mortar library, especially if you are allowed to wander among the bookshelves, can help as well.

Third, academic journals often publish reviews of the state of the art in a field which would normally identify gaps in existing knowledge and outline directions for future research. Encyclopedias, the articles in the *Annual Review of Political Science*, and some 'state of the art' books (for example, Katznelson & Milner, 2003) can be used for such a purpose as well. You can take a lead from what specialists consider promising avenues for future research and develop your ideas from there. The danger is that many academic fields can quickly become detached from the original real-world problems that motivated them and get engaged in internal debates and issues that make little sense to the broader world. As a complementary strategy, consult the classics to restore the connection to the original problems animating social scientific research. An additional problem with relying on published literature reviews is that by the time a literature review appears in print the knowledge frontier has moved (sometimes dramatically), with the result that some of the gaps may have been filled and some of the suggestions for future research might have been implemented already. A new type of literature review that is hosted online and is regularly updated – a living review – exists for some subfields of political science and public administration (for example, on the topic of EU governance, see http://europeangovernance-living reviews.org/) and can help alleviate the problem of delay. Or you could stay up-to-date by consulting the bibliographical databases mentioned above, which are updated very fast. Being familiar with the state of the art ensures that a research project would be valuable to other researchers and could contribute to society as well.

A shortcut to get to know what currently animates an academic field is to look for scholarly exchanges that often find their place on the pages of academic journals. One team of researchers publishes an article, followed by a response by some other scientists who usually disagree with the results, a reply to the response by the original authors, and so on. Such exchanges can be very informative about the major debates in an academic field, the contested parts of existing knowledge, and the needs for future research. They are usually sharper and more polemical than the standard scientific articles, which can be useful to get quickly to the raw nerves of academic contestation in a particular field. Sometimes these academic debates can spill over to the pages of regular newspapers and journals as well, so stay on the lookout: following an academic exchange can make the choice of research topic easier for you.

Successful research projects at any level are born from a match between a gap in our understanding of a topic and some specific knowledge, skill, or perspective one can bring to the issue. Every individual possesses, or can develop, a unique set of intellectual and analytical skills. In choosing a research topic, you should identify your skills that would allow him/her to make a worthy contribution to a field. This skill could be speaking a rare language, for example. Maybe you are a native Georgian speaker. That would put you in a position to contribute to the study of interstate conflicts in the Caucasus, for example, by making use of documents, archives, or interviews – sources that are inaccessible to most scholars due to language barriers. If you are a native Georgian speaker and a beginner in statistical modelling, it would make little sense to start a research project on Caucasian conflicts based on the statistical analysis of existing general databases. You would be in a much better position to make a contribution by putting your language skills to use. Alternatively, if you have had the chance to learn how to do computer simulations of social processes (more on that in Chapter 3) and you want to study a topic that has so far not been analysed using computational agent-based modelling, you would be ideally placed to make a contribution. More prosaically, maybe a high civil servant who has been instrumental in a recent controversial public decision happens to be a relative who is willing to grant you an interview: use that and design a project around the opportunity, provided that the interview can bring novel insights about the case. In sum, be strategic in your choice of research topic and the kind of project you conduct: paying attention to your specific skills (and weaknesses) will not only make it more likely that the project gets finished but also that it will make a contribution to the existing literature.

Taking this argument one step further, plan to acquire the skills that would put you in a good position to contribute to a field. If you feel that the study of political attitudes in relation to morality issues has relied too much on standardized surveys, learn how to conduct research that takes more subjectivity on board, such as Q-surveys (Brown, 1980) or in-depth interviews. If your conclusion from reviewing the literature on government effectiveness is that there is a lot of data available that has not been analysed sufficiently, plan to strengthen your data analysis skills for your project. Of course, learning new skills, languages, or statistical methods takes time, so this advice would only work for longer research projects, but the general point remains: in order to say something new to a field, you need to bring an original perspective.

Sharpening the Research Question

You have finally completed the difficult task of choosing a research topic, and after much hesitation you have settled on your general approach. Now you need to mould the topic and the idea into a real question. This process requires the reformulation of the idea into a single sentence that captures your interest, poses the task to be accomplished, and even frames the way in which it would be done. To achieve so much in a single sentence, the research question needs to be impeccably constructed, both conceptually and grammatically.

Most importantly, the research question defines the type of research needed to answer it: normative or positive; theoretical or empirical; descriptive, predictive, or explanatory; theory building or theory testing. The first part of this chapter clarified at length these crucial distinctions,

Box 2.1   *Tips for choosing a research topic*

- Be inspired by the big problems facing society
- Inquire into the issues currently in the news
- Pursue suspected patterns and regularities
- Look for puzzles
- Visit bibliographical databases (and libraries)
- Read (online) literature reviews (and the classics)
- Follow academic controversies
- Venture outside your academic field
- Stay curious and critical

but how are they reflected in the research question itself? The choice of interrogative pronoun (the 'Wh-' word) reveals a lot. A 'Why' question requires an explanatory account, be that completely theoretical or empirically informed. 'What' questions tend to ask for descriptive research. 'How' questions are usually about causal explanations but with a focus on the causal mechanisms (see Chapter 6) rather than on estimating the causal effects. Normative questions contain value-charged phrases such as 'good', 'optimal', 'natural', 'appropriate', 'virtuous', and so on, while positive questions avoid such language.

Beware that an exclusive focus on the 'Wh-' word can mistake explanatory for descriptive questions. '*What is the cause of state failure?*' is a question that demands a causal explanation despite the fact that it starts with 'What' and not with 'Why'. The same goes for a question of the type '*What has been the impact of labour unions on welfare state development in Denmark?*'

Avoid posing factual questions that can be answered by a simple look-up in an encyclopedia or a quick Internet search. How many parliamentarians voted in favour of giving women voting rights in Britain in 1918 is an important fact that can be relevant for many discussions, but it cannot provide the basis for a full-fledged research project because it can be answered with a simple Internet search or a trip to the library. In contrast, asking a similar question about a less-documented case might be an appropriate question for research into the history of politics. In sum, unless the task of collecting the facts is particularly daunting or controversial, avoid asking purely factual questions as research problems.

Avoid long questions. Less is more when it comes to the formulation of a research question. Distil your inquiry into as few words as possible. Edit until no further character can be deleted. Do not bring unnecessary conceptual clarifications, conditional statements, or rhetorical distractions into the question. There is a place for that in the research report. For example, the question '*How did the nature of the state, as wonderfully portrayed by Hobbes, and no less masterfully by Marx, influence in at least a small but nevertheless important selection of social contexts the disparities in wealth of its citizens, or more appropriately put for some states, subjects?*' is too long. '*How does the state influence economic disparities?*' is better and carries essentially the same idea.

Avoid composite questions. Composite questions contain more than one part, for example, '*What is the state of democracy in Uganda, and how to improve it?*' The first part calls for descriptive (hence, positive) and the second part calls for normative research. As explained at length in the first part of this chapter, positive and normative questions should be kept separate. Like oil and water, they don't mix well. There is nothing wrong with conducting two projects – one focused on establishing the state of democracy in Uganda (descriptive) and another one debating what reforms could improve it (normative) – but the two questions and projects had better be kept apart. Otherwise it is too easy for normative elements to contaminate the description and for descriptive elements to dilute the theoretical normative discourse.

Avoid questions that already contain implicit answers. *'How do cultural differences determine the extent of political corruption in the Middle East?'* already presupposes that cultural differences have a causally important role to play. Unless this has been established by previous research and your aim is to specifically study the causal *mechanisms* through which it happens, it is better to keep the question, and your mind, as open-ended as possible. A better formulation would be *'What explains the extent of political corruption in the Middle East?'*

We already noted that research questions can be about particular cases, such as Uganda or the 'Gun Owners of America' association, or about relationships between general phenomena, such as power and money. Let's quickly point out that questions of the first type have an even bigger challenge to justify their societal and scientific relevance. The second type can be posed in a number of different flavours. You can ask about the effects of something, such as *'What are the societal effects of political corruption?'*, or you can ask about the causes of something, such as *'What are the causes of the Arab Spring of the 2010s'*, or you can ask directly about a relationship, such as *'What has been the impact of political corruption on the onset of societal revolutions?'* The choice has consequences for the style of the research project and the expected output (see Chapter 6).

Questions about the effects of causes tend to be more analytical. By putting the general phenomenon first, you are not constrained in your search for potential effects on other parts of the social system. Questions about the causes of effects tend to be more case-focused and tied to the explanation of particular events. Questions about a possible relationship are quite specific. This is the source of both their power and their weakness. They are powerful because they squarely focus on one possible link in the social fabric and, as a result, they are well positioned to evaluate the possible relationship. At the same time, the hypothesized relationship, as featured in the research question, needs to be carefully selected to have a high chance of revealing something useful about the world, whatever the findings turnup.

In summary, research questions benefit from being structurally simple, short, precise, and open-ended. They set the scene for the actual research project by indicating the type of research that is going to be conducted, the main concepts that are going to be used, and sometimes the major empirical case that is going to be explored. The question should be firmly rooted in existing literature and bear societal and scientific significance, so that the findings from the actual research will deliver a contribution by discovering something new about the social and political worlds.

Box 2.2   *Tips for improving a research question*

- Make it short
- Make it grammatically simple
- Make it structurally simple
- Make it open-ended
- Use general concepts instead of specific variables
- Only refer to cases if you must
- Choose the 'Wh-' word carefully
- Make sure the question reflects the research goal
- Drop normative language (for positive science projects)
- Edit, edit, and edit once more

The research question sets the goal and the final destination for the research project. This chapter provided a basic map that can help you choose the general route to follow in order to reach your destination and answer your question. Many paths are possible. Choosing the right one depends on where you want to get to (the research objective); what you want to discover on the way (the state of existing knowledge); and which paths are traversable with the skills, knowledge, and intellectual toolkit that you have. The map presented so far can serve for general orientation, but it is too crude to be of much help once the real research design begins. The rest of the text provides more fine-grained views of the various components of design (conceptualization, operational-ization, case selection, and so on) and many more examples of actual research to serve as guides and inspiration.

But before all, we need to consider the role of theory in the research process in depth. Theory is what binds disparate research projects together, what makes knowledge accumulation in a field possible, what reflects our state of understanding of a problem in the most succinct form. But what *is* theory anyway? And what about a *model*? And *how* do you theorize? Let's cross into Chapter 3.

Further Reading

On normative research in political science, in addition to the references already cited in the chapter, see the handbook edited by Dryzek, Honig, and Phillips (2008) and the article by Gerring and Yesnowitz (2006). A good collection of classics of political ethics and normative politi-cal theory is Morgan (2011). Normative research has a long and vital tradition in public administration research. A relatively recent handbook is Cooper (2001). Other books with a more focused agenda include Dobel (1999) and Wolff (2011).

For research design in the context of interpretive social science, see Schwartz-Shea and Yanow (2012).

Additional advice on selecting a research question can be found in Gerring (2012b, pp. 37–57); King, Keohane, & Verba (1994, pp. 14–19); and Lehnert, Miller, and Wonka (2007, pp. 21–40). Grofman (2001) collects empirical studies framed as answers to puzzles, and the introduction to that volume discusses the role of puzzles and puzzle solving in political science research.

Chapter 3

Theory in the Research Process

Theory has a bad reputation. It is equally disliked by students who think it is hard, professionals who think it is useless, and some philosophers who think it is unattainable. If we could only cling to the observable facts and forget about theory altogether! Alas, theory is unavoidable. Whether we like it or not, it is theory that provides explanations, allows for the communication and accumulation of scientific knowledge, and even determines what are relevant observable facts in the first place.

By definition theory is abstract. That is what makes it difficult, possibly useless, and often dull. But because it is abstract, theory harbours concepts and ideas that transcend the immediate context in which they were initially developed. Abstract theory has a complex relationship with facts and data. The fit is rarely perfect, but scientists try to reconcile the differences by improving both theory and observation. So we need to learn about the various roles theory fulfils in the scientific process in order to design effective research projects. This chapter takes up the task.

Theory starts with ideas, and ideas are conceived out of intuition, inspiration, intense observation, frustration, or even hallucination. There can be little guidance to inspiration. But once a theoretical idea is born it needs a careful examination – its assumptions need to be spelled out, its mechanisms uncovered, its consistency checked, and its implications teased out. These are more sober and systematic activities, and this chapter will introduce several methods and tools for the rigorous analysis and development of explanatory theories.

Paradigms, Theories, Models, and Interpretations

There is much confusion surrounding theories so, first things first, let us get our terminology straight. This chapter deals with *explanatory* theories; that is, with theories that try to engage with social reality in order to explain it or to make social action comprehensible. Hence, normative political theory – for example, John Rawls's theory of justice (1971) – that deals with questions of good and bad falls outside our scope. We focus on *applied* rather than pure theory; that is, with theories that have empirical import and can be developed to have observable implications that may be tested and falsified. Pure political theory – for example, Kenneth Arrow's impossibility theorem (1951) – can be fascinating, but it falls for the most part outside our interest. Lastly, some things are called theories but, at least for our purposes, are better conceived as methods or tools (for example, game theory).

Theories can also be distinguished according to their intended scope (for a discussion, see Blatter & Haverland, 2012). At the most abstract level, theories are so general that they are better called meta-theories, paradigms, or theoretical frameworks – examples include rational choice theory (Hindmoor & Taylor, 2015; Green & Shapiro, 1996; Friedman, 1996; MacDonald, 2003), constructivism (Adler, 1997), and realism (Donnelly, 2000). Theories that aim to provide grand accounts of politics in general (for example, Easton's systems theory, 1965), social conflict (Marx, 1990), bureaucracy (Weber, 1947), or international relations (Immanuel Wallerstein's world-system theory, 2004) are rather abstract and too broad for our purposes as well. Mid-range theories, which are the ones we focus on, have more modest goals and more circumscribed targets; for example, issues such as democratization in modern societies, coalition building in Western democracies, or policy making in separation of powers political systems.

Theories are similar to interpretations. But interpretations are better considered as the application of a theory to a particular case. We can interpret the 2013 government shutdown in the US on the basis of the spatial model of legislative decision-making. Or we can interpret the failure of the international community to agree on an effective global carbon dioxide reduction treaty in light of the 'Tragedy of the Commons' theory (Hardin, 1968).

What about the difference between a theory and a model? While you can find many formal definitions, truth be told, researchers often use these terms interchangeably in practice. That is, *a model* is often no more than a synonym for *a theory*. For example, one can speak of Anthony Downs's (1957) electoral competition theory or of his electoral competition model. When there is a difference implied in usage, models are usually more specific than theories. A single theory can provide the base for a number of different models that develop and operationalize theoretical postulates into directly measurable variables. For example, rational choice theory has grounded several different models of *delegation*, which develop in different ways the basic theoretical assumptions of rational utility-maximizing principals (politicians) and agents (bureaucrats) (Epstein & O'Halloran, 1999).

To provide one succinct formal definition, a model is a symbolic representation of reality. The symbols used can be mathematical, logical, graphical, or others. The essence is that a model provides a necessarily simplified and schematic picture of a real-world process or phenomenon that is useful for a particular purpose.

As implied by the everyday usage of the term, models can also be implemented as physical objects. This is quite common for teaching and illustrative purposes in the hard and biological sciences – consider for example the physical models of the solar system or of the DNA molecule that you probably encountered in secondary school. Physical models can be used to generate new theoretical insight and predictions as well. In the social sciences, a famous example of a physical model is Bill Phillips's hydraulic model of the British economy, which represented economic processes as the movement of fluids across plastic tanks and pipes and was more than two metres high (see Harford, 2014).

A model is often compared to a map. As maps, models ignore some features of reality in order to emphasize others. Moreover, you need different maps for different purposes – a hiking map would do for trekking, but you would need a different representation of the same area to examine property claims, and yet a third to consult the public transportation lines traversing the region. Similarly, a model built for illustration of a process would not necessarily be a good predictive model. For example, one model will be needed for showing the formal legal steps that need to be fulfilled for a bill to become a law in some legislature, but a different one to show where the politically powerful battles shaping the substance of the bill take place.

Like maps, models do not always benefit from more detail – simplicity and abstraction can improve both as long as enough resolution is retained to serve the predetermined goal. Lastly, just as you would not normally argue that one map is more 'true' than another, you would also not compare models on the basis of how 'true' they are; you would rather consider how well they do their job – prediction, measurement, illustration, explanation, and so on. These remarks about the truth, completeness, and usefulness of models are relevant for evaluating theories as well, as you would expect from the considerable degree of interchangeability of the terms. We will go back to the question of what makes good models and theories towards the end of this chapter, but let us first consider more thoroughly the functions of theory in the research process.

The Functions of Theory

Theories direct attention. They point to the relevant questions to be asked, identify classes of relevant explanatory variables and phenomena, and selectively focus the researcher's gaze on some aspects of reality rather than others. It is instructive to consider at this point what an atheoretical science would look like. Imagine you arrange to spend a month at a public organisation (say, a ministry) with the purpose of understanding how the organization works. Furthermore, imagine that you manage to lose, on purpose or not, all the theoretical background you had acquired over years of schooling – you forget all concepts such as hierarchy, coordination, and authority; all knowledge of organizational structures, roles, culture, and so on. You approach the organization with your mind as a blank slate, *tabula rasa,* with the intention to observe and record everything *as it is* without the interference of theory. But, of course, once you started this atheoretical observation, you would be promptly overwhelmed by a cacophony of impressions, overloaded with information, dizzy from the lack of focus. In the absence of theories to direct attention and provide concepts to structure observations, research is not only difficult, it is downright impossible. For an example of a different kind, consider an atheoretical attempt to make sense of a standard public opinion survey. The possible distributions, correlations, and interactions to explore in the survey dataset are so numerous that without the help of some theory you would be paralysed by the sheer number of possibilities to explore; no feature of the data being more noteworthy, plausible, or significant than any other.

Theories guide observation in a more direct sense as well. They identify empirical puzzles – aspects of reality that are rendered problematic in light of the theory. For example, human cooperation can be considered 'natural' in light of holistic social theories, but it is rendered a puzzle to be explained by theories starting from the assumptions of self-interested individuals. The development of professional merit-based bureaucracy might be viewed as the normal course of state development for modernization theories, but it is considered a puzzle by theories of state capture (see Hellman, Jones, & Kaufmann, 2000). Poor countries with an abundance of natural resources might be considered anomalous according to common sense, but the norm according to 'resource curse' theory (see Humphreys, Sachs, & Stigliz, 2007) – in fact, in light of this theory cases of successful utilization of natural resources for the growth of national wealth will be a puzzle to be accounted for. In short, prevailing theories set the research agenda by identifying puzzles and problems.

But they also predict the existence of facts and practices that would otherwise remain invisible to the observer's eye. Extending the 'standard model' of particle physics (a theory), in 1964 Peter Higgs (alongside other physicists) proposed the existence of a particle now called the Higgs boson. In 2012, scientists finally announced the discovery of a new particle (boson) with a mass consistent with the prediction of Higgs. The discovery was made by monitoring decay products from particle collisions and searching for traces of the brief existence of the Higgs boson. But the measurement of decay signatures is imperfect and, even if it existed, the Higgs boson would be created only in a very small fraction of the collisions – as a result, a very large number of observations were needed. Two teams of scientists working independently at CERN (the European Organization for Nuclear Research) announced the discovery when they had made enough observations to claim a 5-sigma significance each, meaning that there was less than a 1 in 3.5 million chance that the pattern each team registered would have been observed if the Higgs boson did not exist. Scientists needed to make and register more than 300 trillion particle collisions over more than two years, generating more than 50 petabytes of information, before they could detect the traces left by the particle (see Carroll, 2012, for a popular history of the search for the Higgs boson). The point for us is that, in the absence of a theoretical model that predicts what to look for in the particle collision decay products, and without sustained efforts to build and perfect a measurement instrument, there is no chance that somebody would have casually 'observed' or discovered the pattern in the data that would have given away the existence of the Higgs boson.

Political science examples of theories predicting the existence of previously unobserved empirical phenomena are less lucid and lack the drama of twenty-first century particle physics. But they occur nonetheless. The existence of ingenious *institutions for monitoring and sanctioning noncompliance* in managing collective property was recognized, if not discovered, by Elinor Ostrom and her collaborators in the 1970s (see her 1990 book for an introduction). These institutions had existed all along, but they had not captured the attention of social scientists prior to the development of the theory of collective public goods by Ostrom and colleagues. For another example, consider that the importance of risk orientations for a large class of individual decision-making problems was only realized after the development of relevant cognitive theories (see prospect theory and Kahneman & Tversky, 1979). It is not that people did not possess risk orientations before the advent of prospect theory; rather that not many tried to detect, measure, and explain them before they turned out to be crucial for a host of other attitudes and predispositions, including political ones.

Theory not only predicts new phenomena to be observed but also determines what are relevant observations in the first place. In the absence of theory it is easy to get fooled by focusing only on the data that *are* available. Imagine that we are interested in assessing the effectiveness of the United Nations' economic sanctions on target state policies and institutions. Data shows that there are many cases in which sanctions were imposed and countries did not change the offending policies, which would seem to suggest that sanctions are ineffective. But if we try to model theoretically the imposition and reactions to sanctions, we will quickly recognize that it is *the threat* of sanctions that does most of the work in preventing unwanted state policies (see Figure 3.1 for a stylized representation). As a result, the relevant set of cases we need to consider in order to assess the effectiveness of sanctions now includes all cases where *the threat* of sanctions has been present and not only the cases in which sanctions have been *imposed*. If states indeed anticipate and strategically adjust their behaviour to the *possibility* of sanctions, we would have been deceived by our initial

Figure 3.1   *Imposition of and reactions to economic sanctions*

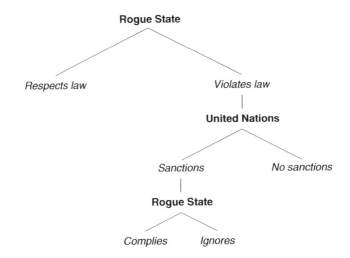

sample of observations (see Lacy & Niou, 2004; Tsebelis, 1990). And
one can push the arguments a step back by arguing that the threat of
sanctions itself is a product of strategic choice and should be included
in the model, which would further extend the universe of relevant cases
for observation.

Theories function as repositories of ideas and existing knowledge.
Theoretical concepts are focal points for practising researchers – they
make knowledge accumulation, as well as disagreements, possible
within an academic subfield. Moreover, they allow for cross-disciplinary
dialogues. For example, the concept of *incentives* brings economics and
political science together; prospect theory – the psychological theory
of risk orientations mentioned above – binds many social sciences that
apply its insights in their respective domains; theories of institutionali-
zation provide bridges between political science and sociology, history,
and anthropology.

The most important function of theory was left for last. Being so
important, it will be discussed in a dedicated chapter (Chapter 6).
Naturally, the main function of explanatory theories is to offer explanations. These explanations are often causal, but we have to wait until
Chapter 6 to make this notion more precise. When fully specified, theories can shed light on *why* and *how* certain phenomena are related,
provide *hypotheses* about previously unnoticed aspects of the world,
predictions about the future state of affairs, and *interpretations* of particular events.

Box 3.1 summarizes the functions of theory discussed so far.

Box 3.1   *What do theories do?*

- Set the research agenda
    Direct research attention
    Identify empirical puzzles
- Direct data collection
    Determine what count as relevant observations
    Predict new empirical facts and patterns
- Enable the accumulation of knowledge and scientific discourse
- Provide and support explanations

The Structure of Theory

Having surveyed the functions of theory, we are ready to discuss its structure. The building blocks of theories are concepts. Concepts are abstract entities that possess a number of carefully defined attributes. Chapter 4 discusses concepts and conceptualization in detail, so for now we can leave it at that. Theories propose relationships between concepts that rest on causal mechanisms and logic explicated in the theory itself. At a minimum, an explanatory theory is a set of internally consistent statements about relationships between concepts linked by mechanisms. As you would expect, each theory has an intended domain of application, which specifies in advance which phenomena should fall under its remit to be explained by its propositions.

To start with an example familiar to most, the theory of evolution is designed to explain the origin and diversity of life on Earth and does so by the two main mechanisms of natural selection and genetic drift; key concepts include heredity, variation, and genes (the last one anticipated but not known in the original formulation of the theory by Charles Darwin).

Faced with the complexity of the social world, all theories make *assumptions* about what to include and what to leave out. Not all of these assumptions can be put directly to the test – they are necessary simplifications. Most models of party competition assume that parties are either motivated by policy goals, or by re-election concerns, or by a mixture of both. Theories of executive–legislative relations routinely assume that the positions of the legislature can be represented by its median member. Theories of international conflict often treat states as unitary actors. As explained above in the section on models, different simplifying assumptions would be appropriate for different research goals. Treating states as unitary actors is obviously unsatisfactory, if we are interested in whether presidential or parliamentary systems are more likely to escalate local conflicts into international wars, but it might be sufficient for an aggregate-level predictive model of the arms race in a bipolar system of international relations.

Combining assumptions with known facts about the way the world works gives rise to the relationships between the core concepts that are at the heart of any theory and to the mechanisms that bind them. A reasonable question to ask at this point is, how do we know which assumptions to make and which 'facts' can we trust to incorporate in the fabric of our theory? A comprehensive answer would take us too far ahead. For now, suffice it to note that tradition, intuition, and received knowledge (often in the form of inductive generalizations from previous empirical work) have major roles to play.

The crucial part of theory development is what follows after the initial idea: once we have identified the assumptions or premises of our theory, we need to tease out in the most transparent, comprehensive, and rigorous way possible all its *implications*. In essence, the process works as follows: we ask, provided that our premises are true, what implications can be deduced from them? In other words, we inquire what is entailed by the set of premises if pushed to their logical limits. The implications can be at the conceptual level or directly about observable phenomena. This is the deductive part of theory development and corresponds to the purely theoretical research, as described in Chapter 2.

It is really hard to infer deductively the implications of even the most simple sets of theoretical premises. That is why scholars use various, more or less formal, tools, including game theory; mathematical analysis; agent-based modelling; causal diagrams; conceptual maps; metaphors; narratives; and explanatory typologies, like Weber's ideal types, in order to get some help in the process. Several illustrations of some of these tools in action are provided later in this chapter. But to get a sense of the challenges involved, try for yourself to deduce informally *all* implications of this simple model of voting behaviour: (A1) voters care to a different degree about different issues, (A2) the preferences of individual voters over different issues are uncorrelated, and (A3) voters choose parties according to how well they represent their preferences. Relevant implications of this model can be derived about individual voting behaviour, party competition, the structure of voters' preference space, the structure of party competition space, the dynamic of party position changes over time, and so on. Considering seriously the implications of the model pushes us to clarify further assumptions left implicit in the model, such as how voters compare the fit of their preference profiles to that of different parties, and so on.

For a more historically flavoured example, think about the implications of the following insightful theoretical statement made by Charles Tilly: 'War made the state, and the state made war' (1975, p. 42). What dynamic of state formation is entailed? Can we derive an implication about the scale and frequency of wars over time on the basis of this simple statement alone?

In practice, deductive analysis rarely proceeds linearly from assumptions to implications and hypotheses. More often, researchers start with a hunch or an idea that can account for a salient feature of the phenomenon they want to explain. Then they trace back the assumptions this idea is based on and try to uncover what is implicit in its logic. Once these premises are exposed, they are ruthlessly analysed until they provide as many and as concrete implications as possible; one of which would of course be the initial idea that started it all. The process is iterative with assumptions leading to clearly nonsensical implications revised or replaced until the researcher is satisfied that his/her model is ready to go out in the open and be matched against additional data and alternative theories. Successful theories would tend to generate their own starting points, so that one proceeds directly from assumptions to hypotheses in order to explore previously untested features or the effect of small changes to the premises.

A major reason to derive theoretical implications is to identify hypotheses. Hypotheses are observable implications; they are testable propositions entailed by the logic of the theory. But do not forget that a hypothesis is also a tentative answer to the question that motivated theory development in the first place. Hypotheses can be stated in various forms, but are usually expressed as 'If X and Z, then Y' or 'The more X, the more Y'. Here are some examples with real concepts rather than symbols: 'If a national minority is politically repressed and has the support of a neighbouring state, then it will start an open rebellion.' 'The closer the election, the higher the turnout.' 'The longer the policy stability, the bigger the policy change that will follow.' 'The more diverse the interests of the negotiating countries, the longer the treaty negotiations.'

Strong hypotheses are deterministic and identify necessary and sufficient conditions that always produce the outcome of interest. They are also very rare, unless trivial (for example, 'All adopted laws have the support of a legislative majority'). They are very rare, because it takes a single aberrant observation to disprove them. Probabilistic hypotheses are weaker in the sense that they posit probabilistic relationships, or tendencies, rather than deterministic associations. Almost all hypotheses that you will encounter and develop will be of the weaker, probabilistic kind, even if they are not stated explicitly as such – after a while it gets tedious to write 'The *probability* of political participation increases with the expected closeness of the election.' The fact that almost all hypotheses are probabilistic also means that they are expected to hold *on average* and given that all else remains equal (the so-called *ceteris paribus* clause). So a fully spelled out hypothesis would state: 'On average, and all else being equal, the probability of political participation should increase linearly with the closeness of the election.' You will note that one more change has been made to the wording – the hypothesis now specifies further what kind of relationship is expected, namely linear (Chapter 7 explains in more detail what a linear relationship implies).

Hypotheses should be stated as precisely as possible. If you can specify the functional form of the expected relationships, do it, as in the example above. If you can narrow down the likely size of the expected effect, do not hesitate. If you can explicitly list the conditions under which the hypothesis should hold, or the contexts in which the effect should be stronger or weaker, do that as well. Of course, your theory needs to be mature enough to allow for this amount of specificity; one cannot just make up precise hypotheses unwarranted by the logic of the model.

Hypotheses often try to account for *a central tendency*, like the average, of the phenomenon or population of interest. If we care about government spending by different ministries, we can trace the spending amounts of ministries over time and develop hypotheses that account for the average spending per year and/or the average spending by a ministry over time (perhaps with reference to the political ideology of the minister, the economic cycle, and so on). But we could also develop hypotheses to account for the *variation* of some phenomenon. We could try to explain and form propositions about the reasons why the *variation* from year to year in spending of some ministries is larger than the variation in spending of others. (Perhaps some ministries have more *discretionary* spending items than others.) Or we could develop hypotheses about how the process of European integration influences the *variation* in welfare spending among European Union member states. For another example, a recent book studied in detail how political institutions affect the *variability* of economic growth (Nooruddin, 2011). In sum, the *variability* of political and policy outcomes can be as relevant for theory and as consequential for practice as the *average* outcome.

Finally, while hypotheses are usually about relationships, they need not be. They could specify expectations about the distribution of some variable and even about the possibility of the existence of some previously unobserved phenomenon (see the paragraph about the Higgs boson above). For example, the punctuated equilibrium theory of policy change developed by Bryan Jones and Frank Baumgartner (2005) posits that the distribution of year-to-year budget item changes over a long period of time would have a peculiar form with a very large number of very small changes and a small number of very, very big changes – a pattern that would not arise under different assumptions of how policies and budgets change. So while the theory is based on a *causal* account of how the policy process works and identifies the relevant mechanisms, the hypothesis it provides is not about a causal *relationship* as such but about the (univariate) distribution of outcomes.

While hypotheses provide tentative answers to a research question, causal mechanisms specify how exactly the hypotheses and the real-world process they represent are supposed to work and why. Causal mechanisms provide the links between the concepts and spell out the background stories that motivate theoretical propositions; they explicate the causal chains that lead from one event to another and from one variable to another.

For example, the hypothesis 'More highly educated individuals are more likely to support European integration' might rely on several mechanisms. One is as follows: education increases knowledge about how the EU political system works, which in its turn induces more trust in the EU, which translates as higher support for integration. Another possible mechanism for the same hypothesis is that more educated people tend to be more competitive in the job market, so they are likely to benefit from increased job competition and mobility; hence they are likely to support integration, which encourages both competition and mobility. Specifying the purported mechanisms behind the theoretical propositions can improve the hypotheses by making them sharper (for example, 'More educated individuals *working in competitive sectors of the economy* are more likely to support European integration') and can provide new expectations as well (for example, Knowledge about the EU moderates the link between education and support for integration).

Causal mechanisms can be provided in the form of stories – narratives that illustrate how the hypothesized effects would work – but can also be embedded in formal models. Sometimes, more specifically when mechanisms are so complex and intertwined that it is not possible to follow them in a narrative, models would envelop the mechanisms in a black box and provide propositions directly. But in any case, mechanisms explicate the analytical level at which the theory is supposed to work; they specify what constitutes an actor in the framework of the theory and which concepts (intentions, structural factors, institutions, and so on) are allowed to play causal roles. We discuss causal mechanisms further in Chapter 6, which deals with explanations and causality.

Causal mechanisms are intricately linked to the question of microfoundations. In political science, by asking for microfoundations scholars demand an explication of how aggregate-level phenomena can be traced back to individual-level actions; that is, to the actions of individual people with their own knowledge, dispositions, and power. For example, if an aggregate-level relationship between the territorial organization of a state (unitary versus federal) and democracy survival in multiethnic societies is hypothesized, the microfoundations would provide the individual-level stories backing the relationship (for example, 'People from geographically concentrated minorities in unitary states routinely are left unrepresented at the national level by elections, which leads them to seek non-democratic means of getting their voice heard, which undermines democracy in the aggregate'). Consider the hypothesis 'Public organizations tend to grow.' What actions, preferences and capabilities at the individual level need to be present to produce the development at the level of organizations that the hypothesis posits?

It is often hard to specify the microfoundations of substantively interesting hypotheses. 'What individual-level dynamics can generate bursts in mass political violence?' 'Which individual-level interactions are important in explaining national foreign policies?' 'Who are the agents behind the impact of policy frames and discourses on public opinion and the actions of the state?' Some theorists would argue that not all social phenomena can be reduced to the individual level and that social entities such as organizations, institutions, states, communities, and more abstract things such as discourses can posses their own explanatory powers and that we need not always push the theoretical analysis to the level of individual people. This view, which goes by the name of methodological holism (in contrast to methodological individualism), argues that there is no reason to suppose that the individual has a more privileged place to start the theoretical analysis than, say, the community.

Furthermore, social groups and institutions have emergent properties – that is, properties at the group level that cannot be reduced to the sum of individual-level properties. Even if individuals are the starting point of the analysis, as with methodological individualism, once they are allowed to interact the properties of the resulting groups cannot be deduced from the individual level. As a result, in some cases the search for microfoundations would be futile. But no matter whether you subscribe to methodological individualism or holism, it is always a good idea to be as specific as possible when describing how exactly the theory you propose or endorse is supposed to work, which inevitably includes statements about the primary level of analysis (individuals, groups, states, and so on).

To recap, explanatory theories are built from concepts on the basis of assumptions and known facts. They are deductively developed systems of internally consistent propositions which provide hypotheses – often in the form of putative relationships between concepts – that have empirical content and are based on explicit causal mechanisms.

Developing Explanatory Theory

In the words of Charles Darwin (1876, p. 9), who knew a thing or two about theories,

> In scientific investigations it is permitted to invent any hypothesis, and if it explains various large and independent classes of facts it rises to the rank of a well-grounded theory.

Different methods can be used to invent hypotheses, but it remains important that, once conceived, hypotheses are analysed to uncover their assumptions and implications. Even the simplest of propositions and the most unassuming of assumptions can have surprisingly rich and unexpected implications when rigorously analysed. To systemically derive implications and follow the logical threads of theoretical ideas researchers have a number of methods at their disposal.

We have already explained the general goal of this type of (purely) theoretical analysis in Chapter 2 (see also Figure 2.2) and mentioned briefly its difficulty earlier in this chapter, when we discussed the structure of theories. In this section of the chapter we will illustrate *how* theoretical analysis proceeds and see a few tools for theory development in action. As with other tools, there is no single one that is fit for all jobs. The task of this section then is to provide you with a general orientation to the range of available choices, so that you do not reach for a hammer when you need pincers. You will need to receive more specialized knowledge and training to master any of the available theory development tools (some suggestions where to start are listed at the end of the chapter). But the overview is important in its own right, because in political science research, as in other crafts, a big part of mastery comes from knowing the right tool for the job at hand.

Informal analysis

Developing explanatory theory in contemporary political science takes many forms, ranging from informal discussion to highly formalized modelling to computer simulations. Informal analysis has its roots in the study of history and the humanities, while formal models are inspired by economics, biology, and the hard sciences.

Inequality and democratization

For an example of informal yet rigorous theorizing consider Charles Tilly's article 'Inequality, Democratization, and De-democratization' (2003). In this text Tilly offers an explanatory theory of transitions to and reversals from democratic forms of government. The major conjecture is that inequality threatens democracy – an old idea which is systematically explored and advanced in the article.

First, the author clarifies the major concepts of the theory – categorical inequality and political regime; in fact, much of the theoretical innovation comes from the careful conceptualization of categorical inequality, which is defined as 'organized differences in advantages by gender, race, nationality, ethnicity, religion, community, and similar classification systems' (p. 37). Then Tilly considers the mechanisms through which governments, including democratic regimes, influence categorical inequality – namely by protecting the advantages of their supporters, by extracting and allocating resources, and by redistribution. Categorical inequality interacts with networks of trust and public politics to make some democratic regimes more vulnerable than others. Democratization provides relatively more equal rights to a wider share of the population, so categorical inequality declines in areas of public politics (p. 39); in a related process, networks of trust start to rely on rather than evade governments. But according to the argument, if this process is reversed, if networks of trust remain outside public politics, participation in the democratic process remains low and erodes protection for the weak in society. So reversal in any of the three – reduction of inequality, broad participation in public politics, and transformations of trust networks – undermines democracy. Note that each element is considered *individually sufficient* to produce the result, although the theory explicates the causal links between all three.

A set of conjectures, such as 'Without compensating changes in government activity, increasing categorical inequality within the subject population decreases breadth, equality, bindingness, and protection of agent-subject relations and thereby de-democratizes regimes' (p. 41), is offered at the end of the analysis. Tilly is clear that the main conjectures of his theory are derived on the basis of close observations of several European cases, hence inductively, but the theoretical analysis pursues and clarifies the logic of the argument to the point that clear hypotheses can be formed – for example, reversal from democracy should be related to failures of governments to co-opt major trust networks in society. It is interesting to ask what the microfoundations of the analysis are, and whether formalization of its logic using one of the tools described below could provide any additional analytical leverage.

Mathematical analysis

Formalizing the theory so that its structure can be analysed and represented by mathematical equations is a common strategy in political science research and one that is often fruitful. The advantages of formalization and mathematical analysis are that all assumptions are explicated, the consistency of the theory is guaranteed, and the implications and hypotheses are crisp and precise. The major disadvantage is that formalization and the subsequent mathematical analysis are hard even for experts, so only models of limited complexity can be treated in this way. The difficulty is not only with the analysis itself but also with the communication of the results and the logic of the model. That being said, many areas of political science have benefited from formalization of their theoretical ideas.

Public opinion and policy

Formal mathematical analysis proceeds by specifying the purported relationships between the theoretical concepts in a system of equations and analysing how the system works. For example, Christopher Wlezien proposed a theory of how public opinion and policy influence each other

(1995). Because it is known that, in general, the public is not very well informed about the details of most policies, it is theoretically problematic to propose that absolute levels of public support for certain policies should be directly influenced by policy changes, and that leaves open the question of how shifting public opinion affects policy. Wlezien proposed that the public acts essentially as a thermostat – the public might not have a very clear idea about its ideal level of, say, military spending, but might know whether the current level is too little or too much (so the public has relative preferences over policy). So when spending increases, the public adjusts its relative preferences similarly to a thermostat reacting to a change in temperature. Once the level is 'right' no further signal is sent to the policy makers by the public. But then outside events or shocks can bring the link with public opinion out of balance, which would trigger a new process of adjustment until the two are in equilibrium again. Wlezien formalizes this argument with a single equation:

$$\Delta R_t = \Delta P^*_t - \Delta P_t,$$

which says that the relative preference of the public R at time t changes as a function of changes in the absolute preference level P^* and changes in the policy P itself.

In some circumstances, formalization allows the researcher to build an appropriate statistical model to test the implications of the theory. The initial empirical test indeed showed support for the 'public thermostat' model, which initiated a small research program devoted to studying the links between public opinion and policy in various democratic societies and policy areas (see, for example, Soroka & Wlezien, 2010). Thermostatic models prove to be useful for understanding other social and political phenomena as well (see Schelling, 2006).

Diffusion of innovations
Another family of models having wide applicability in the social sciences and beyond are diffusion models. They have been used to study the spread of diseases in a population, technological innovations in firms, new public policies among countries, norms among individuals, and so on. To understand the dynamics of diffusion over time, formalization can go a long way. A very simple version of a diffusion model is represented by Frank Bass's single equation (1969):

$$\frac{f(t)}{1 - F(t)} = p + qF(t),$$

where $f(t)$ is the rate of change in the installed base fraction, $F(t)$ is the installed base fraction, p is the coefficient of innovation, and q is the coefficient of imitation. The model supposes that there are two types of individuals – innovators and imitators, who differ in their propensity to adopt innovations. Even such a simple set-up can provide expectations about the speed of innovation, the size of the 'affected' community over time, peak levels of adoption, and other things. In fact, versions of the Bass diffusion model are routinely used in marketing to forecast the life-cycle of new goods.

Diffusion models also generate expectations about the distribution of affected versus unaffected agents over time, which, assuming a fixed population, takes a characteristic 'S' shape. One can then test whether the spread of some policy innovation (for example, smoking bans) in the real world is likely to have arisen from policy diffusion or from states acting independently by comparing the empirical distribution of the policy adoption over time to the theoretically derived shape (Toshkov, 2013).

Many mathematical formalizations of political science theory take the form of *equilibrium analysis* – a tool borrowed from the discipline of economics, where it plays a major role, for example for studying the dynamic relationship between demand and supply. Equilibrium can be understood as a stable relationship between phenomena (public opinion and policy, news volume and political attention, inflation and unemployment, political platforms and electoral dispositions, and so on), but it has a more specific meaning in the context of game theory, which is a special type of mathematical formalization for theory development.

Game theory

Game theory is a tool for analysing the strategic aspects of human inter-actions. It can be employed to model relationships between countries disputing a territory, political parties distributing government positions, individuals haggling over the price of a goat, or any other situation where the outcome depends on the actions of more than one actor. Game theory is useful when actors can be expected to have reasonably stable and clear interests (preferences, desires), which may be diametrically opposed or partially aligned, and it has been used extensively to study problems of social conflict and cooperation. In essence, game theory proceeds by identifying the agents participating in the game, positing on the basis of assumptions or external information a set of preferences and beliefs for each of them, and specifying the rules of the game (available actions and information, sequence of play, and so on). It then asks: what is the optimal course of action for any agent given his/her preferences and beliefs, the preferences and beliefs of the other agents, and the structure of the game? Putting everything together, the analysis provides expectations about the actions of the players and the aggregate (group) level outcome of the game using the concept of 'equilibrium' (a set of strategies or plans for playing the game for each of the players that no agent would want unilaterally to deviate from).

The power of game theory comes from offering a map for a territory that would otherwise be quite intractable – namely what *should* and what *would* rational agents with possibly divergent interests and beliefs do. To see for yourself how maddeningly difficult such questions can be, try to develop predictions or advice on how to play an extremely simple game with two players only (A and B) and two available actions to pick (Left and Right) for each. Choices are made simultaneously. A wins if both players choose Left or if both choose Right; and B wins if there is a mismatch (for example, A chooses Left and B chooses Right). It quickly becomes obvious that it is better for A to choose Left if B chooses Left and Right if B chooses Right, while for B it is better to pick Left if A plays Right and Right if A plays Left. Still that does not help us much as choices are made at the same time – our analysis is trapped in infinite regress. Game theory provides a way out. A complete answer to the above riddle requires familiarity with the concept of mixed strategies, but the intuition of the solution is simple to explain: the best strategy for both players is to randomize their actions so that choices cannot be guessed and adapted to. Similar to a penalty shoot-out in a game of soccer, the moment your action is guessed, you lose.

Game theory has given political science a number of such relatively simple models – the Prisoner's Dilemma, the Game of Chicken, the Ultimatum Game, Battle of the Sexes, Matching Pennies, and others – which have been extensively analysed over the years. These simple models often provide important insights about society and politics at a very general level. Prominent examples include the sum of actions of rational individuals can be collectively disastrous (Prisoner's Dilemma); in the absence of communication, coordination is hard, even if actors share the same interests (Coordination Game); restricting your own set of options or making your opponent believe you are mad can be advantageous (games of deterrence); and so on. But the simple models can also be adapted to fit particular situations and made more complex (for example, by including informational asymmetries between the players) and thus be brought closer to the reality of real-life political interactions and institutions.

Decision-making in the EU

One such application is provided by Robert Thomson and colleagues (Thomson et al., 2006; Thomson, 2011). The big aim of the project was to understand decision-making in the European Union and assess the relative power of the different institutions (the European Commission, the Council of Ministers, and the European Parliament) that decide together on EU laws and policies. The rather complex decision-making rules of the EU can be modelled theoretically in a variety of ways, and the researchers developed several related models, all grounded in game theory but making different assumptions about the structure of the process and the role procedural rules play (see also Steunenberg, 1994; Steunenberg,

Schmidtchen, & Koboldt, 1999). Then they proceeded to gather, through expert interviews, information on the preferences of each actor (EU institution) on a number of different law proposals. Having measured the interests of the actors, the scientists plugged the information into the theoretical models and compared their predictions with the actual outcomes of the legislative negotiations. Testing alternative model specifications, the project concluded that models that downplay procedural rules perform altogether better and suggested that the European Parliament is weaker than the procedural models imply (Thomson et al., 2006).

War and the balance of power
Players, or agents, in game-theoretic models can be individuals; institutions, as in the example above; or even countries – in fact, one of the motivations for the development of game theory since the 1940s has been to analyse international relations and specifically those between the nuclear superpowers USA and USSR. Focusing on wars more generally, Powell (1999) theorizes how war depends on the power between states and shifts in the balance. Exploring a family of related game-theoretic models, he derives implications about the probability of violent conflict in terms of the alignment between the current distribution of benefits and power (it rises with disparity) and in terms of the speed of change in the power balance (rapid as well as gradual shifts can lead to war).

So far, we have seen examples of game theory being employed to provide general insight and to model particular political processes and classes of events. But its utility can be taken a step further by using it *to design* institutional mechanisms with desired properties. It works as follows: first, we build a model that captures the essence of some real-life phenomena. Then, once we are satisfied that the model provides sufficient theoretical understanding, we manipulate its features (sequence of play and so on) to discover a game with a structure that elicits outcomes we like (for example, no actor has an incentive to misrepresent his/her preferences, or no actor can be made better-off without making somebody worse-off – a criterion known as Pareto efficiency). Finally, we translate the model into a real institution used by real people, organizations, and so on. Mechanism design has been successfully applied to set up auction rules, to improve matching algorithms (for example, between schools and pupils, or firms and interns), and to develop mechanisms for organ exchange (for example, kidney-paired donation in the United Kingdom), the latter two applications bringing the Nobel Prize to economist Alvin Roth in 2012 (see his prize lecture for an accessible overview of these topics).

Agent-based modelling

Despite its utility for theorizing about strategic interactions that are ubiquitous in politics, game theory cannot be applied to all research problems. In addition to imposing very strict requirements for the rationality of actors, it can become too complex and intractable with many actors, many different types of actors, and a complicated game structure. The beauty of its mathematical deductions comes at the price of assuming sometimes too much about the consistency of individuals' desires and people's capabilities to reason strategically.

An alternative to game-theoretic analysis is agent-based modelling (ABM), which is a form of simulation or computational analysis. Instead of endowing actors with hyper-rationality, ABM gives them simple behavioral rules to follow – for example, in a world represented by a spatial grid, move left if space is unoccupied, stay put if occupied. Once the model 'world' is populated with various types of autonomous agents following different but precise instructions, we let the interactions play out by repeated application (iteration) of the rules and look for any systematic patterns to appear.

In essence, scientists build a stylized representation of a phenomenon they wish to understand with the hope that the phenomenon will emerge as a result of the unsupervised interactions of agents encoded with rules to follow. Once the model is successful in generating the outcome or pattern of interest, its other properties are explored for further validation or calibration. Nowadays, ABM is performed mostly on computers, which do the necessary iterations in a matter of seconds, but the rules can be implemented with enough patience using any medium.

A paradigmatic example of the use of ABM outside the social sciences is modelling bird behaviour. With an extremely simple set of rules for each bird (steer towards the average position and heading of the neighbours but avoid getting too close to any of them) scientists have been able to generate group movement patterns of surprising complexity reminiscent of the movements of real flocks of birds (Reynolds, 1987). The model has been used for, among other purposes, simulating movements of groups of birds (and bats) for computer animations for Hollywood films.

Segregation

Thomas Schelling's famous segregation model (1969, 1971) demonstrates how ABM can be used to shed light on social-scientific questions. Schelling was intrigued by the puzzle of racial segregation in housing decisions – why people from different races tend to form homogeneous neighbourhoods. One rather obvious possible explanation is that people from the same race just prefer each other's company. Such a preference can certainly account for the pattern of separation, but is it *necessary* for its emergence? Schelling's model showed that, in fact, a strong fondness for the company of your own race is not necessary for segregation to occur at the aggregate level. Even if people have very moderate racial preferences (at least one-third of my neighbours should be from the same race), they will tend to separate into racially homogeneous neighbourhoods as an effect of the sorting process.

Schelling demonstrated this counter-intuitive dynamic with 'a roll of pennies and a roll of dimes, a tabletop, [and] a large sheet of paper' (2006, p. 147), but nowadays you can find computer applications on the Internet that implement his model. The setup of the game is rather simple – the two types of agents (pennies and dimes) are spread (randomly or not) to occupy squares on a chequerboard. Agents look into their immediate neighbourhood (the surrounding squares), and if they find that less than a certain percentage (say, one-third) of their neighbours are from the same type, they move to a new randomly selected square on the chequerboard. Otherwise agents are 'happy' and stay in place. The process is repeated until no agent wants to move. The main result of the model is that a segregation pattern in which pennies and dimes form homogeneous neighbourhoods would arise under very general conditions (including different starting distribution, strength of racial preferences, ratio of dimes versus pennies, and so on). But even more importantly, the model vividly shows the dynamics, the 'unravelling' process by which segregation emerges (which is why Schelling insisted on trying the chequerboard rather than the digital version of the model). It is important to note that Schelling's segregation model does not 'prove' that people do not have segregation preferences. What he does is show that a different mechanism from strong racial preferences *can* equally account for this sorting behaviour, but of course it remains an empirical question whether in any real situation one or the other mechanism holds. Nevertheless, the theoretical model provides a novel insight that motivates an empirical research agenda, has important implications for urban planning, and is one reason why Thomas Schelling got the Nobel Prize in 2005.

Consensus in legislative politics
ABM can also be used to theorize problems of legislative decision-making, as a recent study by Frank Häge shows (2013). His model tackles the puzzle of consensus in the Council of Ministers of the EU, which refers to the fact that a large percentage (more than 75 percent) of all decisions taken by the members of this institution (the number of members ranging from 15 to 27 for the time of the analysis) are taken without any negative votes being recorded, even when a majority of the votes would suffice for a decision. Many have tried to explain this phenomenon before, and one possible interpretation is that there is a strong 'consensus culture' in the Council of Ministers that demands that negotiations continue until every member is satisfied and controversial decisions that go against the interest of any member would not be taken. Häge models the coalition-building process by assuming that each actor groups with others with similar positions until the group is big enough to block a decision they do not like. By adopting a common group of positions the actors make some sacrifices, so it makes sense to group with the 'closest' positions only, and only until the coalition is just big

enough to be able to block adversary decisions. The process is repeated until either one group forms that is big enough to impose its position, or one or more blocking coalitions emerge, which means that the final decision needs to be a compromise that the blocking coalitions would agree to. As a result, under the second scenario the final decision would be approved by all, but the consensus will be just a side effect of the coalition-building process arising from the independent actions of actors who pursue their own policy goals.

So far, the model provides a mechanism for the way in which consensual decisions in the Council of Ministers *could* arise, but that is not all. Running the model many times and examining the effect of changing its parameters (number of actors, majority threshold, and others), Häge comes up with a prediction that the number of actors has only a small effect on the rate of consensual decisions, while changing the majority threshold would have a big impact. These predictions can be tested against data generated by the functioning of the Council of Ministers, given that its compositions and rules of procedure change over time.

Note that both the segregation and coalition-building models provide theoretical results that would not have been obvious from informal analysis of their assumptions. The whole point of using ABM is to examine systematically the implications of your theoretical starting points: implications that cannot be deduced by mere mortals just thinking very long and hard. The difference from game theory is that the implications are not *mathematically* deduced from the premises, rather we have to rely on *simulations* to examine what patterns are generated by the operation of our model: full-fledged mathematical analysis would have been impossible for these models due to their complexity.

ABM has also been used, for example, to theorize about world politics, international conflicts, and state formation, with interesting implications derived about the size of wars over time, the distribution of country sizes, nationalist insurgencies, and so on (Cederman, 1997, 2003).

Statistical models

Statistical models and statistical modelling are ubiquitous in political science, and it is important to clarify how they relate to the formal explanatory models described in this chapter. Altogether, statistical models are not of the same sort as the mathematical, game-theoretic, and agent-based computational models discussed above. Most of the time, they do not even fall under the definition of theoretical models discussed here. Statistical models *operationalize* theoretical models with the aim of estimating structural parameters, making predictions, and testing hypotheses. They do not specify causal mechanisms or microfoundations or bring insight into the process producing the phenomenon of interest. They are no substitute for theory.

In principle, statistical models should directly translate the structure of theoretical models, and, in an ideal world, the two should remain very close. In practice, statistical models make a number of additional assumptions, such as linearity of the purported relationships, which are not always derived from the theoretical model. Political science theory rarely offers sufficiently detailed and specific guidance to specify all components of statistical models. That being said, understanding the assumptions of statistical models (see Chapter 7) can improve theory development by pushing the theoretical analysis towards more specificity.

How to better translate the structure of formal theoretical models into observable implications that can be tested with data is currently an area of active research in political science; for details see the Empirical Implications of Theoretical Models research program (Clarke & Primo, 2007; Granato & Scioli, 2004; Whang, 2010).

What Makes a Good Theory?

We have postponed this crucial question long enough. Now that we have some idea of what theories are, what they are supposed to do, and how they are developed, we need to discuss what makes some theories better than others. The short answer is that there is a combination of criteria that good theories need to fulfil. You may find this answer somewhat disturbing if you assumed that the one and only virtue of theories is their truth.

Truth

There are two rather different philosophical perspectives on the relationship between theory and truth. According to a realist view, the theoretical starting points (assumptions) need to be true and the mechanisms need to closely represent reality in order to produce a satisfactory theory. An instrumentalist view, on the other hand, would insist that we can remain agnostic about the truth value of theoretical assumptions as long as the theory remains useful for our purposes – for example, if the theory predicts well the outcome we are interested in. If empirical patterns match predictions based on the theory, the truthfulness of the axiomatic structure of the theory need not concern us too much. In short, theories do not need to be true, but useful.

Indeed, we already noted that theories and models are by necessity simplifications, so they cannot be expected to be truthful representations of reality. We can devise theories *as if* actors have well-behaved sets of preferences and *as if* they have unlimited power of reasoning as long as the implications of these assumptions offer explanatory or predictive leverage or general insight into a problem. While in the abstract the realist and the instrumentalist views seem worlds apart, in the practice of research they meet somewhere in the middle. A pragmatic view on the matter can be summarized as follows: while theories cannot and should not be expected to provide full, and in this sense truthful, representations of reality, if their assumptions are widely discordant with reality, they are very unlikely to be useful. How could completely wrong assumptions provide consistently useful propositions and predictions? How could we systematically generate good explanations, if we have given the wrong causal mechanisms a central role in our theories? At the same time, simplifications are not wrong by default as long as they allow us to retain *enough* explanatory, predictive, or analytical power.

Parsimony

Simpler theories should be preferred to more complex ones, given the same theoretical power. Models based on fewer and more general assumptions are better if the loss in predictive capacity is minimal. These statements follow from the famous 'Ockham's razor' – if two hypotheses can explain a phenomenon, the one based on fewer assumptions should be preferred. The value of parsimony is well established in the practice of political science explanatory research and has implications for concepts and descriptive work as well – a shorter definition is to be preferred if it allows us to make the same empirical distinctions. The principle may be justified on different grounds – aesthetic, pragmatic, or empirical – but is best regarded as heuristic rather than a law of nature. And while, all else being equal, simpler theories are to be preferred, in reality there will always be *some* trade-off between parsimony and explanatory power, and the principle of Ockham's razor offers no guidance on how to proceed in this case. To paraphrase slightly the words of Albert Einstein: make theoretical statements as simple as possible, but not simpler.

Generality

Similarly, theories should be made as general as possible, but no further. As a principle, researchers should not restrict the scope of application of their theories unless forced to by logical considerations or empirical failures. Thus, a theory of democratization need not be restricted to apply only to the twenty-first century or only to Latin America, unless some of its mechanisms rely on phenomena (for example, digital social networks) that would not have existed in some time periods or places. It is quite important to be explicit about the intended generality of the theory so that appropriate selection of cases for testing and application can be made in the design of empirical research.

Often, political science theories may be framed as more general than they really are. Many theoretical arguments are deeply rooted in

American or West European political experiences but are presented as if having general application. The researchers need to be diligent and specify the boundaries of their arguments: Is the theory supposed to apply only to democracies or to any political regime? Is it applicable only for rich industrialized societies? Is it relevant for all kinds of organizations or only to public ones? And so on.

The reasons to value generality in theories are several. First, generality brings *integrated* understanding. We do not want to have different coalition-building theories for each country or for each government formation process. If the theories are so specific as to apply to a single episode or to a couple of cases, they hardly deserve their name. The purpose of a theory is to enable transfer of insight and understanding from one case to another, to bring seemingly disparate phenomena under a common logic, to illuminate the commonalities and explain the patterns in social and political life.

Ideally, we should have a single theory of individual decision-making and not one for political decisions, a second for economic ones, and third for family ones. While it would be ideal to have an integrated theory, logic and evidence might force us to retain different theories for the various domains of decision-making, but then we should have an explanation for why this is the case, so that the particular theories are brought under a common framework. For another example, a general theory of economic voting should explain how individual economic well-being influences electoral choices in advanced democracies but also in semi-autocratic regimes, in the USA but also in Africa, now but also at the dawn of electoral politics.

Second, generality is related to parsimony – simple theoretical structures necessarily have a wide intended scope of application and vice versa. So generality and parsimony reinforce each other. Third, the search for generality triggers conceptual development as new concepts are crafted to cover previously separate phenomena. Fourth, generality is efficient in the sense that less information needs to be remembered for the same explanatory potential.

Precision

Without any doubt, all theories gain from clarity and precision. Unclear theories having vaguely specified mechanisms, hidden assumptions, and poorly specified structure are to be avoided altogether. A hallmark of a good theory is that it is precise enough so that it can be disproven. It is usually a good test for the quality of a theory to consider the questions: What does the theory rule out? What would *not* be consistent with its logic? What evidence would contradict its propositions? If you cannot answer all these questions, then the theory is no good and should be either further explicated or abandoned.

A fun case in point to consider is conspiracy theory. Conspiracy theories would not qualify as scientific explanations because any empirical findings can be reconciled with them – the absence of evidence that the world is secretly ruled by a select few illuminati living on a big ship floating in the ocean *is the evidence* that the rulers of the world are so powerful that they can hide any evidence of their existence. So it is not possible even in principle to disprove the conspiracy theory, which puts it off the limits of scientific work. Note, however, that this does not preclude the theory being actually true! The impossibility of disconfirmation. only means that the scientific method cannot be applied in the case, not that the theory is wrong.

Many theories may be formulated at such a high level of abstraction as to be invulnerable to empirical disconfirmation. While they could provide useful starting points, to turn them into proper explanatory theories one should develop and translate their logic to a level where the empirical implications are clear and crisp hypotheses can be derived.

To sum it all up, good explanatory theories are built on reasonable assumptions that are as few and as simple as possible, yet rich in their implications and empirically successful in their predictions and hypotheses. Their scope of application is general but above all clearly specified, their structure is transparent and internally consistent, and their propositions are precise and testable.

Practical Considerations about Theory

We have cleared a lot of ground in this chapter already. Now we need to pause and reflect on what all of it means for the *design* of research projects in political science. Important practical concerns remain: Which theory to use for my project? Shall I develop my own theory or apply an existing one? Which tool to use to develop my theory? To answer these questions, to the extent that they can be answered in general, the best starting point is to consider again the goal of your research. To repeat Chapter 2, the goal is key, and the research design, theoretical choices included, follows from the objective.

First, if you are interested in a theory-testing type of research, the questions above are easy to answer – you pick a theory that you deem worth testing; you might need to clarify, extend, or gauge some of its propositions, but then you proceed with operationalizing the concepts and case selection, which are the crucial components of research design for such projects. For example, you might want to test the theory of racial bias in political candidate evaluation (see, for example, Sigelman et al., 1995), but in the understudied case of local rather than national elections. You might have to do some theoretical work to adjust the existing theory to the case of local elections if need be, but the bulk of the contribution, and the work, would not be theoretical but empirical, and problems of operationalization and case selection loom larger than ones of theory development.

Second, you might be interested in **theory development** as such. By this I mean not generating inductively new theoretical ideas (which will be discussed shortly), but purely deductive analysis. A self-contained theory-development project is certainly possible, but it requires rather special skills. The main thing to consider for such a research project is why a new theory is needed in the first place: improvements in any of the criteria listed in the previous section – predictive and explanatory power, parsimony, generality, clarity – can provide suitable motivations. Theory-development projects may take several forms. While you would rarely start completely from scratch, you could explore the implications of changing or relaxing the assumptions of existing models, formalize a promising theory that has been expressed so far only in narrative form, pursue new implications of old theories, or revise old theories in light of new knowledge coming from other scientific fields. Hopefully, the illustrations of several tools with which to do deductive theoretical analysis in this chapter has provided a flavour of these types of research projects.

Third, you can design a project to inductively generate new theories. This strategy is suitable for relatively new problems where little deductive theorizing exists. The idea is to collect detailed information for a small number of cases and develop bottom-up from the data hypotheses that can account well for the current set of cases and can be further tested in the field. By definition, in this type of research project you rely little on prior theory. Nevertheless, existing theories guide what type of data would be collected, which aspects of the cases would be deemed worth exploring, and so on, and you need to pay attention to and explicate these general theoretical orientations, or starting points, even for inductive theory-generating projects.

Fourth, in applied research one might be interested in applying a particular theory to a particular case. In this most simple of situations, a theory is taken off the shelf and its propositions are used to interpret a single case, or a set of parameters is fed into a model to provide a new prediction. Such routine theory application is useful only if the theories are already known to work well and can be taken 'for granted' for the particular explanatory or predictive tasks in hand. So in this mode of research the choice of theory to use should be almost self-evident – if it is not, the scientific field is not mature enough to support theory application as a routine activity.

Fifth, the most tricky situation is when you are primarily interested in explaining a puzzle, a single case, or a unique event, and have little interest in theoretical generation, development, or testing as such. Case-driven research is embedded in theory, but pure deduction or induction is not a good representation of how the research proceeds and offers poor guidance as to which theories to use. A stylized account of the scientific process for explaining particular cases can be summarized as follows (a more comprehensive discussion is available in Chapter 9): start by identifying some salient features of the case, develop hypotheses that can account for these features, explore what other implications these hypotheses have, check if these additional implications receive empirical support, and conclude which one is most likely to have explanatory relevance for the case at hand. The method resembles how detectives and medical doctors work and has been termed 'logical abduction'. Existing general theories relate to abduction in a number of ways: (1) They inform the initial selection of salient case features to observe and measure. (2) The working hypotheses formed need to be consistent with general theories and mechanisms; indeed, they should normally follow from some well-established general theories of the class of phenomena our case belongs to. (3) The conclusion feeds back into the pool of theoretical knowledge by either suggesting a completely new theory, adjusting the scope conditions, or offering unconditional support for existing ones.

There is just one final issue left to consider before we are ready to cross into the next chapter. As important as it is, theory is not all of political science. It should be used to support rather than discourage exploration, not to denounce but to give significance to description, and to inspire rather than constrain experimentation. Theory testing cannot monopolize the scientific agenda. Research should be free to follow where empirical puzzles lead, even if no theoretical explanations are available for the time being. The straitjacket of theory-testing research templates should not be allowed to paralyse the spirit of discovery.

Further Reading

A good introduction to the philosophy of science issues discussed in this chapter is provided by Rosenberg (2000) and the accompanying collection of original texts (Bolshoi & Rosenberg, 2002). Chalmers (1999) is another very accessible introduction. The volume edited by Mantzavinos (2009) offers a more advanced treatment, and one from a social scientific angle.

Stinchcombe (1968) and Merton (1967) remain two of the best discussions of theories and theory development in the social sciences. Elster (2007) offers a more contemporary alternative.

General texts on model building include Jaccard and Jacoby (2010); Shoemaker, Tankard, and Lasorsa (2004); and Rueschemeyer (2009). A good accessible introduction to game theory is Dixit, Skeath, and Reiley (2009) and a more challenging one is Osborne (2003); an advanced textbook with a political science focus is McCarty and Meirowitz (2014). On agent-based modelling consult De Marchi (2005). A good text on building general mathematical (predictive) models is Taagepera (2008).

Chapter 4

Concepts and Operationalization

This chapter deals with the nature of concepts and with their translation into operationalized constructs that can be studied empirically. It takes us from the heights of the most abstract discussions about the definition of definitions and the conceptualization of concepts to the most practical, feet-on-the-ground issues of measurement.

Concepts are the elementary, bite-size units of reason. Yet, they can evolve and become quite a mouthful. The chapter discusses in detail the definition, nature, and structure of concepts to prepare the ground for their analysis, or conceptualization. Once conceptualization has clarified and imposed analytical rigour the concept is ready to be operationalized into observable indicators and 'detectors'.

In the context of research design the processes of conceptualization and operationalization have central roles in mediating between the world of abstract theoretical entities and the world of empirical observations. They translate theoretical propositions into concrete empirical expectations, and they connect real cases to abstract categories. The chapter explains what the process of conceptualization entails and covers the related, and rather tricky, issue of classification. The operationalized concepts and classification schemes constrain in important ways the type of research that would be appropriate to study the processes and phenomena they represent.

The chapter concludes by listing some of the many pitfalls of concept formation and deployment in research in political science. It is easy to identify the dangers of conceptual profusion, stretching, functional equivalence, and beyond, but no single recipe for success will be provided, because there cannot be one. Conceptualization is after all a question of fine balancing. Apply too rigid and strict definitions, and empirical relevance might be lost. Allow too loose and compromising definitions, and the analytical clarity will be gone.

Concepts

The previous chapter posited that theories are logically connected systems of propositions. Propositions are made of concepts and the relations between them. Therefore, the development and analysis of concepts is an integral part of theory development. At the same time, concepts are

83

generalizations and abstractions of empirical events and phenomena: in the words of Giovanni Sartori, they are 'fact-containers' (1970). It is in this sense that the dual processes of conceptualization and operationalization bridge the world of theoretical propositions and the world of empirical phenomena.

Concepts are the *building blocks* of scientific reasoning, and of human cognition in general. They are essential for core scientific activities such as theory formation, description, categorization, and causal inference. What's more, they are indispensable for fundamental cognitive tasks, such as the formation of memories, the use of language, and learning. To think is to use concepts, in science as in daily life.

Defining concepts

But *defining* concepts is difficult. To discuss (conceptualize?) the concept of *concept* is a brain-twister only philosophers and their like can enjoy. Yet, given the central role concepts play in the process of research, we have to try to get more precise as to what they are, how they work, and what makes some better than others.

The Merriam-Webster Dictionary defines a concept as 'an abstract or generic idea generalized from particular instances' and 'something conceived in the mind: thought, notion'. Let us unpack these definitions and see how they apply to the case of *scientific* concepts.

First, concepts are general. While me voting on the 2nd of December 2014 is a concrete event, the concept of *voting* is indeed more general and transcends this particular realization. The imposition of some tough economic policy choices ('austerity') on Greece in the aftermath of the 2008 financial crisis by its international creditors is a concrete event; the concepts of *power* and *debt* are not. So, concepts appear *to be* generalizations of particular instances, which is not to say that they are *created by* generalizing these instances (see below). While it is conceivable that we create the concept '*me voting on the 2nd of December 2014*' that would refer to one and only one event (hence, it would not be general), it is hard to see what the use of such a concept would be. Even when there is only one possible empirical realization of a concept, say the Universe, the concept of *universe* still needs to remain *general* and allow, at least theoretically, for other realizations. In sum, especially in the context of science, concepts can be assumed to be general.

Second, concepts are abstract. Intuitively, if concepts are not about particular instances and events in the world, then they must be abstract. In this case, the intuition is correct, but some concepts can still be more abstract than others. Linguists, neurolinguists, and other cognitive scientists have introduced the distinction between abstract and concrete concepts. The latter are more familiar and readily imagined and are often acquired directly through sensory perception rather than verbally or by reading the appropriate entry in an encyclopedia. *Voting* would be an example of a concrete concept (at least for people lucky enough to have had some direct experience of this activity), while *representation* would be an example of a rather abstract concept; similarly for *desire* and *utility*, *conflict* and *neutrality*, *meeting* and *coordination*. Admittedly, the distinction is not always clear-cut, especially when it comes to political *science* concepts which are all situated towards the abstract end of the continuum. For instance, consider the concepts of *money* and *power*: are they abstract or concrete? It is hard to answer, because they seem to be both very abstract and very concrete at the same time. Yet, the distinction between abstract and concrete concepts is important because, if cognitive scientists are to be believed, they are processed by the human brain quite differently (see, for example, Crutch & Warrington, 2005, and, for a meta-analysis, Wang et al., 2010). Concrete concepts have a significant cognitive advantage over abstract ones (Jelec, 2014, p. 56). To sum up, concepts are in principle all abstract, but some can be said to be more concrete than others, especially when we consider everyday concepts lumped together with scientific ones.

In the context of research design and conceptualization, it is not entirely clear what to make of the finding that humans process concrete concepts easier, faster, and more reliably. On the one hand, ease of processing is not necessarily a virtue of *scientific* concepts, if it comes at the expense of clarity or generality (see below for these and other criteria of good concepts). On the other hand, if scientific results are to be communicated and understood, ease of processing the concepts should be a consideration. One possible resolution of the dilemma is to employ, in research, concepts that are as abstract as needed, but to translate the results into more concrete concepts and terms when they need to be communicated to a wider audience.

Beyond the properties of generality and abstractness, the ontological nature of concepts (what concepts really *are*) is even more hotly contested. There is an ongoing debate in philosophy whether concepts are abstract *entities* (hence, in some sense objective), mental *representations* (hence, psychological), or even some sort of cognitive *abilities* (see Margolis & Laurence, 1999, 2007, for overviews). Currently, the most popular view, especially among practising scientists, seems to be that concepts are the mental representations of a class of objects. As mental representations, concepts have physical existence in the brain. So defined, concepts appear subjective. But it is important to clarify that they are still *shareable* (Laurence & Margolis, 1999) – they can be communicated between people forming subjective mental representations. Furthermore, even as representations, concepts are not completely divorced from objective reality, so any mental representation of a concept can be evoked at will. Different people would think of different prime examples when they think of the concept *negotiation*, for example, but the individual mental representations can still be sufficiently similar to be shareable (Laurence & Margolis, 1999, pp. 7–8).

The nature of concepts

It has already been said that a concept refers to a class of objects. But, we have to add, a concept cannot be defined simply by listing all objects that it covers. For one, that would be rather impractical even when the number of referent objects is finite. What's more, the list would still fail to point out what the *essence* of a concept is. We cannot understand the concept of *democracy* by simply listing all possible instances of democracies around the world and over time. Some analysis would be required to single out what are the *essential* features of democracies, how they relate to other types of government, and so on.

The classical view

According to the so-called classical view, or classical theory, concepts have rule-based definitional structure. That is, a concept is defined by a set of individually necessary and jointly sufficient conditions that delimit unambiguously what qualifies as its empirical realizations. Say we define democracies as these political regimes that hold contested elections for state power. This leads to a simple model for categorization. The experience of contested elections would be a necessary and sufficient condition for a country to qualify as a democracy; all countries, and only those countries, that satisfy the condition would do so. If we consider this definition too minimal and add the requirement that a large part of the population should be able to vote in the elections, we would have a definition of the concept that has two conditions that are individually necessary and jointly sufficient for a country to qualify as a democracy, and we can apply the new rule to recategorize the countries.

Definitions under the classical view have appealing logic and clarity. It is easy to see why they are still the preferred way of defining political science concepts. A civil war is an armed conflict between the state and organized military opposition challenging the internationally recognized sovereignty of a state which causes a large number of deaths (based on Doyle & Sambanis, 2000, 2006). A public organization is an organization that is directly or indirectly controlled by the state and works in the interest of the public. Examples can be easily multiplied. We will explore in more detail how to construct and analyse concepts with the help of necessary and sufficient conditions later in this chapter, but let's first consider alternatives to the classical view.

The prototype view

As attractive as rule-based definitions are, it turns out that humans just do not learn and process concepts like that, at least not all of the time.

If definitions delimit which objects correspond to a concept and which do not, then no object that satisfies the rules should have a privileged position as an example of the concept. Yet, when asked to judge whether *apples* and *figs* are examples of the concept fruit, people (Americans at least) are much more likely to point to apples than to figs (Rosch & Mervis, 1975). More generally, people consistently rate some members of a concept as more typical than others (Rosch, 1973). This suggests that, although both apples and figs satisfy the definition of being a fruit, apples are somehow more *central* to the concept and that they better exemplify what the essence of being a fruit is about. Empirical work in psychology has demonstrated that this effect is not confined to fruit categorization but is pervasive. In many domains – birds, colours, and so on – people show a preference for some objects that are considered as a prototype or an exemplar of the concept. It has been found that exemplars have many of the properties of the other members of the concept and are thus considered more typical than others that share only some of these properties (Rosch & Mervis, 1975).

Another challenge to the classical view comes from the fact that people tend to classify objects into different concepts depending on the context (Lakoff, 1987). Even more importantly, for some concepts it is not really possible to list the necessary and sufficient attributes. Consider colour, for example: being, say, 'red' has no clear boundaries. Colour distinctions are graded, which seems to defy a simple application of a rule-based definition; at the same time, people have no problem in evoking a prototype of 'red' in their minds.

These and other problems for the classical view (for an overview, see Laurence & Margolis, 1999) have led to the development of the so-called prototype or exemplar view (theory) of concepts. Under this view, concepts are not defined by clear rules based on necessary and sufficient conditions but have a 'family resemblance' structure. That is, an object is considered to belong to a concept if it sufficiently resembles a prototype member of this concept. For example, we wouldn't judge whether a country is a democracy by reference to a strict definition but by comparing it to a prototype democracy, such as the United Kingdom. If the country is sufficiently similar to the prototype, it would be a member of the concept; otherwise not. Note that the categorization rule is much more fuzzy than in the case of rule-based definitions. Under this view, it is neither possible nor productive to specify exactly which and how many features of the 'candidate' country need to resemble the prototype for the candidate to qualify as a 'democracy'. It only needs to satisfy 'enough' of them. In effect, concepts do not have a rule-based structure but a *statistical* one, for which what matters is the *distribution* of properties that the concept members tend to posses.

The lack of clarity is certainty problematic from a scientist's point of view, but, as psychologists would argue, this is only fair to the way in which people actually form, use, and process concepts. The prototype view claims to be a better descriptive theory of concepts (what concepts are and how they work), rather than a prescriptive one (what concepts should be). It is undeniable that some examples of concepts are more central than others in the realm of politics and in political science as well. Most people in the world are more likely to think of the United Kingdom and the United States rather than Brazil and Botswana as examples of the concept *democracy*, despite the fact that all four would satisfy most definitions. The American Civil War (1861–1865) is more likely to be evoked than the one in Sri Lanka (1983–2009) as an example of a civil war. Similarly, ministries are considered more central to the concept of public organization than semi-independent regulatory agencies.

There have been attempts to use the 'family resemblance' idea to construct and operationalize concepts in political science (see Goertz, 2006), but it is fair to say that this approach is not as popular as that of rule-based definitions. Another important way in which political science makes use of 'prototype' concepts is the notion of 'ideal types'. Introduced by Max Weber, ideal types are prototypical representatives of each category of a concept. The ideal types need not be real cases; they can combine features from several real-world case and analytical considerations to form an idealized example that captures the essence of what it is to be a member of the type. For example, Weber famously posited three ideal types of grounds of legitimate authority: rational, traditional, and charismatic (Weber, 1947). The analytic ideal types serve similar purposes as reference points and exemplars of the conceptual types, as *apples* do for the concept of *fruit* in everyday language. The difference is that they need not be concrete and 'real'.

There is one other way in which the 'prototype' theory of concepts is relevant for the process of concept formation in political science, even when this process adopts a classical rule-based definitional standpoint. If the definition composed by a strict set of necessary and sufficient conditions does not unambiguously cover what would intuitively be considered a prototype of the concept, it is a poor definition and should be abandoned. A rule-based definition of democracy had better cover the UK, and a rule-based definition of public organizations had better cover ministries. Since people do process concepts in terms of prototypes and family resemblance, our rule-based definitions should take into account these intuitions. Otherwise, communicating scientific research results would become even more cumbersome than it already is.

Other views

A third influential perspective on the nature of concepts is the rather confusingly titled 'theory' view. According to this view, concepts can be defined only in reference to mental theories in which they are embedded (Carey, 1985), and categorization works like the process of scientific theorizing. Yet another alternative is the neo-classical view, which only requires that concepts are defined by necessary conditions and underplays the role of sufficient conditions for conceptual definitions. For our purposes of discussing scientific concepts and conceptualization, however, there is only so much philosophical baggage that we can take. The overview has already demonstrated the most important points: (1) there are different ways in which to define a concept and its structure; (2) a rule-based definition employing necessary and sufficient conditions is in many ways a standard approach, but one that is not very good in describing how people actually use concepts; (3) for some concepts at least, a prototype or family resemblance view in which objects can be more or less typical members of a concept based on the number of concept attributes they posses is an attractive alternative option for thinking about concepts.

The structure of concepts

Concepts come in different shapes and sizes, but all have several common elements: term, intension, extension, and indicators. The term is the concept's label. The intension gives its defining attributes. The extension specifies the objects it applies to. And then, depending on the concept's complexity, several levels and dimensions can be distinguished before we reach the level of indicators, which are the interface between the concept and the empirical world. Figure 4.1 illustrates the basic structure of concepts. Let us discuss each element in more detail.

Terms
What is a scientific *term*? A term is a label, a symbolic shortcut – most often, but not necessarily, in the form of a word – for referring to a

Figure 4.1   *The structure of concepts*

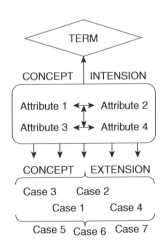

particular concept. It is used for convenience so that we do not have to evoke the entire definition of a concept all the time. In scientific discourse, terms are to concepts as words are to ideas in everyday language (compare with Sartori, 1975). Unlike everyday words, which can have multiple and shifting meanings (think of the word 'party' for example), a term has a fixed and unambiguously defined referent, namely its concept.

Sometimes an everyday word and a conceptual term would be the same, while the idea behind the word and the concept behind the term would only partially overlap. *Rational behaviour* is a good example. As an everyday word, it can mean a number of different things, such as acting with reason, self-interest, purpose, intelligence, infallible knowledge, egoism, cleverness, or unemotionally. But when used as a political science term, rational behaviour refers to a very specific concept – namely acting in accordance with one's preferences and beliefs, with a set of technical conditions imposed on the structure of preferences and on the formation of beliefs (see Elster, 2007, for an excellent discussion). It is clear that the everyday idea and the scientific concept are not entirely the same, even though their symbolic representations (the word and the term respectively) are. And it is easy to see how the discrepancy can lead, and has indeed led, to endless confusion when scientific results are expressed with scientific terms but are interpreted with the everyday meaning of the words. The lesson from this is that researchers need to be very clear about the definitions of their concepts and the terms they use, especially when there is the danger that the meaning of the term can be confused with the meanings of an everyday word.

Intension and extension

If the term is just the label, the analytic *definition* of a concept is also called its '*intension*'. The intension specifies the attributes that an object must posses in order to fall under the scope of a concept. (The attributes can also be referred to as properties or aspects.) As explained above, these attributes would often be expressed as a set of individually necessary and jointly sufficient conditions.

The '*extension*' of a concept is the set or class of objects in the world that it refers to. For example, the intension of a concept can be specified as '*a radical left party which has won a parliamentary election in a European Union member state since the beginning of the twenty-first century*'. The extension of this rather narrowly defined concept, as of the time of writing, would contain only one party, the Greek SYRIZA (Coalition of the Radical Left), which got a plurality of the votes (36.3 percent) at the January 2015 elections for the Hellenic Parliament.

Generally, when we limit the attributes that are part of the intension of a concept, its extension expands, and vice versa. To continue with the previous example, if we drop the condition that the radical left party has won an election, the extension of this new concept will cover additional cases, such as the Red–Green Alliance in Denmark and the French Communist Party. Relaxing the temporal condition would make even more cases qualify, such as the now-defunct Italian Communist party. The principle is clear: in general, the more conditions we include in the intension, the fewer cases will fall under its scope. This is true as long as the conditions are necessary, necessary-and-sufficient, or additive. If the conditions are only sufficient, by increasing their number, the extension of the concept is also enlarged as more objects become eligible via different ways of membership in the concept (Gerring, 2012b, pp. 122–123). But defining concepts only with sufficient conditions is rare, and neo-classical views of concept formation (see above) limit the use of sufficient conditions in definitions altogether.

The ladder of abstraction, or ladder of generality, is a related idea (Sartori, 1970; Goertz, 2006). When concepts are nested, the more abstract the concept, the greater its extension. By moving up and down the ladder of abstraction, the extension of the concept, hence the number of objects covered, expands and contracts.

The practical implications of the inverse relationship between intension and extension and the ladder of abstraction/generality become clear when we realize that by adjusting the intension, abstractness, and level of generality of a concept we can manipulate its empirical scope. This can be desirable in several situations. First, if a theory is shown to be deficient when defined in terms of general and abstract concepts, we can reformulate it with more concrete and narrowly defined concepts in the hope that it will account for the smaller number of relevant cases better. Alternately, if a theory has been shown to work for a small and narrowly defined set of cases, we can reformulate it at a more general and abstract level and see if it performs well at that level, which would bestow upon the theory broader relevance as it would cover more cases.

Intension attributes and minimal definitions
Normally, one of the attributes in the definition of a concept specifies its referent class: the broader set of phenomena the concept is a part of. The example of '*a radical left party which has won a parliamentary election in a European Union member state since the beginning of the twenty-first century*' tells that this is a type of *party*. *Parties* will usually be defined as some kind of *organization*; *compromises* would be defined as types of *decisions*; *hostility* would be defined as a type of *attitude* or *predisposition*; and so on. In many ways, the referent class is the crucial part of the concept definition, because it connects the concept to a large family of concepts and because it directs attention towards the class of phenomena that we would consider categorizing with the concept. Other attributes, such as spatial and temporal modifiers can delimit the extension.

From the remaining attributes in a definition some relate to internal or intrinsic properties, such as *being radical left*, and others refer to external or extrinsic properties, which are about how the concept connects with other concepts, such as *having won elections*. According to Fred Riggs, wherever possible, extrinsic properties should be dropped from a definition (1975, p. 72). To sum up, definitions contain a list of several attributes of the concept; one of the attributes points to the broader referent class of the concept, others delimit the extension; some attributes are intrinsic to the concept, others are extrinsic. Taken together, the attributes of a conceptual definition must clearly specify not only what the concept is but also how it differs and relates to semantically related concepts.

Relationships between concepts

So far we discussed the nature and structure of concepts in isolation. But concepts are entangled through their definitions in complex relationships. These relationships involve hierarchical links between 'parent' concepts and their lower-level counterparts and lateral links among concepts in conceptual fields.

Let us first look into lateral, or non-hierarchical, links. These involve the use of concepts as attributes or dimensions in other concepts. For example, a recent definition of populist political parties defines them as parties with a thin ideological core (Mudde, 2007). To understand this definition one needs to know what 'political ideology' and 'political party' are. Both have a long history of conceptualization, with the result that there are myriads of ways to define them. Ideology, in particular, is a concept that has been stretched so much that some eminent scholars consider it meaningless (Sartori, 1970; Mullins, 1972). In their turn, ideology and parties evoke concepts such as beliefs and organizations, respectively. Starting from any relatively abstract concept, a large conceptual network can be reconstructed. Therefore, disturbing the definition of any single concept in the network can affect the meanings of other directly and indirectly connected nodes. This is one reason to avoid unnecessary conceptual innovation.

Concepts are also embedded in hierarchical or parent–child relationships. Note that we use the term 'concept' to refer both to the 'parent' concept, for example 'political system', and to a particular value or category of the parent concept, for example 'democracy'. At one level, *democracy* is a concept. We can define its attributes in various ways, and we can categorize cases into democracies and non-democracies. At a more abstract level, however, democracy is only one *type* of a political system or, if you will, one *endpoint of a scale* with autocracy being the other endpoint. Irrespective of the level of measurement, the point is that *democracy* is now *a value* that the higher-order concept of political system can take. What is a concept at one level of abstraction becomes the value of a concept at another. And as with Russian dolls, the process can continue for a number of iterations. At one level *direct democracy* is a concept, which can be defined with a combination of necessary and sufficient conditions. At a higher level, it is just one value or a type of the higher-order concept *democracy*.

This can be confusing for several reasons. First, we use the same term – *concept* – to refer to the concept proper *and* to a particular set of values that the concept can take; to a class of objects and to (a subset of) objects that are part of the class. Both *colour* and *red*, *political system* and *democracy* are concepts. Second, what are often presented as indexes of democracy, for example, are in fact indexes of political systems of which democracy is just one possible value, or an endpoint of a scale (see, for example, the project '*Varieties of Democracy*' at https://v-dem.net/). When democracy is defined as a set of individually necessary and jointly sufficient conditions, empirical cases would either fulfil the criteria or not; they would either be classified as democracies or as non-democracies; there are no shades of grey. However, once we recognize that the concept being measured is not *democracy*, but *political system*, then assigning empirical cases a number on a scale starts to make more sense. Third, note that if the parent concept is many-valued or continuous (for example, *colour*), it is somewhat arbitrary that some of its values are concepts as well (for example, *red*, which can be defined as a colour with a wavelength approximately between 620 and 740 nm), but others are not (for example, a colour a with wavelength of 512.5 nm).

To avoid these sources of confusion when defining and using concepts, always be clear about the parent concept of which your concept can be thought of as a value or a type of. While specifying the types and values a concept can *take* is standard in the process of operationalization, looking up the ladder of abstraction is not, but should be. Some concepts are so abstract they would have no parents. For example, *political system* can be considered as a type of *social organization*, but it would be hard to imagine what the parent concept of *social organization* would be (but see De Landa, 2000, who draws parallels between mechanisms of organization in the physical, biological, and social domains). But Most of political science research operates at lower levels of abstraction, so looking up remains good advice.

There is another important lesson for research design here as well. Research often starts with an interest into the causes or effects of a particular concept – direct democracy, meritocratic civil service, bicameral legislatures, professional army, and so on. When the concepts have adjectives, as in all these examples, it is relatively easy to recognize that they are all but *types* of higher-order parent concepts – democracy, civil service, legislature, army, and so on. When they lack adjectives, it is harder but still as relevant. Often the key to productive research is recognizing what your main concept of interest is a type or a particular value of, so that comparisons between different ways to run democracies, organize civil services, structure legislatures, and finance armies are made possible.

The rather important implication for the design of research is that initial research questions would often need to be reformulated at a higher level of abstraction to unlock empirical inquiry. Even when the research motivation is to understand the impact of meritocratic civil service systems on government effectiveness, the underlying theoretical relationship of interest is between the civil service system (of which *meritocratic* is just one type) and government effectiveness. Hence, the research question needs to be pitched at the more abstract level. Realizing this point is critical for understanding why researchers should investigate cases that *lack* meritocratic civil service even when all they want to know is the impact of having a meritocratic civil service, as the chapters on specific research designs would try to convince you.

Definitions

Altogether, methodologists argue that *minimal definitions* of concepts are to be preferred (Sartori, 1975). Especially if an attribute of the intension does not affect the extension – if dropping a characteristic from the definition would leave us with the same set of objects that qualify – it should be left out (Riggs, 1975, p. 67). Additional, non-essential properties of concepts should be treated as hypotheses to be tested and only retained if they prove useful for delimiting the extension or help to categorize dubious cases. The separation of a concept's definitional properties from those that are merely accompanying is a major task for the social sciences (Teune, 1975, p. 85).

Note that in contrast to dictionary definitions, scientific definitions of concepts are always *stipulative*, meaning that they 'legislate' what the concept is about. It helps to think of dictionary definitions as inductive, because they try to document and summarize how words are used in practice (see Pinker, 2014). Scientific ones stipulate what the use *should* be.

There are two main strategies to arrive at definitions. The first and most common one is to analyse dictionary definitions and common use by removing inessential properties, clarifying the nature of links between the remaining attributes, and so on. The second one is constructive. It starts by examining the relationships between concepts and assigning labels to some particularly useful ones. For example, the ratio of a country's wealth and population size is so central to many research projects that it is defined as a separate concept, usually operationalized as '*gross domestic product per capita*'. The effective number of parties in a political party system, which adjusts the total number of parties by their electoral weight, is another example of a constructively-defined concept (Laakso & Taagepera, 1979).

Explaining how to build definitions of our concepts of interest already brings us into the discussion of conceptualization, as the elaboration of definitions is an integral part of this process. Let us focus squarely on what conceptualization and the subsequent process of operationalization entail.

Conceptualization

It is useful to distinguish between two phases in the analysis of a concept. In its totality, the analysis is performed to enable, support, and interpret empirical research. In the beginning of the first phase, the concept is still fuzzy; amorphous; expressed verbally rather than formally; its definitional structure is not completely spelled out; its boundaries are unclear; its dimensions or attributes are not enumerated; and its meaning is possibly conveyed with reference to intuition, everyday usage, or tradition. We have some idea about what the concept is about, but not a very sharp one. This phase is roughly equivalent to what Sartori refers to as *conceptions* (1975), to what Adcock and Collier call *background concepts* (2001), and to the *basic level* in Goertz's (2006) three-level framework. In the second phase, the concept is clearly defined by spelling out all its attributes and how they combine in the definition. This phase is what Sartori would call *concepts* proper, Adcock and Collier refer to as *systematized concepts*, and roughly corresponds to the *second level* of Goertz's framework. *Conceptualization* is the process of getting from phase one to phase two; from conceptions to concepts proper; and from background to systematized concepts. Conceptualization is also about clarifying how the concept under scrutiny connects to other related concepts. Once at phase two, a concept can be further *operationalized* into indicators which allow for the measurement and classification of empirical cases into the categories of the concept. Figure 4.2 illustrates these processes.

Conceptualization itself comprises two main activities. The first one – the careful elaboration of a definition – has already been discussed. Importantly, the definition not only stipulates what the concept is and what falls under its remit, but also clarifies how the concept relates to more general 'parent' concepts. The second main activity of conceptualization is clarifying how the various objects falling under the concept's definition group together. In other words, the second activity is elaborating the intensional classification structure of a concept. If the definition looks up and sideways on the ladder of generality, intensional classification looks down the ladder.

Figure 4.2   *Conceptualization and operationalization*

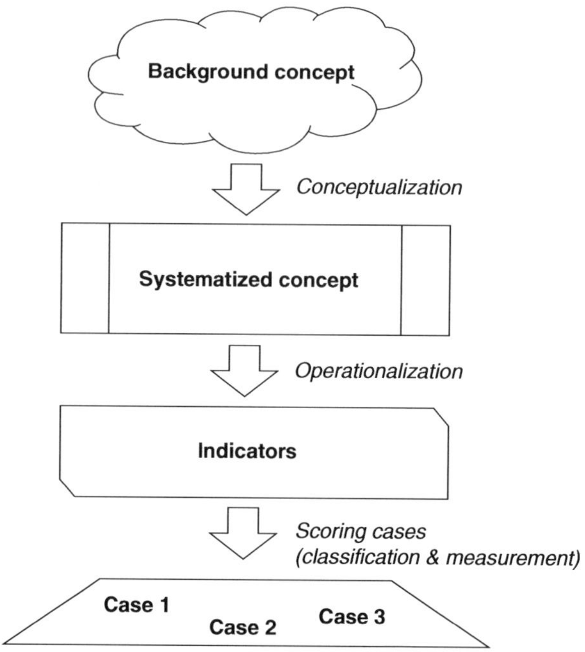

Classification (intensional)

Classification is another term that, rather confusingly, is routinely used to denote several different things (for an extensive discussion, see Marradi, 1990). (It is quite ironic that the study of definitions, concepts, and classification – which should be a paragon of clarity – is marred by such conceptual confusion!) First, classification can refer to the *process* of classification but also to the *product* of this process. We reserve the term *classification scheme* for the latter. Second, the process of classification can refer to three different processes: (1) intensional classification (also called division or categorization), (2) extensional classification, and (3) classing. Intensional classification is a process of conceptual elaboration in which the intension (definition) of a concept is 'unpacked' in order to subdivide its extension into several narrower classes. The division into lower-level classes is performed with respect to one or several attributes (aspects) of the intension, and can be iterated in a chain. This is a purely analytical exercise. The products are collections of conceptual labels (categories) arranged as classification schemes, typologies, or taxonomies. In this sense, classification is part of conceptualization and we will discuss it in more detail below. In contrast, extensional classification is inductive and starts with data instead of conceptual analysis. It groups observed objects that are part of the extension of a concept into subgroups on the basis of similarities among the objects along one or several of their properties. In this sense, extensional classification is akin to description, measurement, and data reduction, and will be discussed in detail in the next chapter. The same for classing, which is the process of assigning empirical cases into an intentionally developed classification scheme. Table 4.1 summarizes the four common different meanings of classification and where to find more details about each.

Let us discuss intensional classification. It starts with a focus on one attribute or property of the concept which is used as a basis for division or, in other words, as a classificatory principle. Subsequently, the principle is applied to delineate a number of lower-level classes (which, as explained below, can also be referred to as concepts). In their turn, the classes can be further subdivided on the basis of the same or different classificatory principles, and so on. If this all sounds too abstract, it will be made more accessible with a few examples.

To ease exposition, let us call the original concept the parent and the lower-level concepts the child concepts-classes. In principle, all child concepts inherit all other attributes of the parent concept but one. So they differ with respect to the classificatory principle but remain similar in all other aspects. If the parent concept is *organization*, the classificatory principle is *ownership*, and the child classes are *private* and *public organizations*; both types of organizations retain the defining attributes of the parent concept *organization* (for example, having a goal and a structure) and only differ in ownership. If the parent concept is *terrorism*, the classification principle is *motivation*, and the child classes are *political*, *religious*, and *other*; all three classes retain the defining attributes of the parent concept (such as the use of violence or having a political or social goal) and only differ in motivation.

The classification principle dividing parent concepts into lower-level classes need not be part of the explicit definition of the concept, but it

Table 4.1 *Various meanings of the term 'classification'*

	Details	Other terms	Discussed in
Classification (intentional)	Part of conceptualization; theoretic	Categorization; division	Chapter 4
Classification (extensional)	Grouping of empirical cases; inductive	Clustering	Chapter 5
Classification (classing)	Scoring cases into an intentionally developed classification scheme	Categorization; classing	Chapter 5
Classification scheme	A product of either intentional or extensional classification	Taxonomy; typology	Chapter 4

should be an attribute that all objects that are part of the extension of the concept share. For example, the fact that all people eat is not usually included in the definition of humans (because it is not very useful for differentiating between humans and other animals), but since it is a property that all humans share, it can be used as a classificatory principle to divide people into, say, meat-eaters and vegetarians.

The simplest classifications, such as the ones discussed so far, are unidimensional: they are based on a single classification criterion and the division is applied only once. The product, as mentioned, is called by the generic term *classification scheme*. When more than one classificatory criterion is applied at the same time, the result is a *typology*. Types are formed by the intersection of these multiple classificatory criteria. For example, we can classify organizations on the basis of ownership (public or private) and goals (economic or not). Hence, we end up with four possible types: private organizations with economic goals, private organizations with non-economic goals, public organizations with economic goals, and public organizations with non-economic goals. Typologies can be made more complex by adding a third, a fourth, and more, classification criteria, but this leads to an explosion in the number of possible types and is, as a result, not very practical.

When more than one classificatory principle is applied *in sequence* (*chain*), the result is a *taxonomy*. The well-known biological 'tree of life' is a hierarchical taxonomy with several ranks (levels) from *domain* to *genus* to *species*. The classificatory principle applied at each step need not be the same. And not all child classes from the first step need to be divided by the same classificatory principle at the next step. For example, a taxonomy of political parties might start with classification according to the importance and integrity of ideology for the party, producing two classes – parties with and without ideological cores. The former can be further split according to the substance of their ideology (socialist, liberal, conservative, other), and the latter can be divided based on the breadth of their issue focus (single-issue or not).

Figure 4.3 visualizes the taxonomy of classification products that we have outlined so far. The first division is based on the number of classificatory principles employed. At the second level, the division is based on whether the multiple classification principles are applied simultaneously (leading to a typology) or in sequence (leading to a taxonomy).

Vertical or hierarchical taxonomies are a special class of taxonomies in which each level is at a lower level of abstraction than the preceding one (the 'tree of life' fits the label). For example, the taxonomies of research designs presented in Chapter 2 are hierarchical, because the types of research discussed are nested and the distinctions are at progressively lower levels of abstraction. Hierarchical taxonomies can be extremely powerful conceptual schemes for organizing knowledge, but they are difficult to construct.

Figure 4.3   *A taxonomy of classification products*

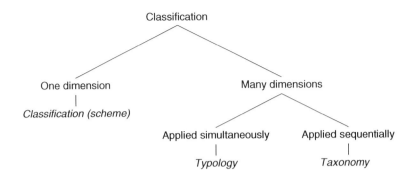

In contrast to typologies, the order in which we apply the several classificatory principles that make up a taxonomy matters. Therefore, different classificatory schemes can result if we first apply classificatory principle A and then principles B and C to the resulting classes, than if we first apply B and then A and C.

According to Giovanni Sartori (1975, p. 17),

> hierarchical classifications, or taxonomies, remain a major, nonreplacable, logical backbone of scientific (empirical) enquiry. The genus and differentia unpacking of concepts not only helps us detect – via the unnamed cases – our cognitive voids; it also appears to be the only systematic technique for arriving at standardized fact-seeking and fact-sorting data containers.

Evaluating concepts and classifications

Let us turn to the question of what makes simple classifications, typologies and taxonomies good and useful. The two crucial requirements for classifications are that the resulting classes are collectively exhaustive and mutually exclusive. This means that each (relevant) empirical case can be classified in one and only one class, and that all relevant cases can be classified. The use of residual categories (such as 'other') is usually employed to satisfy exhaustiveness. Clear definitions and delineations of borders between classes ensure that mutual exclusiveness is respected. Importantly, only one classification principle must be applied to produce the classes at each level. These requirements are easy to articulate, but what is also needed for a good classification is relevance or utility, and this one is much harder to define. It is easy to come up with logically sound and unambiguous classification schemes. It is much more challenging to develop intensional classifications that reflect theoretical knowledge and are useful for organizing the messy empirical reality. In short, they should bring insight as well as rigour. Henry Teune (1975) posed two very similar criteria for evaluating concepts: precision and theoretical relevance. Precision is related to the mutual exclusiveness criteria above, and theoretical relevance to the need for insight.

Classification and measurement

Classification schemes are usually nominal. That is, they divide the parent concept into a small set of classes, and the classes are not ordered in any way. The labels of the classes do not imply any order of the classes or other more fine-grained comparisons. In the simplest case, the classes are just two or three. For example, a classification of party ideologies can divide them into socialist, liberal, and conservative: a nominal classification, since the three classes are not ordered or ranked in any way; the labels of the classes are obviously just that – names – and names cannot be meaningfully ordered, weighted, or compared. There is nothing to prevent us, however, from creating more lower-level classes from a parent concept and ordering them in a meaningful way. For example, imagine that we divide party ideology not in terms of broad ideological families but with respect to how favourable it is in relation to social redistribution. The resulting classes can be 'Very favourable', 'Neutral', and 'Very unfavourable'. These three classes are not nominal but ordered or ranked (an ordering is a ranking without ties). And there is nothing to stop us from creating an even larger set of ordered classes in which to divide the parent concept. We can also posit that the distance between the classes is the same, which would result in an interval scale. And if we can meaningfully assign one class as a 'zero', we end up with a ratio scale.

At this point you might suspect that something strange is going on, since rankings, intervals, and ratio scales are terms usually encountered in the discussion of *measurement*. And you would be right! By extending the idea of classification, we reached the notion of measurement. In a sense, measurement is nothing more than a form of classification. Admittedly, a rather peculiar one, but a classification nonetheless. Moreover, the same way the term classification can be used for the process of developing a classification scheme and for assigning objects into classes (the latter also called 'classing'), measurement can refer to the process of developing measurement schemes and scales, and for the process of assigning ranks and numbers to cases. Measurement will be dealt with at length in the next chapter. But the process of operationalization, which prepares concepts for classing and measurement deserves some more attention.

Operationalization

Operationalization is the translation of abstract concepts and their attributes (dimensions), into less abstract ones that can be detected, classified, and measured in the empirical world. It is said that operationalization provides indicators of concepts. But it is useful to distinguish between two types of concept indicators. The first one genuinely and directly translates an attribute of an abstract concept into a measurable variable (for the definition of variables, see below). For example, the *intensity* attribute of the concept *war* can be operationalized as *the number of casualties from military activities.*

The second type of indicators are indirect and usually do not allow for a precise measurement of a concept or one of its attributes, but only for detecting presence or absence in a rough-and-ready way. (Fred Riggs, 1975, p. 69, calls these 'detectors'.) For example, at least one peaceful government turnover following contested elections is a very good detector of democracy in practice (Przeworski, 2010), even though an actual government turnover might not be part of the definition of democracy as such.

Note that we differ on this point from Gary Goertz's view that indicators are part of the concept definition. Here is why. You might remember from secondary-school chemistry that, litmus test papers provide a very quick and cheap way to detect acids because they turn red when exposed to acids. But acids are never *defined* as the substances that turn litmus paper red, and there are more precise (but slower and more expensive) tests of acidity. In the practice of political science research, it is important to clarify whether an indicator is used as a direct operationalization of a concept or as a 'detector'. If all we need is a quick test of whether a country is a democracy or not, checking whether it has recently experienced a peaceful post-electoral government turnover might be sufficient. If more precise and fine-grained comparisons between political regimes are needed, a different operationalization would be necessary.

Sometimes, the concepts of interest in empirical research would be so concrete that they would be the same or almost the same as the indicators used to detect and measure them. In an evaluation of the effect of the provision of free bed nets against mosquitoes on malaria-related mortality in Africa, the provision of a free bed net is pretty much the concept *and* the indicator used to measure it. (Malaria-related death might be more or less directly measurable, depending on the type of evidence available.) Note that the concreteness of this concept might be very appropriate for the hypothesis-testing research objective at hand, but it certainly impedes the possible generalization of the research findings.

When there is no such direct correspondence between the concept and the observable indicator used to detect and measure it, operationalization provides for indirect proxies. Hence, the operational definition of a variable to be used in empirical research and the intension of a concept might correspond less than perfectly. Rather than an occasional aberration, this is a standard state of affairs in political science research. And it is to a large extent unavoidable. The concepts political scientists grapple with are rather abstract, intangible, and cannot be observed directly. To make matters even more complex, they are often dispositional (for example, aggressiveness) (Teune, 1975): dispositions are hard enough to detect when they refer to internal states of people, and only become harder when they refer to internal states of abstract aggregate entities such as states.

The same intensional definition of a concept can be developed into different operational definitions in the context of different research projects. This might be necessary for theoretical or practical reasons. In the former case, different research projects emphasize different aspects of a concept, so they require a different operationalization. In the latter case, data availability issues often dictate a preference for one operationalization versus another. There is little use for empirical research projects of operationalizations that faithfully capture the essence of a concept but cannot be measured with data. Hence, the quality of operationalization is not absolute but context-specific, and it depends on the research objective and theoretical focus of the research and on the type and kind of empirical data that can be collected and used.

Sometimes, a very rough and indirect proxy of a concept could provide a reasonable indicator for the research task at hand. An operationalization cannot always be dismissed simply because it does not capture directly the essence of a concept. Especially in the context of theory and hypothesis-testing research, establishing a relationship between two concepts operationalized only indirectly can still be highly important and inspire future work improving on the operationalizations.

The fact is that there is seldom one operationalization that would satisfy all scholars; it is an important research task to examine whether relationships of interest are robust to different operationalizations of the underlying concept.

Pitfalls of Conceptualization

Conceptual profusion

The unchecked profusion of new concepts is a disaster in any field of research and is crippling political science in particular. The introduction of a new concept should be a last resort and backed by a demonstration of a clear deficiency of the existing conceptual vocabulary. So one must be aware of the existing definitions in the scientific field.

Unfortunately, there is a flip-side to this requirement. Too often, the discussion of definitions and the different ways in which existing research conceptualizes a phenomenon consumes a great number of research papers without a clear goal or conclusion in sight. Conceptualization is not empty scholasticism or an exercise in demonstrating command of the existing literature but one part of the research process that supports the link between theory and the empirical world. Few things can be more off-putting in scientific writing in the social sciences than endless paragraphs on various ways scholars have defined globalization, e-government, or sustainable development, to give but a few examples. In short, conceptualization, and especially the review of existing efforts, should be instrumental.

Conceptual stretching and functional equivalence

Conceptual stretching is an oft-discussed potential problem, especially for comparative cross-case designs. It refers to the muddling of a concept's definition to accommodate more and more empirical cases. It is a mistake easy to commit when a concept, such as the welfare state, is developed in one historical and institutional context and transferred to a completely different setting – either in space or in time – where its applications would be totally inappropriate.

Yet, to enable comparisons, concepts need to be reconsidered in light of experiences in different time periods or parts of the world. Parochialism – studies avoiding established general concepts – can be as damaging as conceptual stretching. For example, throughout much of human recorded history, and even now in certain parts of the world, social functions such as help for the poor have been provided not by the state but primarily by religious organizations. This is the problem of functional equivalence: different institutional and organizational forms provide essentially the same functions or services. By failing to recognize functional equivalence we might fail to realize the potential for comparisons across time and space and we might also reach the wrong conclusions: for example, we might conclude that because there was no welfare state in the sixteenth century, there was no organized help for the poor. While it would be preposterous to apply the welfare state concept to that historical period, by redefining the concept of interest either at a higher level of abstraction or in functional instead of institutional terms, we can gain a more general understanding of how human societies support the poor.

The legal–bureaucratic context

In political science, the problem of (non-)equivalence is intensified by the fact that scientific concepts and terms are often rooted in legal and bureaucratic definitions that tend to differ across national jurisdictional borders. To give a simple example, what counts as a 'ministry' differs even within the relatively similar set of European states. A comparative project that aims to study, say, convergence in government structures across Europe will be hampered by the fact that what is called a ministry in France might not be what counts as a ministry in Greece and that units that are not called ministries in the UK are actually functional equivalents. To mitigate the problem of shifting legal and bureaucratic definitions, scientific concepts need to be refined without reference to the legal and bureaucratic terms but, rather, analytically. For example, a ministry can be defined as a central government unit that is directly headed by a member of the cabinet. This still leaves room for improvement (for example, what counts as a 'cabinet member' might still differ across states), but it is a step in the right direction.

Some concepts are easy to define but devilishly difficult to operationalize and measure. Salience is a case in point. In a political science context, salience is usually defined simply as the importance of certain issues for a class of people or organizations. The problem is not with the definition, but with devising a strategy that can detect and measure salience. One possible strategy is to operationalize as salient these issues that people single out as important when asked in surveys. While feasible, this strategy produces measures that have been shown to vary considerably as a function of seemingly minor and theoretically trivial factors, such as the wording of the survey question and the availability of answer categories to choose from. Another strategy – operationalizing salience as what makes it to the media – suffers from obvious potential biases and restricts the definition of the concept to *media salience* at best. The conclusion is not that concepts of this kind should be abandoned but that care is advised when interpreting research based on a particular operationalization of such concepts.

Contested concepts

In political science, concepts are often contested. The application of concepts such as 'democracy' or 'good governance' or 'administrative efficiency' to real-world cases is not only important to political scientists but to politicians and ordinary people alike. Hence, often, not only the classification of cases into conceptual categorizes is contested but the nature of the concepts themselves.

For example, the concept of 'illiberal democracy' has been coined to accommodate cases that exhibit some features of democracies, such as contested elections, but lack protection of fundamental human rights or press freedoms. We can argue that the latter two features are essential for a definition of democracy (and many would agree). But others can argue that what we have described is just a particular type of democracy. Such debates are not purely academic, because whether a country is formally democratic matters for many practical purposes, for example for membership in the European Union. So when the Hungarian prime minister indicated that for him not all democracies need to be liberal, the German chancellor remarked that for her an illiberal democracy is a contradiction in terms (see the article by Adam Halasz in the *EU Observer* from 3 February 2015 at https://euobserver.com/beyond-brussels/127468). Behind this fight over the meaning of words or concepts is a very real struggle over the appropriate limits and responsibilities of the state.

Similarly, there is an ongoing conceptual debate over the concept of 'good governance' (see Fukuyama, 2013). While for some any definition of 'government capacity' and good governance must include a reference to democratic government and citizen participation in policy making, others argue that these are non-essential elements of the definition and that state capacity and professional state bureaucracy are sufficient.

Political science concepts are often contested because they have emotional, in addition to normative implications. Concepts such as 'third world', 'developing states', or the currently popular 'Global South', stir powerful emotions among those being classified and described by them. Because of the emotional charge of such concepts, they are rarely left to political scientists to work with in isolation. For example, scientists might define the concept of political party 'objectively' as any organization that pursues a goal of placing its avowed representatives in government positions (Sartori, 1970). But since the label stirs powerful and often negative emotions for the citizens in some countries, organizations that would be classified as parties according to the scientific definition adopt other labels, such as 'movements' and 'blocks'. And these organizations would publicly repudiate being classified as parties, irrespective of what scientists have to say.

Summing Up

Conceptualization mediates between our intuitions, abstract definitions, and operationalized rules that assign cases to categories. Traffic is in all directions. Intuitions motivate the elaboration of concept intension, which, if successful, sharpens our intuitions. Intension directs the scope of extension, but if a paradigmatic case happens to be classified in the wrong class, the intension itself would need to be amended.

Some of the most celebrated scientific achievements come in the form of a new concept, the discovery of a new type of an important concept, in showing that two concepts considered separate are actually related on a deeper level, or in relegating a concept to the dustbin of history. Social capital – a concept advanced by Robert Putnam (2000) was a conceptual rediscovery that is regarded by some as one of the most important achievements of social science during the twentieth century (others such as Jon Elster are not convinced). Arend Lijphart's 'discovery' of a new 'species' of democracy – consociational democracies, with the Netherlands as a prototype – is similarly heralded.

Further Reading

There is relatively little literature on concepts and conceptualization in political science. The work by Gary Goertz (2006) is a rare book-length treatment with a general scope. Several articles by David Collier written with different co-authors are central to the methodological literature in political science (Adcock & Collier, 2001; Collier & Levitsky, 1997; Collier, LaPorte, & Seawright, 2012). John Gerring's textbook (2012b) on social methodology has extended and very useful discussions of concepts as well (under the heading 'Description').

The works of Giovanni Sartori are seminal in the field and are so often cited, if not read, that to the casual observer it would appear that they are the last word on conceptualization. But the grand project of conceptual clarification and discipline that Sartori advanced throughout his career does not seem to have had the desired effects on the field of political science. If anything, the problems have increased in scale and presence after the creation of his Committee of Conceptual and Terminological Analysis. Do consult the texts collected in Sartori (1975), which can be read both as a methodological manifesto and a practical program for standardizing the use of core concepts in political science. Despite the institutional backing of the International Political Science Association, the International Sociological Association, and even UNESCO during the 1970s and 1980s, however, little standardization, discipline, or methodological sophistication can be seen in the broader field as a result of this program. This does not make Sartori's contributions less valuable, but it does hint that there are deeper challenges to conceptualization in the social sciences than his analyses discerned.

Bevir and Kedar (2008) offer a critique of what they call the Sartori–Collier approach to conceptualization from an anti-naturalist point of view.

The edited volume by Margolis and Laurence (1999) and the book by Murphy (2004) are good entry points into the philosophical and cognitive science literature on concepts.

Chapter 5

Measurement and Description

This chapter is about measurement and descriptive research in its various manifestations. It discusses in detail the purpose, types, challenges, and limitations of descriptive research. Description is considered a fundamental goal of science and one that is valuable (if currently undervalued) in its own right rather than *merely* as a stepping stone towards explanation.

We start by making clear how measurement and description are intrinsically related and go on to introduce the basic terms that we will use throughout the rest of the chapters: cases, samples, populations, and the many kinds of variables.

Next, we discuss different measurement strategies popular in political science and what makes some measures more appropriate, valid, and reliable than others.

The sections on description cover widely different modes of analysis – from surveys to cluster analysis to networks to regressions to ethnographic observation and historical research. We review cases of description when the goal is to learn about the distribution of a variable in a sample and in a population, when it is to inductively recover and represent the structure of a population, when it is to learn about the associations among variables, and when it is to understand a single case in-depth. These are all important goals of descriptive inference – a major part of the research process and one that has considerable theoretical and normative implications as well.

Preliminaries

First, a confession: what is going to be discussed under the heading of 'Measurement' in this chapter would not be considered *measurement* by many scholars; for example, Otis Dudley Duncan (1984), Giovanni Sartori (1975), and Martyn Hammersley (2007). And, formally, they would be right. In a strict sense, measurement is the process of assigning numerical values to objects or their aspects. The numerical values must retain their arithmetical properties. Only when a ratio scale is used (some more compromising methodologists would occasionally allow an interval scale as well) can we speak of measurement proper. Binary classification and nominal scales, even when ranked and ordered, do not count.

Technically, such a narrow definition of measurement is true to the meaning and usage of the term in the sciences. However, if we separate the discussion of classification of empirical objects into a list of nominal or ordered categories (classing) from measurement proper, we can easily lose sight of the fundamental commonality of these two activities. Classing and measurement are but two ways of assigning facts and objects from the empirical world into a set of classes. In some cases, the classes are equally spaced and are so many that they can be assigned numbers. In others, the differences between the classes are such that only labels (names, words) can be meaningfully assigned to them. But, fundamentally, the process remains the same. Unfortunately, there is no good umbrella term that covers both nominal classing and measurement proper. Hence, we choose to employ 'measurement' for the generic (umbrella) term as well, with the qualification that measurement in a strict sense requires interval and ratio scales. Figure 5.1 clarifies these distinctions.

Alternatively, instead of 'measurement' we could have used 'observation' as an umbrella term, but 'observation' suggests passive perception of the world around us, while 'measurement' has the benefit of stressing the proactive role of the researcher in the process. Perception and registration of social and political processes and phenomena are rarely if ever passive and unmediated. It takes instruments and active probing, laborious 'soaking and poking', to compartmentalize social and political reality into cases, variables, classes, and measures. To call the process 'observation' is to seriously underestimate the work and ingenuity required.

It is also not very common to find the discussion of measurement and description in the same chapter. Measurement is usually associated with a rigid, hard-nosed, cold-blooded administration of measurement instruments to anonymized populations, while description is often considered the province of ethnographers and historians, who generally abhor quantification and care deeply about qualities, idiosyncrasies, and context. Researchers who rely exclusively on words cannot be seen too often rubbing shoulders with scientists who put their trust in numbers. Yet measurement (in a broad sense) and description *are* intrinsically

Figure 5.1　*Types of measurement*

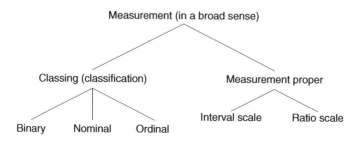

related. Measurement can be conceived as a 'shallow' description of many cases along a small set of variables. Description of a case is then a 'deep' measurement of one unit along a large set of variables. But what is a variable? And what is a case, for that matter?

A Glossary of Research Terms

Before we are ready to delve into the intricacies of measurement and description, we have to get familiar with a set of terms related to the theory and practice of empirical research in political science and beyond. These terms will serve us throughout the remaining chapters and have relevance both for description and for explanatory research designs; indeed for any research project that engages with the empirical world.

What is a case?

The basic unit of scientific observation and analysis is called *a case*. A case is a spatially and temporally bounded object, phenomenon, or event in the world. A case can be an individual such as Mary, a country such as Angola, an organization such as the International Criminal Court, a process such as European integration, an event such as the secession of Bangladesh from Pakistan in 1971, a phenomenon such as the convergence of banking regulation around the world, a historical period such as the Reformation in Western Europe, and so on.

An empirical case is something in the world. But what constitutes a case is not entirely objectively given. What counts as a case depends on the conceptual framework of the particular research project, on certain assumptions about the salient features of the empirical world, and even on the measurement instrument. Cases are *carved out* from the raw material of the empirical world. Charles Ragin refers to this process as 'casing'. (He has also co-edited an entire book that attempts to answer the question 'What is a case?: Ragin & Becker, 1992). For example, a country such as Italy might be a single case in the context of one research project, but can be separated into various regions such as Umbria and Tuscany for another, or segregated diachronically (over time) into country-years for a third one.

A case must be sufficiently separable from other phenomena and aspects of the world and have a sufficient degree of homogeneity and stability (see also Chapter 10). The first requirement is about being able to delimit more than roughly where one case ends and another one begins. The second requirement is about a case being and remaining the same over the period of observation. These two requirements seem trivial to satisfy, but in the practice of research they are not, and require careful consideration.

For example, an individual person is always a sufficiently separable, homogeneous, and stable entity to constitute a single case, right? Well, it depends. For many research purposes, an individual person would be a single case. But for others, an individual person might provide either more or less than one case. Imagine that we are interested in the effect of a drug that has just a short-term effect that does not carry over and accumulate in the body. We administer the drug every Monday for a month to a single person to examine the reaction. Would we say that the research consists of one case (the person) or of four cases (the same person observed at four time periods)? Both answers can be given depending on further assumptions about how the person relates to the relevant *population* (see below). Under the strong assumption that all individuals would react to the drug in the same way, the single individual can confidently be considered to provide four cases. (Think about it for a minute. If people would react the same, it does not really matter who is tested. Four tests on the same person are exactly the same as four tests on four different persons. Hence, the number of cases in both situations must be the same.)

How can an individual person provide less than one case? This one is easy. Imagine that we are interested in the effect of a new teaching method (for example, repeating everything being said exactly three times) on student achievement. One teacher of one class of 20 students adopts the new method and the comparison class of another 20 students is taught using the old method. Again, assume that all students in a class react in the same way to the teaching method and that the teaching method is the only determinant of student achievement. How many cases does this research study have – 40 (the total number of students) or two (the number of classes)? Although there are 40 individuals being tested, in essence the study provides only two relevant independent data points, hence, two cases.

Ambiguities about what exactly counts as a case are not rare in the practice of research, and are ubiquitous when objects and processes are observed and analysed over time. The temporal boundaries of cases are usually harder to draw than the spatial ones. Careful conceptualization and attention to the autonomy, independence, stability, and intrinsic (internal) homogeneity of units can help in deciding what exactly constitutes a case for a particular research project.

Sometimes, what are initially considered *cases* interact in groups so much (for example, individuals in families) that the definition of a case would have to be lifted to a higher level of abstraction (from an individual to a family). In other situations, what are thought of as single cases would exhibit so much intrinsic heterogeneity that they would have to be disaggregated into smaller chunks (for example, a country observed over a long period of time can be disaggregated into several cases defined by several distinct time periods). Occasionally, no straightforward solution would be possible. Consider again the examples from the previous paragraph. What if the drug has some minor leftover effect from week to week; do we still have four cases, or only one, or some number in between? What if different students in the same class differ in how receptive they are to the teaching method, and their individual learning achievements are neither entirely independent nor completely dependent on the ones of their peers in class? How many cases would we have: two, two times 20, or some number in between? In the context of large-N research, various techniques have been developed to address such problems at the data analysis stage (for example, multilevel statistical models or clustered standard errors; these are too technical to be discussed here, but you can consult Gelman & Hill, 2007, to learn more about them.) For our purposes, it is enough to note that the definition of what constitutes a case in any research project deserves attention and careful consideration.

Cases, samples, and populations

Quite literally, a case is a case because it is *a case of* something. Therefore, speaking and writing about cases implicitly assumes that there is a more general class (set) of objects, events, and phenomena to which the case belongs. The entire set of cases to which the case belongs is called *a population*. All difficulties in defining a case carry over to the delineation of a relevant population, and new ones arise. The boundaries of populations are even trickier to draw than the boundaries of a case. For example, is the 1789 French revolution a case of revolutions, of bourgeois revolutions only, or of a broader category of social revolts? Such questions can be settled only after careful conceptualization and only relative to a specific research project. In any case, a researcher should always be explicit about the relevant population.

A *sample* is a subset of cases from the population. Usually, we study a sample of cases to infer something about the broader population. The selection of cases to form a sample from the population (or 'case selection' for short) is one of the crucial issues of research design. Case selection is often done with the goal of learning something about the broader population from studying the cases in the sample. A sample can be formed (or drawn) from a population in various ways: actively or passively, randomly or purposefully, at once or in stages, and so on. For example, if we are interested in the political opinions of American citizens (which would constitute the relevant population), we can select randomly a sample of 1,500 individuals from a list of all Americans, or use a convenience sample of ten American students in a single class in a college we happen to be visiting, or we can put an advertisement on the internet and interview the Americans who get in touch, or we can survey our American friends, and then their friends, and then the friends of their friends in a snowball fashion, or we can just collect expressed opinions in the online forums of digital newspapers. These would all be different ways of case selection.

For another example, if we are interested in the fate of regional economic integration communities, we can select one of these relatively rare entities to form a sample (so we would have a sample of one case), or we can select two that appear most interesting, or we can select all (so the sample contains all cases from the population).

All these various ways to select a sample from a population have important implications about what can be learned about the population from analysing the sample. Some of these implications will be discussed shortly in this chapter. For now, it is sufficient to understand what a sample is, and how it relates both to cases and to populations.

The total population of potential cases must be distinguished from the population from which cases *could have been drawn* to form the sample. The latter is also called a *sampling frame* or *target population*. The total population and the sampling frame need not coincide. A sample of 900 British citizens can be drawn randomly from the list of the entire population of one British city, say, Oxford. As we shall shortly see, that would make the sample representative of the population part of the sampling frame, so that we can be confident that what we find in the sample has a very high chance of being true for the sampling frame population as well. But the total population of interest might be broader than the population of Oxford and extend to all British citizens living now, all British citizens who ever lived during the past 400 years, to all Europeans, to all citizens of affluent secular societies, or even to all humans. The point is that even a randomly drawn sample is representative only to the sampling frame population, and further assumptions are needed to decide how relevant the results from studying the sample are for the general population of all potential cases beyond the ones included in the sampling frame.

The total relevant population is defined on conceptual and theoretical grounds. The sampling frame is often delimited by practical concerns. In more complex research designs, at a first stage a sample of sampling frames can be selected from the total population, and at a second stage samples of cases can be selected from each sampling frame. This can increase our knowledge of how the results from studying the sample cases generalize to the total population. Figure 5.2 illustrates the relationships between total population, target population, sample, and cases (cases selected for observation are shown as solid black dots; the remaining ones are white).

Variables and observations
There are two ways to get to variables: one starts with concepts and works its way down a ladder of abstraction; the other starts with cases and works its way up. Along the first route, variables are defined as single operationalized dimensions of concepts. Along the second one,

Figure 5.2   *Cases, samples, and populations*

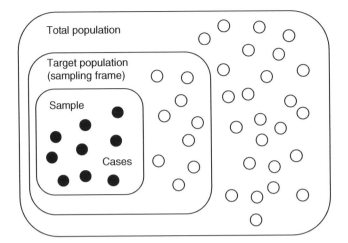

variables are aspects or attributes of cases. Indeed, variables are both operationalized concepts and case attributes. Their Janus-faced nature – one pair of eyes looking into the empirical and another into the conceptual realm – is what makes variables so central to the research enterprise.

A variable is also, quite literally, something that must be able to vary, in other words, to *take* different values. Cases *receive* different values with respect to a variable in the process of measurement (including both classing and measurement proper). The assignment of values to cases is also called scoring or coding the cases. Each score of one case on one variable provides a *data point*, or *datum*. The collection of data points constitutes the *data* of the research project.

In science, the process of observation or measurement in a broad sense can be considered as the evaluation of cases with respect to variables (so it covers both classing and measurement in the narrow sense). An observation relates to scoring one case on a variable or assigning one case into a class (category). But when a case is studied and described in depth, tens and even hundreds of different aspects of the case fall into the researcher's focus. Technically, each of these aspects of the case can be considered a variable and each observation on one of these aspects can be considered a measurement. For example, we can make the observation that the German prime minister opposed sending weapons to Ukraine in February 2015 for support against the insurgents in the east of the country. Equivalently, we can say that the dichotomous variable 'support by the German prime minister' takes the value '0' or 'absence'. But using the language of variables in the context of in-depth case descriptions can quickly become rather tedious and feels unnatural. Therefore, usually one talks and writes about making observations rather than scoring variables in the context of single in-depth case studies. But fundamentally, the process is the same. The chapter on single-case study designs (Chapter 10) will have more to say about observations in case study research and will provide further examples as well. We would discuss 'causal-process observations' (and not 'causal-process variables'), which are the analogues of explanatory variables in large-N research. One additional terminological clarification: when observations are relevant for a particular causal hypothesis, they are sometimes referred to as 'evidence'.

Types of variables   There are several types of variables. Actually, there are several relevant criteria according to which variables can be classified. First, variables differ with respect to the level of measurement precision they allow. A *binary* (dichotomous or dummy) variable can only take two values – yes/no, 0/1, presence/absence, food/not food, and so on. With only two possible states, this is the most coarse level of measurement possible. It corresponds to a classification scheme with only two classes (categories). A nominal (also called categorical) variable can take several values but they are not ordered in any way. For example, the types of political regimes can be classified as 'parliamentary', 'presidential', and 'semi-presidential'. With respect to the vertical distribution of power, states can be classified into 'unitary' and 'federations'.

The differences between the nominal classes (categories) are ones of kind and not of degree. An ordinal variable has a set of categories that are ordered from 'high' to 'low', from 'full agreement' to 'full disagreement', from 'fresh' to 'exhausted', and so on. Importantly, the distance between the categories need not be the same. The 'distance' between 'fresh' and 'tired' might be different from the one between 'tired' and 'exhausted', although the three can still be ranked or ordered. Interval variables are ordered variables that satisfy this additional requirement of equal distance between the classes. Ratio variables add the requirement of a meaningful zero. For example, the vertical distribution of power in a state can be measured not as a binary or nominal variable, but as a degree of regional self-government, which might be assigned a meaningful number, implying either interval or ratio scale.

Obviously, ratio and interval variables allow for more precise and fine-grained comparisons between the values of the variables than nominal ones. This in turn enables the use of more complex mathematical tools to describe and analyse these variables. But not everything can be made to fit a ratio variable. More on how to choose the type of variable and the level of measurement will follow shortly.

Note that there are further distinctions to make when it comes to the type and level of measurement of variables. Variables can be bounded, when the range of values they can take is limited (for example, a percentage, which can only vary between 0 and 100) or unbounded; they can also be discrete (for example, count data) or continuous, which can take *any* value on the underlying scale. These distinctions are important when it comes to the statistical analysis of data.

Another dimension on which to classify variables is their role in theoretical models. The variable capturing the outcome that the researcher is interested in describing, explaining, or predicting is called the 'outcome variable'. The designation 'dependent variable' is also popular in the methodological literature, but that choice makes most sense in the framework of regression models, and we want a term that is more general. Alternative terms are 'response', 'effect', 'explanandum', and many others. The variable that captures the main hypothesized causal factor is called the 'explanatory variable'. Alternative designations are 'independent variable', 'treatment', 'cause', 'explanans', and many others. When a researcher is interested in the impact of one or a small number of explanatory variables on an outcome, we would refer to them as *main explanatory variable(s) of interest*. This is necessary in order to distinguish them from other potential causes of the outcome, which might be present but are not of central interest for the particular project. When these additional, potentially causal variables are at the same time potential causes of the main explanatory variable of interest, they are called *confounders* or omitted variables (see also Chapter 6 and Chapter 8). When they are possibly related to the outcome only, they can be called predictors, or just covariates. There are additional 'special' cases such as colliders, mediating variables, and moderating variables, but they need to be introduced in the framework of building and testing causal arguments, so the discussion will have to wait until Chapter 6. Note that in the context of predictive rather than explanatory research, all variables that help model the outcome of interest can be referred to as 'predictors' or 'covariates'.

Conditions versus variables   In some corners of the social sciences, researchers prefer to use the term 'conditions' instead of 'variables'. Namely, practitioners of Qualitative Comparative Analysis (QCA) and other set-theoretic methods (see Ragin, 2000, and the extended discussion in Chapter 9 of this text for details) insist on calling the aspects of cases that they observe and analyse '(causal) conditions' rather than '(explanatory) variables'. 'Conditions' emphasize the essentially dichotomous nature of the aspect of the case being evaluated – a case either qualifies as a member of the set defined by the condition or not (fuzzy scores can accommodate partial membership in the set, but the point remains). A person is either rich or not. In set-theoretic terms, it makes little sense to refer to membership in the set of rich people as a 'variable', so the term is avoided at the expense of '(causal) condition'. While 'condition' perhaps resonates better with the spirit and underlying philosophy of QCA, there are few practical consequences of using '(binary) variables' and 'conditions' interchangeably. In any case, be aware of this terminological subtlety.

Levels of analysis and observation

Observations and measurements are performed at a certain level which also defines what counts as a case, or a unit. For example, the level of observation can be individuals, or organizations, or states, or ties between states, and so on. In quantitative research, the level of observation corresponds to the row in the data matrix. In qualitative research, it is trickier to define, since the cases themselves are more amorphous.

Often, the level at which the data are collected and observations are made would be the same level at which the analysis (descriptive or explanatory) is performed. But sometimes the two would not coincide. Therefore, we need to introduce the distinction between level of observation and level of analysis, and correspondingly between unit of observation and unit of analysis (see also King, Keohane, & Verba, 1994, pp. 52, 116–117). For example, observations may be collected at the individual level, but the analysis may be performed at a higher level of aggregation, say schools or organizations. Alternatively, several observations can be made for the same individual over time, but then the data can be aggregated and analyzed at the individual level, disregarding the variation over time. Such aggregation would be appropriate when the units at the level of observation cannot be considered completely independent. By pitching the analysis at a higher level of aggregation, we make sure that what counts as a 'case' in the analysis is a truly independent realization of the underlying data-generation process. In sum, the level of observation is the level at which the data are collected, while the level of analysis is the level at which the analysis is performed and, importantly, at which the conclusions are pitched.

The distinction between levels and units of observation and analysis is more relevant for large-N research, where the independence of observations is a central assumption for the statistical analysis of data. Multilevel models, discussed briefly in Chapter 9, are one method of handling data with complex structures of dependence across different levels of aggregation. In the context of qualitative research the distinction is harder to draw and less consequential for the analysis and interpretation of the data.

In sum, determining the levels of observation and analysis is a crucial step in the process of research design. Often, and especially in qualitative research, the two would coincide. When there is a difference between the two, they would need to be defined separately and the researchers should be careful to take the difference into account when analysing the data and frame the conclusions of the analysis at the appropriate level.

Measurement Reliability and Validity

Whatever the level of observation, measurement needs to represent in a valid way the underlying variables and theoretical concepts. There are several aspects of measurement reliability and validity, and a related set of requirements that appropriate measures should fulfil.

First, measures should be reliable. The application of the same measurement instrument or technique to the same data should result in the same estimates. Reliability implies that if different researchers were to apply the same measurement approach (or the same researcher at different periods of time) they would get the same or at least very similar results. Failures of reliability can happen for a variety of reasons; some related to shortcomings of the measurement instrument or the researchers applying it, and others related to natural random variability or elusiveness of the phenomenon of interest. Rarely will perfect reliability be achieved. But then we should strive to estimate the uncertainty of the measurements and to quantify how reliable the measures are.

Second, measures should be as precise as possible. They should capture real differences between units, when these differences exist, and quantify precisely the amount and scale of these differences. At the same time, measurement should not create false precision by pretending to be more exact than it actually is. That is, the measurement level – nominal, ordinal, interval, or ratio – should be true to the underlying nature of the differences between the units *and* to the precision with which we can detect these differences. If all we can say is that Party A has a more extreme ideology than Party B, we should not impose a precise number on the scale of the differences, since the quantification would be unwarranted. It is a matter of fine judgement to decide what is the appropriate level of measurement for each particular research project. But the general advice is that measures should be as precise as possible, but no more.

When we get it wrong, it is useful to distinguish between two general types of measurement error (King, Keohane, & Verba., 1994). Random measurement error results in measures that deviate from the 'true' values, but in a non-systematic way. Random error is of course not nice, as it implies that measurement would be often off the mark. But if the errors are really nonsystematic, they would tend to cancel each other so that the average of many measurements would tend to converge on the 'true' value. Therefore, measures with random error will be inefficient, as we would need to repeat the measurements to get a good estimate, but they would not be *biased*.

Conversely, when measurement error is non-random, it will always bias our estimates, no matter how many measurements we take. Non-random measurement error systematically errs on one side, either over-estimating or underestimating the quantity that we try to measure. That would be easy to fix, if we know the direction and magnitude of the bias. But in the general case, we don't. Systematic measurement error is bad news for descriptive inference. Obviously, when the measures are biased, anything we want to infer about the cases and populations we want to describe would be wrong. But if the measurement bias is the same for all observations that are being measured, causal inference can still recover the 'true' relationship between variables. Imagine that we are interested in the impact of countries' wealth, measured in GDP per capita, on the probability of transition to democracy. If our measure of GDP per capita is systematically biased (say, it overestimates the wealth of nations) but the bias is the same for all countries, it would still be possible to estimate the strength of its real effect on democratization (although, the precise number we put to quantify the effect would be biased). If the measurement bias, however, is systematic – for example, if stronger totalitarian regimes overestimate to a greater degree their GDP per capita – this would invalidate all causal inferences we want to make about its effect on democratization.

In the context of causal inference, random measurement error would not bias the estimation of the causal effects, but the estimation would be inefficient, meaning that we would need more observations to detect a relationship in the data. This is important to realize, since a common critique of large-N studies is that the variables they use are measured less than perfectly. But variables that are imperfectly measured make it actually harder to find a relationship in a given dataset, provided that the measurement errors are truly random. Therefore, one could critique the statistical power (see Chapters 7 and 8) of such analyses, but it would be in general wrong to conclude that a relationship that is detected in data with measures subject to random error is an artefact of the measurement process and, as a result, illusory.

In real research projects in political science, measurement is never perfectly precise and totally reliable. Researchers should strive to improve the measures they use. But when this is not possible, they should consider the nature of the bias that their measures are likely to have and its possible effects on the inferences that they want to make. Even with imperfect measures, it would still be possible, and necessary, to anticipate how much and in what direction the conclusions are likely to be biased. And there are tools to account for measurement error at the data analysis stage (see Blackwell, Honaker, & King, 2015).

When variables are properly operationalized and measured, they provide valid representations of the concepts they refer to. To assess the extent that they do so, several assessment approaches are possible. Face validity refers to the 'common sense' validity of the measures used and evaluates whether the measures reconstruct the phenomenon of interest at 'face value'. Convergent validity refers to the extent to which different operationalizations and measures of the same concept lead to similar representations. Nomological validity captures whether previously established relationships can be replicated using a new measure. Content validity is about the extent to which the measure covers all aspects of a concept. Concurrent validity is about the ability of the measure to assign units to their proper classes. Additional adjectives to characterize measurement validity have also been proposed, but the list is already quite long.

What is crucial to realize is that assessing measurement (and operationalization) validity relies on existing knowledge and theoretical ideas about the concept and its relationships with other concepts. When the new measure does not fit – when it flies in the face of common sense, when it cannot reproduce previous findings about the concept, when it produces inferences that deviate from previously established facts – its validity is suspect. But, of course, the very reason to search for a new measure is dissatisfaction with the existing state of knowledge. If we were confident in the state of the art of the research field, we would not need new measures in the first place. So the fact that a new measure does not produce the same descriptive and causal conclusions as existing ones cannot be taken directly as a reason to disqualify it. That is why, in political science at least, the utility of standards of nomological, convergent, and face validity is limited. When a new measure fails on these accounts, it should be examined with extra care, but it cannot be dismissed right away. It remains a matter of fine judgement and academic debate when new measures provide enough novel insight to justify attention, but not too much to provoke rejection.

Measurement Strategies in Political Science

So far we discussed the nature of measurement in the abstract and considered many of the challenges of its reliability and validity. But we said little about the practice of measurement in political science and its relationship with empirical research in the field. In fact, political science harbours a great variety of measurement practices and currently displays fervent innovation when it comes to measurement strategies. The data political scientists use to devise measures of their concepts of interest ranges from readings from magnetic resonance imaging to historical archives, and from highly structured official documents to open free-flowing conversations with ordinary people.

Measures of phenomena and processes of interest for political science come from coding events in the world – for example, the occurrence and intensity of wars and other conflicts, diplomatic and trade ties between nations, national elections, protests, and negotiations. A large number of the measures come from the analysis of written sources, ranging from memoirs to official documents, laws, party programs, political speeches, international agreements, regulatory orders, and so on. Political scientists use words expressing opinions, making claims, and trading political accusations. But they also track actions: voting at polling stations and voting with the feet by relocating to another place, going on strike and going to demonstrations, voting for legislative bills and implementing laws at the street-level. Measures are constructed by passively recording what goes on in the world, at the micro-level in individual organizations and the macro-level of the global international relations system. And measures are actively elicited by surveys, experiments, and interventions in the world. A big chunk of the data political scientists use comes from efforts to track and map the opinions, predispositions, beliefs, and attitudes of ordinary people (the public), but also of special groups, such as political elites, lobbyists, policy entrepreneurs, and even fellow political scientists and other experts. It is futile to attempt to cover the diversity of measurement and data collection strategies in the field. Several of these are discussed later in the chapter under the heading of 'Description'. But we can illustrate the diversity by reviewing briefly the various operationalization and measurement strategies that have been employed to tackle one particular concept, namely the policy positions of political parties.

Measuring policy positions of political parties

Political parties are central actors in democratic political systems, and their preferences and positions on policy issues play leading roles in theories of political decision-making and accounts of policy change.

While it would appear straightforward to retrieve measures of the positions of political parties on policy issues, this is not the case. First, preferences can be expressed in words (for example, in official documents or interviews), but they can also be revealed in actions (for example, in supporting a legislative bill or sabotaging its implementation). Expressed and revealed preferences would not always lead to the same conclusions about the favoured positions of actors. This is especially true for political parties, which by their nature are aggregate actors, so the preferences of the core supporters need not be the preferences of the party leadership or of the party base. Furthermore, policy positions are expressed strategically, because these expressions are used as weapons in political bargaining and negotiations. Note that the first problem of measuring policy positions stems from deep and rather elaborate theoretical issues about the nature of the concept of 'preferences' and not from operational disagreements about data sources or the level of measurement precision.

The second challenge of measuring policy positions of political parties is that we often want measures that capture their general positions in an abstract policy space and not necessarily support for or opposition to particular policy choices. While the latter can be all that is needed for some research projects, for broader theories and questions a more general measure is called for, a measure that would allow us to compare parties to each other and across time, and that would have validity for a sufficiently broad set of policies. If the policy choices of political parties were completely unstructured so that a position on one issue was not predictive at all about what positions parties would take on another, such a general measure would be impossible. But policy positions are, in fact, structured across parties. Indeed, they are structured to such a great extent that usually one or two underlying latent dimensions are enough to capture sufficiently well the variation in party positions. The dimensions of the resulting policy space can be given on theoretical grounds – for example, it is normally assumed that the main dimension is a socio-economic one related primarily to issues of redistribution. Dimensions can also be identified inductively by the analysis of many concrete policy positions using a data-reduction technique such as factor analysis, cluster analysis, or item-response models (see below). Because spatial metaphors of political competition and spatial theories of legislative decision-making are so prominent, the reconstruction of the policy space and positioning the political parties in it is a major task of political science. It is also one that has been attacked from many angles.

One approach measures the positions of political parties by surveying experts who have deep substantive knowledge of individual political systems and parties. Experts are asked to assign to parties numbers on a scale representing a small number of analytically derived dimensions, such as left–right, liberalism–conservatism, or support for European integration (see Benoit & Laver, 2006; Bakker et al., 2015; Hooghe et al., 2010; Steenbergen & Marks, 2007). The individual expert estimates are then aggregated into an average. Using this approach, party positions are derived through the proxy of the judgements of political experts. As such, the measurement is subjective, but through the aggregation of many different opinions, it is hoped that the measure will converge on the 'true' party positions. (This has a higher chance of being correct for comparison of parties within rather than between different political systems.)

A second approach relies on the analysis of written text, hence on expressed policy positions. One prominent source of policy positions is provided by the electoral manifestos of political parties (Budge et al., 2001). Party manifestos for many parties and elections have actually already been coded for the parties' positions on many issues (see https://manifestoproject.wzb.eu/), and a smaller number of scales have been constructed from these opinions as well. But the source of such measurement need not be confined to party manifestos, and researchers have used many other texts such as political speeches, statements during the legislative process, and written contributions to policy consultations to recover policy positions from text (see, for example, Giannetti & Laver, 2005, and Laver, Benoit, & Garry, 2003), often using some form of automated text analysis (see Lowe et al., 2011).

Yet a third approach is to examine the voting behaviour of parties to reveal their true preferences regarding policies. When voting is open and recorded (which is not always the case), the so-called roll call voting records can be analysed to recover the main dimensions of political contentation in a political system and to measure the actors' positions in this space (Poole & Rosenthal, 1997; Poole, 2005; Jackman, 2009; Clinton, Jackman, & Rivers, 2004; see also http://www.voteview.com). Because parties and legislators vote on individual issues (which might not be entirely representative of the overall population of issues facing society), while what we want to measure is more general positions, some form of data analysis has to be employed that can combine the information from the individual voting records in a small number of positions. There are various data-analytic techniques to do that, and they are all based on more or less different assumptions about how to combine the observations into composite measures. These assumptions are rather technical, but the point to recognize is that they embody particular 'deep' and subtle theoretical assumptions about the nature of political preferences. For example, they would make different assumptions about how fast the utility actors derive from certain policies declines with policy distance (see Clinton & Jackman, 2009). Such assumptions of the data-analytic technique are often hidden 'under the hood' of packaged statistical programs, but they can have important implications for the output measures we get from the raw data. This is a powerful demonstration of how theory affects in subtle but often unavoidable ways the very process of measurement in science.

The measurement of policy positions of political parties is an active and exciting field of research (for example, a novel approach is crowd-sourcing expert evaluations of political texts; see Benoit, forthcoming), despite decades of ongoing efforts (for a recent overview, see Laver, 2014). Clearly, different approaches are possible and are being employed to tackle the measurement of the same concept. Because preferences are a latent, abstract, and intangible concept, there can be no 'silver bullet' or 'gold standard' approach to their measurement. Expert opinions, written text, and political actions all provide partial perspectives, each of which might be more or less appropriate for particular research projects. But even if not, perfect, measures of policy positions of parties, legislators, and other political actors have already delivered plenty of theoretical insight and input into policy discussions.

Descriptive Inference

Description is one of the major goals of research. It is important both in its own right and as a necessary stepping stone towards explanation. Description includes what others call 'exploration', which can be regarded as 'analytically enhanced' description that probes for possible explanatory ideas and prepares the ground for more systematic analysis.

We mentioned at the beginning of this chapter that description is closely related to measurement conceived as the process of assigning numbers and categories to aspects of cases. If there is a difference between description and measurement, it is that the former often takes a more holistic approach – a case or a population is *described* along many dimensions and in more depth than the notion of measurement suggests.

One can describe a single case and also a population of cases. When describing a population, often a sample is studied. The characteristics of the unobserved population of cases are inferred from the characteristics of the observed sample. But inference is involved at another level as well: what we describe and observe are operationalized variables, while we usually want to say something about more abstract theoretical concepts. In a study of public organizations, we observe how often co-workers meet and how they talk to each other, but eventually we want to learn something about *hierarchy* and *coordination* in organizations, not only about what Todd told Jane during the 2012 Christmas office party and what she did in response. Hence, description involves inference from observed cases to unobserved populations, from observed variables to unobserved concepts, and also from observed words and actions to unobserved meanings. When we get to the next chapter, we will see that the process of explanation adds yet another layer of inference, namely from observed *associations* between variables to *causal relationships*.

Description is truly intimate with the empirical world. It is a projection of the empirical world onto analytical dimensions. But description does not exist in a theoretical and normative vacuum. Theory is relevant to description at many levels. At one, it provides the concepts that help organize and make sense of raw sensations and perceptions. At another, more operational level, theoretical knowledge and assumptions are needed to support the process of descriptive inference. As we will shortly see, theory is needed to project findings from a sample to a population and various sub-populations of interest. At a third level, theoretical and causal models are often needed before we can even attempt to measure an abstract concept, such as preferences, and characterize a population in terms of the concept.

Lastly, descriptive inference in political science has rather obvious normative connotations (although political scientists often pretend that it does not). While an *amoeba* couldn't care less if it is classified as *eukaryote* or *bacteria*, it matters a great deal to countries whether they are classified as democracies or not, because, whatever state leaders think of the actual practice of democracy, the label itself can stir powerful emotions in society. Any measure of 'good governance', however meticulously defined, is bound to provoke normative reactions from the populations of states being described and ranked with the measure.

The definition of what constitutes a case in the first place can be equally normatively charged, for example when it concerns political formations that have not received international recognition, or ethnic communities without a state. To pigeonhole people, communities, and states into analytical classifications, to sort them from top to bottom, and to assign them numbers, inevitably bears normative connotations, and these should be acknowledged in the process of research. Which is not to say that they should be allowed to limit the questions researchers ask or be an excuse to compromise the integrity of the research process. But we, who describe, sort, classify, and attribute meanings to political entities and processes, have a certain responsibility to bear.

Goals of Descriptive Research

Descriptive research can have a number of very different goals. These goals can be classified with respect to the subject being described – a case, a (sample from a) population, or several populations – and the number of variables that are part of the description. When a single case is described on a single dimension (variable), we usually speak of measuring or scoring the case. When a single case is described along many variables, the description is extensive, often qualitative, and usually conducted via ethnographic or historical methods (see below).

When a population is being described (more often, it would be a sample from the population) and the focus is on a single dimension, we talk of univariate description. Depending on the level of measurement of the variable, this can take the form of classification, ranking, or analysis of a more complex distribution. Surveys (of public opinion, for example) and document analysis are common methods for such description.

When a population or a sample is described along several or many dimensions, the interest could be in the population or in the relationships among the variables themselves. This type of description may take the form of data reduction, which searches for structure behind the variables.

Finally, when our interest is in describing how populations differ along one or several dimensions, we explore the associations of variables with

Table 5.1 *Types and goals of description*

	Variables	
	One	*Several*
Single case	Measurement *classing and scoring cases*	Description (extensive) *various modes*
Sample of cases	Univariate description *classification, ranking,* *distributions*	Multivariate description *data reduction, population* *structure recovery*
Several samples	Exploration *analysis of variance and associations*	

characteristics varying in these populations. Such exploration is often a stepping stone to causal modelling with explicitly explanatory goals.

Table 5.1 summarizes the discussion of descriptive research goals and types.

Describing Populations

Let us first look into some of the ways in which political and other social scientists describe populations. A population can be described along one dimension (variable) at a time with the goal of learning how the variable is distributed in the population. Alternatively, we can attempt to describe a population along multiple dimensions at the same time, which usually requires some technique for reducing the complexity of data. Relatedly, we can group the cases with respect to their similarity along their values on the variables.

Univariate descriptions of populations

The description of a population along a single variable of interest is perhaps the most common research task in political science. Note that even when we describe a population in terms of more than one variable but do that in sequence, one variable at a time, without exploring connections between the different variables, we are still doing (a series of) univariate descriptions.

Nominal variables: filling in the boxes of classification schemes
When the variable of interest is binary or nominal, the basic way to describe the population would be to put the cases into the appropriate categories (classing) and compute a frequency count of the number of cases in each category (class), and/or the relative frequency (which is the

absolute frequency divided by the total number of cases in all categories). For example, if we want to describe the population of sovereign
states in the world in terms of their system of vertical distribution of
power (unitary or federal), we will end up with 27 states in the 'federal'
and the remaining 168 in the 'unitary' category. The relative frequencies
are 14 percent and 86 percent, respectively. The class with the highest
number of cases is called the *mode*. Of course, a real research project
would not leave it at that but would collect additional information on
other variables, for example, whether the states are republics or mon-
archies, whether there are additional lower levels of regional autonomy
in the states, how autonomous are the local levels of government, how
the regional units of federations are represented at the central level, and
whether federal units can raise their own taxes. The information from
these multiple descriptive dimensions could then be combined together
to fill the boxes of an intensionally defined typology or taxonomy, as
presented in Chapter 4.

What could be the purposes of univariate description with nominal
variables? First of all, we learn something about the cases themselves by
assigning them to the appropriate category. But, in addition, we uncover
the distribution of important variables in a population, which can be
important in its own right. In the case of federalism, the description has
already been done, and the results can be looked up in various encyclopedias, but for other questions and other variables the mere putting
together of the data can be a valuable contribution in itself. For instance,
a simple but comprehensive classification of the types of civil service systems that exist in the world, even along a small number of dimensions
(variables such as how much turnover there is at the top of the administration, what are the recruitment procedures, and what is the relative
power of bureaucrats versus politicians) would be a most welcome scientific contribution. Given the challenges of defining and operationalizing concepts for comparative research on a global scale, even such
relatively coarse classifications of fundamental aspects of the political
and administrative worlds are no easy feats to accomplish.

Often, merely identifying, listing, and crudely classifying a population
can add value to a research field. For example, identifying the population
and types of organizations that lobby the institutions of the European
Union is a major ongoing research effort (the EU does not yet require
lobbyists to register, so we cannot easily keep track of them) (Berkhout
& Lowery, 2008; Wonka et al., 2010).

Filling in the boxes of typologies and taxonomies can also be suggestive of deeper causal structures. If it turns out that no empirical cases
go into some of the boxes of the classification scheme, perhaps there
is a theoretical reason for that. More generally, the distribution of
cases along the classificatory dimensions can inspire hypotheses about
which variables are related to each other and why. Moreover, when

different populations or the same population at different points in time are described in this manner, the relative distribution of the variables can be compared, which can be another source of empirical research puzzles and causal hypotheses. Finally, well-thought out and meticulously executed classifications organize information efficiently, so later research projects can easily use them to test and probe theories and arguments that might not have even been conceived when the initial process of descriptive classification was performed. Of course, to fulfil all these promises, the assignment of cases to classes needs to be valid and reliable and the classificatory dimensions (variables) need to be carefully selected to capture salient and novel features of the social and political worlds, as explained in Chapter 4.

One example of a major effort to classify objects into a previously intensionally developed classification scheme that has had enormous influence for the study of politics and public policy is the already-mentioned Comparative Agendas Project. The project is based around an exhaustive classification scheme of between 20 and 35 (depending on the different versions) major topics and more than 200 subtopics. The topics range from 'Macroeconomic issues' to 'Nuclear energy' to 'Cultural policy', and cover the entire range of governmental activity. The scheme allows for the comprehensive classification of a wide range of activities and items, for example, political speeches, budgets, party manifestos, policy actions, public attention, and many others. The common classification scheme then supports research on various political and policy-making processes, such as agenda setting, problem definition, policy responsiveness, and legislative decision-making (see Baumgartner et al., 2009, and the bibliographies at http://www.policyagendas.org/ and http://www.comparativeagendas.info/). In short, the descriptive work that goes into the classification of real-world data into the analytically developed scheme provides the bedrock for a great number of exploratory and explanatory research projects.

Rankings   When the categories of a nominal variable can be ordered, descriptive research can provide rankings of the members of a population along a single dimension. The dimension can be related to a single operationalized variable, but it can also be a composite index combining information from several variables.

For example, the population of judicial systems in the world can be classified in terms of their level of autonomy, and conceptualized and operationalized as an ordered variable with three classes: independent, semi-independent, and dependent. The distribution of cases along the three classes can be presented and summarized with (relative) frequency counts; we can identify the mode class and the class containing the *median* (the midpoint) case. With a true ranking scale, all cases can be sorted from, say, most independent to most dependent.

Developing and marketing descriptive rankings are a favourite pastime for think tanks and other non-governmental institutions. Prominent examples include the Corruption Perceptions Index, provided by Transparency International (http://www.transparency.org/research/cpi/), the Democracy Index of the Economist Intelligence Unit (www.eiu.com/democracy2014), the Press Freedom Index of Reporters Without Borders (https://index.rsf.org/), and many others.

Rankings automatically point to leaders and laggards and identify top performers and worst offenders. As a result, they often generate media buzz. And occasionally these indexes provide useful data for quick orientation into a topic. But the scientific validity of such rankings is sometimes questionable, and the information they provide should be taken with a pinch of salt. Often, they will have poor operationalizations of the concepts they purport to measure, overestimate the scale of differences between units, and fail to report the uncertainty of the estimates.

Numerical variables: distributions and their moments   When the variables are defined and measured with the use of interval and ratio scales – in other words, when we assign numbers to cases – there is more to do to describe the population along a single variable. Ordinal variables allow for rankings and comparisons across classes. But interval and ratio measurements allow for a more complex descriptive analysis of the distribution of a single variable in a population. Since variables measured with such scales by definition have equal distance between the classes (values), we can apply a multitude of mathematical operations to derive properties of interest. Presenting the distribution of a numerical variable is often the first step.

The *distribution* of numerical variables generalizes the idea of frequency counts across a small number of categories and shows at a glance how the empirical cases are spread out along the values of the variable. A graphical representation of empirical distributions (the distribution of the observed cases) can take various forms – bell-shaped, uniform across the range of values, with a peak at one end and a long tail at the other, with two peaks at two different values, and others. While the empirical distribution can take any form it wishes, usually it will resemble, more or less closely, one of several well-known *theoretical* distributions, such as the Gaussian, the uniform, or the Poisson. It can be highly useful when an empirical distribution corresponds well to a theoretical one. One reason is that we know the type of processes that can produce a certain theoretical distribution, so when we see a match with an empirical one, we can infer something about the factors and processes producing the empirical distribution of cases; in other words, we can learn something about the world.

For example, the famous Gaussian (or 'normal') distribution is known to arise as the sum of many small independently acting forces, and the Poisson distribution is known to show up from counts of rare events over time. Assigning an empirical distribution of cases to a well-known theoretically defined one is also useful for comparing populations and the estimation of statistical models. In fact, it is so useful that many researchers automatically assume that one of a small number of distributions (most often, the 'normal' one) characterizes their empirical distribution of cases and conduct the analyses on this assumption. In descriptive analysis in particular, there is much to be learned from the empirical distribution before we rush to subsume it under a theoretical one, which might have useful mathematical properties but be inappropriate for the data at hand.

Normally, we are interested in some measure of the *central tendency* of the distribution – the mean (average), the median, or the mode(s). What is the average level of support for the death penalty in the US? What is the median number of months for a draft law to be adopted? What is the mean level of election campaign spending by political parties? Furthermore, we can examine how *spread out* the distribution of cases is, by reference to a measure of variation such as the variance, the standard deviation, or the absolute deviation. As we noted in Chapter 3, how *variable* a population is can be as relevant for theoretical and practical purposes as its central tendency. Another quantity of potential interest is how many and how high the '*peaks*' in the distribution are. For example, this can give us a clue about how *polarized* public opinion on a certain question is. Yet another useful feature of distributions to note is how 'long' and 'fat' its tails are, meaning how likely we are to encounter extreme values relative to the mean (in technical terms, the *kurtosis* of a distribution characterizes how sharp the peaks and how fat the tails are). How skewed the distribution is can also be informative about the (lack of) symmetry around the mean.

All in all, when numerical measures are appropriate to describe a variable, its empirical distribution can provide not only an efficient summary of the population for which it is measured but plenty of insight about what are the likely processes that produce the variable and the deep structure of the analysed population. For example, by analysing the distribution of changes in spending on individual budget items from year to year, Bryan Jones and Frank Baumgartner (2005) have developed their famous 'punctuated equilibrium' theory of policy change, where the causal mechanism of 'institutional friction' gives rise to a very peculiar empirical distribution, and one that happens to be observed in reality in many different contexts – across countries, policy areas, and indicators of policy change (Baumgartner et al., 2009).

Figure 5.3   *Four examples of empirical distributions generated from simulated data (the number of observations for each plot is 200)*

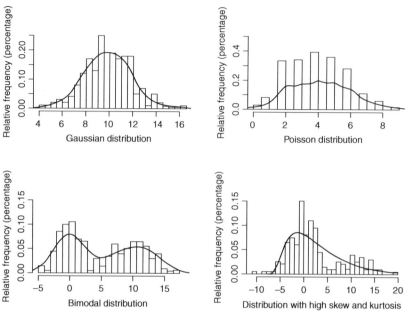

Figure 5.3 shows four examples of empirical distributions of simulated data. Each plot (called a histogram) is based on 200 observations. The bars indicate the relative frequency (as a percentage) of each value, and the lines show the density of the distribution. The top left one is generated by a Gaussian process giving rise to a normal distribution. The top right one shows a realization of a Poisson process. The one in the bottom left corner is bimodal, meaning that it has two modes, or most popular values. It is often generated by a mixture of two separate processes giving rise to the data. The histogram in the bottom right shows a distribution that is highly skewed (asymmetrical around the mean) and a high degree of kurtosis (note the fat 'tail' of the density curve at the right side).

All good textbooks on statistical data analysis will give you the technical background needed to work with and understand empirical and theoretical distributions. Without this background, this is as far as we can go in our discussion. Having acquired an idea of what the descriptive analysis of numerical variables entails, let us look back at an important issue of descriptive research *design*: sampling.

Sampling and surveys
So far we have (implicitly) assumed that all members of the population of interest have been part of the descriptive analysis. But we do not *have*

to score all cases of a population on the variable of interest. In many situations this is impractical or plainly impossible – imagine trying to get hold of *all* voting-age Indians, or all clandestine political independence movements in the world. Fortunately, under certain circumstances we can learn a lot about a population from studying a sample. Again, a sample is a subset of the population we want to learn something about, so the critical question is how to select a sample so that we learn as much as possible about the population.

Consider that we are interested in the opinion of Europeans on gay marriage. The population of interest is more specifically defined as citizens of the member states of the EU, age 18 and above. The variable of interest is whether the individuals approve of legal marriage between members of the same sex. For now, it is not important whether this is conceptualized and measured as a dichotomous variable (approve or not) or on some form of ordinal or interval scale (for example, five equally spaced categories from 'totally approve' to 'totally disapprove'). It is out of the question that we pose our question to all Europeans, so we have to sample. But how?

When we can safely assume that all cases (individuals) in a population are completely alike, it does not really matter which one and how many we choose. *Any* single one would do. But cases in a population are never completely alike, otherwise we would not need a description of the population in the first place. When there is only *random variability* in the population with respect to the variable of interest, it also does not really matter how we select cases (individuals) to study. If all values of the variables (answers to the opinion question) are random and equally likely (and we know that), there is no point in the research. When some answers are more popular than others but who takes what position is randomly given, we would need to measure the opinion of a number of individuals to get a sense of the population, but how we select them does not really make a difference. This scenario is also unrealistic.

In reality, there will be *some* systematic factors that would be related to how the variable is distributed in the population, and a fair amount of non-systematic random variation as well. Approval of gay marriage is probably systematically related to factors such as the age, place of residence, and political preferences of the individuals, but these factors would not completely account for the opinions. Older people are probably more likely to oppose gay marriage than younger people, but it is not the case that all old people would be against and all young people would approve. When there is a mixture of systematic and random variation in the population, as in practice there always will be, how shall we sample?

It turns out that the best way to select individuals is to sample *randomly*. (Complete) random sampling means that each individual in the population has exactly the same probability of being selected in the sample. This method is *best* in the sense that the sample will represent the population with respect to the distribution of the variable of interest, and representation will be achieved *efficiently* with a rising number of individuals in the sample. For an extended account of why random selection works, see Chapter 7 and the law of large numbers. In short, it guarantees that the sample is not biased with respect to a systematic source of variation of the variable of interest. If age is systematically related to approval of gay marriage, random sampling guarantees that as we sample more and more individuals, the age distribution of the people in the sample will converge to the age distribution of the people in the population. Not only that, but the distribution of *any* characteristic, no matter whether we suspect that it affects opinion or not, will become very similar in the sample and in the population. Thus, random selection will make the sample and the population alike in all respects, so that any bias is avoided.

You probably intuitively feel that asking only your friends whether they approve or not of gay marriage will not provide a picture that is representative for the population as a whole because your friends systematically differ from the average members of the population. By selecting a sample randomly, this bias is avoided. But how *many* cases are needed for random selection to work its magic?

The more individuals in the sample, the closer the distribution of the variable in the sample will resemble the one in the population. But there are diminishing returns to getting more and more individuals in the sample after a point. The precise answer to the *size* question depends mainly on the size of the population, the precision we want, and the error we are willing to tolerate. There are many available formulas and tools to calculate the necessary sample size (there are also many free sample size calculators on the internet, but if you use them make sure that their assumptions, for example about the type of measuring scale used in the survey, are met). For example, if we have a binary variable (approval of gay marriage or not), the population is eight million individuals, and we want to be 95 percent confident that the estimate of percentage approval in the sample will be within three percentage points of the true value in the population, we would need around 1,050 individuals in the sample. If the population is eighty million instead, the necessary sample size does not change; but if the population is 800, it drops to just a few short of 500. If we want to be 99 percent confident (instead of 95 percent) that we are within three percentage points of the true value, the required size almost doubles to 1,850. If, in addition, we want to be more precise – within one percentage point of the true value in the population – we would need 16,600 individuals in the sample. All these numbers assume that every individual has *exactly* the same probability of being selected in the sample: an assumption with very powerful and useful implications, but one that will be rarely satisfied in practice. After all, where do you get the list and contact details of all Europeans?

In the practice of social and political science research, one would often use a mixture of theory-driven and random sampling. Big surveys representative of national populations are based on complex multistage sampling procedures using stratified and cluster samples. If we suspect that a certain factor is important in affecting the variable of interest, it might be more efficient first to separate the population according to this factor (for example, into six age groups), and then sample randomly *within* the group. That would be a simple example of stratified sampling. In cluster sampling, some individuals, within a close geographical region, for example, are more likely to be sampled than others, with the aim of reducing the costs and other practical inconveniences of complete random sampling (which, however, comes at the cost of an increased total number of cases needed to achieve the same level of precision).

Operational details on how to design, administer, and interpret multistage sampling and surveys can be found in one of the many available specialized textbooks (for example, Valliant, Dever, & Kreuter, 2013; Lumley, 2010). But even with the cursory knowledge gained in this section, it is already clear that sampling and other questions of survey design are not completely removed from theory. Stratification and clustering require that we have some idea about the possible determinants of the variable of interest. Moreover, no survey has a perfect response rate (not all people who should be contacted are possible to reach or cooperate to provide answers.) Nonresponse needs to be taken into account in order to recover the representativeness of the sample for the population, and the 'corrections' involve analysis, which in turn requires theoretical knowledge and assumptions.

In addition, surveys based on random sampling produce estimates that are representative of the population as a whole, but sometimes we are also interested in some subpopulation, for example, the very rich, or the inhabitants of a particular region. To derive better estimates for the subgroups, the information from the random sample can be complemented with theoretical knowledge about possible determinants of the variable of interest and the distribution of these determinants in the population (a process called multilevel modelling and post-stratification) (see Gelman & Hill, 2007).

In short, despite their primarily descriptive nature, descriptive surveys make use of substantive theoretical and causal knowledge to improve the process of inference from a sample to a population. The weight of such theory-based 'adjustments' is only greater when sampling is not random but based on convenience, self-selection, snowballing, or when the sampling frame (see above for a definition) is not representative of the total population. Non-random samples are almost always guaranteed to be biased, so we should not even dream of using the raw estimates they provide as a measure of the total population. For example, how likely is it that surveying your friends and your friends' friends – an example of snowball sampling – would give a picture of gay marriage attitudes that is representative of the total population in a country? Or consider an alternative strategy – opening an online poll on the website of a popular newspaper and collecting the responses of those who decide to fill in the survey (self-selected sample). How likely is it that people from different ages and occupations would participate with the same probability in the poll? How likely is it that people having the same *intensity* of opinion on the issue as the average citizen would take part? If you agree with me that the answer to both these questions is 'Not very likely', can we extrapolate to the general population findings from a sample biased to significantly over-represent young, urban, well-educated, internet-savvy people who care enough about gay marriage and have the free time to fill in an internet form? No, we cannot (although many newspapers and some pollsters would have you believe that we can). Adjusting the raw information with the help of theoretical models (for example, by increasing the weight of the opinion of the one old village-dweller who self-selected into the sample) can help to some extent. But even then, convenience and self-selected samples are not always likely to provide valid and reliable inference about the population. The greater the selection bias and the nonresponse in random sample surveys, the greater the weight that our substantive theoretical assumptions and models will have in producing the final descriptive estimates. The border between descriptive and explanatory research certainly ain't as sharp as we drew it in Chapter 2!

Multivariate descriptions of populations

Surveys and other forms of description collect information on more than one variable, of course, but so far the analysis focused on one variable at a time. That is appropriate when the research goal is to describe how a variable is distributed in a population. Another goal for which descriptive analysis can be used is to discover the underlying structure of the population or to identify natural groups (clusters) in the population of cases. This goal corresponds to the second meaning of classification we discussed in Chapter 4, namely extensional classification. Having collected data on several variables for a set of cases, we can inductively infer how the cases tend to cluster. The inference is usually based on how similar the cases are. Similarity is measured with respect to the values of the cases on the variables. The output of the process – some form of extensional classification scheme – can be valuable in a purely descriptive sense – for example, when it discovers which states have similar foreign policy profiles and how they group – but it can also be suggestive of a 'deeper' causal structure behind the classification. The inductive clue can become the basis of a hypothesis that can be tested in subsequent research.

There are different similarity measures that can be used to summarize the data, and there are many statistical techniques that can be used to infer the groupings from the similarity measures. Cluster analysis (which itself has many variants such as hierarchical clustering or k-means clustering) and multidimensional scaling are the most popular techniques for classification in political science. (Note that decision trees, neural networks, and other statistical classification techniques that are part of the scientific field of machine learning, are used for a related but slightly different purpose, namely to automatically classify *new* cases into *existing* classification schemes. That would correspond to the process of classing according to the terminology endorsed in Chapter 4 and is related to prediction.)

Nowadays, of course, computer programs implement the algorithms and calculations involved in producing the extensional classifications. The remaining tasks for the researcher are to select the relevant dimensions (variables) on which the cases should be compared, to delimit the sample or population to be clustered, and to select the appropriate way to define the similarity measure (by considering questions such as should differences on all dimensions have the same weight in the computation of the distance measure) and the precise clustering method. Some of these tasks are informed primarily by substantive theoretical knowledge, such as the issue of which variables to include, but others require understanding the technical assumptions of different similarity measures and clustering algorithms. Seemingly innocuous choices (that the default settings of statistical software programs often make on your behalf), such as using Euclidean versus city block distance metrics, can reveal important theoretical assumptions (for example, about how utility declines with preference distance in the context of preferences measurement models; see Laver, 2014 for details) and have significant consequences for the output of the classification. So handle with care.

As an example of the output of cluster analysis, consider Figure 5.4, which shows how 27 of the EU member states (as of 2013) group when we take into account how similarly they vote in one of the legislative institutions of the European Union, the Council of Ministers. The data consists of the recorded votes on 352 draft bills which were considered between 2007 and 2014. Each of these 352 dossiers can be considered a binary variable taking the value '1' if the country voted in favour and '0' if it expressed dissent. Countries that are part of the same fork in the figure have the closest voting profiles. At each stage of the hierarchical tree, new clusters appear, again grouping more similar mini-clusters together. The figure can answer questions such as which is the most similar country to Spain (ES) – the answer is Portugal (PT) – or which are the two main opposing camps – the answer is given by the partition at the highest level of the classification tree (shown with additional lines).

Figure 5.4   *Hierarchical cluster analysis of 27 EU member states according to the similarity of their voting records in the EU Council of Ministers. Country codes are according to the ISO 3166 standard*

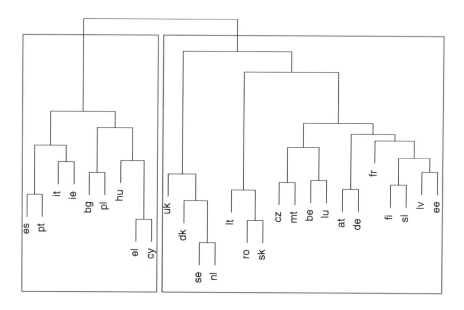

The figure above computes the similarity on the basis of all 352 dossiers (proposals for legal acts) at the same time. But we might suspect on theoretical grounds that there are two quite different types of dossiers that would lead to two quite different groupings of countries – for example, dossiers that concern issues of redistribution and those that concern regulatory policies. To explore this possibility we can conduct a different type of analysis – multidimensional scaling, which first identifies how the 352 variables can be best summarized in two underlying dimensions and then how the countries can be projected on these two dimensions. The result is again a visual representation of similarities between countries, but now on two dimensions. The dimensions can be interpreted in theoretical terms, if such an interpretation would be warranted, but are inductively derived. Whether they mean anything is a call that the researcher needs to make. Figure 5.5 shows an example of a multidimensional scaling plot based on the same data as Figure 5.4.

In general, purely inductive classifications such as the ones above bring insight to the extent that the resulting clusters and proximities can be meaningfully interpreted in terms of established concepts and theoretical ideas. They can also be used to create rankings and measures of latent concepts. For example, if we interpret the horizontal dimension in Figure 5.5 as 'support for redistributive policies', we can use the positions of the countries on this dimension as measures and rank the

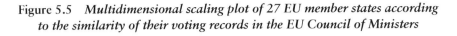

Figure 5.5 *Multidimensional scaling plot of 27 EU member states according to the similarity of their voting records in the EU Council of Ministers*

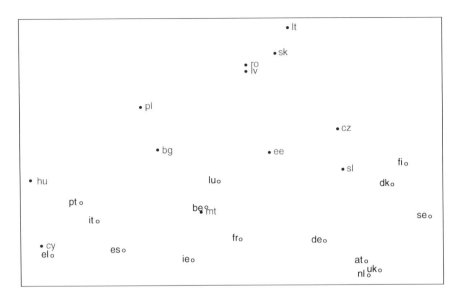

countries from the most pro-redistribution (on the left) to the ones most opposed (to the right). The ranking would be *relative* but could still inform further analysis.

Another method for describing and exploring relations between cases is network analysis. In network analysis the connections (called *ties* or *edges*) between the cases (called *nodes*) are defined not by similarity measures but by the existence and strength of 'links' between the cases. The links can stand for various kinds of relationships, such as contact within organizations, or family links, or being together at a set of events. The collection of *ties* can be visualized as *networks*. Just looking at the network representation can often be informative about its structure, but there are more formal methods and measures to detect different properties of the network, such as the degree of clustering or cohesion, and to identify cases (nodes) with special positions in the network. In the study of politics and policy making, network analysis has been employed to study diffusion of policy innovations (Cao, 2010), terrorist networks (Krebs, 2002), the structure of the American Congress (Fowler, 2006), the evolution of political attitudes (Lazer et al., 2010), and other topics. See Ward, Stovel, and Sacks (2011) for an overview of applications.

If we look back at the data used to illustrate cluster analysis and multidimensional scaling, we can decide to treat each country as a node and each instance of two countries opposing a legislative dossier together

Figure 5.6   *Network visualization of 27 EU member states voting patterns in the Council of Ministers: environmental policy*

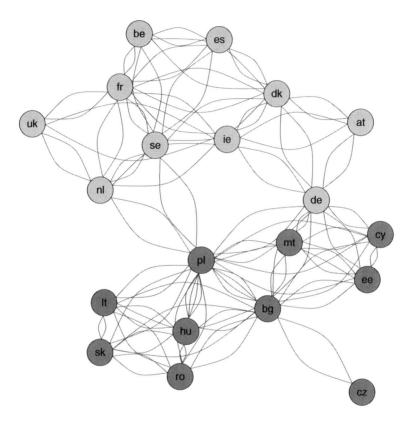

as a tie. We can then use one of the many available programs and algorithms to plot the resulting network. For the subset of legislative dossiers related to the field of environmental policy, the resulting network is shown in Figure 5.6.

Just by looking at the figure we can detect two 'cliques' (clusters) of countries that tend to vote together with members of the same clique but not with members of the other clique, and we can see that two countries – Poland (PL) and Germany (DE) – 'bridge' the two cliques. The visual representation of the data in the network, while purely descriptive as such, is highly suggestive of causal hypotheses which can become the starting points of explanatory theory-testing research designs.

Describing associations between variables

The focus in the previous section was on describing a population or a sample of cases. The goal was to learn something about the population, and the variable scores and the network ties were used to reveal its structure. Descriptive analysis of a set of cases can be employed with a different goal as well, namely to learn something about the relationships between the variables themselves by observing their associations in a set of cases. Of course, in doing so we also learn something about the cases, but the primary focus is on exploring how different variables covary, and not on how the cases are distributed or how they cluster with respect to the variables.

There are many different statistical techniques that can be used to approach this goal – from the most simple bivariate scatterplots to factor analysis to analysis of covariance (ANCOVA) to regression analysis. Each technique is appropriate for a slightly different research objective, and they are all based on different technical assumptions that need to be well understood to allow appropriate inferences to be drawn from the data. These are techniques of data analysis so their detailed presentation falls outside of this text. There are tens of hundreds of statistical textbooks that can guide you in how to use them (on regression analysis in particular, the introductory-level texts by Achen, 1982 and Berry, 1993, the intermediate-level texts by Scott Long, 1997 and Gelman & Hill, 2007, and the advanced-level text by Shalizi (forthcoming) are recommended).

If you have already been taught about regression, you might be surprised to see it introduced in the chapter on descriptive analysis. But this is no mistake. Without additional causal assumptions, which will be discussed in detail in Chapter 8, the output of statistical regression is best perceived in descriptive terms. Despite the fact that the variables on the right-hand side of a regression are often referred to as 'effects', 'determinants', and 'explanatory' variables, without further causal assumption, this is not strictly speaking warranted. Regression coefficients are sometimes a very good way of summarizing associations between variables in a set of cases, but nothing more than that. Under certain conditions, the associations between variables recovered in a regression analysis might be extrapolated beyond the cases part of the analysis. They can be projected from a sample to a population, if the sample is drawn randomly from the population, or they can be projected into the future to provide predictions about how variables will be associated in future realizations of the process we study (for example, the association between the state of the economy and approval of the president). But even these projections that require their own set of strong assumptions fall short of a truly causal interpretation, which needs to satisfy an even stricter set of requirements. These assumptions will be the subject of Chapter 6, and the design of research that can satisfy them will be the topic of Chapters 7, 8, and 9. For now, remember that without further assumptions, regression provides nothing more than a description of the data at hand.

Factor analysis is another very popular statistical technique for summarizing relationships between variables. Its goal is different from the projections to populations and to the future that regression is usually used for. Factor analysis is often employed to uncover latent unobserved variable(s) from a larger set of observed variables. For example, the concept of intelligence is not directly observable. What we can observe is how individuals answer various test questions that probe their verbal and numerical abilities, memory, and so on. Exploring the relationships between these observable variables, we can discover a common factor that accounts for a large share of the variation in how people perform on the various tests, and we can decide that this common factor is, in fact, general intelligence. There are debates whether in this particular example the common factor can be interpreted as a valid measure of the latent concept 'intelligence' (see Shalizi, forthcoming), but for us it is the principle that is important. When one or several factors are identified, the cases can be characterized by how they score on the factors, compared, and ranked (for example, from most intelligent to least so).

In political science factor analysis is routinely used to uncover unobserved personality traits and predispositions from answers to multiple questions from public opinion surveys, essentially in any field where more than one measurement indicator of a concept can be used and no single one among them is a perfect operationalization of the concept. Item-response models are a related technique (Treier & Jackman, 2002; de Ayala, 2009).

Describing Individual Cases

Description is not always about numbers, populations, and statistical associations. There are radically different ways of doing descriptive research. In fact, there are entire social scientific disciplines – above all history and anthropology (ethnography) – devoted primarily to description. But historical and ethnographic description operates in a very different mode from the one discussed so far; a mode that puts a premium on context, detail, and comprehensiveness, rather than abstraction, quantitative measurement, and complexity reduction.

In this section of the chapter we are going to introduce description focused on an individual case. Instead of coding variables for a sample, we will consider collecting qualitative observations for a case. But one of the salient features of qualitative description is that the case *itself* is much harder to define with fluid boundaries, blurred dimensions, and a fuzzy core. In qualitative descriptive research we cannot easily delimit cases, identify populations, and point to their salient 'variables'. That being said, the differences from description as presented in the previous section should not be exaggerated. For all its attention to context, qualitative description still needs to make inferences from observable words and actions to unobservable concepts and meanings, which requires the use of replicable and valid procedures; in other words, it requires the use of the scientific method.

In this section, we only concentrate on case-focused *description*. The use of case studies and qualitative observation for causal inference and explanation is discussed in detail in Chapter 10.

Participant observation and ethnographic fieldwork

When the research interest is in describing a case comprehensively and holistically (as a whole), we often need to resort to intensive methods of data collection. These methods require that we get to know the subject of the research in intimate detail, by observing it closely, from various angles, and for a continuous period of time. Such methods go by the name of participant observation, or ethnographic fieldwork, or often just 'fieldwork'. Moreover, when we study people or social groups, we need to get to comprehend the world from the subject's point of view, to emphatically see what they see, and then translate these subjective world views into a text that communicates them to the broader research community.

It is not only that description in this mode provides more information about a case. The type of information is different. The researcher not only codes variables that he or she has previously considered important. What is considered an important aspect of a case and a situation is itself a matter that is shaped and discovered in the process of research. So the difference between intensive case-focused description based on ethnographic fieldwork and quantitative surveys or standardized measurement is both that the former provides richer and more detailed data about each case being studied *and* that the type of information being collected is less structured.

Ethnographic fieldwork and participant observation are the core methods for interpretative social science, which, as explained in Chapters 1 and 2, often distances itself from the positivist ambitions to develop explanations and uncover systematic causal effects in the social and political worlds. But there is nothing to prevent these methods from being employed in positivist research projects, especially descriptive ones. While there are specific challenges when it comes to the replicability and reliability of observations provided by participant observation research, fieldwork is certainly compatible with a positivist outlook (Wedeen, 2010). And as explained in Chapter 3, observation is never completely divorced from theory, despite even the best efforts of researchers to see all things purely as they are, uncontaminated by prior theories and concepts.

Ethnographic work features prominently in research on organizations, policy implementation, social aspects of criminal behaviour, urban studies, state formation, and other fields of relevance to political science.

It usually involves 'immersion' into a social group or organization, such as a government department, a local agency, a minority group, or even a criminal gang, and then observing and recording all aspects of the social and political interactions that appear salient, to the researcher and to the subjects of the research. Since no book can record all these observations at the same level of detail, the researcher then selectively weaves some of the evidence into a descriptive narrative. The narrative recreates the social or political phenomenon of interest from the subjective view points of those directly involved, as interpreted by the researcher. Recurrent themes of such narratives are relationships with power and the state, the dynamic between formal and informal hierarchies and institutions, the invisible mechanisms of social control, the development and change of social norms, language and discourse, and the production of shared meaning of social actions.

Participant observation and fieldwork seem to be the only viable descriptive modes when the phenomena we are interested in are not captured by formal documents and official statistics, and would not be revealed by a short telephone conversation with a pollster or a census administered by an official government agency. In fact, such methods provide an often needed 'reality check' on the shortcomings of official documents and standardized surveys to detect and describe the important aspects of social reality. And they provide context for the interpretation of other data by disclosing the real-life experiences behind social measurements and statistics. As such, they can inspire and ground new efforts to develop better surveys, more appropriate questionnaires, and more relevant statistics to be employed in subsequent large-N or comparative research.

A recent example of the use of ethnographic participant observation for the study of public bureaucracies is provided by Thorbjørnsrud (2015). The researcher's goal is to describe and explore the mediatization strategies of contemporary government organizations, or, in other words, the ways in which government organizations deal with the media and how the media context (re)shapes the organizations. The author spent a year at the central administration dealing with immigration issues in Norway and meticulously observed how the department reacts to and tries to influence its relationships with the media. Based on the extensive fieldwork, the research uncovers the overt and subtle ways in which mediatization challenges key bureaucratic values, goes hand-in-hand with growing politicization of the department, and slowly transforms the government organization. The evidence for such processes could not have been collected through standardized questionnaires or document analysis only, as the processes are novel, fluid, and complex. But the case study can inspire new research projects that can reframe the insights in more explicitly causal terms and probe the generalizability of the descriptive findings to other government organizations and countries.

Archival historical research

Next to ethnographic approaches, the other great tradition of rich, qualitative, contextual, case-focused description in political science is based on historical methods, which themselves are very often based on archival research. Historical political science focuses on the detailed reconstruction of events of political importance, but also of broader social and political processes, such as the glacial evolution of institutional forms over centuries or the dialectics of social and class conflicts in the past. Because historical work deals by definition with the past, data sources such as interviews and surveys are rarely available. Most of the research needs to be based on written sources kept in various archive collections. This is simultaneously a disadvanatge for historical description but also an opportunity, because many important documents become available to researchers only after a long period of time has passed.

We cannot do justice to the variety and complexity of historical description in one section of one chapter, but it is nevertheless important to note its relevance to problems of political science and governance. And there are methodological parallels to draw between historical work and the other forms of descriptive inference that we have already discussed.

One example of a historical study of a problem of significance for scholars of politics and public administration is Kerkhoff's study of the evolution of public norms concerning political corruption and unethical behaviour of public servants in the late eighteenth century in the Netherlands (2011). On the basis of extensive archival research, the author identified a number of pamphlets and other public statements from the period discussing contemporary scandals involving the corrupt behaviour of tax collectors and other public administrators. The discourse in these documents was used to reveal the changing standards of appropriate behaviour and the evolving public values and beliefs in which public service is embedded. In a way, the written documents operationalize the elusive concept of public values and, as such, are subject to all the rules of descriptive inference (see also Kerkhoff, 2013), such as replicability, reliability, and construct validity. The study is more than purely descriptive, but even the descriptive aspects are revealing about how much of what we take for granted nowadays in our understanding of corruption and bureaucracy is contingent on the social and normative context of the time.

* * *

The variety of descriptive modes and strategies used in political science is nothing short of amazing: from the statistical tools of sampling and public opinion surveys to the complex hidden structures revealed by cluster and network analysis to the rich contextual worlds evoked by ethnographic and historical work. This chapter reviewed the research design choices involved in descriptive research when the goal is to summarize populations, to characterize associations between variables, or to comprehensively describe individual cases. Yet, despite its variety, description is not all of political science. What more could we ask for? The answer is, the promise of control and of a deeper understanding of not only how things are, but why. In other words, explanation.

Further Reading

A rare general reflection on the place of descriptive research in political science, as well as its types and normative significance, is Gerring (2012a).

Detailed discussions of issues of measurement validity are available in Cook and Campbell (1979) and Shadish, Cook, and Campbell (2002).

On sampling and survey analysis, consult the excellent Lohr (2009) and Valliant, Dever, & Kreuter (2013). On the design of complex surveys, see Lumley (2010). Kish (1995) and Cochran (1977) are older classics of the field. Note that the practice of surveying is currently experiencing an uneasy transition to an age of declining response rates and usage of the traditional communication channels used by researchers to reach people.

For an introductory text on cluster analysis, see Aldenderfer and Blashfield (1985). Applications in political science include Ahlquist and Breunig (2012) and Jang and Hitchcock (2012). Sharma (1996) is a textbook on factor analysis and related techniques; Rummel (1970) is an alternative. On inverted factor analysis or Q-methodology, used to discover and describe the structures of subjectivity, see Brown (1980).

Goodin and Tilly (2006) is a great source on a variety of contextual approaches to political science, including the ethnographic and historical ones discussed here. Schatz (2013) is an edited volume on political ethnography. A guide to field research is provided by Kapiszewski, MacLean, and Read (2015).

An early review of the use of archives in political science is Skemer (1991). Hill (1993) is a general introduction to archival methods. A contemporary guide for the US is Frisch et al. (2012). Kreuzer (2010) makes the case for the importance of historical knowledge for the study of institutions and institutional change (see also the reply by Cusack, Iversen, & Soskice, 2010). Raadschelders (2000) is a handbook on administrative history.

Chapter 6

Explanation and Causality

The Ancient Greek philosopher Democritus allegedly once said, 'I would rather discover one causal law than be King of Persia.' Much of contemporary political science is fuelled by a similar ambition to offer explanations rather than 'mere' descriptions, although not necessarily in the form of causal laws. How to test for and discover causes and explanations in empirical data is the subject of Chapters 7–11. But we have one question to answer before that. What exactly *is* explanation? While we have used the term extensively already (especially in Chapters 2 and 3), so far we left its meaning deliberately vague. In this chapter we go beyond an intuitive understanding of explanation to suggest some possible forms and definitions. We conclude that *causal* explanation is the most relevant one for political scientists.

Causality, however, turns out to be a rather difficult notion as well. Forced to explicate what it means, we endorse a *counterfactual* definition. The idea of counterfactual causality might appear unscientific at first sight because of the irreducible uncertainty at its heart, but, as the chapter will try to convince you, it is unavoidable.

The major benefit of a counterfactual understanding of causality is that it allows us to express clearly the fundamental problem of causal inference. The problem is that we only observe one version of the world but want to form reasonable expectations about what would or could happen (or could have happened) under alternative scenarios. The solution is to approximate the observed and the hypothetical as much as possible – while the approximation is never perfect and the inference never completely certain, once we have defined the problem in counterfactual terms, we can examine how various research designs provide partial solutions.

Types of Explanation

First, a warning – the problem of the nature of explanation has bemused philosophers for millennia, and we cannot hope to resolve it here. Our aim is modest – to arrive at a workable definition that can provide clarity and guidance for empirical research in political science. With this warning in mind, let us explore what some of the possible paths, cleared for us by centuries of philosophizing, are. We are going to briefly discuss

145

nomological (in its deterministic and probabilistic variants), functional, intentional, and mechanistic causal types of explanation. These types differ in their underlying explanatory logic and in their primary focus. The last type to discuss – mechanistic causal explanation – is the one that will prove most relevant for our purposes, but the rest have more than historical importance as they introduce valuable ideas about what explanations are and how they could work.

Covering laws

The idea of explanation via reference to covering scientific laws has an appealing logical structure. Simply put, science is supposed to explain by subsuming empirical phenomena under covering laws. An outcome is explained if it can be deductively subsumed under principles having the character of general laws. That is why this type of explanation is also called 'deductive-nomological' (*nomos* is the Greek term for 'law'). Deductive-nomological explanations are associated with the philosophical school of logical positivism and the work of Carl Hempel in particular (1965).

Here is a short example of how this works. We can explain the observation that John voted at the last elections by the particular fact that John is rich and the general law that rich people always vote. Of course, there is no scientific law that rich people always vote, but imagine for the moment that there were. If we believe the general law, the particular fact of John being rich is sufficient to explain the outcome; hence, the explanation is also deterministic.

In science, laws posit *strong* relationships between different phenomena (for example, speed, time, and distance). Theories explain why and under what circumstances these laws hold. Laws are more than empirical generalizations and require a certain necessity rather than the existence of mere regularities (which might after all be accidental). The classic illustration of the difference is the comparison between the statements: 'Any solid ball made of gold weighs less than 100,000 kilograms' and 'Any solid ball made of plutonium weighs less than 100,000 kilograms'. Both statements happen to be true on the planet Earth, but only the latter is backed by a necessity (plutonium balls would explode before reaching such mass), while there is nothing to prohibit *in principle* the existence of a ball made of gold that big, other than the accidental fact that currently on Earth it just so happens that there is not enough gold to produce it (Balashov & Rosenberg, 2002, p. 41).

When scientific laws in the strong sense defined above are available, explanation of particular facts is straightforward, according to the deductive-nomological model. But when they are not, explanation would appear to be impossible, and this is the Achilles' heel of this type of explanation. In modern political science, and the social sciences more

generally, scholars rarely, if ever, speak of laws. And even when they do, they mean an empirical generalization rather than a relationship backed by theoretical necessity. Furthermore, these political science 'laws' have plenty of exceptions as well, so at best they refer to probabilistic tendencies rather than strict regularities as would be expected from real laws.

For example, the so-called Gamson's law proposes that parties in a coalition will get a cut from the available government portfolios proportional to the share of the seats they contribute to the coalition. While observations of real-life coalition formation generally support this tendency (although exceptions abound), theories not only fail to posit any necessity to the pattern but actually have a hard time reconciling it with standard collective decision-making models (Gamson, 1961; Carroll & Cox, 2007).

Another case in point is Duverger's law that electoral systems based on plurality rule within single-member districts tend to produce two-party systems (Duverger, 1954; Cox, 1997). Altogether, the relationship receives strong empirical support (yet, again, counterexamples exist) and rests on plausible mechanisms, its theoretical foundations are not universally accepted (for example, the direction of causality between the electoral and party systems is contested – see Benoit, 2007; Colomer, 2005).

While real laws in political science do not exist, theories abound. The search for laws itself is discredited, which makes the quest for theoretical understanding more difficult and more pressing.

In sum, the deductive-nomological type of explanation is not very useful for political science research, both because it is (too) deterministic and because it requires laws to be more than mere empirical generalizations. An alternative, also associated with the name of Carl Hempel and logical positivism, is the so-called probabilistic explanation.

Probabilistic-nomological explanation

If determinism is too strong a requirement, we can relax it and reformulate laws in probabilistic form – rich people have a high probability of voting, plurality electoral systems have a high probabil   f producing two party systems, and so on. Combined with particula   icts (John is rich, the UK has a plurality electoral system), probabili   c laws confer very high probability on the outcomes and by virtue of this explain them. The explanation is still nomological, yet no longer deterministic, but probabilistic.

Probabilistic-nomological explanation appears to be an attractive alternative for social scientists, but it comes with its own set of problems. First, it still needs to be based on something more than empirical generalization: the probability in question is a relation between statements and not between facts. Mendel's laws of inheritance, which you might remember from secondary-school biology (if not, see Bateson & Mendel, 2009), are probabilistic in nature, but they still possess a necessity that is more than an inductive empirical generalization – a necessity that seems unattainable in the context of political science. Second, probabilistic-nomological explanations, at least in their original formulation by Hempel, suffer from a logical flow – some probabilistic laws confer a small rather than a large probability to an outcome, but they nevertheless provide a sufficient explanation of why the outcome occurred (Scriven, 1959). For example, only a small proportion of smokers would develop mouth cancer, but smoking nevertheless would provide a sufficient explanation for many of those who do. Only a small proportion of repressed societies might experience revolutions, but political repression might still be a sufficient explanation for the ones that do. Despite Scriven's critique of the probabilistic-nomological model, the idea that an explanation does not have to be deterministic is a valuable one and we shall retain it and return to it later in the chapter.

Functional explanation

Another form of explanation completely does away with the notion of laws. Functional explanation accounts for a phenomenon by showing that it fulfils a function that is vital or beneficial for an organism, firm, state, or society. So the spread of professional bureaucracy in the early modern period can be explained by virtue of the fact that it fulfils a basic need of the state, organizational differentiation can be explained by virtue of the fact that it helps organizations perform better, and the rise of the welfare state can be explained by virtue of the fact that it fills the vacuum left by the dissolution of communal life in modern society. Functional accounts are a form of teleological explanation – explaining in terms of the purpose or utility of the cause. To put it even more succinctly, the consequences of the behaviour *are* its causes (Stinchcombe, 1968). Functional explanations have been quite popular in the social sciences, especially in cultural anthropology since the 1920s and sociology since the 1950s, but their prominence has declined steeply in the past few decades.

For functional explanations to work, there needs to be a causal mechanism that rewards and filters beneficial behaviour or traits in order to make them dominant or prevalent in a population. Such a mechanism, for example, is provided in the case of biological evolution by natural selection. It is possible that similar mechanisms operate in the social world as well. For example, in an ideal market efficient firms survive while the rest perish. So we can in principle explain the prevalence of some practice, such as professional management or organizational differentiation, in a population of firms by virtue of the fact that firms that have not adopted this practice will be destroyed by the competition. If the selection mechanism is sufficiently ruthless, we could in' ed account for the prevalence of a trait by its effects, thus teleologic 'y. Note that in the case of functional explanations, the causes (cc· s⌐ ⌐nces of behaviour) come only *after* the 'effects' (the behaviour '.se ,.

Apart from the market, there are other contexts that could potentially support functional explanations in the social sciences. Wars and internal conflicts wipe out unsuccessful states and communities, strife for resources filters efficient from inefficient organizations, individual-level traits such as altruism or risk-aversion could provide evolutionary advantage. But in all these cases, the selection mechanisms are often weak. In other words, there is quite a lot of 'slack' (Hirschmann, 1970) that allows suboptimally adapted individuals, communities, or states to survive. Consider, for example, the case of public organizations. While in the (very) long term under-performing ones would probably be reformed, dismantled, or otherwise exit the pool, as we all can testify, inefficient public organizations can survive for a long time even in the face of scarcity of resources and other environmental pressures (such as citizens angry at the poor service they provide). The same is true for private organizations as well, if we abandon the *assumption* of ideal market competition.

If the selection mechanisms are not brutal enough or the rewards strong enough, functional explanations break down. The requirement to demonstrate not only that a certain behaviour or trait is beneficial but also that there is a generative mechanism that would make it dominant in a population is often very difficult to satisfy, so researchers in social and political science have increasingly looked away from functional explanations.

Intentional explanations

Explanations in terms of beliefs coupled with intentions (desires, wants, interests, needs, reasons, and so on) are also teleological and have their part to play in political science analysis. It seems only natural to try and explain why John votes in terms of his desire to express his preferences, why Great Britain fought Argentina for the Falkland Islands in 1982 in terms of its intention to do so, or why Russia joined the World Trade Organization in 2012 in terms of its interest from accession. Intentional explanations are also popular, if not predominant, in everyday discourse about politics. For laymen uninitiated in the art and craft of political science, it is perfectly natural to discuss and explain the latest domestic political scandals, international conflicts, or approaching elections in terms of the intentions of the actors involved.

While intuitive, intentional explanations face several challenges. First, individual intentions do not combine in a straightforward way to produce collective outcomes, as demonstrated in passing in Chapter 3. Second, intentions are not directly observable, so they are of less explanatory value than appears at first: even if individuals' wants and desires are major reasons for social action, if we have no direct method of ascertaining what they are *before the fact*, then their explanatory utility is limited. Third, intentions are seldom, if ever, *sufficient* for explanation. We might explain the latest reorganization of the Department of Agriculture in terms of the intention of the minister to improve its work, but that would probably be insufficient and the intention could even be unnecessary. In short, while admissible, intentional explanations in political science would be at best incomplete.

Mechanistic causal explanations

We could go on our tour of social-scientific explanatory modes, but we had better zero in on the type that should prove most relevant – causal, and more specifically, mechanistic explanation. Non-causal explanation sounds a bit like an oxymoron akin to 'dark light', and in fact philosophers have different opinions about whether nomological, functional, and intentional explanations qualify as causal or not (for example, Lewis, 1986, p. 221; or Elster, 2007, p. 14, who says that 'at the most fundamental level ... all explanation is causal'). There are some complications in treating all explanations as causal. The difficulty with covering laws is that, at least when expressed as equations, laws imply strong relationships but no directionality (Russell, 1948). The difficulty with functional explanations is that the effect precedes the cause (reversed temporarily). The difficulty with intentional explanations is that it is unclear, to philosophers at least, whether intentions can ontologically be regarded as proper causes. In any case, in this section we consider a particular notion of causal explanation, namely *mechanistic*, that is sufficiently distinct from the types discussed above.

A mechanistic explanation identifies causes and effects *and* the causal paths linking them. It answers the question *how* the cause produces the effect by tracing the links of a causal chain or the interactions of the elements of a mechanistic model. We have already discussed the importance of explicating mechanisms in the process of theory development in Chapter 3. And mechanisms are intricately related to the method of process tracing discussed in Chapter 10. In practice, a mechanistic causal explanation identifies a number of different causal paths through which the cause and the effect are linked, and mediating and moderating variables provide ways to operationalize and eventually test these conjectures. Mechanisms often unfold in time so that the causal paths specify a sequence of events. They can also start causal cascades in which the effects propagate simultaneously. But the temporal aspect is not essential for a mechanistic causal explanation: a characterization of how a system-level behaviour arises from the interactions of its constituent parts would also qualify (Glennan, 2002; Hedström, 2005). A mechanistic explanation of a particular event can either specify a robust causal process that produces the event or the actual sequence of steps that led to it. Both options are put to use in actual political science research.

Table 6.1 summarizes the main types of explanation discussed in this chapter. But the differences should not be overstated. The idea of mechanistic explanation is sufficiently broad that functional and intentional explanations can be considered as particular mechanisms producing, in some circumstances, necessary and/or sufficient causal accounts of processes and events. (So they are compatible with and, in a way, subtypes of mechanistic explanations.) And at a deeper level, the notion of a robust causal mechanism is not that different from the notion of a causal law. But it is the persistent attention that mechanistic explanations pay to *how* an outcome is produced that is its defining feature.

Mechanistic causal explanations encompass a wide variety of specific approaches to understanding social and political phenomena and provide the basis for a number of particular research methodologies. Nevertheless, let us demarcate what they do and what they do not imply. First, as explained in detail above, they shift attention from covering laws, be they deterministic or statistical, to mechanisms the operation of which is almost always contingent. Second, they are not teleological, unlike functional and purely intentional explanations. Third, they endorse scientific realism as a grounding philosophy at the expense of both pure empiricism (which rejects the very notion of causality, see below) and radical subjectivism (which rejects the idea that social reality is 'dense' enough to support objective causes and effects). Fourth, mechanisms can, but do not have to, be specified at the level of individual persons – they are compatible with, but not wedded to, methodological individualism. Fifth, causal mechanisms are compatible with statistical

Table 6.1   *Types of scientific explanation*

Type	How it works	Major limitation
Deductive-nomological	Subsumes facts under deterministic covering laws	Rigid and deterministic
Probabilistic-nomological	Subsumes facts under probabilistic-statistical laws	Rigid and problem of low probability
Functional	Teleologically (in terms of the utility of the cause)	Requires strong selection mechanisms
Intentional	Teleologically (in terms of goals, intentions)	Intentions unobservable, rarely sufficient
Mechanistic	By specifying causal mechanisms	Mechanisms unobservable and uncertain

explanations; in fact, they provide a major way for statistical analysis to deliver casual inferences. The last point requires further elaboration, if only because of the misunderstandings concerning the nature of statistical explanation widespread among its critics and proponents alike.

How is it that mechanistic and statistical notions of explanation are compatible? On the one hand, mechanisms require that *each outcome* can be traced back to a chain of causes and their effects. On the other hand, statistical explanations speak of probabilities and work with *distributions of outcomes* (see Chapter 7). A statistical explanation in the form '*Poor people have a high probability not to vote*' seems to be able to explain both that Mary, who is poor, did not vote (high probability of this event) and that she did vote (low, but not zero probability of this event). If we consider 'wealth' a causal factor, we have a problem, because probabilistic explanations do not seem to be *contrastive*, as the problem that X (wealth) seems to be able to explain both 'Y' (vote) and 'not Y' (no vote) is known in the philosophical literature (Salmon, 1984). Relatedly, because statistics deals with populations, it does not seem to be able to derive a causal story (etiology) for any single unit within the population (for example, Mary), which would seem to imply that it cannot in fact explain individual cases.

A resolution of these apparent contradictions is provided by Bruce Glymour. In his own words (1998, pp. 468–469):

> Mechanistic explanations ... answer how-questions about the origin of property frequencies or distributions in particular populations. They do so by individuating the kinds of causal traces productive of the relevant property or properties, and then specifying the frequencies of these trace kinds in the history of the relevant population or sub-population.

An example can illustrate how this works. Assume that a population consists of rich and poor people. Rich people always vote, while only a small proportion of poor people vote (say 20 percent). The population of poor people is further subdivided into those who are highly educated (few, say 20 percent) and those who are not. Imagine that there are two mechanisms that produce the outcome 'voting': (M1) being rich and (M2) being highly educated. In other words, there are two alternative causal paths that lead to voting. On this account, every individual in the population has a particular causal story or etiology (rich, poor and uneducated, poor and educated) that completely determines the individual outcome (votes or not). However, when we compare the distribution of voting at the population level, wealth appears as a *probabilistic* cause. Suppose that the researcher is aware of mechanism M1, but not of M2. This imperfect understanding of the causal structure of voting will make wealth appear only probabilistically related to voting, while each individual's outcome is deterministically produced, and wealth is in fact a causal factor part of a relevant causal mechanism. Had we known the full causal structure, no statistical explanations would have been necessary.

Alas, there is a multitude of possible mechanisms behind practically all social and political phenomena of interest. Furthermore, in the general case, we are aware of the existence and workings of only a part of these mechanisms, and imperfectly so. Therefore, even if at the bottom of social reality there is a deterministic process producing each individual-level outcome, our imperfect understanding of the causal structure would lead to probabilistic causal relationships at the level of observation. The limits of our knowledge would be reflected in the 'noise', or residual variation, of statistical models *and* in the variability of the estimated causal effect. The former can be thought of as the influence of alternative mechanisms not accounted for in the model and the latter as population heterogeneity (diversity), which, in its turn, results from the ways in which the context influences the mechanism represented by the variable in the model.

More prosaically, even if we knew the causal structure in all its glory and complexity but had imperfect measurement instruments, we would still be able to detect causal relationships only as probabilistic. Measurement errors can be thought of as additional mechanisms that can produce the observed data.

To sum up the argument, statistical explanations are compatible with a causal mechanistic definition of explanation. But do not take this to mean that statistical analysis is the only way to get at causal inference and explanation.

Notions of Causality

So far we have posited that causal mechanisms provide an appropriate, if somewhat minimal in its requirements, notion of explanation for the social sciences. Apparently, this demands that we have a corresponding notion of causality. We agree that explanation is an account that reveals the mechanisms linking causes and effects, but what is a cause in the first place?

A counterfactual definition

Cutting short centuries of rather perplexing philosophical debates and disagreements, we will endorse a counterfactual definition of causality. According to this view, something has causal relevance if changing it (without disturbing the rest of the system) would affect the outcome. In other words, the outcome counterfactually depends on the cause.

Causes are difference-makers (Lewis, 1973). If the causal factor were to be different, the outcome would have been different as well. (Note that an outcome can be a single event or a distribution of events. For example, two roulette wheels – one with standard and one with rigged mechanics – can both produce the outcome 'ball in a red pocket', but the distribution of outcomes will be different.)

An intuitive understanding of explanation tells us that it has to do with knowing how something came about, why it is the way it is, and how it can be made any different. There are different shades of meaning at play, so let us try to unpack them. Consider the set of statements in Box 6.1. Initially the statements might seem innocuously similar, but they are not – beyond first appearances lie important differences in meaning and implications.

General patterns and particular facts

One of the first things to note is that some of these statements – (1) and (5) – refer to a particular event while others generalize about an individual – (6) and (8) – and beyond to an entire, not very well specified, population, 'people' – (7) and (10). Some philosophers would contend that (causal) explanation is only relevant for general patterns rather than for individual

Box 6.1 *Varieties of causal(?) statements*

- (1) 'John voted at the last election. He is rich.' [association]
- (2) 'When John was poor, he did not vote. When he became rich, he started voting.' [association, exploration]
- (3) 'If he is rich at the time of the next elections, John is very likely to vote.' [prediction]
- (4) 'Wealthy people are more likely to vote.' [generalization, association]
- (5) 'John voted at the last election, because he is rich.' [causation]
- (6) 'John's wealth makes him more likely to vote.' [probabilistic causation]
- (7) 'All, and only, wealthy people vote.' [deterministic necessary and sufficient causation]
- (8) 'If John had not been rich, he would not have voted at the last election.' [counterfactual causation]
- (9) 'If we deprive John of his wealth, he would not vote.' [manipulation]
- (10) 'If we make poor people rich, they will vote.' [generalization, manipulation]

facts or events. Political science should be about the discovery and explanation of regularities and the study of variation, according to this view. We will do well to disagree. Political science explanations can be about particular facts/events *and* about general patterns/variation. Indeed, they *need* to be about both. It was already explained above how statistical explanations, which focus on variation in populations, and causal histories, which focus on individual events, can be reconciled. Moreover, Chapters 8 and 9 will argue that pattern explanations are of little use if they do not help account for individual cases, and Chapter 10 will show that causal explanations of individual events can only be supported by recourse to general relationships established previously. Whether one is interested in causal explanations of patterns or of individual events is a matter of taste, professional upbringing, and societal need. But let us go back to the statements – there are more nuances to uncover.

Complete and partial, deterministic and probabilistic explanations

Some statements involve probabilities and likelihoods – (3) and (4) – while others leave no such uncertainty – (7) and (8). This refers to the distinction between deterministic and probabilistic causality and to complete and partial explanations. To explain is to account fully for a fact, event, or a pattern, according to typical everyday usage and the opinions of a few scholars. Such a standard is unattainable for political science. Partial explanations that are translated as probabilistic statements to be explored with statistical methods cannot be excluded from the realm of science, because not much will be left. More to the point, it was already explained above how incomplete knowledge of deterministic causal mechanisms gives rise to probabilistic relationships in the world we observe.

In scientific usage of the term, to explain is not necessarily to account for. This is extremely important to keep in mind when interpreting political science literature making causal claims. Often, the factors and variables called causal, deterministic, influential, and so on, would be making only marginal 'explanatory' work. They will be (very, very) partial explanations, even if the claims they make are taken at face value (which you should rarely do). The preponderance of partial explanations in political science makes it possible that in many subfields we have a plenitude of significant causal factors (partial explanations), but at the same time we can only poorly account for the actual problems and puzzles in the field. This goes for general patterns as well as for individual events.

To provide a complete explanation is to identify a set of causal factors and underlying mechanisms that are *individually necessary and jointly sufficient* to produce an outcome. *Individually necessary* means that if any of the factors is missing, the outcome would not occur; and *jointly sufficient* means that nothing else is required for the outcome to occur. Such a strong standard for causal explanation is useful as an ideal and a reference but is ultimately too high for real research in political science. In practice, identifying anything that comes close to either a necessary *or* a sufficient cause of a political phenomenon, event, or pattern is considered a success, even if it provides for a partial explanation only.

A partial cause may be defined as *an insufficient but nonredundant part of an unnecessary but sufficient condition*: the so-called INUS condition (Mackie, 1965). We will have more to say about necessary and sufficient conditions and how to use them for causal analysis in Chapter 9.

Prospective and retrospective causation

A common distinction related to the one above is between prospective and retrospective causation. Prospective causal questions are about the *effects of causes*, about projecting what an intervention or manipulation can achieve in the future or in a different population. Examples include: 'What would be the effect of changing the electoral threshold?' 'What would be the impact of decreasing development aid to Africa?' 'What influence will increasing the salaries of civil servants have on their job satisfaction?' Retrospective causal questions are about accounting for events that happened in the past or, more generally, about the *causes of effects*. Examples include: 'How can we explain the fall of the Berlin wall and, with it, most communist regimes at the end of the 1980s?' 'What accounts for Barack Obama's victory at the 2012 presidential elections in the USA?' 'Why did Russia support the Syrian government in the civil war in 2013?' With these questions we are not only asking for prospective evaluation of the likely effects of particular variables (causes), but for retrospective accounts of how an event came to be. Different strategies for causal inference are appropriate depending on whether one is interested in the former or in the latter. Experimental and large-N analyses are better suited to tackle prospective questions. Within-case analysis is tailored towards building retrospective accounts. But these affinities between research approaches and types of causal questions are not absolute.

Association, prediction, and causation

Looking back at Box 6.1, we note that the first statement is purely associational, and hopefully all would agree that it is descriptive rather than explanatory. The second one is still associational, but by the mere fact that it explores the association it seems to suggest something more. Despite the lurking suggestion, the statement, phrased as it is, remains descriptive. It shows a correlation but not causation. For a long and distinguished tradition of philosophers (such as David Hume, 2000, who perhaps started it) and scientists (such as Karl Pearson, who expressed it in statistical terms, 1911, 1920), constant association is all we can get at, so that any 'deeper' notion of causality is unattainable and pseudo-scientific.

Our view is less extreme. Getting at causality beyond association is difficult, but it is possible and a worthy scientific endeavour. Explaining how and why is the purpose of much of the chapters that follow. Nevertheless, this anti-realist view of causation, as outlined above, should come as a warning to those making frivolously causal claims – many learned men have considered that *no information at all*, much less unguided observation or the collection of anecdotes, can substantiate conclusions about anything more than mere association.

The third statement in our list goes a step beyond and extrapolates to the future, making a prediction. The fourth statement similarly entails a prediction, but for the general population level. There is still no notion of causality implied in these two statements. They do suggest association and extrapolate the association to the future and to a broader population. So they make inferences (from the observed to the unobserved), but not causal inferences. (The extrapolation could well have been for the past rather than for the future in which case it would be referred to as 'retrodiction' or 'postdiction').

To understand how even successful prediction is different from causation, consider the following example. Having yellow fingers is rather strongly associated with the presence of cancer in the lungs. You can actually predict (probabilistically) lung cancer from the presence of yellow fingers in an individual. However, the link between the two is not causal, because both yellow fingers and lung cancer are caused by smoking cigarettes. While not causal, the link between yellow fingers and cancer can still be useful when all we need is a quick indicator that somebody has an elevated chance of having lung cancer. But because it is not causal, we cannot influence or control lung cancer by manipulating the colouring of the fingers – there is no causal mechanism from one to the other. But there are causal mechanisms that link smoking with both. A big task for research design for explanatory inference is to plan projects that can distinguish between association and causation. Chapters 7 to 11 present in detail the major ways this can be achieved.

Intervention, manipulation, and causation

A crucial distinction between association and causation appears to be the fact that the latter implies manipulation and control. The counterfactual definition of causality also seems to point in this direction. In fact, for some scholars (notably Holland, 1986), the possibility of intervention and manipulation is a necessary condition for something to be a causal factor, and hence to provide explanations. That is, no intervention, no causation. Only if something can be directly manipulated and changed under outside control can it be considered causal. This standard and definition of causality are also too unrealistic for political science. Requiring that causal explanation always refers to factors that can be directly manipulated would rule out too many relevant and interesting questions that political science needs to address but for which no imaginable, for practical or for ethical reasons, interventions exist.

Nevertheless, this 'strong' view of causation is illuminating in two distinct ways. First, it is often fruitful to consider causation *as if* interventions would be possible. We cannot manipulate social class, for example, but it sharpens our thinking about causation to consider the causal impact of social class *as if* we could actually intervene and change it without altering the whole ensemble of related social phenomena. This is the heart of the counterfactual notion of causation. Second, even if admissible on logical or pragmatic grounds, 'causes' that cannot be controlled or manipulated even in principle are of limited utility. If knowledge of causes and mechanisms does not allow us to intervene and control, then the borderline between causation and association becomes increasingly hard to define. In addition, it is often argued that without intervention one cannot *know* causation, but this is a different thesis altogether and one that is not endorsed in this text. In sum, while in principle causation does not need to imply intervention, political scientists are well advised to pay more attention in theoretical and empirical explanatory analysis to factors that at least in principle can be manipulated.

Summing up

Table 6.2 summarizes five common notions of scientific inference that can rarely be found explicitly compared in the methodological literature but that, nevertheless, implicitly inform the work of political scientists. At one extreme, a weak notion of description (I) would insist that all we can infer from an association between variables (or coincidence of evidence) observed in a sample is, well, nothing more than that – an association in a sample. A stronger notion of descriptive inference (II) would insist that, using appropriate methods and assumptions, we can project the directly observed sample association to a broader population of interest. Similarly, predictive inference would argue that, again using appropriate methods and assumptions, we can project an observed association to the future to predict how things will be or to the past postdicting how things have been. A weak notion of explanation (I) would add that we can infer what the effects of interventions, manipulations, and other forms of control would be. A stronger one (II) would insist that we can, and should, also gain *understanding* of a phenomenon from observed associations between variables to provide a satisfactory explanation. (The two notions of explanation presented here roughly correspond to level-one and level-two causality in Cox & Wermuth, 2004.) These five

Table 6.2 *From association to causality: different shades of meaning*

	Descr. I	Descr. II	Prediction	Explan. I	Explan. II
(Sample) association	x	x	x	x	x
Projection to a population		x	x	x	x
Projection to past/future			x	x	x
Intervention and control				x	x
Understanding					x

positions are typical, but others that combine the inferential claims in the first column of Table 6.2 in different ways are possible as well.

Clearly, to explain how John votes in terms of his wealth can mean different things to different people. And in the practice of political science, it does mean different things to different researchers. In terms of the statements in Box 6.1, some scholars would use (5) but deny that it implies a prediction (3) or any other generalization like (4). At the other extreme, others will insist that only an explanation that can support intervention (9) is worth its name. One can use a counterfactual explanatory statement, like (8), and still deny support for intervention, like the one implied in (10), on the grounds that no feasible manipulation can affect only John's wealth without disturbing other factors, for example his emotional state, which are causally important for voting decisions. To recap, *my* view is that causation is most appropriately expressed in counterfactual terms; it can provide explanations of particular facts/events and patterns/variations; it can be expressed in deterministic or probabilistic terms; it is more than association and prediction, but does not necessarily require the possibility of manipulation. This view implicitly informed the chapters so far and will guide the ones that follow.

You are free to make up your own mind about what counts and what does not count as proper causation and explanation. But you have to be clear about it. Because people mean different things by explanation and causality, in the practice of research it is of primary importance to be explicit about which view you embrace and what exactly you mean by a statement like 'X causes Y'. The importance is much more than purely academic. Imagine the confusion if you offer your explanatory model of electoral behaviour to a newspaper interested in predicting turnout at the next elections, but you forget to mention that according to your views of explanation and causality, successful prediction is not implied. Things can get even worse. Imagine you advocate an explanation of economic growth that attributes causal importance to labour union repression, and only when the government decides to act according to the theory do you remember to note that in your perspective successful explanations are not supposed to analytically support manipulations and interventions.

In general, do not use explanatory language – words such as causes, determinants, impacts, effects, influences, and so on – if all you mean is association (and if all the evidence you have is associational – but this is a slightly different matter with which the next four chapters deal). Avoid explanatory language even if prediction is what you are solely aiming at. Clarify whether and to what contexts your causal statements are supposed to generalize. Explain whether your explanations can support real-world manipulations and interventions, and if not, why not.

Causal Inference

The problem

Defining causation in counterfactual terms helps to clarify what we mean by causation – namely that the outcome would be different if the cause was different, one way or another. It tells us that something else would have happened if the cause was absent or took a different value. Expressing causation in these terms immediately makes the fundamental problem of causal analysis clear: since we cannot go back and change history (or travel into the future) to see what would have happened under different circumstances, the counterfactual scenario is by definition hypothetical. But the comparison between what really happened and the hypothetical scenario is how we know if a factor makes a difference (whether it is causally relevant) or not. We can hypothesize that John would not vote had he not been rich, but he happens to be rich and we cannot go back in time and make him poor while leaving everything else the same. We can see whether John would still vote if by some accident he loses his fortune, or we can look at his twin brother Jim who is poor, but all that is just not the same. Hence, we can never be *certain* that something is causally relevant. That is, we can never be certain no matter how hard we look, how many cases we study, samples we take, experiments we conduct, and so on. The uncertainty is irreducible. This is the fundamental problem of causal inference, as it is known in the literature (see Holland, 1986; King, Keohane, & Verba 1994).

The problem appears a good reason to despair, or at least to do away with the counterfactual definition of causality. However, there is no need to do either. First, any conception of causality shares the same problem which is more fundamental than definitional issues. Hence, abandoning counterfactual language to express causal relationships does not remove the inherent uncertainty of causal claims. Second, while we can never be entirely certain, we can still get more or less confident that a causal relationship exists. While we can never achieve absolute certainty about causal claims, we can get close. For many purposes, this would be enough. It is not that since nothing is absolutely certain, anything goes. Moreover, we can qualify our confidence in the causal claims we make.

Thus, the difference between the use of causality in (political) science and normal life is not that science sticks to a faulty definition while in daily life we have stumbled upon something better. It is that science recognizes the irreducible uncertainty of causal claims and tries to limit and qualify it, while in our daily lives for the most part we can just ignore it. But the fundamental problem of causal inference shows its ugly head every time causal inferences need to be made – judicial convictions, medical diagnoses, public policy decisions, and so on. As opposed to description and prediction, causal statements not only promise understanding and control but also assign responsibility. Hence, we have good reasons to take the problem seriously.

Partial solutions

Causation is inferred by comparing two scenarios in which only the suspected cause changes while everything else remains the same. We agreed that, bar access to parallel universes, this is impossible. However, we can try to get as close as possible to a counterfactual scenario in which only the hypothesized cause changes. In other words, we can *approximate* the counterfactual scenario. There are different ways to approximate the counterfactual – one is by using the power of chance (see randomization in Chapter 7), another is by controlled comparisons (Chapters 8 and 9), a third is by relying on the the law of large numbers to even out differences (Chapter 8); mixing the three is also possible and often advisable. In essence, the counterfactual approximation controls for alternative explanations. Under certain assumptions, to be explicated in the next few chapters, the procedure would allow deriving valid causal explanations.

What the counterfactual definition of causality makes clear is that we cannot make causal claims and provide explanations only based on empirical data without any assumptions. But the quality and reasonableness of such assumptions will differ and they might be more or less, or not at all, appropriate in specific research contexts. In general, the stronger the assumptions we are willing to make, the more precise the causal inferences we can propose (Manski, 2007). But the price of strong assumptions is, of course, higher risk that they would be in fact wrong and that, as a result, the causal inference they support would be invalid.

The exact nature of particular assumptions that need to be made to move from observational to causal inference will be clarified in the chapters that follow. Many of these are connected to specific research methodologies (experimental, large-N, comparative, and so on) and they are usually most explicit in the tradition of statistical analysis. This does not mean that case-study researchers can avoid making assumptions to

Box 6.2   *General steps for causal inference*

1. Form, by whatever means, a causal hypothesis $[X \rightarrow Y]$
2. Detail the causal mechanisms it is based on $[X \rightarrow M \rightarrow Y]$
3. Derive additional observable implications of the hypothesis $[X \rightarrow Q]$
4. Outline alternative explanations and draw their observable implications $[Z \rightarrow Y; Z \rightarrow X; I \rightarrow X; U \rightarrow Y]$
5. Compare with data
6. Conclude

derive explanations. A general procedure for causal inference that is relevant both for cross-case and within-case inference is sketched in Box 6.2. The procedure should appear familiar because it is entailed in the discussions of Chapter 3, but is now offered through the prism of causal inference rather than theory development.

Even this toy model of Y embedded in Box 6.2 is rather complex, and the details of what is supposed to influence what are easily lost. A useful tool to summarize and represent visually the hypothesized relationships is offered by so-called causal graphs or diagrams. The details and definitions are rather technical and cannot be presented here. Readers are encouraged to consult an introduction to causal graphs (such as the excellent but demanding Pearl, 2009b, and the more accessible Morgan & Winship, 2007). But even relying only on intuition one can get a sense of the added value of causal diagrams.

Figure 6.1 below is an example of a causal diagram that represents the hypothesis presented above in Box 6.2. The letters stand for variables, and the arrows indicate (purported) causal relationships (flowing in the direction of the arrow). If no direct links and paths exist between variables, they are assumed to exert no direct or indirect causal influence on each other. For example, according to the graph in Figure 6.1, I causes X; X causes Q, M, and Y; Z causes X and Y; and U causes Y. X has both a direct and an indirect, mediated (through M) effect on Y. Z is a confounder of the direct relationship between X and Y (as it causes both).

Different styles of research follow different routes towards the goal of causal inference. Single within-case studies focus on the observable implications about the mechanisms through which X is supposed to causally influence Y, and the additional implications of X about things other than Y, and argues that the traces left by the data for each step of the way are compatible with the hypothesis that X is a cause of Y, and

Figure 6.1 *Example of a causal diagram*

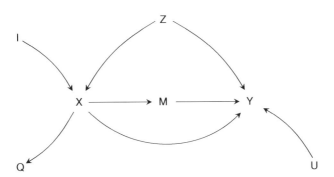

at least some of it is incompatible with evidence about the effect of the alternative causal factor Z. This is within-case evidence. So the study will look at all X, Y, Z, M, Q, I, and U for a single case.

When more than one case is available, one can complement (which leads to qualitative comparative and mixed designs) or almost completely replace the within-case evidence with more observations on a subset of these variables (for example, ignoring Q, P, R, N, and U), but for more cases (leading to experimental or observational large-N designs). In these designs the primary evidence for causal claims is the joint and conditional distributions of the variables in the population of cases you study. Deciding which variables to ignore and which to include and which and how many cases to have in the study are questions to be dealt with at length later. But even with an unlimited number of cases, valid causal inference would still be difficult and never entirely certain. For example, observing an association between X and Y is not enough, because it could have been induced by Z, if Z is a factor influencing both. How and under what conditions one can be partially successful is the topic of Chapters 7–9. But here is a taste of things to come.

Experimental designs break the contaminating influence of Z by using randomization (natural experiments do as well). In observational large-N studies, there are several routes to take. First, one can 'condition' on Z, that is measure and include Z in the analysis, hence controlling for its effect so that the suspected influence of X on Y can shine through the net of any direct and indirect effects of Z on Y. Second, one can use the fact (often it would be no more than an assumption) that M stands between X and Y but is not related to Z to identify and estimate the indirect (through M) effect of X on Y (mediation). Third, one can use the facts (well, in most cases these would be more or less credible assumptions) that I influences X but not Y directly and that it is unaffected by Z to filter out the influence of Z (instrumental variables).

The first two approaches are also known as the front-door and back-door criteria respectively (Pearl, 2000). You can specifically design empirical research projects to make use of any of the routes to causal inference described above, for example, by selecting appropriate cases for analysis.

What the discussion already made clear is that even if the effect of X on Y is all you are interested in, to make a causal inference you need to consider the fuller picture and identify mechanisms and mediating variables, alternative explanations of Y, and additional implications of X.

This is as far as we can go without getting into the details of particular research designs and methodologies. This chapter provided a frame for thinking about explanation in political science, discussed the fundamental problem of causal inference, and outlined possible solutions for empirical work. Practitioners of experimental, statistical, comparative, and within-case research all stake claims to uncover the deep structures of the political world, bringing understanding, prediction, and perhaps control, and specialize in different methodologies to do so. We are going to examine each methodology at length with a focus on issues of research design. After reading the following chapters, you should obtain a good orientation into the main research options available nowadays to an aspiring political scientist interested in explanation, the general pros and cons of each option, and the critical choices involved in designing research projects.

Further Reading

From a philosophy of science point of view, explanation and causality are subjects of lively debates. Salmon (1984, 1998), Woodward (2003) and Cartwright (2007) all present important, and different, perspectives. Little (1991) is focused on mechanistic explanations. David Lewis (1973) developed the philosophical notion of counterfactual causality (see also Lewis, 1986).

Illari and Russo (2014) is a recent and accessible overview of the philosophical issues surrounding causality written for the practising scientist. The contributions in Vayda and Walters (2011) provide illustrations of different notions of causality at work in the social sciences in particular. Hoerl, McCormack, & Beck (2011) is a volume that brings together philosophical and psychological studies of (counterfactual) causality.

The methodological literature on counterfactual causal inference is equally rich, and its importance cannot be overstated for the practice of contemporary social and political research. Morgan and Winship (2007) is a comprehensive, rigorous, and mostly accessible if demanding introduction. As mentioned in the text, Pearl (2000, 2009b) provides a framework for counterfactual causal analysis using causal diagrams. For an alternative approach rooted in statistics – the potential outcomes framework – see a recent overview in Rubin (2005). Dawid (2000) presents a critique of counterfactuals from a statistician's point of view, and the contributions in the ensuing academic discussion provide a powerful defence of the utility of counterfactual understanding of causality.

Chapter 7

Experimental Designs

Experiments are probably not the first thing that come to mind when you think about political science research. More likely, experiments evoke visions of white-coated men running around sterile rooms or, in a more social-scientific context, people behind glass windows hurting each other just because they were told to do so by the scientists (I am referring of course to the famous Milgram experiment). Yet experiments have a large role to play in research on politics and governance. There are at least three reasons why you should care about the topic.

First, the experimental method is held by many to be the gold standard for producing causal inferences. Indeed, for some the experimental method is the *only way* to uncover truly causal effects. Even if we choose not to go as far as dismissing all non-experimental explanatory research, understanding why experimental research is so powerful remains crucial. The first goal of this chapter is therefore to introduce the logic and workings of experimental designs.

Second, experiments *are* in fact already quite popular and are getting increasingly prominent in research on politics, public policy and administration. From social network-based experiments on voting to field evaluations of foreign aid effectiveness to lab experiments on social cooperation, experimental forms of research are everywhere. The second objective of this chapter is to introduce in some detail several examples of actual experiments run in the real world. The examples will serve both to illustrate how experiments work and, hopefully, to inspire you to design some form of experiment to address your own research questions.

Third, results derived from experimental research feature all the time in the news and the public sphere more generally. As an informed citizen and even more so as a public manager or policy maker one needs to have at least a basic understanding of experimental research in order to critically evaluate research results about new drugs, health regimes, teaching methods, management practices, website designs, chemical threats, interventions in the economy, shampoos, or different ways to mix beer ingredients.

In short, experiments are ubiquitous and even if not intending to become a master of the art and craft of experimentation, a student in the sciences of politics and government should understand the set-up, the strengths, and also the weaknesses of experimental designs. This chapter presents the logic, the design, and the analysis of experiments and discusses possible complications, validity issues, and the limitations of experimental research. The discussion of weaknesses and limitations of experiments will also serve us as a bridge to the world of observational designs discussed in Chapters 8–11. But, first things first, it is time to uncover the power of experiments.

The Basics of Experimental Research

Experiments, randomized controlled trials, and quasi-experiments

Experiments are a form of research where the researchers have some control over the environment and intervene in the natural state of the world in order to study the phenomenon they are interested in. The control need not be complete but the element of deliberate intervention is essential: if there is no intervention, the research project is observational, meaning that the researchers draw (descriptive or causal) conclusions by simply selectively observing and recording the data produced while the world works undisturbed.

The deliberate scientific intervention can take many forms: providing people with rewards for certain actions and punishment for others, or selecting only some families to receive a new social assistance program, or making sure that some people visit a political website, and so on. For a research design to qualify as a *real* experiment, however, a very special form of control needs to be exercised by the researchers: the ability to randomly select the group of individuals (or other units) who receive the treatment from those who do not (the control group). This *real* experiment also goes by the name 'randomized controlled trial', or RCT for short. Experiments that do not use random assignment of subjects into treatment and control groups are also called 'quasi-experiments'.

Quasi-experiments differ from RCTs because of the lack of random assignment, but they also differ from purely observational research because the researchers retain some form and extent of control over some aspects of the study (for example, they can still choose who gets the treatment and who doesn't, or they can manipulate the incentives of the subjects, or limit the amount of information some subjects are exposed to). In this text, we adopt the convention that we call only RCTs 'experiments' and we discuss them in the following sections. Quasi-experiments are briefly mentioned in the current chapter, while observational designs are covered in Chapters 8–11. Note that the popular Shadish, Cook, & Campbell (2002) textbook uses the label 'quasi-experimental' differently: it applies it to observational designs that try to approximate experimental inferential strategies. Consequently, many

Table 7.1   *Experimental and observational research designs*

		Random assignment	
		Yes	No
Experimental control	Yes	True experiments (RCT)	Quasi-experiments
	No	Natural experiments	Observational research

of the quasi-experimental designs they discuss are covered in this text in Chapter 8, which deals with large-N observational research.

In sum, as you can see from Table 7.1, true experiments have random assignment and are subject to experimental control. Quasi-experiments lack the former but might have some form of the latter. In natural experiments (discussed in Chapter 8) we have random assignment of units into groups but no experimental control – the random assignment is provided by nature. And, finally, when neither random assignment nor experimental control are available, research is classified as 'observational' – a category that groups together a number of distinct approaches differing in the strategies for causal identification they rely on.

When discussing experiments and quasi-experiments we often use 'treatment' (or 'intervention', or 'manipulation') to refer to the major phenomenon the impact of which we want to study. These terms obviously have origins outside the social sciences. In the context of social-scientific experiments they sound distinctly out of place, but their use is so entrenched that we have no choice but to follow it. Please try to suppress the associations with hospitals, white coats, and social engineering that treatment, intervention, and manipulation evoke, and focus on the underlying ideas which have broader relevance than the clinical language they are expressed in.

The goals of experimental research

The goals of experiments and quasi-experiments are usually explanatory, theory-testing, and focused on the prospective evaluation of purported causal effects. By definition, experiments rely on empirical data to draw conclusions, so they are *par excellence* the type of research that embraces positive (rather than normative) goals and positivist empiricist scientific philosophy. Experiments are usually set up to test a theoretically derived expectation or to establish and estimate a causal effect of practical importance: a new program, policy, institution, technology, communication mode, electoral tactic, website design, marketing campaign, drug, and so on. While experiments can be used to derive purely descriptive inferences (for example, what would people do in a certain situation), the costs and difficulties of setting up experiments that can provide reliable and valid conclusions make them much more likely to be used to put to trial a proposition strongly embedded in an important general theory (for example, a game-theoretic implication about altruistic behaviour) or to evaluate the impact of possible interventions in the social world that could have important practical consequences (at least in the eyes of those commissioning and/or paying for the research). The costs of RCTs in particular are effectively prohibitive for use as casual exploratory projects probing some intuitively derived proposition. That being said, small-scale experiments run on convenience samples (for example, your network of friends or your classmates) can be used as pilot projects for preliminary exploration of the plausibility of new theoretical ideas or intuitions.

Experiments can be useful not only to evaluate impact and establish and estimate causal effects but also to study the micro-level causal mechanisms through which the causal effects are exercised. As explained in Chapter 6, an explanatory proposition is not worth much unless a plausible causal mechanism links the purported cause and its effects. Very often these mechanisms run at the micro-level (between or even within individuals), even if the effects are exercised (or only visible) at a macro-level (societies, countries, and so on). Experiments can provide a sort of microscope through which social processes that remain hidden in the real world are made visible in a laboratory. A more extended discussion on the use of experiments for the study of causal mechanisms, including an example, is featured later in this chapter.

The logic of experimental research

No matter the field of application, the underlying logic of experimentation is one and the same. And it is one that is quite straightforward to describe and understand. In this section we will go through the elements of an idealized experiment (an RCT) to understand the source of its power; afterwards we will discuss what deviations from this idealized template imply and how they can be handled.

First, we start with random selection of a sample from the relevant population. As discussed in Chapter 5, the population is the set you want to generalize about. It can be a population of actual people but also a population of organizations, or a population of countries, and so on. (The population can even be a single person if that is the unit you want to generalize about; in this case the sample could be observations of this one person at different points in time.) It all depends on the levels of analysis and observation (also defined in Chapter 5). How you could possibly fit a country into a lab will be discussed below. For now just bear in mind the fact that we start with a random selection of individual units (cases) from a population.

Once we have selected our sample, we conduct a pre-test which provides a measure of what we are interested in (the outcome variable) for all individual units before we have conducted the experiment. The pretest will later serve as a baseline.

Next, the sample is randomly divided into two groups that can be designated as 'treatment' and 'control' (generally, the two groups are of equal size). The crucial part of the process is that the assignment is random in the sense that every individual (or unit) has the same chance of ending up in the treatment as in the control group. After the assignment, the experimental manipulation (treatment) is applied to one group, but not to the other. Importantly, the two groups are not aware of their condition, meaning that they do not know whether they are 'treatment' or 'control'. If the scientists are also not aware of the individual assignment into groups, the experiment is called 'double-blind'.

After the experimental manipulation is applied, a post-test is given to the individual units to measure the outcome of interest after the intervention of the scientists. The results of the treatment group are compared with the results of the control group, and a conclusion is formed about whether the manipulation makes a difference and how much of a difference it makes. In essence, that's it. Indeed, if in reality research always worked according to this experimental template, this chapter could have ended right here and now. Of course, real research is more challenging than that, but before we see what could go wrong, let us see why it works when it does.

The first step of random selection of the sample guarantees that the sample is representative of the population, so that the results from the experiment would generalize to the population. It is also a step that is

Box 7.1   *Steps in experimental research*

- Research question definition
- Conceptualization and operationalization
- Experiment design
- Performing the experiment
  - Random selection
  - Pre-test
  - Random assignment
  - Manipulation administered
  - Post-test
- Data analysis
- Conclusion
- Communication of results

often skipped for a variety of reasons. Unfortunately, this comes at a cost. If the sampling is not random, one needs to consider how the sample differs from the population, whether the intervention is more or less likely to work with the particular sample, whether the raw results from the experiment conducted on the sample need to be adjusted to project better for the population of interest, and other complications, some of which will be discussed below. For now we also skip over the important question of how many individuals or units you need to recruit.

The second 'pre-test' step establishes a baseline for comparison of the effects of the manipulation. It is also a step that is often skipped. Sometimes, the 'natural' or pre-intervention state of affairs is pretty clear, so that a pre-test is not necessary. In other cases, it is impractical to conduct a pre-test without alerting the subjects to the nature of the experiment (which is often undesirable). In general, and only if random assignment works, this step might also be unnecessary as the control group's post-test results should be the same as both groups' pre-test results (provided that there are no common developments over time, and subject to random error). Finally, the researcher might be only interested in whether the intervention makes any difference no matter what the baseline level of the phenomenon is, so that a simple post-intervention comparison between treatment and control groups would do.

The third step – random assignment into groups – is at the heart of the method. If the subjects are not selected into treatment and control groups randomly, then the design does not qualify as a real experiment (RCT). Obviously, random *assignment* requires that the experimental manipulation, or intervention, is actually under the control of the researchers. Using a randomization device (such as coin flips, dice, a deck of cards, or a digital random number generator), the researcher decides which units should receive the treatment and which units should not. In principle, no individual (unit) assigned to the control group should get the treatment (via the researcher or any other means), and all individuals (units) assigned to the treatment group should receive the treatment. Of course, in the real world things often do not go exactly as planned, and how to deal with some of the possible complications is discussed below. But the point remains that, notwithstanding some minor unavoidable errors introduced by nature, in order to qualify as an experiment the research project needs to separate treatment from control units randomly.

Why randomly? Well, in short, randomization ensures that the groups are as similar as possible in all respects. So if we suspect that some characteristic such as gender, education level, or wealth confounds the relationship between the intervention we want to study and the outcome of interest, then randomization would produce groups that are similar in their average level of wealth and education and have a similar gender distribution. Randomization achieves that by the magic of the law of large numbers. Getting similar groups will ensure that if we observe a difference after the experimental manipulation it will be due to our intervention and not to something else, such as a pre-existing characteristic distributed differently in the two groups. In the language of Chapter 6, a randomly assigned control group provides a counterfactual to the treatment group; a comparison case that is as similar as possible in all ways except for the experimental treatment (the intervention or manipulation we apply).

But why randomly? If we know that gender, education, or wealth confound our hypothesized relationship, doesn't it make more sense to create two groups similar with respect to these characteristics *by design* rather than relying on *chance* (which is another word for random)? Well, we *could* control for all these things by design by creating groups that have the same number of men and women and similar distributions of wealth and education. But what if there is another confounder the existence of which we are not aware of? For example, age. We can't control for age by design if we don't know that we should control for age. The trick and magic and beauty of random assignment is that it automatically controls for all possible confounders, even for the ones we don't know about! Remember, the groups created by random assignment resemble each other in all respects – relevant and irrelevant, known and unknown. So, this in a nutshell is why experimentation works.

Interestingly, while the intuition behind the logic of experimentation has been familiar to mankind for millennia, a rigorous formalization of the intuition and its application to real research work had to wait until the end of the nineteenth and the first half of the twentieth century respectively. While scientists have been doing experiments at least since the time of Galileo, the practice of using randomization rather than trying to control everything explicitly and by design did not become widespread until the work of Sir Ronald A. Fisher in the 1920s and 1930s (see in particular Fisher, 1925, 1935). The idea of random assignment opened a door to progress for many sciences such as biology, agriculture, ecology, medicine, psychology, sociology, education, economics, and not least political science, where full explicit control by design is often and truly impossible (see Box, 1978; Salsburg, 2001 for the history of the discovery of the experimental method and the role of Sir Ronald Fisher).

It is useful to review how experimental designs address the list of common threats to causal inference. First, we are able to show that it is indeed our intervention and not something else that is driving the observed differences, because the groups we compare (treatment and control) differ only with respect to our intervention due to randomization which produces groups that do not differ (in the limit) in any other way. If they don't differ in any other way, then it must be our intervention that is the cause of the differences. Or it could be due to chance. We use statistics to guard against this possibility, and some intuition about how this is done is provided just below. As a result, alternative explanations, including chance, can be ruled out. Second, we are able to show that it is indeed our intervention that is driving the observed differences in the outcome and not the other way around, because the intervention is under our control and comes first in time before the observed change in the outcomes. As a result, endogeneity (reversed causality) is ruled out. Voilà!

Validity

In the literature, validity is usually separated into construct, causal, statistical, and external. These four categories supplant and grow from the simpler distinction between internal and external validity.

Statistical validity is about the validity of the estimation of the relationship between the treatment and the outcome. As we are going to discuss shortly below, the major purpose of statistics in the analysis of experimental data is to estimate the likely effects of the treatment on the outcome and to show whether, if there is any link between the two, the link is likely to be due to chance alone or not. Statistics quantifies the uncertainty of our conclusions, so statistical validity is about the trust we can have in these estimates of uncertainty.

It is important to emphasize that statistical validity is not about deciding whether a relationship we observe is causal or not. That is a separate issue of causal validity. Causal validity is addressed by blocking the impact of potential confounders, making sure that the causality flows in the hypothesized direction and not the other way around, and showing that there are plausible mechanisms linking cause and effect. The causal validity of experimental designs depends on successful random assignment and the aids to randomization (blocking, measurement and control of pre-test characteristics, and so on).

Construct validity concerns the relationship between the operationalized concepts used in the empirical research and the theoretical concepts that the study attempts to study. We discussed construct validity in detail in Chapter 5.

To recap, external validity is about the generalization of the experimental results to the population of interest. A research project can have high causal validity within the selected sample, but this does not guarantee that the results would generalize outside the sample. If the sample is randomly selected from a target population, the results might generalize about the target population, but it still remains uncertain whether they will have any relevance for different populations.

A hypothetical example

Before we move on, let us go through a hypothetical example that will put some meat on the bones of the abstract ideas presented above.

Imagine that you need to study the elections for the university board of your local academic institution. Your research goal is to evaluate the impact of acquiring information about the platforms of the student parties on participation in the election. Your assignment could be either commissioned by one of the parties planning a campaign or based on a purely academic interest in the well-studied informational theory of voting (a line of inquiry stretching back to Anthony Downs). In any case, the assignment clearly calls for an explanatory, hypothesis-testing research design, so an experiment is deemed appropriate. You start by operationalizing your concepts; you define the outcome of interest as the declared intention to vote on a five-point scale ranging from '*very likely to vote*' to '*very unlikely to vote*'; you define the main explanatory factor as the level of information about the platforms of the two competing parties measured through the number of correct answers to five factual questions about the content of the programs.

Having operationalized the concepts, you proceed with defining the population of interest, which in this case is all students at the particular university. You need to generalize about the students at *your* university only, so a random sample from these students will do. At the same time, if you want to claim that your results would generalize for all students in the country or all students in world, you would need to convince that your sample is representative for those populations as well (which would be pretty hard). Practically, to draw a random sample you need to obtain the full list of students currently enrolled at the university. If that is not possible, you can proceed in steps by first getting a list of all programs at the university (which is certainly available) and their sizes, then drawing a sample of programs, and finally selecting randomly students within the selected programs. If carefully conducted and adjusted for, such a process, called stratified random sampling, can sufficiently resemble the results from simple random sampling. Using either method you identify, say, 200 students for the sample.

For a pre-test you administer a short survey to the individuals in the sample asking about their intention to vote in the forthcoming university board elections and testing their level of information about the student parties' platforms.

Next, you randomly assign the 200 individuals from the sample into a 'treatment' and a 'control' group. To make the assignment random you can use, for example, the last digits of the students' university ID numbers (after making sure they are not related to gender, program, student year, and so on), or use coin flips, or the random number generators included in many statistical packages. To make sure that the randomization has worked well, you can compare the pre-test scores and the distribution of certain characteristics across the two groups – none of these should differ significantly.

Having divided the two groups, you administer the treatment only to the first group and not to the control group. The treatment in this case is showing the students the websites of the two student parties and making sure that the websites are indeed visited and the information they provide is read. So you manipulate the level of information individuals have about the election by making them read these websites. You can either not do anything with the control group units or, even better, make them visit a website irrelevant to the university elections to conceal the fact that they are the 'controls'. After the intervention, in order to obtain the post-test scores, you administer a second survey which again records the intention to vote and the level of information possessed.

The effect of the treatment (information provision) can be estimated simply as the difference in the average post-test intention to vote between the treatment and the control groups. Alternatively, you can define the effect of the treatment as the difference in the average *increase* between pre- and post-test intention to vote between the treatment and control groups. The latter will be more appropriate if both groups are expected to have shifted their intention to vote during the duration of the experiment, which is likely if the university elections are getting closer. You should provide information about the uncertainty of the estimated effect by reference to the within-group variability of the results (more on the analysis of experimental data in the next section).

You can use the information from the survey questions measuring the actual level of information acquisition to check whether the treatment really increased the levels as expected; this can provide valuable clues as to whether the treatment worked according to the proposed theoretical mechanism. Finally, based on the experiment and the data collected you can (1) conclude whether providing students with more information about the university election is likely to increase the turn-out, and (2) provide some reasonable expectations about the size of the increase if all students in the university were provided with more information about the election. Such information can be valuable, for example, to a student party interested in mobilizing students to vote or to the university administration concerned about low turnout rates at university elections, and it might have relevance for the theories of voting as well. The project could be extended to evaluate alternative methods of information provision (such as newsletters versus websites), levels of exposure to information (such as seminars versus individual reading of websites), or effects within certain subgroups of the population (such as for those most unlikely to vote).

Even if our hypothetical yet realistic example is rather stylized, it already raises important further questions. Why were 200 and not 20 students selected for study? Can we really make sure that the students read the information provided on the websites? What if students in the control group actually visit the 'treatment' websites on their own initiative? What if the two groups actually talked to each other during the duration of the experiment? Is a reported intention to vote a good measure for the real thing we are interested in – whether the person would actually go and vote on election day? Would our results be relevant for the next election cycle? All of these concerns are legitimate and need to be addressed. Some of them touch upon the details of research design, while others require that we relax the assumptions that everything goes according to an idealized template. Some concern the internal validity, while others relate to the external validity of the results. Knowing the basics of experimental research, we can turn towards these complications.

The Design of Experimental Research

In this section we will go through the main elements of research design for experiments. The research design, as always, concerns the questions which and how many observations to choose, how to translate the theoretical concepts into measurable variables, and what kind of comparisons need to be made. Some of the advice on the practice of research design for experiments is generic: everything about the selection of a research topic and its transformation into a research question from Chapter 2 and everything about the conceptualization and operationalization of concepts from Chapter 4 remains directly relevant for experiments as well and need not be rehearsed again here. In addition, the discussions about the role of theory in the research process from Chapters 3 and 6 apply. But case selection needs to be explored in more detail.

Level of analysis

The importance of sample selection was emphasized above. But before one selects a sample, the level of analysis needs to be established, and this can sometimes be tricky in experimental research (as well as in observational studies). For example, if you study pupils within a school and the treatment is a new teaching method, it might not be appropriate to define the individual pupil as the unit of analysis if pupils within classes cannot be isolated into different treatment and control groups – the teaching method needs to be provided at the class level, so effectively the unit of analysis becomes the class and not the pupil. As a result, sampling and calculations of the required number of experimental units need to be performed at the class and not at the individual level. Similarly, if you need to analyse the effect of organizational symbols on public service motivation, and if all public servants working in the same building have to be exposed to the same symbols, then the building and not the individual is the proper level of analysis. To take one final example, if you study the effect of a public service such as building a small park on the subjective welfare of citizens, the unit of analysis needs to be defined as the neighbourhood or some other aggregation that captures the extent of the possible influence of the park.

More complicated scenarios in which the treatment effects span several levels (for example, a main effect at the individual level and smaller residual effects at the family level) are easy to imagine, and things get even more tricky when one introduces time as a separate dimension of variation. The general principle to follow in order to determine the level of analysis is to consider at what level the treatment can be isolated; if a treatment 'contaminates' or spills over to larger units, they should be considered the unit of analysis.

Sample size

With the level of analysis defined, we need to decide on the number of units to include in the research. This problem has two aspects: how many cases do we need so that our sample will be representative of the underlying population and how many cases do we need to be able to show a difference between the treatment and control groups? Both aspects have to do with the sample selection and its size. To clarify, the sample includes both the treatment and the control units, so even if you end up just observing the treatment units, the controls are included in the size calculations. The first aspect relates to the external validity or generalizability of the results from the experiment to the target population. Because we dealt with this problem in our discussion of descriptive surveys (Chapter 5), we only need to recall here the general conclusions that there are diminishing returns to including more and more observations after a point, and that the number depends on how much error we are willing to tolerate. The second aspect of the sample size question has to do with the sensitivity of the causal analysis and needs to be examined further.

Sensitivity is about the ability of the experiment to detect increasingly small causal effects. As with other tools, the more sensitive the design, the finer the measurements that could be taken, the greater the precision of the estimates, and the smaller the effects that will register. Because experimental data are analysed using statistics, sensitivity can be transformed into a question of statistical power. In short, determining the number of units you need to include in the experiment is an issue of statistical power.

Statistical power in its turn depends mainly on (1) the size of the causal effect you attempt to uncover and (2) the within-group variability (which is a function of unit heterogeneity). In agreement with intuition, the bigger the hypothesized effect and the lower the within-group variability, the fewer observations you would need in order to detect the effect of interest. Additional factors to consider include the quality of the measurement (how good your measures are), the consistency of the experimental protocol (how rigorous the implementation of the experiment is), and the exact data-analytic technique (statistical test) that is going to be used. As you would guess, the more messy and uncertain the measurement and procedures, the more observations you would need.

Once these quantities (at the very least, the likely size of the hypothesized causal effect and the within-group variability) are approximately known, there are statistical power calculators and tables adapted for different types of variables (dichotomous, categorical, continuous) that can provide precise estimates of the required number of units to include in the sample. It is beyond the scope of this chapter to explain how the actual calculation is performed and to reference the required values for different combinations of expected effect size and variability – these can be found in a number of sources, such as Duflo, Glennerster, and Kremer (2006) and Lipsey (1990).

The hard problem in considering statistical power is not calculation but obtaining reasonable estimates of the likely causal effect size and the within-group variability. Usually, there are little prior research and data to answer either of these two questions. The researcher needs to employ previously available data, existing theory, and common sense to deliver a reasonable estimate of the expected size of the effect of the specific treatment. In many cases, the range of the expected size could be narrowed down considerably by carefully examining the measurement scales and existing estimates of the effect of other treatments on the same outcome variable. For example, if the outcome is a survey response on a five-point scale and alternative treatments have never produced any effect greater than two points, it would be reasonable to assume an expected size between 0.5 and two points. The lower boundary could come from a consideration of what would be the smallest effect that, if discovered, would still be useful for theory or practice. Even if we could design an experiment sensitive enough to detect size effects of 0.01 on a five-point scale, what could be the possible use of this knowledge?

Delivering reasonable estimates of within-group variability, or unit heterogeneity, is even more tricky. If one has access to previous datasets using the same outcome variable, these can be used to derive estimates. If not, there is not much one can do but entertain various scenarios and see how the different assumptions about variability affect the required number of observations. If, for lack of data, a statistical power calculation is not possible prior to the execution of the experiment and the collection of the data, at the very least the researchers should conduct a post-experimental power calculation, which would use the actual data to estimate within-group variability and check what effects *could* have been detected given the collected number of observations.

Table 7.2   *Types of errors*

		Hypothesis of no effect is	
		True	*False*
Research finds hypothesis of no effect is	*False*	Type I	Correct
	True	Correct	Type II

What would happen if you fail to recruit a sufficient number of subjects for the experiment? The research will be under-powered, which means that you are likely to conclude that the treatment doesn't make any difference, while in reality it does but your design is not sensitive enough to register it. You might consider this to be a more acceptable error than concluding that there is an effect of the treatment when in reality there is none. But it makes no sense to embark on a research project to evaluate a possible causal effect if *by design* your project lacks the power to detect the effect even if it was there.

Table 7.2 presents a useful and commonly used overview of the main types of errors hypothesis-testing research may commit. Imagine that we are researching a possible causal effect (or we could be testing whether two populations are different with respect to some trait, no matter whether the difference is causal or not). A Type I error is finding evidence for an effect, when in reality there is none (false positive). A Type II error is finding no evidence in support of a hypothesized effect, when in reality there is an effect (false negative). In general, this is the type of error that underpowered research projects are likely to make, because they lack the sensitivity to detect small but real causal effects. However, due to a combination of selective reporting of research results and the higher variability of effect estimates in studies based on small samples, underpowered studies can also greatly overestimate small or non-existent effects (Gelman, 2009).

Blocking and randomization

In the presence of great heterogeneity in the population, provided that the source of this heterogeneity is known, we can group (cluster, stratify) the population within blocks and sample randomly within blocks. For example, in the student elections example we would expect general interest in politics to be an important source of variation for whether a student would vote. To incorporate this information in the design, we can stratify the student population into several groups depending on their level of interest in politics and sample randomly within each group. We would need to take the clustering into account when doing the data analysis, but the additional step can guarantee that our sample covers students with different levels of interest in politics and that we have reduced the additional variability in intention to vote that is not related to our treatment.

Now we have naturally reached the idea that, although random assignment can work wonders, often it is even better to make the design more complex to reflect prior information we have about the relationship we want to study. Let us look in more detail at some of the possible ways to augment the simple, completely randomized, design.

The idea of blocked, or stratified (also called clustered), randomization is to create groups that are more alike with reference to some important characteristic before the random assignment of the treatment. Randomization is then applied within the blocks. The advantages of blocked design is that we can gain efficiency (see Cox & Reid, 2000) and precision (Imbens, 2011; Gelman & Hill, 2007) in the estimation of the average causal treatment effect because of the reduced variability within blocks.

In a sense, blocking assists randomization to create groups as similar as possible by incorporating known predictors of the outcome of interest in the design – these are the characteristics we use to create the blocks. Importantly, even if we happen to block on a variable that turns out to be irrelevant, the design would not suffer in terms of statistical power or efficiency (see the references in Horiuchi, Imai, & Taniguchi, 2007).

Pairwise randomization (also called matched-pair designs) takes the blocking approach to its limit by initially creating pairs of units that share one or a number of important characteristics, and then picking randomly one unit from the pair to receive the treatment while the other unit remains as a control (see Horiuchi, Imai, & Taniguchi 2007). Instead of observable characteristics such as gender, age, or wealth, an analytic quantity that measures an artificially defined 'distance' between units which incorporates information from many variables at once can be constructed and used (see the discussion of matching in Chapter 8 and Imai, 2005).

It is difficult to give a general recommendation as to when one should use complete randomization, blocked randomization (clusters), or matched-pair designs. Imai, King, and Nall (2009) recommend always pairing when feasible. Guido Imbens summarizes his advice as follows (2011, p. 2):

> use stratified [*blocked*] randomization with relatively many and relatively small strata (to capture as much as possible of the precision gain from stratification), rather than either complete randomization or paired randomization (which would capture all of the potential gain in precision, but at the price of the analytical complications).

Sometimes it would not be possible to block the sample before randomization. In these cases it can still be useful to conduct pre-tests and to collect pre-test information about the subjects of the experiment which can be used during the data analysis in the estimation of the treatment effects. Some of what is lost due to lack of clustering can be recovered in the data analysis stage, but in general stratification is the preferred option.

An alternative route to 'assist' randomization is to repeat the randomization until it produces groups that are similar with respect to characteristics we suspect to be important and that can be measured in advance.

In summary, while the complete simple randomization design was useful to discuss in order to highlight the logic of randomization, in practice researchers would incorporate existing information in the research design by blocking or pairing, collecting data on covariates, or at least making sure that the randomization has indeed produced comparable groups. From a research design perspective, all these additional steps are performed in order to recreate as convincingly as possible a counterfactual scenario for the treatment group.

In our discussions so far, we drew a sharp line between experimental and observational research. Now that we have a more sophisticated understanding of experimentation, the gap separating it from observational studies doesn't seem so wide any more. Yet, for any sort of explanatory design, it would help to ask: *what would have been the ideal experiment to test this proposition?* Observational research can benefit from an explicit benchmarking vis-à-vis the 'pure' experimental template, even if randomization remains impossible. What serve as secondary aids to experiments – blocking, clustering, covariate adjustment, and so on – become of primary importance in observational designs. But we are getting ahead of ourselves. Before we reach Chapter 8 we have to consider the choice of experimental setting, discuss common complications, and go through some real-world examples.

The experimental setting

One of the most fundamental questions related to the design of experiments is where the experiment should take place. The choices range from the completely controlled environment of the research laboratory to the noise and complexity of the real world. Survey experiments (in which respondents answer manipulated questions) fall somewhere in between as they can be performed in a variety of contexts, including the university classroom and the respondents' homes.

One can further distinguish between experiments that rely on direct observation of the outcome of interest (for example, voting in an election), or on some kind of simulation or approximation (declared intention to vote in a survey or vote in a decision-making game designed in the lab).

The advantage of the laboratory is that the researchers can control to a large extent the environment, isolate the nuisance variables that would obstruct the observation of the phenomenon of interest, and manipulate the incentives, impressions, information, and communication between subjects. At the same time, it is exactly the artificiality of the laboratory setting that is its biggest disadvantage. If we are interested whether people exhibit altruism in collective decision-making, for example, perhaps studying students in a laboratory playing small-stakes games is not the ideal context.

Field research, or studying individuals and collectives in their undisturbed social and environmental setting, has less of a problem with realism but has the disadvantage that the treatment effect is much harder to isolate from everything else that goes on in the field. One immediate implication is that, in general, field experiments need a larger number of observations because there is more random variability in the field than in the laboratory.

Laboratory experiments are better suited to examining causal mechanisms due to the higher control over the context. As such, they are more relevant for theory-driven research that studies the micro-foundations of human decision-making. In contrast, field experiments are more appropriate for evaluating substantively interesting causal effects. If we are interested in what effects a new policy would have in reality, a field experiment would often be more appropriate than a lab-based one. Of course, different types of experiments can be used in combination to compensate for their relative strengths and weaknesses. But whatever the location, measurement instruments, and delivery modes of experiments, they all face threats to validity stemming from a number of possible violations of the experimental protocols.

Complications

So far we have outlined what makes experimental designs sound, and we assumed along the way that the experimental template is executed without any complications. The real world, however, is rarely so disciplined. In practice, the conduct of experimental research is faced with common and important deviations from the ideal template which need to be recognized and addressed. This section will focus on a few of the most often encountered ones and suggest ways of dealing with them. For more in-depth discussions, see the references included here and in the 'Further Reading' section at the end of this chapter.

Noncompliance

Let us begin the overview of common complications with the problem of noncompliance (Angrist, Imbens, & Rubin, 1996). Noncompliance means that the participants in the treatment and control groups do not follow the course of action they are supposed to. Table 7.3 shows the possible types of experimental subjects with respect to their compliance

Table 7.3   *Types of experimental subjects*

Assignment	Treatment	Control
	Receives treatment?	
Always-taker	yes	yes
Never-taker	no	no
Always-defier	no	yes
Complier	yes	no

behaviour. The entries in the cells of the table indicate whether the subjects *get* the treatment or not and whether they are *assigned* to the treatment or to the control group.

Always-takers get the treatment no matter whether they were assigned to the treatment group or not. For example, in the university elections example, an always-taker will visit the websites of the student parties irrespective of the experimental condition that he or she was in. Even if part of the control group, he/she will visit the website on his/her own initiative and thus receive the 'treatment' without being supposed to. Never-takers are the subjects who would not get the treatment under any of the two conditions. They cannot be induced to receive the treatment. If assigned to the treatment in the university elections example, they ought to access and read the website, but they will not. It would often be impossible for the researcher to make all subjects comply. Always-defiers are those who will always do the opposite of what they are assigned to do. They would visit the website only if assigned to the control group and not visit only if assigned to the treatment. Finally, compliers act according to their assignment.

The problem of noncompliance demands more precision from the terms we use to describe experiments. So far we have used intervention and treatment interchangeably. But if subjects can get the treatment on their own initiative, we have to be careful to distinguish the *intervention* of the scientist, which is applied to those and only those who were assigned to the treatment group, and the actual *treatment*, which may not have been received by some (never-takers and defiers) or received by some who should not have (the always-takers and defiers). Often, the intervention can be no more than an encouragement to receive the treatment, as in the example of the university elections.

Furthermore, the presence of noncompliers complicates the design and analysis of experimental data. Noncompliance breaks the comparability of treatment and control groups achieved through randomization. If noncompliance occurs non-randomly (which will usually be the case), different estimates of the treatment effect need to be considered (see below). In sum, noncompliance on a small scale does not imply the end of the validity of the experiment but needs to be taken into account in order to produce valid and reliable inferences.

Nonresponse and attrition

Another common complication of experimental research is nonresponse, which occurs when researchers are unable to obtain post-test scores for all of the participants. Again, if nonresponse occurs non-randomly, it undermines the design of the experiment and, unless the complication is addressed, can render the conclusions from the analysis invalid.

The researcher can try to model the nonresponse in order to clarify its likely effects on the estimation of the main relationship of interest. The nonresponse model will use existing information to check what types of subjects are more or less likely to have missing post-treatment values and correct to some extent the estimates of the main causal effect being studied accordingly. This is another reason for collecting pre-tests and pre-test characteristics for all subjects. We can use this information to model the nonresponse and try to adjust the estimates of the causal effect of the treatment.

A specific form of nonresponse is attrition. Attrition happens when individuals drop out of the experiment between the random assignment and the completion of the measurement (Behaghel et al., 2009). It is especially common in longer field experiments and experiments employing several waves of post-test measurements. Individuals can drop out of the experiment for various reasons – relocation, losing interest, or even death. The remarks about the general phenomenon of nonresponse apply to attrition as well.

Spillover and learning effects

A spillover or diffusion effect is the indirect effect of the experimental intervention on subjects who were not supposed to receive the treatment. The problem is greater for field experiments where researchers are not able to control effectively the communication flows between people. Spillover effects can arise from treatment subjects talking to control subjects or from more generalized diffusion effects. For example, if the treatment is a social assistance program applied to individuals within a small neighbourhood, positive wealth effects of the program can affect the entire neighbourhood, and not only the treated individuals, due to increased consumption, gifts exchange, and so on.

Such indirect effects of the treatment can be interesting in their own right, and sometimes rather than getting rid of them researchers should try to induce and measure spillover effects. For examples of how to study spillover effects, see, in particular, Bond et al. (2012) and Gine and Mansouri (2011), as well as the study by Sinclair, McConnell, and Green (2012); the first two are discussed later in this chapter as well.

A learning (or testing) effect results from the fact that subjects might change their behaviour in the course of an experiment because they get familiar with the test (if given more than once) or adapt to the experimental protocol (for example, in decision-making games). The effects of learning can either obscure or attenuate the effect of the treatment, depending on whether only control or only treatment subjects experience it. Having pre-tests available can help in this situation, since one can rely on gain scores (see below) rather than raw post-test comparisons of the groups to estimate the effect of the treatment.

Relatedly, there is evidence that sometimes even the fact that one participates in an experiment and is being surveyed can alter behaviour (Zwane et al., 2011). The fact of being 'watched' by scientists can motivate people to be more information-seekuing or to act in socially desirable ways.

Convenience samples

Convenience samples are samples that are not selected randomly from the target population but because it is convenient for the researchers to recruit these individuals for the experiment. In most cases, convenience samples consist of undergraduate students. Even if not students, participants in laboratory experiments in particular are often WEIRD (White, Educated, Industrialized, Rich, Democratic). The actions, opinions, attitudes, predispositions, and so on of students and WEIRD people are not always representative of other people who might have less formal education, different cultural backgrounds, less money, or more time. There has actually been extensive research to examine these claims. Existing studies based on student samples sometimes (but not always) cannot be replicated with other people. For details, see chapter 4 in Druckman et al. (2011) and chapter 9 in Morton and Williams (2010).

Apart from the general advice to try and recruit participants for experiments outside the pool of undergraduates from the local university (which is easier said then done), researchers can try to account for the peculiarity of the sample during the data analysis stage if it is known how the sample differs from the target population in ways that could affect the hypotheses being tested.

And more

The list of possible complications can be extended, but we have already identified the most common potential problems one should be aware of when designing and analysing experiments. The classic texts of Shadish, Cook, & Campbell (2002) and Cook & Campbell (1979) provide a comprehensive overview of additional threats to validity, and experimentalists within various substantive fields have catalogued yet more possible ways in which the ideal experimental template can be violated. The bottom line is that even if one is able to assign treatment randomly, additional care must be taken that the compared groups are, and remain throughout the duration of the research, as comparable as possible.

The Analysis of Experimental Data

Average treatment effect

With both random sample selection and random assignment, and in the absence of any of the complications presented above, experimental research produces data that are relatively straightforward to analyse. We could take the effect of our intervention (treatment) to be simply the difference between the treatment and the control groups in their post-test results. Let us call this the *average treatment effect*. Alternatively, to make sure that the randomization has worked well, we can take into account the information from the pre-tests (if available) and measure the effect of our intervention as the difference between (1) the change in the treatment group results before and after the intervention and (2) the change in the control group results before and after the intervention. In essence, we would compare the *average* change in the one group with the average change in the other group. This would produce the so-called gain score or a difference-in-difference estimator of the average treatment effect.

Adjusting the estimates

Even if the experiment is completely randomized and the randomization has worked well, we can still improve the precision of the estimates of the average treatment effect by including information about pre-test scores or other pre-test characteristics of the units in the statistical model (Gelman & Hill, 2007, p. 177). An important caveat is, however, that we should only include variables that could *not* have been affected by the treatment itself. If we include (control for) mediating variables that stand in the causal path between the treatment and the outcome, we can no longer interpret the estimated treatment effect as the average causal effect.

If the randomization of the treatment assignment has not produced completely comparable groups, including pre-test scores and other pre-dictors (again with the exception of mediating variables) in the statistical model can improve the estimate of the treatment effect itself, and not only its precision (Gelman & Hill, 2007).

When randomization has been performed within groups (clusters), we obtain the average treatment effect by first calculating it within each group, and then average these estimates using the proportion of treated units in the cells as weights (Duflo, Glennerster, & Kremer, 2006, p. 48). With more complicated experimental designs, such as randomized block designs or paired comparisons, we could use hierarchical (multilevel) regression models to estimate the average treatment effects. With a multilevel set-up, not only can we estimate a single average treatment effect, but we can let this estimate vary across the different blocks and even model this variation.

No matter the statistical estimation technique, we have to remember that what we estimate is the population-level causal effect of the treatment and not individual-level causal effects. If our initial experimental sample is not a random sample of the population, more care is needed to interpret the output of the statistical models as estimates of the population average treatment effect. Usually, further modelling is needed, for example post-stratification, which adjusts for the fact that our sample differs systematically from the population we want to generalize about (if we know how the sample differs).

Alternative definitions of treatment effects
The discussion of data analysis has so far ignored the possibility that there is noncompliance and nonresponse. But as explained, both are common and consequential for the interpretation of the experimental data. In the presence of non-random noncompliance and/or nonresponse the comparability of the treatment and control groups breaks down, so a simple (or covariate-adjusted) comparison between the average results of treatment and control groups is no longer a valid estimate of the average effect of the experimental intervention. We are led to consider alternative definitions of causal effects that are possible to estimate even in the presence of noncompliance and nonresponse.

Table 7.4 gives an overview of the most often used alternatives to the simple ATT (average treatment effect). If we stick to the estimate of treatment effect as the (adjusted) difference in averages between the two groups (as introduced above), in the presence of noncompliance or partial compliance this estimate is better thought of as the effect of the intention to treat (ITT). ITT would still capture the effect of the 'intervention' (what the researchers do), but not necessarily of the treatment

Table 7.4 *Different definitions of treatment effects*

Abbreviation	Full name	Definition
ATE	Average treatment effect	ATE in the sample
ITT	Intention to treat	ATE in the sample with noncompliance
LATE	Local average treatment effect	ATE among compliers
CACE	Sample complier average causal effect	ATE among compliers
ETT	Effect of treatment on the treated	ATE among compliers and always-takers

itself. In some circumstances ITT is actually what we are interested in –
for example, if we want to know whether encouraging people to visit
political websites will increase turnout – because in any real electoral
campaign there is no way in which people can be *made* to read the information from the websites. But we have to bear in mind that ITT would
not be the effect of the treatment, as conceptualized in the theory, but
would be the effect of the *intention to treat*.

Under certain assumptions we can use the ratio of ITT and the fraction
of treated units in both the treatment and control group as an estimate of
the true causal effect of the treatment (and not only of the intervention).
This is the so-called LATE or local average treatment effect, which gives
us the treatment effect among the compliers (those who comply with
their assignment into treatment and control). It can also be referred to as
CACE or sample complier average causal effect (see Horiuchi, Imai, &
Taniguchi, 2007). For details on LATE and its use, see Angrist, Imbens,
& Rubin (1996), and for a more gentle introduction, consult Duflo,
Glennerster, and Kremer (2006). Another slightly different estimate of
the treatment effect is the so-called effect of treatment on the treated, or
ETT, which represents the effect of treatment on compliers and always-
takers (hence, all who have received the treatment one way or another)
(Freedman, 2006).

Under many circumstances ITT will be smaller than the LATE and
will provide a conservative estimate of the treatment effect. This would
be the case, for example, in the presence of significant spillover effects or
many non-compliers who are assigned to treatment but do not receive it.

This is just one example of why it is truly important to recognize the
differences between the various treatment effects definitions. These push
us to consider very carefully what exactly is the causal effect that we
want to measure; they force us to define meticulously the counterfactual
that we are trying to evaluate. The care taken when discussing the causal
effect being estimated in the research has practical utility, because it
specifies what the expected impact of real-world interventions would be,
and it also brings methodological rigour, because it delineates what can
and what cannot be inferred from the data.

From a research design perspective, the lesson to take from the discussion of data analysis is the following: with randomization and no
significant noncompliance and nonresponse problems, the analysis of
experimental data is relatively straightforward. This is actually one of the
main attractions of the experimental method. Nevertheless, one should
plan to collect as much information as possible about the participants
prior to delivering the treatment. This information can help during the
analysis phase to efficiently derive better estimates of the causal effect
of the treatment. Even in the presence of significant noncompliance and
nonresponse, it is possible to retrieve causal estimates from the data
generated by the experiment, but one needs to be careful how exactly

the causal effect is defined (the effect of the intervention, the effect of receiving the treatment, or something else) and adjust the data-analytical technique accordingly.

Quantifying uncertainty
In any real-world experiment there will be some variability in the effects we want to study. If our sample is composed of families (thus, the family is the level of analysis), our intervention is a new social assistance program (compared to no social assistance), and our outcome of interest is political participation (measured as votes at the local election), not every family who received the program would be expected to vote and some of the families who didn't receive the program would be expected to vote *even if* the social assistance program has a causal effect on voting and even if we have successfully designed the experiment to detect the effect. This is quite intuitive. Going to vote or not depends on many factors; some of them systematic and others random. Our treatment could still make a difference at the margins so that families who receive the assistance would be more likely to vote, but there will be variability within both the treatment and control groups. No experimental intervention would be expected to eliminate all variability *within* the groups. Still, the outcomes in the treatment and in the control groups can be captured by a measure of the central tendency, such as the average, which would give us a good initial idea whether the groups differ overall, but we have to take into account the variability within the groups. Enter statistics.

In the simplest case of a completely randomized experiment with one treatment and one control group, a statistical t-test can provide an indication of whether the differences in the averages between the two groups are 'significant'. 'Significant' in this context means that the difference between the two averages is not likely to be due to chance only (at some predefined level of confidence, usually set at 5 percent), in view of the observed within-group variability and given some assumptions about the distribution of the group averages. Instead of a t-test one can use analysis of variance (ANOVA) or regression analysis, which are tools that can achieve the same purpose but are more easily extended to more complicated contexts with more treatment levels, continuous treatments, blocked designs, or more complex designs testing several treatments simultaneously. The details about the assumptions, estimation, and interpretation of these statistical techniques can be found in any textbook on statistical methods, and it is outside the purpose of this text to provide a complete description of how they work. For the particularly important issue of what statistical significance means (and what it doesn't mean), see Chapter 8.

Having covered how experiments work, what challenges they face, and how one goes about analysing the data they produce, we are ready to look at some real-world applications.

Experiments in Political Science and Public Policy Research

So far we have discussed the principles of experimental designs mostly in the abstract and with the help of hypothetical examples. But experiments are already commonplace in actual research on various topics of politics and administration. This section will present a number of real-world research projects based on experimental designs with the double purpose of illustration and inspiration.

The experiments presented below take us from the slums of Mexico to university lecture halls in Germany and involve a number of participants that ranges from a low of 88 to a high of 61,000,000. The selection showcases the variety of substantive questions one can tackle with experimental designs, as well as some of the practical challenges of doing experimental research.

The examples are grouped according to the physical context and method of delivery of the intervention. As discussed above, laboratory settings are better at controlling for the 'noise' of the real world. On the other hand, field experiments provide more realistic context by performing the experiment in the usual environment of the participants. Survey experiments are conducted in a non-controlled environment – either using a captive audience such as students during a lecture or at the leisure of the participants' homes or offices. The Internet and digital social networks are increasingly used both as a channel for delivering standard survey-based experiments and as an experimental environment in their own right.

Survey experiments

Audience costs and international commitment

Tomz (2007) is interested in the idea that audience costs (leaders being wary about what citizens think of them) can make international commitments credible at the domestic level. The hypothesis plays a prominent role in theoretical explanations of why national leaders would stick to their international commitments, but it is difficult to evaluate using observation designs due to possible selection bias effects.

The researcher employs a series of survey experiments that focus on the idea that citizens will 'punish' domestic leaders who make empty promises and threats during international crises. I will describe here the first of the reported survey experiments; the rest are similarly designed. Tomz starts by selecting a random sample of 1,127 US citizens representative of the US population. The participants read on the internet a scenario about a country sending its military to take over a neighbour. The scenario has four different variants that describe slightly different regime types, motives, power, and interests. The major experimental difference in the stories is that in half of them the US president does not get involved, while in the other half the US president makes a threat to send troops but eventually does not carry it out. So the president's actions are the treatment of the study. After reading the scenarios, the participants answer a series of questions about whether they approve of how the president handled the crises; the questions are then used to construct a seven-point scale ranging from strong disapproval to strong approval. The approval of the president is the outcome of interest.

Tomz finds on the basis of the experiment that the approval rating of the president who makes a commitment and then backs down is significantly lower than that of the president who doesn't get involved at all. The percentage of people who disapproved somewhat or very strongly of the 'empty threat' president was 49, while the corresponding number of the 'stay out' president was 33. The difference of 16 percent is rather large and substantively important. The rest of the article reports experiments that test whether the *level* of commitment (threat) matters (it does) and explores whether the effect *varies* with the international context described in the scenarios (it does) and the level of political participation of the participants (also, it does).

In terms of research design, it is important to note that in this case no pre-test is applied (and it is difficult to see what that would be in this case). The author examines whether the random assignment had produced balanced groups with respect to predictors of presidential approval (based mostly on demographic and political characteristics). No indication of nonresponse rates is given and no formal power analyses are reported.

The author himself raises some questions about the broader validity of the research, for example: 'Do citizens behave differently in interviews than in actual foreign policy crises?' and, if not, what are the likely differences? (p. 825). These open questions notwithstanding, the article is a nice example of how international relations theories and processes can be examined in an experimental setting.

News framing and support for European integration

Schuck and de Vreese (2006) aim to study the effect of news framing on public support for the European Union. More specifically, the frames relate either to 'risk' or 'opportunity'. Attitudes towards the recent enlargement of the EU to the East are the outcome of interest, and the hypothesis is that framing the enlargement as a risk rather than as an opportunity will decrease public support. The study combines content analysis of news and a relatively small-scale experiment.

The experiment is organized in a (German) university faculty and the subjects are undergraduate students. Hence, no random sample has been drawn. No pre-test is given, but some background information about the participants is recorded. In total 88 students take part in the experiment. The students are made to read a news article about EU enlargement that has two versions: one in which EU enlargement is framed as a 'risk' in four different parts of the article and another in which it is framed as an 'opportunity'. The outcome is measured using a series of six five-point-scale questions about support for the EU and enlargement in particular.

The results of the data analysis show that framing has the expected effect on support for enlargement. The average level of support for the 'risk' group is 2.7 (on the five-point scale), while the average level for the 'opportunity' group is 3.2 with the difference estimated as statistically significant. The results are also found to be *moderated* by levels of political knowledge, so that participants with low levels of political knowledge are more likely to be affected by the framing. No indication of nonresponse rates is given and no formal power analyses are reported.

Some additional questions raised by the research include: What is the likely generalizability of the results beyond the sample of (German) students on whom the experiment is conducted? Would the reported effect be stable over time? Is the size of the effect substantively important in addition to the statistical significance?

Field experiments

Conditional cash transfer programs

This example presents not a single study but the evaluation of a novel welfare policy that is now implemented in more than six countries around the globe. The policy, or rather the new way of delivering a social policy, in question is conditional cash transfers. These programs provide money to poor families if the families fulfil certain criteria such as sending their kids to school or visiting a health centre on a regular basis. Unlike traditional social assistance, conditional cash transfers try to improve the human capital of the families rather than provide emergency support only.

Starting with the Mexican Progresa program, conditional cash transfers have been subjected to a rigorous evaluation including the use of field experiments (RCT). From the population of families eligible for support under the program, some have been selected to enter the program two years earlier than the remainder (control). For example, in Mexico 4,682 households from 186 localities were selected as controls and 7,887 households in 320 localities were selected for the treatment group. This variation in the starting date allowed for a sound assessment of the educational and health effects of the program.

In their article, Rawlings and Rubio (2005) summarize the results from the evaluation, mostly on the basis of RCT, of conditional cash programs in six countries. They report that the program leads to significant improvement in primary school enrolment (for example, between 0.96 and 1.45 percentage points for girls in Mexico), school attendance, and a range of health outcomes (for example, a 4.7 percentage point reduction in illness rates).

The studies are methodologically sophisticated, measure many potential confounders in addition to the randomization of the treatment, distinguish between various treatment effects (ATT, ITT), report a number of estimates of substantive as well as statistical significance of the effects, and discuss the implications of the estimated program impact for future decision-making about national social policies. Furthermore, the article and the studies referenced in it provide an interesting discussion of the practical challenges of implementing a massive social experiment in the field, such as the coordination of the timing of the impact evaluation and the policy implementation, technological delays in the delivery of the transfer, or the interference of natural disasters as in the case of Jamaica.

The program and its evaluation spur many questions. For example, what is the proper comparison to the new policy: the old policy, no policy at all, or a new policy with a minor modifications? Was it ethical to provide some families with cash transfers before others? Is it likely that the effect would be similar for the entire country populations when the program is enforced in full? Would we expect significant differences in the impact of the program when implemented in different countries? Could such country differences be incorporated in the evaluation design?

Female voting in Pakistan
In another example of experiments in the field, Gine and Mansuri (2011) conduct a study of female voting behaviour in two regions in Pakistan. The issue has immense social significance, since women remain systematically less likely to vote and participate in the political process in many parts of the world. It also speaks to a large existing literature on the determinants of political mobilization.

The intervention that Gine and Mansuri design is an information campaign that explains the importance and mechanics of the electoral process. The information campaign is delivered only to the women within each household. The intervention is applied to several villages in two rural districts in Pakistan. The selection process has two steps: first, within each of the two regions, several villages are selected; second, the villages are divided into geographical clusters each of which is then randomly assigned to receive the treatment (the campaign) or not (so we have a blocked randomized design). Importantly, within the treated clusters some households were left untreated so as to measure the indirect spillover effects from the experiment. Although the study uses random assignment, in the data analysis it controls for polling station, household, and individual woman characteristics that might not have been perfectly balanced by the randomization.

The study concludes that the treatment increased female voter turnout on average by 12 percent. It also finds that there indeed exist geographical spillovers – the close neighbours of the treated women were more likely to vote as well even though they were not directly shown the information campaign. Given the costs of the campaign, the authors conclude that it is effective and efficient in increasing female voting.

Apart from the substantively important conclusion, the study demonstrates the importance of choosing the right level of analysis. If the researchers had selected the individual woman as the unit of analysis, the results would have been contaminated by the likely spillover effects. Instead, by focusing on the village, spillover effects become a hypothesis to be evaluated rather than a bug in the experimental design.

Since all individuals and spatial units included in the experiment are located within a relatively small area in Pakistan, a natural question to consider is whether the results from the intervention would generalize for the entire territory of the country and to other developing countries. In fact, it is an interesting question whether we can expect the results to be relevant for developed countries with longer traditions of female political enfranchisement, which can still suffer from lower turnout rates for women as well.

Social network-based experiments

2012: Social influence and political mobilization
In what is perhaps the biggest social-scientific experiment to date, Bond et al. (2012) conducted an experimental study of the effect of social influence on political mobilization that used 61 million participants. The issue is important for practical purposes (if one wants to influence voter turnout) and for theoretical reasons since the effect and contagiousness of impersonal mobilization messages is not well established.

In the framework of the study, political mobilization messages were delivered to Facebook users during the 2010 US congressional elections. The sample consisted of all US users who logged in to Facebook on 2 November 2010. The treatment group (more than 60 million people) were shown a message encouraging them to vote, and tools to share and access information about their own voting behaviour. A control group of 613,096 people were not shown the message (and a third group were shown the message and a slightly modified version of the sharing tools). The researchers were able to track several different indicators of whether people voted and whether they shared voting information on Facebook. These indicators allow for the operationalization of the theoretical concepts of interest: political self-expression, information seeking, and actual voting.

In short, the authors found that the messages they sent influenced all three variables: political self-expression, information seeking, and voting behaviour. But in addition to these direct effects on the 'treated' individuals, the effects were transmitted among the close friends of the subjects, so that the total effects of the intervention were much bigger than the direct ones. The researchers report that those who received the social message were 0.39 percent more likely to vote than those who did not receive any message; the difference is statistically significant at the 5 percent level according to a t-test. They also quantify the indirect effects using the randomized design and combine this information to estimate that the total effects of the campaign amounted to 340,000 additional votes in this particular election.

The scale of the study is no doubt impressive, but it also raises several questions. For example, what is the meaning of statistical significance tests in a sample with 61 million observations? Why were the treatment and control groups so unbalanced in size? Would there be different effects for different elections (with higher stakes)? Is it ethical for researchers to conduct studies that directly increase turnout, which might benefit certain parties?

Laboratory experiments

Self-interest and fairness in majority decision-making

Sauermann and Kaiser (2010) use laboratory experiments to examine whether social preferences (people caring for the utility or welfare of others) exist in majority decision-making. The laboratory setting is deemed appropriate for the research question because the effect of preferences can be isolated from the myriad of other possible influences on majority decisions in the real world. The controlled environment of the lab helps block the impact of these nuisance factors so that, if there is any effect on social preferences, it would become visible.

The sample is 120 people, predominantly students of economics and related disciplines. The set-up of the experiment is as follows. Participants are divided into five-person committees that need to select by majority one alternative among eight proposals. The decision-making rule is pure majority, each member has one vote, and voting is simultaneous. If no majority is reached in the first round, the participants are given information about how the others have voted, and new voting rounds occur until a majority decision is reached. The whole procedure is repeated 20 times with changing composition of the committees: for each round the five members of a committee are randomly chosen from a pool of ten people.

The preferences of the participants are induced by the experimenters: participants get a different number of points for each alternative chosen, and their pay-off depends on the points earned. The pay-off is real money, so each point gained during the game means a higher monetary reward for the individual. Importantly, each participant knows the pay-off structure of every other committee participant for each round of the play. The table of pay-offs is constructed by the researchers in such a way that there is a unique decision that should emerge at each round of play if actors act according to their preferences and the predictions of rational choice theory. The experiment controls the level of information and communication during the game and prevents face-to-face interaction between the participants since these are potentially important predictors of social preferences. The decision-making game is implemented via a computer network.

The study finds evidence both for self-interested and for fairness motivations in the experimental data. In one of three cases the alternative selected by the committee was different from what rational choice theory would have predicted. The authors conclude that a theory that integrates concerns for equality, reciprocity, and fairness performs best in accounting for the patterns in the experimental data.

As with every lab-based experiment, questions exist as to what extent the insights from the research are applicable to real-world cases and which aspects of the situation need to resemble the controlled environment for the experimental conclusions to hold. It is also important to speculate (and perhaps test) whether the fact that the sample was mostly composed of students in economics influenced in important ways the results. Would other people have more social preferences? Or perhaps less?

Limits to Experimental Research

Despite their methodological strengths and increasing popularity, experimental designs have some important limitations. For some questions at the core of political science, they are strictly impossible. For others, they are just impractical. And in many cases while in principle possible, experimental research will be controversial from an ethical point of view.

Researchers in political science are interested not only in the behaviour of individual people but also in institutions. Experimental research designs have been designed with humans in mind as potential participants, but if one is interested in the functioning and output of institutions, experiments are rarely of help *directly*. The influence of the committee system on the legislative productivity of parliaments, for example, could not be studied using an experiment, because it is never under the control of the researchers to assign countries randomly to different types of committee systems. That being said, we can examine experimentally the theoretical mechanisms that we hypothesize to underpin legislative productivity (for example, specialization). And we can turn towards the data produced by the world to try and find data *as if* produced by an experiment. How to do that will be the topic of the next chapter.

Even when possible, experimental research is often impractical. Experiments are expensive to run, especially if one is after representativeness (external validity) and needs to avoid noncompliance and nonresponse (so that extensive monitoring during the duration of the experiment is applied). Money and time are only two of the reasons why in practice people would refuse to support an experimental design even when from a scientific point of view the contributions would be worthwhile. Policy makers are not easily persuaded by the benefits of randomized evaluation. Hopefully, with the increasing visibility of experiments for evaluating aid effectiveness and other policies around the world, they will became more receptive to the idea.

Still, many questions will remain outside the reach of experiments for ethical reasons. Many of the important issues that animate international relations and conflict management could not be subject to experimentation – questions of war, civil conflicts, and revolutions – are just some of the most obvious examples. Randomization of the delivery of different forms of social assistance is also potentially unethical in the eyes of many. Participants themselves might also object and boycott experiments if they feel they breach fairness and other social norms. Furthermore, experimentation often requires that the participants are not aware of the exact purpose of the research, but deception is potentially unethical. We will have more to say on the ethics of research in Chapter 12.

In some circumstances concerns about poor external validity can render the usefulness of experimental results rather low. This goes mainly for underpowered experiments conducted on convenience samples, but it is an issue for well-designed field experiments as well. Due to their costs, experiments are usually run in a small number of localities. Whether causal inferences will travel in space and time is always an open question, and here observational analyses of institutions and social systems can help to probe the generalizability of experimental results.

Finally, while methodologically attractive, experiments do not provide a silver bullet solution to the problem of causal inference. As we have seen, the dividing line between experiments and observational studies is not as sharp as many believe. But how is it even possible to think causally within a counterfactual framework when experiments are not available? Chapter 8 explains.

Further Reading

There has been a small explosion of interest in experimental research in political science and public policy recently. Three edited volumes present excellent overviews of the substantive and methodological variety of experimental research in political science: Druckman et al. (2011); Kittel, Luhan, and Morton (2012); and Morton and Williams (2010). While the interested reader can find plenty of examples of actual experimental research in these texts, as well as in-depth discussions of certain methodological issues, none of the three would serve very well as an introductory learning tool for the design and analysis of experimental data.

Gerber and Green (2012) is a textbook (focused on field experiments) that covers introductory as well as some fairly advanced topics. The 'Randomization Toolkit' by Duflo, Glennerster, and Kremer (2006) is an excellent source for advice on the practice of experimental design and, although written for development economists, can serve political and policy scientists wishing to design field experiments just as well.

Banerjee and Duflo (2009) present an overview of the use of field experiments for policy and program evaluation. A very useful source of up-to-date information and in-depth discussions of randomized trials for program and policy evaluation is the World Bank's blog 'Development Impact', available at http://blogs.worldbank.org/impactevaluations/. Another online source is provided by the International Initiative for Impact Evaluation (http://www.3ieimpact.org/en/evaluation/).

The hypothetical example of university elections discussed in the chapter is loosely based on the study of Japanese elections reported in Horiuchi, Imai, & Taniguchi (2007).

For an introduction to data analysis of randomized experiments, see Chapter 9 in Gelman and Hill (2007). There are many textbooks on the topic (for example, Gonzalez, 2009), but most focus predominantly on the statistical rather than on the causal inference issues. Most of the textbooks, even if written with a general social science audience in mind, approach the problem from the angle of psychology, which is not always helpful for researchers in politics and administration.

The discussion of different treatment effects and their estimation is deeply rooted in the Rubin causal model and the potential outcomes framework (see, for example, Rubin, 1974), which we encountered in Chapter 6 and will reference again in the chapters on observational designs.

On power calculations see Duflo, Glennerster, and Kremer (2006). For a 'cookbook' on calculating and interpreting statistical sensitivity, see Lipsey (1990).

For an in-depth treatment of nonresponse and missing data, see Imbens and Pizer (2000) and Horiuchi, Imai, & Taniguchi (2007) (which also has a useful discussion of noncompliance). A more theoretical treatment of experimental design for detecting spillover effects is Sinclair, McConnell, & Green (2012). Imai (2005) is helpful for understanding the implications of choosing the right definition of a treatment effect and estimation technique.

On the early development of randomized experiments and the statistical methods associated with it, see the highly enjoyable book *The*

Lady Tasting Tea by David Salsburg (2001). For a biography of Sir R. A. Fisher, see Box (1978). An additional source is Armitage (2003).

On using experiments for studying causal mechanisms, see Imai et al. (2011); Imai, Tingley, and Yamamoto (2013); and Imai and Yamamoto (2013).

Morton and Williams (2010) has an excellent coverage of the ethical issues surrounding experimental political science.

Chapter 8

Large-N Designs

The merits of experimental research notwithstanding, for many questions of primary interest to political scientists an experimental design would too often be infeasible, unethical, or both. We cannot abandon such questions on account of a methodological difficulty. We have to do the best we can in situations where random assignment and experimental manipulation are unavailable. Welcome to the realm of observational research designs.

Observational research brings together a variety of approaches that are traditionally separated on the basis of the number of observations they work with – one, several, or many – and on the closely related distinction between qualitative and quantitative data. We follow this admittedly rough categorization as each of the three types of observational design emphasizes particular solutions to the common problems of causal inference and deriving valid explanations.

This chapter deals with observational designs when many observations are available. In other words, the 'N' (which stands for the number of observations) is large; hence the shortcut 'large-N designs'. The main advantage of large-N research over comparative and single-case designs is that it can, in principle, identify and estimate weak and heterogeneous causal relationships. Indeed, the fundamental assumption and motivation for large-N research is that, even if real, our hypothesized explanations and causal effects would only be partial and probabilistic and would vary from one unit to another. As a consequence, one needs plenty of observations to detect the systematic 'signal' from the noisy data the world provides. The analysis of noisy, weak, and heterogeneous relationships also invites the use of the tools of mathematical probability theory or statistics.

Statistical analysis as such, however, provides no automatic solution to the problem of causal inference. Only when coupled with careful research design – appropriate case selection, valid operationalizations, and measurements, and so on – can it help in the discovery of causal relationships and the testing of hypothesized explanations.

This chapter will present the logic of causal large-N data analysis and introduce several different approaches for inferring causal inferences from quantitative observational data. Next to causal identification (inference) strategies, it will outline how the estimation of causal effects proceeds and will discuss in detail the major issues of large-N research design, such as the selection of variables and cases to observe.

The Logic of Large-N Research

Large-N analysis in the social sciences is built on a number of fundamental premises that often go unspoken. The first one is that there is
enough structure to the social and political worlds for information about
one case to be useful for understanding another. Knowing about democratic legitimacy in England is relevant for democratic legitimacy in
Brazil. Understanding why Carlos from New York votes is relevant for
understanding why Carla from Portland does not. Information about
corruption in Italy is pertinent for the study of corruption in Egypt. The
second premise is that the structure of the social and political worlds is
loose and the causal links holding it together are weak, partial, and contingent. If that was not the case, we would only need to closely examine
one democracy to know about all and study one individual to understand
all people. But causal links being weak, partial, and contingent we need
plenty of observations to detect the fragile, evolving, and elusive structure they provide to our social world. Therefore, causal relationships are
to be uncovered in patterns of variation rather than individual outcomes,
in changing distributions rather than any particular fact, in subtle trends
and tendencies that need to be filtered from the noise of randomness. In
short, the fundamental premises of large-N research are, one, there is
signal and, two, there is noise. The task is of course to separate the two.

To do so, the grand strategy of large-N research designs is to bring
together quantitative data on many cases but relatively few aspects of
each case. When operationalized and measured, these aspects become
variables. In contrast, small-N comparative and single-case designs rely
on collecting data, possibly qualitative, about many aspects of few (possibly one) cases. Having collected data on many cases, in large-N (quantitative) research with explanatory goals we investigate whether the
individual, joint, and conditional distributions of the variables conform
with the expectations of our theoretical hypotheses. In less technical language, we examine whether the pattern of associations between the variables in our set of observations fits with what the theory predicts. If not,
we conclude that it is unlikely that the process suggested by our theory
has generated the data. If yes, we conclude that the data are compatible
with the implications of the theory.

Usually, there will be more than one theory that the data are compatible with, so the researcher needs to bring in additional considerations
to decide which theory or explanation is more plausible than the others.
Some possibilities that are always implicated and need to be considered
are that (1) there are no systematic relationships, and the data can be
explained entirely by reference to chance; and (2) there are measurement
problems that either prevent the data from exhibiting the patterns suggested by the theory, or, on the contrary, generate the same patterns as
the theory would suggest, even if the theory is in fact false.

An example

Let's put these ideas in the context of an example. Imagine our favoured theory proposes that political revolutions are caused by economic collapse. A straightforward implication of this theory is that we should observe political revolutions in periods of economic collapse but not in periods of flourishing economy. If we take our theory to be deterministic, so that economic collapse is a necessary and sufficient condition for political revolutions, any case we discover that does not conform to this very strong and clear expectation would in principle disqualify our theory. There is no place for uncertainty, no use for statistics, and little need for a large-N study.

But of course we rarely if ever take our theories to be so deterministic. What we usually propose is that economic collapse is one cause *among others* and that it leads to political revolutions *only when* some other conditions, for example political repression, are also present. But how are we to evaluate such a 'weak' but more realistic theory, when the list of alternative causes and enabling conditions can never be fully specified in advance? Even if economic collapse *is*, in fact, a cause of political revolutions under certain conditions, any single case we study might fail to reveal the effect because some necessary enabling conditions are not realized. Alternatively, we can find that both economic collapse and political revolution are present in a certain case, even if in reality there is no causal connection between the two but some alternative cause of revolution is also present in the case we happen to research. So if the information from single cases has little bearing on how we should evaluate a non-deterministic theory, what are we to do?

The core idea of large-N observational research is that even if the outcome of any *individual* case may not be fully determined, the *distribution* of outcomes should still conform with certain patterns if our theory has any bearing on reality. The effects of other causes and moderators, even if unknown, will recede to the background if we have many observations, so that the average difference observed in the data would approach the 'real' causal association between the variables (*nota bene*: this will only hold given a set of important conditions to be discussed below!).

Even if in each particular case economic collapse may or may not be associated with a political revolution, we should still expect that when we look into a large number of cases there would be more instances of revolution under conditions of economic collapse than under conditions of economic prosperity, if our theory is correct. That is, the *relative frequency* of political revolutions should be related to the state of the economy.

Table 8.1 shows an example of a hypothetical dataset collected for a large-N study. There are four variables – *economic collapse*, which is the main explanatory variable; *war defeat* and *political repression*,

Table 8.1   *Example of a (hypothetical) dataset collected in the framework of a large-N study*

Observation	Economic collapse	War defeat	Repression	Revolution
Country 1	1	0	1	1
Country 2	1	0	1	1
Country 3	1	0	0	0
Country 4	0	0	0	0
Country 5	0	0	0	0
Country 6	0	1	0	1
...	...	...	...	...
Country 60	0	1	1	1

which are additional covariates; and the *occurrence of political revolution* in the last column, which is the outcome variable. The dataset has 60 cases, 7 of which are printed. Assume for simplicity that a case is a country observed at a particular point in time and that the variables are measured as the presence [1] or absence [0] of the condition.

The printed hypothetical data illustrates the situation in which economic collapse is a cause of political revolution, but (1) war defeat is an alternative cause, and (2) political repression is an 'enabler' of the effect of economic collapse (it needs to be present for the economic effect to work). The causal model representing these relationships is illustrated in Figure 8.1.

Accordingly, in Country 1 and Country 2 economic collapse and revolution are observed together. In Country 3 economic collapse is present but revolution is not observed (due to the lack of repression), and

Figure 8.1   *Causal diagram illustrating a simple model of political revolutions*

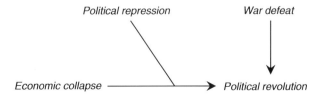

in Country 6 and Country 60 revolution is observed despite the lack of economic collapse (due to the presence of war defeat).

Imagine for a moment that we are unaware of the alternative causal and enabling effects of war defeat and political repression and that we can afford only one case to study. From the seven cases printed in Table 8.1, only in four would we observe the expected association between economic collapse and revolution – if we happen to pick Countries 1 or 2 (where both are present) or Countries 4 or 5 (where both are absent). In any of the three other cases the expected association between the two variables is not to be found, even though economic collapse *is* a probabilistic cause of political revolution.

However, if we collect information only on economic collapse and political revolution but for many cases, we will find that the relative frequency of occurrence of revolution will be higher under conditions of economic collapse. There is a small step from relative frequencies to probabilities. If we rephrase our theoretical hypothesis as '*The probability of political revolution is higher under conditions of economic collapse*', we would clear a straightforward path from a non-deterministic theory to empirical analysis and back. By comparing the relative frequencies of revolutions under different economic conditions we infer the conditional probabilities, which should conform with our probabilistic hypothesis even if any single particular case may or may not fit the argument. If the outcome we study is continuous, such as the number of victims during political revolutions, rather than binary (the occurrence of a revolution or not), we would compare the distributions rather than the relative frequencies, but the principle remains the same.

The relative frequencies for the seven cases listed in Table 8.1 are presented in Table 8.2. We can see that the frequency of revolution under conditions of economic collapse is higher (2 out of 3 cases, or approximately 66.7 per cent) than otherwise (2 out of 4 cases, or 50 per cent), which, if the results hold for the entire dataset, would lead us to conclude that economic collapse and political revolution are probabilistically associated. By collecting information on more cases we have allowed the probabilistic association to shine through the additional variation in the data.

Table 8.2   *Relative frequencies for the cases listed in Table 8.1*

	Revolution	*No revolution*
Economic collapse	2 out of 3	1 out of 3
No economic collapse	2 out of 4	2 out of 4

Note that the last sentence speaks of *association* and not of *causation*. But what we are really after is the *causal* impact of economic collapse on revolutions, not merely their association. Can we claim that the association we have discovered in the data implies that economic collapse has a causal effect? Under what conditions can we make the quantum leaps from association to causation and from description to explanation?

Pitfalls on the Way from Association to Causation

In general, association is not causation. Two variables can be empirically associated without any causal link between the two. And there can be a causal relationship that is not manifested in an empirical association. Data alone cannot reveal causality. But data coupled with certain assumptions can. To the extent that the assumptions are trustworthy, the causal inferences from observational data will be reliable. Let us first demonstrate why association need not imply causation and then discuss what assumptions are necessary and sufficient to derive causality from empirical observations.

First, consider a likely familiar situation. You and your best friends probably like similar music – there is an association in your musical preferences, but we cannot conclude from this empirical association that *you* determine what music your friends like. While that is possible, it is also conceivable that (1) affinity in musical taste (partly) determines who becomes your friend, and/or that (2) you and your friends share some characteristics (for example, growing up in the same neighbourhood or attending the same school) that affect the type of music you all like. And there are many more possibilities as well.

In general, an empirical association between two variables X and Y can result for any of the reasons listed in Box 8.1 and illustrated in Figure 8.2 (Glymour, 2006, p. 390).

Box 8.1 *What can produce an observed association between two variables X and Y?*

1. X causes Y
2. Y causes X
3. Both X and Y share a common cause
4. Conditioning on a common effect of X and Y
5. Chance (random variation)

Figure 8.2   *Causal graphs: what can produce an observed association between two variables X and Y?*

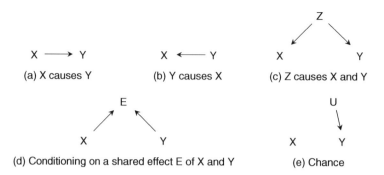

The first item in the list corresponds to the case in which the association is generated by a real causal relationship in which X determines Y. However, exactly the same association would be observed if it was in fact Y that causes X. An empirical association between economic collapse and political revolution does not reveal whether it is the former leading to the latter or the other way round. This problem is known as reversed causality (simultaneity, endogeneity).

Association could also arise if X and Y have no direct causal link whatsoever but are both partly or fully caused by a third factor that is their common cause. To see why, imagine that in reality war defeats lead to both economic collapse and political revolution, but there is absolutely *no* causal link between the latter two. What patterns of associations would we observe in such a world?

Table 8.3 provides an illustration. The occurrence of economic collapse and political revolution appear perfectly associated, but that is only because they are both produced by war defeat, which *confounds* the relationship. Assume we cannot measure or that we are unaware of the confounding

Table 8.3   *Example of association generated by a shared cause*

Observation	Economic collapse	War defeat	Revolution
Country 1	1	1	1
Country 2	1	1	1
Country 3	0	0	0
Country 4	0	0	0
...	...	...	...

effect: the observed strong association between economic collapse and revolution will mislead us into concluding the two are causally related.

This problem is known as omitted variable bias (or confounder bias), because if we omit such a variable from the analysis the relationship between X and Y estimated from the data would be biased. The omitted variable need not be perfectly correlated with X and Y to do damage, but the stronger the links, the greater the bias would be. To correct for omitted variable bias, we try to isolate or adjust for the influence of confounders in the analysis (see the section on conditioning below) in which case they become 'control' variables.

The fourth scenario in Box 8.1 is less intuitive to grasp and less commonly discussed in the literature, so let's first consider an example. Imagine that there are two distinct ways in which politicians get to be successful – either they have great charisma *or* they have great policy expertise. In the entire population of politicians these two traits occur independently – there is no causal relationship and there is no association between being charismatic and having policy expertise. Knowing whether a politician is charismatic gives no information whether he/she has policy expertise or not. However, imagine our sample of observations consists only of politicians who *are* successful. *Within* this sample, charisma and policy expertise would turn out to be negatively associated. Observing a politician who lacks charisma, you can guess that she has great policy expertise; observing one who lacks expertise, you can guess that he has charisma – otherwise they would not have become successful. Table 8.4 shows a numerical illustration, in which two traits that are independently distributed in the population are associated in a sample selected by conditioning on an effect they share (in this case, by observing only the first three cases where *success* is present).

This problem is known as selection bias due to selecting on a common effect (or collider bias). There are other types of problems that can arise during the process of selection of cases to observe. We will discuss in detail case selection and selection bias later in this chapter.

Table 8.4 *Example of association generated by a shared effect*

Observation	Charisma	Policy expertise	Success
Politician 1	1	1	1
Politician 2	1	0	1
Politician 3	0	1	1
Politician 4	0	0	0
...	...	...	...

Lastly, the fifth item in Box 8.1 reminds us that association can arise purely due to chance, or in other words, random fluctuations of the variables. This problem is statistical, and many statistical tests are designed to examine how likely it is that a certain association observed in a sample is due to chance only.

So far we have established that association need not imply causation, but can there be causation *without* empirical association? Can two variables be causally related but exhibit no link in data? In short, yes. One scenario under which this can happen is when the causal effect is *heterogeneous*, meaning that it works differently in different subpopulations. For example, economic collapse might lead to political revolutions only in autocracies but have no effect in democracies. If all the cases we happen to study are democracies, we will find no evidence for an effect, while for the population of all countries one would exist. This would be yet another problem due to selection bias.

A confounder can also *conceal* an association between two variables. Imagine (1) motivation and (2) intelligence both increase study success, but (3) motivation decreases with intelligence. In a random sample containing units with various levels of motivation, we will observe no association between intelligence and study success. But for units with the same level of motivation, intelligence *does* increase success; possibly even for *any* level of motivation.

Figure 8.3 illustrates the situation. The diagram encodes the existing relationships between the three variables with the signs of the causal effects. The scatterplot shows data simulated from such a causal model. The dashed linear regression line summarizes the relationship between intelligence and study success in the entire sample. The line is very close to horizontal, implying a very weak link between the two.

Figure 8.3   *A confounder concealing a true causal relationship*

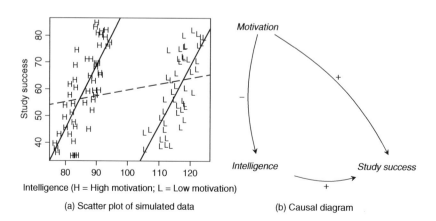

Intelligence (H = High motivation; L = Low motivation)

(a) Scatter plot of simulated data   (b) Causal diagram

The two solid lines are also linear regression lines but estimated, using first only the High-motivation units and then only the Low-motivation ones. The lines are much steeper because within each level of motivation the positive relationship between intelligence and study success is really strong. But unless we measure and control for motivation, looking at the observed association between intelligence and study success will suggest the wrong conclusion of no causation. This example is a special case of the more general phenomenon of a relationship reversing signs in subsets of the data (Simpson's paradox), which we will discuss again below in the context of selecting the right level of analysis.

Evidently, the absence of empirical association does *not* need to imply lack of causation. In sum, observational data *alone* cannot help us to uncover causal structures and test hypothesized explanations. This remains true no matter whether we have observed one, a handful of, or a million units. A greater number of observations is useful in order to rule out that empirical associations are due to chance and to estimate the relationships more precisely in the presence of noisy data. But a large-N as such does not provide a remedy against the remaining problems of inferring causation from observations. These other issues – reversed causality, confounders, collider bias, and so on – are addressed through appropriate *research design*.

Conditions for Causal Inference

Despite the long list of potential pitfalls, there are conditions under which observations can support causal inferences. Unfortunately, not all of these conditions can be tested; many have to remain *assumptions*. We can choose to make certain assumptions based on prior knowledge, experience, or intuition. In general, the more and stronger the assumptions we are willing to make, the sharper and stronger our inferences from data would be. At the same time, the more and the stronger assumptions we make, the less credible they, and by implication the causal inference they support, would be. Furthermore, having more and better data – for example, measured with less error or for a broader set of variables – means that we would have to make fewer and weaker assumptions. The task of research design can be seen as crafting a project that requires the minimum of assumptions to produce the strongest causal inferences possible given practical constraints.

We can distinguish between general assumptions that are related to the particular analytical framework for causal analysis and specific ones that are related to the concrete research problem being studied. For example, in the potential outcomes framework (Rubin, 1974, 2005) the most fundamental assumption is known as *SUTVA* (stable unit treatment-value assignment). In the causal diagrams (DAGs) framework

(Pearl, 2000, 2009b), the general assumptions are the so-called *causal Markov condition* and *faithfulness*. The precise formulation of such general assumptions is highly technical and requires that we are familiar with the language and formalizations used by the particular analytic framework; hence, they cannot be presented here. But remember that each framework for causal analysis is built on a set of such fundamental assumptions that delimit what kind of casual questions can be posed and answered within its structure.

More important for our purposes are the specific assumptions one has to make about the particular problem being studied in order to derive – identify and, subsequently, estimate – causal inferences from observations. These assumptions concern the presence or absence of relationships between variables and, if relationships are hypothesized to exist, their direction, form, magnitude, constancy, and so on.

For example, if we assume that (1) the many possible causes of political revolutions act independently from each other and (2) economic collapse can *lead* to a political revolution but cannot be *produced* by one, we can identify the average causal effect of economic collapse on the probability of political revolution by comparing the relative frequencies in a large set of observations, as illustrated above. Well, we can still get fooled by associations occurring by chance, but we can quantify how likely that is in view of the number of observations we have collected and the variability of the data.

For another example, imagine that we are interested in the impact of leadership on the performance of public agencies. More specifically, we want to know whether the age of the leader is related to public satisfaction with the work of the agency (as measured in a survey). Suppose that we find that agencies led by younger people have higher levels of public satisfaction with their work. Obviously, the difference in outcomes can be due to a myriad of other factors – the difficulty and importance of the agencies' tasks, the resources they have at their disposal, the kinds of people they serve, and so on. But as long as we are willing to assume that (1) all these additional factors act independently and (2) public satisfaction with the work of the agency is not itself influencing the age of the leader, we can interpret the difference in outcomes relative to age in causal terms (again, given enough observations to rule out chance).

The two assumptions would suffice, but how credible are they? In this last example, clearly not at all. It is all too easy to imagine that young leaders get to head less important organizations doing easier tasks, for instance (which would violate the first assumption), or that agencies that have poor ratings are given to more experienced and older leaders (which would violate the second assumption). Some of these concerns can be tested against the data, but not all. In fact, for the examples presented in this paragraph the assumptions made are so implausible that the causal claims they support are not worth much. And, in general, one would be hard pressed to find any problem of significance for political scientists where causes can be neatly separated and assumed to act independently.

Fortunately, while these two particular assumptions above are *sufficient* for causal interpretation of observed associations, they are not *necessary* – there are other sets of assumptions that can help identify a causal effect. These alternatives impose potentially weaker and more realistic requirements on how the relevant variables should be related to each other. The next section of this chapter considers four different strategies for causal identification from large-N observational data relying on four quite different sets of assumptions. These strategies suggest solutions to the *logical* problem of causal inference. If we are able to identify causal effects, the next step is to estimate them. This is a *statistical* problem, and it will be discussed separately.

Strategies for Causal Inference in Large-N Research

To recap, to tackle the problem of causal inference, we need to approximate a counterfactual situation in which only the purported cause changes while everything else remains the same in order to see what its effects are.

There are four main strategies to infer causation from large-N observational data. The common problem they address is, to put it in very simple terms, that something else can account for any association we may observe in data between the hypothesized causal factor and the outcome we are interested in. The first strategy – natural experiments – relies on randomness introduced by nature to solve the problem. The second strategy – instrumental variables – relies on finding a variable that is related to the hypothesized cause but not directly to the outcome. The third strategy – mediation analysis – relies on finding a variable mediating the influence of the main hypothesized factor but insulated from other potential causes. The fourth, and by far the most popular in contemporary political science, strategy is conditioning, or filtering out the influence of confounders by adjusting for or blocking their influence or partialing out their effects. Let us look in more detail at how each of these strategies work.

Natural experiments

Remember that the core power of experimental research stems from random assignment – we control which units get the treatment and which not, and because the assignment is random we can be pretty sure that any differences we find in the outcomes are a result of our intervention only. By definition, this is not possible in observational studies. But occasionally nature will do the randomization for us. In some rare situations the assignment of units into different categories of our main explanatory variable is effectively random despite being outside our control. As it were, we get random assignment for free.

Lotteries are a good example: although we do not control who gets to win the lottery, the selection of winners is purely random. So if we were to compare lottery winners to other people who play the lottery (one hesitates to call them 'losers'), we would expect that, prior to the lottery draw, the two groups do not differ systematically in any respect. If we were interested in the impact of wealth on voting, for instance, we could study how individuals' voting behaviour changes after they win the lottery in order to isolate the *causal* impact of wealth.

Natural experiments resemble real ones as random assignment is available, but they differ from them as the researchers have no direct control over the process of assignment or other features of the study. What researchers still control is the selection of cases to observe, and the case selection makes use of the random variability induced by nature (or by accident). In sum, the assumption that a causal identification strategy based on natural experiments needs to make is: 'The process of assignment of units to different values of the main explanatory variable is random, which implies that it is unrelated to the outcome variable and to any factor confounding the relationship between the main explanatory variable and the outcome.' Note that there is nothing intrinsically 'large-N' about natural experiments. In fact, they can as easily provide a template for a small-N comparative case study as they do for quantitative research.

There are different natural mechanisms that can give rise to random assignment. Lotteries and other games of chance are one, but peculiarities of geography and history provide others. Let us go through some examples of real research based on the logic of natural experiments to see it in action and appreciate its strengths and weaknesses.

Lotteries and voting

If you thought that the case of studying lottery winners to understand politics was purely hypothetical, you were wrong. Doherty, Gerber, and Green (2006) identified and interviewed a large number of lottery winners in one American state in order to assess the causal impact of affluence on political attitudes. They compared the opinions of lottery winners within the sample (the prize money collected by each winner ranged from less than $50,000 to more than $15 million) with those provided by a survey of the general public.

The researchers found that the people who had won large amounts (in excess of $5 million) were much less likely to support estate tax, but overall there was not much evidence that winnings were related to broader opinions about the role of government and redistribution. At the same time, the survey of the general public showed that income is related to attitudes towards redistribution.

How credible is the causal identification strategy used in this study? Lottery winners are picked by chance from the people who do play the lottery, so the assignment of winners can be treated as random. The relative target population is, however, not *all* people but the subset who play the lottery. These might be not truly comparable to the population at large due to their different attitudes to risk, prior wealth, and so on. To avoid this complication, the authors compare political attitudes *within* the sample of lottery winners, all of whom have, obviously, participated in the lottery in order to win. Furthermore, the authors point out that the impact of *winning* may be different from the impact of *earning* or *inheriting* large amounts of money. These remarks notwithstanding, this article offers an important insight into how wealth shapes political attitudes that goes further than purely associational studies.

The conclusions about the impact of winning the lottery would have been even stronger if we knew what the attitudes of the winners were before they had won. A recent paper by Powdthavee and Oswald (2014) does just that, and it finds that winning the lottery, and the associated increase in wealth, makes people less egalitarian and more supportive of right-wing parties. In another study of lottery winners in the US, Peterson (2015) claims that especially those who had not been registered to vote before winning were more likely to start voting for the US Republican party after winning the lottery.

Geography, TV coverage and support for the communist regime in East Germany

How vulnerable are authoritarian political regimes to information coming from their democratic neighbour countries? It has been suspected that during the final decades of communist rule in Central and Eastern Europe, information coming from Western European media eroded support for the communist regimes by providing citizens behind the Iron Curtain with a glimpse of the more prosperous life in the West, by spreading democratic values, and by increasing the appetite of Eastern Europeans for liberty and an open political process. As intuitive as these propositions are, it is not that easy to demonstrate empirically that exposure to Western media really had any *causal* influence on the political opinions of Eastern Europeans. Even if a negative *association* between support for the communist regime and exposure to Western media existed, it could well have been that people who already had more liberal political dispositions found a way to watch Western TV or read foreign newspapers, rather than the other way round (formally, the problem is self-selection leading to reversed causality). Furthermore, access and availability of Western media would be generally higher in communist regions bordering the West, which might be home to more democracy-supporting populations for all kinds of other reasons – more trade links with the West, for example. Alternatively, communist regimes might have been extra diligent in policing anti-regime opinions in the border regions given their strategic importance (these would be examples of omitted variable bias). In any case, it seems rather hopeless to isolate the causal impact of exposure to Western media on political attitudes in the East by simply observing their association at the personal or at some aggregate level.

But Kern and Hainmueller (2009) found an ingenious way around the problem. They focused on the case of East Germans' exposure to West German TV during the 1980s. First, they managed to obtain previously classified surveys of the political attitudes of East Germans collected originally by the East German state. Second, they propose a credible strategy to identify the causal effect of foreign media based on a natural experiment. By the laws of physics, the spread and penetration of a TV signal depends on the geography and topography of a region. Hence, there is variation in the availability of the signal: some East German cities and villages had no access to West German TV purely because of the peculiarities of their geographical and topographical position and not due to state policy. In effect, the 'assignment' of cities and villages into the two conditions [has access to West German TV] and [has no access to West German TV] can be considered as entirely random for the purposes of political analysis. As a result, we would *not* expect to see, on average, any systematic differences in the political attitudes of the East Germans living in the two types of localities (with and without access to foreign TV) *other than* the ones caused by exposure to West German television.

On the basis of this natural experiment Kern and Hainmueller find that, in fact, exposure to foreign media had the opposite from the hypothesized effect on the political attitudes of East Germans. The people living in regions that had no access to West German television were, on average, *less* supportive of the ruling communist party than the ones who had the opportunity to watch West German TV. If anything, it seems from the data that the availability of foreign media solidified support for the authoritarian East German regime. While this finding is quite counterintuitive, it is hard to suggest alternative explanations that can account for the positive association found in the data, because the random variation in terrain should have made the regions with and without access to Western television comparable in all other aspects (and the authors of the study make sure that the regions are, indeed, very similar). To account for the empirical finding, the authors of the study hypothesize that in the late phase of communist rule in Eastern Europe, foreign TV served mostly as a source of entertainment rather than political news and ideas, so it had little or even a detrimental impact on the development of liberal opinions among the people behind the Iron Curtain. Possibly, watching West German TV actually made life more bearable and provided an escape from the dull communist reality for East Germans and, as an effect, reduced their dissatisfaction with the regime. But whatever the actual causal mechanism behind the empirical association, this study alerts us that the effects of foreign media on authoritarian regimes can be much more complex than assumed by many theories of democratization (for example, Giddens, 2000; Nye, 2004).

Regression discontinuity designs
A variation of the natural experiments strategy is the regression discontinuity design, which relies on quasi-random selection of units into 'treatment' and 'control'. Many sorting rules in the social world – for example, which families qualify for health insurance support, which scholars receive research grants, which state regions get national subsidies – while far from random, include some degree of arbitrariness around the qualifying threshold. Thus, if families with annual incomes of less than $20,000 qualify for publicly funded health insurance, while the rest do not, income would be, obviously, systematically related to receiving free or subsidized health insurance. However, for families just above and just below the threshold – say, those with incomes between $19,900 and $20,100 – the selection into the 'subsidy' or 'no subsidy' group can be considered almost or quasi-random (but only if incomes cannot be purposefully manipulated in view of the threshold). Families on both sides of the threshold would be expected to be very similar in all respects other than receiving the health subsidy, because of the large role of chance in determining whether they fall just above or just below the threshold set by the sorting rule. As a result, if we are interested in evaluating, for example, the impact of having health insurance on the number of visits to the doctor per year, a comparison of families just below and just above the threshold for publicly funded insurance would provide a good causal identification strategy.

Some arbitrariness in sorting rules is regularly encountered for issues of political and policy significance. The quasi-randomness involved in such arbitrariness can be employed for causal inference via a regression discontinuity design. For instance, national governments might consider too small or too big municipalities suboptimal in terms of administrative efficiency. In consequence, they might decide to merge the really small ones (for example, Denmark's reform in 2007) and split up the really big ones. Any rule that specifies how small or big municipalities need to be to get reformed would involve some degree of arbitrariness at the margin. Municipalities just above and just below these thresholds would provide good counterfactuals to each other if we need to evaluate the impact of the reform on, say, administrative efficiency, even if the 'assignment' or reform is systematically related to efficiency (which would normally introduce bias).

Altogether, natural experiments, regression discontinuity designs included, are a clever way of approaching causal analysis. When a selection mechanism can be plausibly assumed to produce random assignment, the strategy can provide compelling causal inferences. But in reality such selection mechanisms are rare. And for the majority of questions of interest for political scientists, they are unavailable. Also bear in mind that natural experiments do not instantly solve other issues of research design such as proper measurement and operationalization. But if you find a previously unexplored natural random assignment mechanism or a quasi-random sorting rule relevant for a political process, there is a good chance that you can use it to make a scientific contribution.

Instrumental variables

The instrumental variable approach, the second large-N strategy for causal inference we are going to discuss, is built around another clever idea. Imagine we find a variable that can be safely assumed to be (1) strongly related to the main explanatory variable of interest, (2) otherwise unrelated to the outcome variable, and (3) that there are no common causes of this variable and the outcome. We can then use the variation in the main explanatory variable *induced* by this 'instrumental variable' to screen off all other influences by potential confounders and, as a consequence, isolate the effect of our main explanatory variable on the outcome.

Figure 8.4 illustrates with the help of diagrams what causal models can and what causal models cannot rely on instrumental variables for causal identification. In all the diagrams, variables that are measured and

Figure 8.4   *Causal identification using instrumental variables represented in causal diagrams*

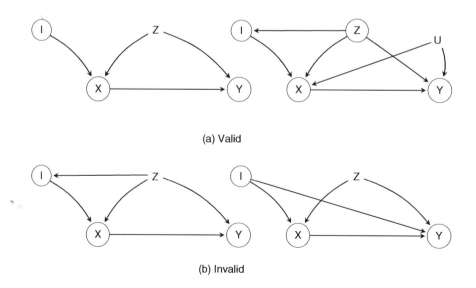

(a) Valid

(b) Invalid

included in the analysis are circled, while variables that are relevant but are left out are not. In the top-left of the figure, the simplest scenario is illustrated where Z is an unmeasured confounder (omitted variable), but I is a valid instrument and can help identify the effect of X on Y. Even if I, X, and Y share a common cause, if we can control for its influence (by some form of conditioning, see below), I remains a valid instrument in view of other omitted variables such as U. However, if a common cause of I, X, and Y remains unmeasured, or if I is directly causing the outcome Y, an instrumental variable analysis would not provide a valid estimate of the causal link between X and Y (see the two bottom diagrams of Figure 8.4).

Note that experimental and natural random assignment can be considered as special cases of instrumental variables. The assignment rule is perfectly (or very strongly) correlated with who gets the 'treatment' and who does not (hence, with the main explanatory variable), while it is uncorrelated with the outcome or with any potential confounder (as it is based on chance alone).

For an example of the instrumental variables strategy, assume that we are interested in the impact of economic growth on civil conflict. Experimentation is obviously not possible, and it will be painfully hard to identify and measure all possible factors that are related simultaneously to these two variables: the list would include type of political regime, trade policies, relationships with neighbours, and war. But in economies based primarily on agriculture and pastoralism, rainfall is strongly related to economic growth. At the same time, rain is probably not very strongly related to civil conflict as such (other than through the influence on the economy) and to the list of confounders. So we can investigate how variation in rainfall is related to variation in civil conflict (see Miguel, Satyanath, & Sergenti, 2004; for a critique of this application, see Sarsons, 2011). If we find a link in data and if our assumptions about the network of relationships are correct, we would have brought compelling evidence that economic growth is causally related to civil conflict, even if we cannot directly control for all possible omitted variables.

Instrumental variables strategies are popular in political science and even more so in the sister discipline of economics. Below are only two examples that illustrate the use of instruments for causal analysis.

Political rhetoric and support for the war in Iraq
Kriner and Shen (2014) study the political rhetoric in the American Congress in relation to the war in Iraq. One of their objectives is to estimate the impact of anti-war speeches made in Congress on mass public support for war. Kriner & Shen look into the number of anti-war speeches made by each member of Congress and relate that to the average public opinion about the Iraq war in their respective electoral

districts. It is easy to imagine that the anti-war positions of congressional members are at least partly responsive to the public mood in their election districts. Therefore, an empirical association between the two alone would not be very informative about the potential causal effect of congressional anti-war speeches. To circumvent the problem, the authors introduce the *level of seniority* of individual members within each chamber of Congress as an instrumental variable. Seniority is highly correlated with the number of speeches congressional members make, but there is no reason to believe that it is related to either public support for the war at the district level or any confounding variables. On the basis of this approach, the article finds that anti-war speeches have had a rather strong negative effect on public support for the Iraq war.

Labour market opportunities, commodity prices, and piracy
Jablonski and Oliver (2013) attempt to explain the variation in intensity of maritime piracy attacks over space and time, and focus on the effect of alternative labour market opportunities available to the potential pirates. The study employs variation in the prices of rice, sugar, and petrol – important commodities produced in the countries traditionally supplying maritime pirates – to measure labour market opportunities, with higher prices associated with more demand for labour. However, commodity prices are probably related to the number of pirate attacks at a time in a region through additional mechanisms other than labour opportunities. For example, higher commodity prices will be associated with more trade and more cargo ships, which increases the number of potential pirate targets. To address such potential problems, the authors rely on an instrumental variable approach. The instrument they use is the level of precipitation in a region, which should be strongly linked with the commodity prices of rice and sugar but unrelated to piracy *other than* through its effects on labour opportunities. The empirical analysis supports the view that the availability of labour opportunities decreases the intensity of piracy attacks.

You would have noticed even on the basis of these short examples that, as with other strategies for causal identification, the assumptions we are willing to impose on the data about the network of relationships between the variables play a crucial role in making the instrumental variable strategy work or not. If the instrumental variable is not strongly related to the main causal factor we study or if it actually exerts a direct effect on the outcome, the strategy falls apart. Frustratingly, one cannot directly test these assumptions (pretty much for the same reasons we cannot infer causation from association). In general, the instrumental variable approach also requires that the relationships in the model are linear. And finding plausible instruments is a difficult endeavour. Similarly to natural experiments, instrumental variables are a clever strategy but one that is unlikely to apply to many research questions, because plausible instruments, such as random variation induced by nature, are rare. Of course, one can turn things around and ask not what instrumental variables can I find for my research question but what research questions can be answered with the instrumental variables (or natural experiments) I have found? This can be a productive approach, if it is not allowed to dominate the broader research agenda in the field.

Mediation analysis

The third strategy for causal inference from observational data relies not on random variation or instrumental variables, but on analysing the mechanisms through which the effect of the main explanatory variable is exercised. Even if we cannot control for all possible confounders, if we find a mediating variable that is (1) influencing the outcome of interest only because it is itself being affected by the main explanatory variable we care about, but (2) has no direct independent influence on the outcome, and (3) is not affected by confounders, we have a way to identify causal relationships.

Figure 8.5 showss examples of models in which causal mediation analysis would be valid (top) and invalid (bottom part of the figure).

Figure 8.5 *Causal identification using mediating variables represented in causal diagrams*

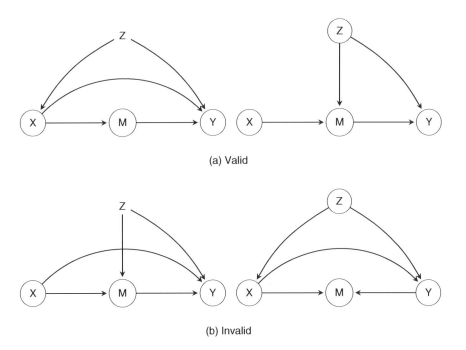

(a) Valid

(b) Invalid

Importantly, a variable that confounds the link between the mediator and the outcome variables needs to be measured and included in the analysis (top right versus bottom left). Furthermore, if the purported mediator is in fact an effect rather than a cause of the outcome Y, the strategy cannot work (bottom right).

The variable we use is called a mediator because it mediates (translates, carries over) the effect of X on Y. For example, think about diplomats bargaining over a treaty. We could hypothesize that spending time together increases trust, which leads to better negotiation outcomes: in this case, trust mediates the relationship between time spent together and the outcome of negotiations; it provides the mechanism through which the two are related. So even if time spent together and negotiation outcomes as such could have plenty of confounders – prior friendship, geographical proximity, complexity of the issue being negotiated, and so on – we have a way out. If we are willing to assume that (1) there is no way by which time spent together influences negotiation outcomes other than by affecting trust, and (2) there are no confounders of trust and time and trust and negotiating outcomes, we can identify the effect of time on the outcome by analysing the associations between time and trust on the one hand and trust and negotiation outcomes on the other hand.

Voting and economic performance

Becher and Donnelly (2013) provide an example of the application of causal mediation analysis to the question of how aggregate economic performance influences individual voting decisions. The authors theorize that the mechanism through which the state of the national economy should influence voting choice is the individual assessments of the economy that people have. Using data on 18 countries for the period between 1979 and 2001, the analysis finds a strong mediated effect but no direct link between the state of the economy and voting choice. Hence, the economy matters, and it matters exclusively through affecting the economic evaluations of individuals, which in their turn influence how people vote.

Conditioning

The last, and by far most popular, strategy to derive valid causal inferences from observational data is based on an altogether different approach. We no longer rely on experimental manipulation or nature to randomly assign units and, as a consequence, create truly comparable groups to approximate a counterfactual situation. Instead, we try to explicitly identify all possible confounding factors and take away their influence, so that the actual relationship we are interested in can shine through. We still want to approximate a counterfactual situation, but the route we take to achieve that is different. We *condition* on potential confounding variables.

Figure 8.6 *A causal model of government attention*

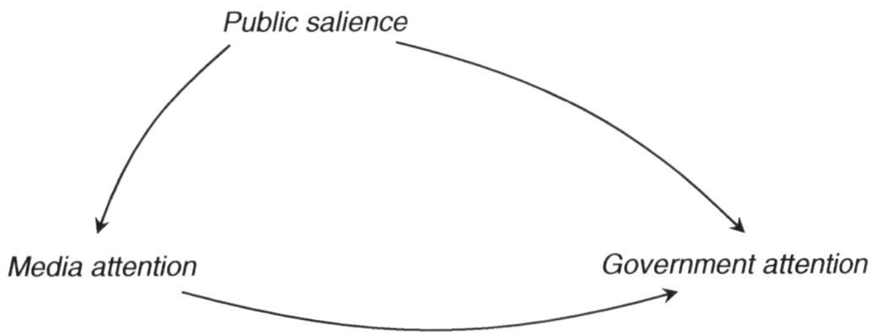

A short example can clarify the basic idea before we move toward the details. Imagine a theory holds that (1) the government pays attention to the issues that the media pays attention to, (2) the media pays attention to the issues that the public finds important, and (3) the government pays attention to the issues that the public finds important. The causal model is summarized in Figure 8.6.

Our assignment is to identify the independent effect of media attention on government attention (if any), net of the effect of public salience. The main explanatory variable is media attention, government attention is the outcome variable, and public salience is a confounder. The level of analysis is an individual issue (such as public safety, unemployment, or the environment).

If we could randomly assign the amount of media attention issues get, conducting the research would be easy: apply varying amounts of media attention to issues, track the amount of government attention they get, compare the numbers, and conclude. But it is not very practical and perhaps outright impossible to randomly assign media attention (feel encouraged to try for yourself). Natural experiments, quasi-random sorting rules, and instrumental variables are not available neither. So we are left with a set of *observations* of how media and government attention covary in some real-world setting (say, we obtain data for the United Kingdom during January 2012). It is tempting to go ahead and just compare the two sets of numbers, but we already know that this will be foolhardy. Even if we observe an association between media and government attention, it could well be that the association is driven entirely by the confounding influence of public salience which we have not taken into account yet. Even if there was absolutely no effect of media on government attention, it would still appear so because when issues gain public salience, both the media and the government increase attention to them. Adding more observations would not really help. We have no instrumental or mediating variables to use. What are we to do?

Well, we could add data on the public salience of issues to the two variables we already have. Then, we can partial out the effect of public salience by holding it constant at different values and examining whether there is any residual association between media and government attention at each level of public salience. In statistical terms, we *condition on* salience. By first taking into account the potential influence of public salience, we let any additional independent influence of media be revealed. And such independent influence would be necessary to call media attention a real cause of government attention.

In sum, if you suspect that a third variable is related to both your explanatory and outcome variables, measure it, partial out its effects, and then compare the residual association between the two main variables of interest. The approach is generalizable so that many potential confounders can be taken into account at the same time. In practice, the 'partialing out' or conditioning will often be done by building a multivariate statistical regression model that would include the main explanatory variable and the confounders on one side of the equation and the outcome variable on the other. The output of such a model run on observational data will be an estimate of the independent (net, additional) effect of the main explanatory variable after all other possible influences (that we have measured and included in the model) have been taken into account and some information about the uncertainty of this estimate (that allows for deciding on the statistical significance of the effect, see below).

And what if we turn out to be wrong about the potential influence of third variables? What if public salience is not in fact a confounder of the link between media and government attention? The good news is that even if we include the variable and it turns out to be unimportant, our estimate of the effect of the main explanatory variable on the outcome would still be generally fine (it would be unbiased), although we would lose efficiency in the process of estimation.

Figure 8.7 shows several situations under which a conditioning strategy would and would not be valid. Again, variables that are measured are circled. The main point is that all paths contaminating the relationship between X and Y need to be blocked by conditioning on a variable that is on the path. For example, in the top-left model, both Z and U need to be measured. But it is enough to measure only one variable on a path (in the top-right model, only Z needs to be measured. At the same time, we have to be careful not to condition on a collider (as in the bottom-right model).

Are we *guaranteed* that our supposed explanatory variable truly causes the outcome if the two remain significantly associated after the influence of all possible confounders we can think of has been taken into account? Disappointingly, the answer is no. First, in the social sciences we can never be sure that the theory has identified all potential confounders so that we can measure and include them. (Now is the time to appreciate again the power of randomization, which, with

Figure 8.7 *Causal identification using conditioning represented in causal diagrams*

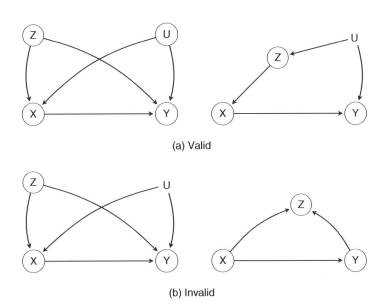

(a) Valid

(b) Invalid

enough numbers, controls for all possible confounders, even those we do not know about!) Second, even if we could include all, there is nothing in the remaining association that excludes the causal effect running in either direction between the two variables (reversed causality). We might *hypothesise* that it is media attention that causes government attention and not the other way round, but there is nothing in the data that can decide – both interpretations would be equally consistent, and it is up to theory, existing knowledge, and additional research to decide which direction of the causal relationship is more plausible. Third, the approach works only if the confounder does not *perfectly* determine the main explanatory variable of interest (which would lead to a problem of colinearity). If media attention perfectly followed public salience, there would be no residual variation to use in order to estimate its independent influence on government attention. For a different example, if all *direct democracies* happened to be always and everywhere in *federal countries*, there would be no way to estimate the independent effect of either of these two on, say, citizen satisfaction with democracy, no matter how many observations we collect and how many other variables we include in the model. Last, the set of variables we condition on must not include colliders (joint effects of the main explanatory variable and the outcome).

Conditioning can be achieved via different means. One, as explained above, is to measure the confounding variable(s) and partial out (adjust for) their effects, calculate the residual association between the main explanatory variable and the outcome for each value of the confounder(s), and get a weighted average of these conditional effects to obtain the average causal effect (this is what a multivariate regression does). A second approach is to block the effect of a confounder by conducting the analysis only for observations for which its value does not change. A third approach is balancing: first, we match observations with the same or very similar characteristics (or some synthetic measure derived from them), but different values of the main explanatory variable, then we calculate the difference in outcomes within each group, and then we average over all groups to get the average causal effect. The matching characteristics (which should be related to the main explanatory variable we are interested in *and* to other potential causes of the outcome) can be just thought of as a different type of confounder. There are other techniques for conditioning (such as stratification) and the individual techniques can be combined (for example, matching on one confounder while the influence of another is blocked by being kept constant). But they all share the core idea of measuring and accounting for additional variables to filter out the real effect between the two variables we are interested in.

The use of conditioning for causal inference is ubiquitous in political science research. We can consider here only two of the many possible examples of published research using this strategy in order to illustrate the strategy in action.

Political appointments and bureaucratic performance

Lewis (2007) is interested in the question of whether political appointees or career bureaucrats make for better public managers. This is a question at the very heart of the study of public administration, and although many normative theories exist as to whether the bureaucracy should be insulated from the political level or not, there is relatively little empirical evidence about the effect of administrative autonomy on organizational performance.

To answer this question, Lewis uses data on 558 US public programs and 229 managers. Some of these programs were headed by career civil servants (bureaucrats) and others by political appointees. To measure the outcome – program performance – the study relies on ratings provided by the Office of Management and Budget that combine various aspects, such as program design, planning, management, and results, to produce an evaluation score – the so-called program assessment rating tool, or PART.

Clearly, an association between PART scores and the management type alone can reveal no causality. There are plenty of possible confounders and concerns for reversed causality. Political appointees might be given programs and agencies that are harder to manage. Or they may take over programs that have already failed under a professional civil servant. Or they may be given bigger and more expensive programs. To take into account these concerns, Lewis presents a multivariate model that includes, in addition to the PART scores and the type of manager, a number of possible confounders, including the program budget, type of program (federal, regulatory, and so on), and organizational characteristics. Even after partialing out these effects, there is still an association between the type of manager and program performance (professional career managers do better than political appointees), so Lewis concludes that leadership matters for organizational outcomes.

In addition, he explores the purported mechanism through which career managers achieve better scores – namely having more experience than political appointees – and shows that the PART scores vary reliably with experience as well, which lends further credibility to his conclusions. While an individual empirical study can never single-handedly overturn normative debates, this analysis provides important evidence with clear policy-making implications for the design and management of public organizations.

Economic shocks, foreign aid, and civil wars

For a rather different example of the application of conditioning strategies to identify causal effects, we look into a study of the effect of foreign aid on civil war. Savun and Tirone (2012) start with the observation that negative economic shocks often lead to civil war and ask whether foreign economic aid can help prevent such wars by attenuating the impact of the economic crisis. They look into a period of 15 years and more than 100 countries. Because certain characteristics of countries, such as the political regime (democracy or not), the relative wealth, and the population, are probably related to both the outcome variable – a civil war conflict – and to the main explanatory variable – the amount of foreign aid received – the study includes these possible confounders in the multivariate regression model. Even after accounting for these contaminating effects, the amount of foreign aid and its interaction with the scale of the economic shock suggest that aid has a preventive effect on civil war.

Summary and additional approaches

Box 8.2 below summarizes the four main strategies for causal inference in large-N observational research.

There are other approaches as well, but they play more of a supporting role and would rarely be used on their own. One such idea is to examine whether the purported causal factor is associated with an outcome that should *not* have been affected if the hypothesized causal relationship were to be true (see Glynn & Gerring, 2013).

Box 8.2   *Main strategies for causal inference in observational large-N research*

1. Natural experiments, including
      Regression discontinuity
2. Instrumental variables
3. Mediation
4. Conditioning
      Adjusting (partialing out)
      Blocking (keeping constant)
      Balancing (matching)

For example, consider that we are interested in the impact of lower intercity highway speed limits on traffic accidents, but all we have is data for two time periods before and after the implementation of a new (lower) speed limit. We can compare the number of accidents before and after the new policy but, even if we find a reduction, we cannot be certain that it is an effect of the speed limit rules. The reduction can result from newer and better cars travelling on that road, better quality of the road itself, less intensive traffic, and so on. Not all of these additional factors can be identified, measured, and controlled for in the analysis. But what if we could compare the number of accidents of a particular type that should *not* have been affected by the speed limit policy change, like accidents due to vehicle malfunction, or accidents involving only trucks which are not subject to the general speed limit? If we see that there is no difference in such accidents before and after the policy change, that would bring additional evidence that the association of accident reduction and the speed limit in the remaining cases is causal. If we see that the number of accidents that should not have been affected also changes similarly to the ones that should have been affected, that would suggest that there are confounding factors that we have not accounted for.

A similar idea is to use the supposed heterogeneity of the effect to help in causal identification. For example, consider the example of the link between rainfall, incomes, and civil wars briefly outlined in the section on instrumental variables. To be a proper instrumental variable, rainfall needs to be associated with the onset of civil war *only* through its effect on income (less rainfall leads to less income, which increases the chances of civil war). As we explained, such assumptions cannot be tested directly. But, if the assumption is correct, rainfall should not be associated at all with civil conflict in situations where it is very weakly or not at all related to income. That is, where income is less dependent on rainfall (because the major economic activity is not dependent on water or there is ample water available throughout the year), there should be no association between rainfall and conflict. Sarsons (2011) uses this reasoning to check whether in Indian regions with economies less sensitive to rainfall there still exists an association between rainfall and conflict. As it turns out, an association exists, which casts doubts on the assumption that rainfall influences conflict only through its effect on income and, as a consequence, it undermines the rationale for its use as an instrument for income.

Common Designs for Causal Inference

In this chapter we already outlined several different strategies for causal inference with observational data and mentioned that the most popular one is to isolate the main causal effect of interest by conditioning, or adjusting for, the confounding influences of other variables. In this section we will present a number of designs that are commonly used in the practice of political science research to achieve this goal. To help organize things, consider the practical designs discussed below as different *ways* of implementing the major strategies to derive causal inference from observational data discussed so far. These practical designs mix matching on prior characteristics of the units, blocking the influence of some confounders, and adjusting for the influence of others.

Empirical research in political science relies on two main axes of variation to derive observations – over time for the same units and across units. These two can be combined, and additional levels can be added by aggregating the units at different levels. Observing the same unit over time leads to time series designs; different units at the same time to cross-sectional designs; different units over time to panel (cross-sectional time series) designs, which can be generalized to multilevel designs if the units are aggregated at different levels (for example, individuals clustered within states). Table 8.5 summarizes these possibilities.

Let's introduce a single research problem in the context of which we can illustrate how each of these designs works. The goal of our hypothetical project is to identify the causal effect of public subsidies to political parties on the number of parties competing at elections. In other words, we want to know whether a policy that provides public money to political parties (perhaps after they reach a certain number of votes at elections) increases politic competition. This public policy can vary over time, across space, and within states as well.

Time series

Pure time series designs trace one unit over time and provide repeated measurements of all variables of interest for this particular unit. In the

Table 8.5   *Types of observational designs*

	Axes of variation		Levels of
	Over time	*Across units*	*aggregation*
Time series	Yes	No	One
Cross-sectional	No	Yes	One
Panel	Yes	Yes	One
Multilevel	Yes or No	Yes	More

simplest case, we have only two observations at two time points. For example, we observe country A in the years 2000 and 2010. Clearly, there is not much to be learned about the effect of any variable, such as party financing policy, if it does not vary at all in the set of observations we have. (Well, there is something we can learn – if the policy stays the same but the outcome varies, we know at least that the policy is neither a complete determinant nor a necessary condition for change of the outcome – see Chapter 9. And using within-case analysis we might still evaluate alternative causal scenarios – see Chapter 10.) But if country A had one policy in 2000 and a different one in 2010, we could take the difference in the outcome variable (number of competing parties) between the two periods as an estimate of the causal effect of the policy (see Figure 8.8a). This would not make for a very convincing causal claim, but it is a start.

The fact that we observe the same country implies that no factor that remains constant over the period can confound the effect of the policy we want to identify. Its geographic position, political regime, electoral system, relative wealth, and so on, can be ruled out as confounders (provided that they don't change between the two observation points), *even* if it is plausible that they are related both to the adoption of the policy and to the outcome. The time series design has blocked their influence.

But there are, of course, many factors that *do* change over time within a country that could still confound the effect of the policy. With two observations, there is not much we can do to filter out their influence, but if we have more observations of the same unit, we can measure, include, and partial out such potential omitted variables in the usual way described in the section on conditioning above.

Even if the policy changes only once during the period of observation (interrupted time series design), we can at least see if the outcome followed any trend *before* the policy change and compare how the extrapolated trend compares with the observations after the change. This would

Figure 8.8 *Examples of time series data*

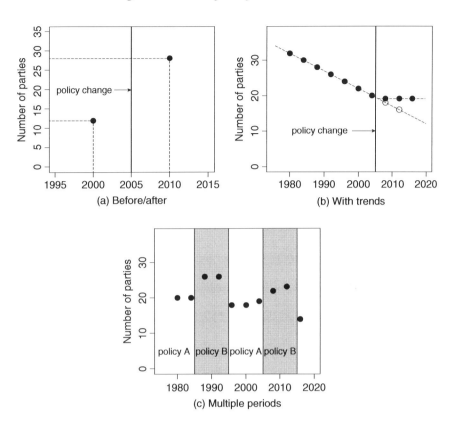

(a) Before/after

(b) With trends

(c) Multiple periods

implicitly control for the major determinants of the outcome, provided that they do not change with the policy.

See, for example, Figure 8.8b. The solid dots represent observations and the empty dots represent *extrapolations* from the pre-policy period to the post-policy one based on the trend that the variable followed prior to the policy change. The effect of the policy can be estimated as the difference between observed values after the policy and the extrapolated values of what would have happened if the policy was not installed.

Even better, we would want to have many changes in the policy over the observation period (Figure 8.8c). This will provide additional leverage to isolate the effect of the party financing policy from other determinants of the number of parties competing at elections. But other sorts of complications arise when we have longer time series and more variation in the explanatory variable over time.

First, we have to decide on the appropriate time lag of the effect (if any). Often, it would not be obvious *when* the effects of the purported cause should become visible. For example, how many years would be needed before more public money for political parties translates into a higher number of parties competing: one year, one election cycle, or more?

Second, the effects of the explanatory variable should be possible to *reset*, once the variable changes values again. That is, there should be no influence carried over from one period of observation to another. Imagine that once parties get some minimum amount of financial resources, they fortify their position in the political system and manage to exclude any newcomers, however endowed with resources they might be. An initial switch in policy from 'no public subsidy' to 'subsidy' will increase the number of active parties, but afterwards any further changes in the policy would exhibit no effect.

Third, the statistical estimation of causal effects (which will be discussed in the next section) requires that observations are *independent* realizations of the data-generating process. In time series analysis, this assumption will often be difficult to sustain. Many political attitudes, for example, are, once set, rather static. Institutions as well tend to remain stable for a long time. Moreover, often even the time unit at which observations are to be taken would be difficult to define. Such stability and ambiguity of defining the unit of observation creates difficulties for the estimation of causal links between variables observed over time (see spurious correlation, Granger & Newbold, 1974). Problems with non-independence of observations can be (partially) corrected, if the potential bias is known.

A more fundamental limitation of time series designs is their uncertain validity beyond the particular unit being observed over time. Even if a causal relationship can plausibly be identified for the unit under study, we have to make assumptions about how well the established causal effect will generalize to other units. The weather might have a big and very persistent over time causal impact on *my* political attitudes but not necessarily on yours. Even if a study convincingly shows that public subsidies for political parties increase political competition in country A, we have to make further assumptions to conclude that adopting the policy in country B would lead to a similar effect.

In some cases, for instance when the study involves fundamental biological processes which differ little from one person to another, it might be plausible to assume that a causal effect found by studying one person over time would vary little in the population and, as a consequence, generalize. In other cases, such assumptions would be debatable at best. But one can theorize how the casual effect might vary in a population and, subsequently, test whether these expectations are correct, which would provide evidence for or against generalizability. And we should not forget that sometimes generalizability beyond the particular unit being researched is not necessary: establishing a causal relationship between economic performance and political stability for the US during the twentieth century via a single country time series design would be important in its own right, and generalization, while desirable, might not be essential.

Cross-sectional designs

While in pure time series designs we follow one unit – a person, a country, an organization, and so on – over time, in pure cross-sectional designs we compare a set of units – persons, countries, organizations, and so on – at a single point in time. In the simplest case, we might only have two cases to compare. Strategies for cross-sectional causal inference with a small number of units to observe will be discussed in detail in Chapter 9. Here we focus on the situation in which more than a handful of observations are available.

In large-N cross-sectional designs we try to identify a causal effect by comparing the distribution of the outcome across the subsets of units defined by a particular value of the main explanatory variable. If the latter takes only two values – such as a policy or an institution that can be either absent or present – we compare the two groups. For example, we can observe which European countries provided public subsidies for political parties in 2014 and examine the distribution (or just the average) of the number of political parties competing at the last elections in the two groups of countries: the ones that have, and the ones that do not have the policy. (Note that even if our observations are taken at different points of time for different units, the design is still cross-sectional if we do not have more than observation per unit over time).

Although we observe a set of units at a single point of time, we usually want to derive expectations about would would happen if a single unit or a collection of individual units experience a change in the explanatory variable. We observe countries A to Z, some of which have public subsidies for parties and others do not, but what normally interests us in the context of explanatory research is how would polit-ical competition *in a particular country*, A, change, if the country was to adopt or drop the policy. For a different example, suppose that we observe a set of poor families, some of whom have access to free school buses and others who do not, and the outcome of interest is whether families send their kids to school. There are a number of relevant causal questions to ask. Would family X start sending their kids to school if they had access to a school bus? How much would school attendance increase if all families had access to school buses? What is the optimal way to distribute a limited number of school buses to maximize school attendance?

It is only with many and very strong assumptions that cross-sectional designs can provide answers to such causal inquiries, as they are prone to all the threats to inference from observational data discussed in the previous sections, unless the explanatory variable is distributed randomly in the set of units (which is very rarely the case). For example, assume that the group of European countries with public subsidies for political parties in 2014 has on average a lower number of parties competing in elections than the group without the policy. The difference could be an effect of the policy. But it is also plausible that countries that have a low number of competing parties have adopted the policy *as a response* to this phenomenon (reversed causality). Or it could be that both having public subsidies and a low number of active parties at elections are direct or indirect results of some feature of the electoral systems of these countries, such as the electoral threshold (see, for example, Casal Bertoa & Spirova, 2013), which would constitute confounder bias.

All these problems of reversed causality and confounded relationships almost always loom large in cross-sectional designs, because the only set of variables that are blocked by design are common time effects. For instance, if we study the distribution of asylum-seeking applications in Western Europe in, say, the year 2000 as a function of the economic attractiveness of the host countries, the relevant factors the influence of which is blocked would be the ones related to the overall demand for asylum at this particular point in time – such as civil conflicts, wars, and famines – and then only if they affect all host countries in the same way: so geographical distance to the conflict should not matter, for example (see Toshkov, 2014).

In view of these considerations, we have to conclude that cross-sectional designs are rather limited in their potential to support causal claims, because they need to control for many possible biases and selection effects through other forms of conditioning than blocking – namely adjusting and matching, both of which require the measurement and inclusion of relevant variables and a sample of units that has enough variation in these variables.

Panel designs

It is only natural to join observations across time and space to make use of the combined strengths of time series and cross-sectional studies. The resulting designs are called panel, or time series cross-sectional. (Pooled data are similar but the difference from panel is that the cross-sections do not have to be the same over time). In panel designs, several units are observed at a number of points in time. For a simple illustration, look at Figure 8.9, which shows two groups of countries A and B: in period I (2000) both groups had no public subsidies for political parties; in period II (2010) group A had adopted this policy while group B still had not.

Figure 8.9 *An example of panel data and the difference-in-differences estimator*

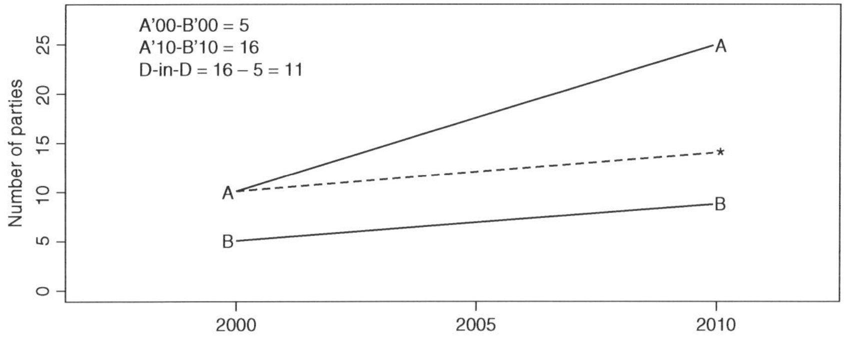

A'00-B'00 = 5
A'10-B'10 = 16
D-in-D = 16 − 5 = 11

Difference-in-differences

What is the likely causal effect of the policy? Given this set-up, there are different estimates we can make that rely on different sets of assumptions. As in pure time series designs, we can take the effect to be the difference in the outcome for countries A between 2010 and 2000. Or, as in pure cross-sectional designs, we can take it to be the difference between countries A and countries B in 2010. Finally, we can take into account both axes of variation: first, we measure the difference between A and B in 2000; then do the same for 2010; and finally we take the difference of these two differences. This approach is, appropriately, called difference-in-differences. Equivalently, we can compute it as the difference in the before/after comparisons of the two groups of countries. We already mentioned the difference-in-differences estimator of the causal effect of interest in Chapter 7 in the context of experimental research.

What do we gain in relying on the difference-in-differences rather than on the simpler comparisons over time or across units? First, the pre-policy comparison (A and B in 2000) takes into account any stable systematic differences between the two groups of countries. Second, the trajectory of countries B over time takes into account any common trends that would have affected all countries. In essence, the difference-in-differences estimate compares countries A to a counterfactual (represented by a star [*] in Figure 8.9) created on the basis of two pieces of information: (1) the changes countries B experienced during the period of observation, and (2) how countries A and B differed prior to the policy intervention.

We still have to make assumptions to interpret the difference-in-differences estimate as a causal effect, but these would be weaker and generally more plausible than in the case of either pure cross-sectional or time-series designs. The main assumption is that there is nothing

Table 8.6   *Blocking by design*

Design	Time series	Cross-sectional	Panel
Estimator	(before/after)	(contemp. difference)	(D-in-Ds)
Common time trends	No	Yes	Yes
Individual time trends	No	No	No
Stable unit features	Yes	No	Yes
Variable unit features	No	No	No
Estimated causal effect	ETT	ATE	ATE

relevant for the outcome that affected *differentially* countries A and B during the period of observation. Another is that countries in the two groups will react in the same way to the policy (homogeneity). And yet another one is that there is no interference between the countries (so the choice of policy for country C has no influence on the outcome in country D).

To sum up, Table 8.6 lists the sources of variation contaminating the causal effect we want to estimate that are blocked by particular observational designs. The before/after estimator of the causal effect used in time series designs blocks the influence of features of the observed unit which remain stable. The contemporaneous difference estimator used by cross-sectional designs blocks the influence of common time trends. The difference-in-differences estimator used in panel designs combines the two but is still vulnerable to differential changes in the units. Finally, the last row of the table points out that the causal effect estimated by time series designs is the ETT – the effect of the treatment on the treated (introduced in Chapter 7) – and a further assumption is needed to interpret this as the average causal effect (ATE).

If we are not willing to commit to some of these assumptions, we can still provide estimates of the likely effect of the policy, but they would be in the form of intervals rather than point predictions (Manski, 2007). That is, we can identify, on the basis of the data, an interval of values within which the causal effect of interest can be reasonably expected to lie. For example, the difference-in-differences might suggest that the average causal effect of the party-financing policy is an increase in the number of parties competing at elections by five. On the basis of weaker assumptions, the data might bound the likely effect between –1 and 9. While less precise, the interval might reflect better the actual uncertainty of the estimate derived from an observational study. In the words of Charles Manski and John Pepper (2011, p. 13):

Imposing assumptions strong enough to yield a definitive finding is alluring, but strong assumptions may be inaccurate, yielding flawed and conflicting conclusions.

If there are reasons to believe that the assumptions necessary for point identification of a causal effect (for example, via a difference-in-differences or a before/after comparison) are violated, reporting intervals of the likely causal effect rather than, or in addition to, a point estimate is the more prudent approach. (Note that these 'causal' intervals are different from the statistical confidence intervals that reflect sampling variability of the estimate; for the latter, see below.)

When the main explanatory variable of interest can take more than two values (for example, the amount of public subsidy given to parties rather than the existence of any subsidy), the difference-in-differences approach as such cannot characterize the relationship between the policy and the outcome. But the ideas just discussed about how the underlying structure of variation in the data and assumptions need to be combined for causal inference are carried over to the new context. With more data available we can complement the blocking of certain influences achieved by the panel design with adjusting for the influence of any remaining confounders and/or by matching on certain characteristics of the units.

Synthetic case controls

Often we are interested in the effect of the introduction of some novel policy or institution. Being novel, the policy or institution could be present only in one state, so even though we have access to panel data (many states over time), in practice the relevant comparison would hinge on a single case.

A relatively new method developed to use panel data for such questions is the so-called synthetic case control (Abadie & Gardeazabal, 2003; Abadie, Diamond, & Hainmueller, 2015). Here is how it works. Say we have 50 states, only one of which (Colorado) has adopted a policy (soft drugs liberalization), and we are interested in the impact of the policy on some outcome of societal relevance (such as hard drugs use). We have managed to obtain yearly measures of the outcome for fifteen years before and two years after Colorado has instated its policy.

In a nutshell, the idea of synthetic case control is to approximate the counterfactual of what would have happened in Colorado, had it not adopted the policy, from the information about what happened in the other states. However, the comparison is not made to any single state from the remaining 49 (or a simple average of those), but to an artificial 'case' which is created as a weighted average of the real 49 states so that the trajectory of the 'artificial' case resembles the trajectory of Colorado *prior to the policy introduction* as much as possible. In practice, first, using the data from the 15 years before the policy was introduced, we make a predictive model of drug use in Colorado over time as a function (weighted average) of the same variable in the remaining 49 states. States with developments that resemble closely the ones in Colorado will contribute a lot to this weighted average, while states that experience divergent trends will contribute little or not at all. Then, as a second step, we extrapolate from this predictive model for the period after the policy introduction based on the real developments in the 49 states after the policy change in Colorado. Third, and finally, we compare the projections with the realized values of drug use in Colorado. The difference would be the estimate of the causal effect of the soft-drugs liberalization policy.

Synthetic case controls approach the idea of causal identification from panel data differently, but the underlying rationale is the same: create a comparison that approximates best a counterfactual situation. The method and design can be used for retrospective policy evaluation and, if it is reasonable to assume that different units will react in the same way to a policy innovation, as a prospective analysis of expected average causal effects as well.

Multilevel designs

The ideas behind panel designs can be generalized even further if the variables can be aggregated at different levels. For example, observations of individual students over time (which would provide panel data) can be aggregated in schools, and observations of individual voters can be aggregated in voting districts, which can, in their turn be aggregated in states. More levels of aggregation provide additional sources of variation and, as a consequence, can be helpful in identifying and estimating causal effects. However, one has to be careful that the aggregation or disaggregation provides real information rather than just an artificial formal increase in the number of observations.

There are many different ways to analyse multilevel (also called hierarchical) large-N data. Gelman and Hill (2007) is an excellent introduction to the issues involved and presents a comprehensive overview of the possibilities available to the researcher. From a design perspective, multilevel data provides more opportunities for blocking (turning-off) additional sources of confounding than the simple time series cross-sectional panel. For instance, turning again to the public financing for parties problem, it could be the case that in the same countries the rules for party financing differ at the subnational level. Contemporaneous comparisons at this level will implicitly control for all time-related and country-specific factors. Not all potential problems would be solved – selection into the policy would still be probably non-random – but the additional dimension of variation can complement over time and cross-country comparisons for additional analytical leverage. One should be careful, however, when drawing individual-level inference from data aggregated at higher levels (see the problem of ecological inference discussed below).

To conclude this part of the chapter, let's recap the exposition so far. First, causal inference from observational data is difficult and prone to a number of biases. Second, there are several different strategies to address these potential problems, each embracing a different approach – find a (quasi-)random source of variation, focus on the mechanism, or condition (block, match, and/or adjust) on confounders. Time series, cross-sectional, panel, and multilevel models provide different ways to implement the conditioning strategy by blocking certain classes of potential confounders, while remaining vulnerable to the influence of others. Large-N causal inference is a function of design, not the number of observations. But with more observations, we can rule out chance as an alternative explanation of any associations we see, and we are better able not only to *identify* but also to *estimate* causal effects.

Estimating Causal Effects

Assume for the moment that we have managed to devise a credible identification strategy for the causal effect of interest – either through an experiment, an instrument, or a mediator, or by conditioning on all the confounders. We are left with a residual association between the main explanatory variable and an outcome variable which could reveal any causal connections between the two. The next step would be to estimate this association. But before we are ready to do that, we have to get more precise as to the meaning of 'association'.

Varieties of association

Two variables can be associated in a variety of ways. In principle, large-N analysis assumes probabilistic relationships, which means that each value of one variable can be associated with an entire distribution of values for another variable. Assume for the moment that we have a binary explanatory variable (such as the presence or absence of a seatbelt policy) and a continuous outcome variable (such as the number of traffic accident victims) observed in 100 countries that differ with respect to the policy. For each of the two states of the world [policy] and [no policy] there will be a *distribution* of victims per country due to random variation in the outcome, even after we have taken into account possible confounding variables. We can choose to focus on the difference in the means of the two distributions as the quantity of interest and, provided that we have a credible causal identification strategy, declare that this is the causal effect we are interested in.

But there are other aspects of the two distributions we can compare that would also provide information about how policy affects the number of traffic victims. For instance, we could compare the medians of the two distributions. Alternatively, we could compare how spread out the two distributions are if we care not only about the central tendencies but also about the *variability* of outcomes under the two policies. If the outcome is a binary variable, we could compare odd ratios or risk ratios instead of a difference in means. If both the explanatory and the outcome variables are continuous, their association can be summarized by the correlation coefficient, or by the covariance, and a host of other measures. In fact, there are statistical techniques that would allow us to compare entire distributions.

In practice, political scientists focus overwhelmingly on the difference in means or, more generally, on the mean effect of one variable on another, but this need not be the case. Two rather different distributions of outcomes can have the same mean. For some applications, the mean would not capture all aspects of the distribution that we care about.

Size of the association

Once we have established that two variables (or rather, the distributions of two variables) are causally related using one or a combination of the strategies described in the previous sections of this chapter, we would want to quantify the direction and size of the association. Such estimates would provide answers to questions such as: If we increase the value of the explanatory variable by one point, how would the outcome variable change? If we install a new traffic policy, what would be the expected number of traffic victims? What would be the probability of a revolution if a country experiences economic collapse next year?

Questions like these demand that we quantify our conclusion about the causal effect of the explanatory variable. A quantitative estimate would indicate the direction of the effect (positive or negative) and the size. For example, the size of the effect can be expressed as a regression coefficient or as a predicted probability of the outcome for a certain value of the explanatory variable. The scientific field of statistics provides the methods to estimate these quantities. In this text we cannot get into how the estimation works but can only focus on some fundamental issues of interpretation.

To express a causal effect as a single number we have to make a lot of *additional* assumptions. The more precise the estimate, the more and the stronger assumptions need to be maintained. These assumptions needed for estimation are statistical, and they are distinct from (though related to) the causal assumptions we have to make to identify a causal effect in the first place. The precise assumptions depend on the particular estimation method used. For example, a multivariate linear regression model would assume that the effects are linear and additive, and that the residual errors of the model are independent, have equal variance, and are normally distributed (Gelman & Hill, 2007).

Uncertainty and statistical significance

The conditions and strategies for causal inference discussed above help with the problems of reversed causality, selection bias, omitted variable bias, and so on, but they do not address the problem that any association we observe in the data can be due simply to chance or random variations. Tests for statistical significance examine precisely this possibility and, again based on certain assumptions specific to each test, can quantify the extent to which any association we observe in the data is likely to have been produced by chance alone. Many people, including some political scientists, confuse tests for statistical significance with tests for causality, and statistical significance with substantive importance of the effects. You should already realize that statistical significance should not be confused with causality, because chance is only one of the reasons why two variables can be associated but not causally related (see again the list in Box 8.1). It is also important to explain why statistical significance should not be confused with substantive importance of the effects.

To begin with, imagine that we observe *some* difference between the probabilities of political revolution under different economic conditions. How do we decide when the difference is big enough to be significant? The classic route to approach this problem is (1) to construct a 'null' hypothesis that there is *absolutely no difference* between the probability of revolution under economic collapse and under a different economic situation; (2) calculate what probabilities would we expect to see in the data, if the null hypothesis were true but the occurrence of revolutions still varied for other random reasons, (3) examine how these made-up probabilities compare to the ones observed in reality; (4) conclude: (4a) if, on the one hand, the empirically observed difference in probabilities turns out to be very far away from the range one would expect if the null hypothesis of no difference were true, we can conclude that it is unlikely (one can get very precise how unlikely) that the difference is due to chance only. This does not imply that our theory is true. It only means that if in reality there was exactly zero difference in the expected probability of revolution under different economic conditions, it is unlikely that we would have observed the data that we did. (4b) If, on the other hand, the empirically observed difference in probabilities is within the range one would expect if the null hypothesis of no difference were true, we can conclude that the observed difference *could* be due to chance only. This does not imply that our theory is false. It only means that the observed data are compatible with a hypothesis of no difference.

What we have just outlined is the logic of standard statistical hypothesis testing and statistical significance. Currently, the use of statistical significance tests to decide whether some variable is causally related to an outcome of interest is ubiquitous and even required by many academic journals in the field of political science. Usually, one reports empirical findings with reference to statistical significance: if there is less than 5 percent chance that the observed difference would have been realized if the 'null' hypothesis of no difference held, the relationship is considered 'statistically significant'. The threshold of 5 percent is largely arbitrary and different standards, such as 10 percent or 1 percent, are also often used. Its ubiquitousness notwithstanding, serious objections have been raised to the dominance of statistical significance.

One, statistical significance does not necessarily imply substantive or practical significance. Imagine that a statistical test results in the rejection of the hypothesis of exactly zero difference in the probability of revolution under different economic conditions. Does it mean that the difference is large? No, it only means that it is unlikely to be exactly zero, but it could still be arbitrarily small. A very, very small difference, corresponding to a very, very small effect of the economy on the probability of revolutions, can still be 'statistically significant'. In some contexts a very, very small yet statistically significant effect can be important. For example, if we were to discover a very small but distinguishable from zero causal effect of some variable on cancer survival, that would still be important given the scale of damage the disease inflicts and the number of people who suffer from it. In other contexts, only effects of sufficiently great substantive size would be truly important. If we estimate that periods of divided government (the situation where the main law-making institutions are run by different parties, such as a Democratic president cohabiting with a Republican Congress in the US) lead on average to two fewer bills adopted per year than periods of united government, even if the effect is statistically significant, it would probably have very limited practical importance.

At the same time, an effect that is not statistically significant can still be substantively important. An effect can fail to be statistically significant, one of the reasons being that there is no effect in the real world. Another reason could be, however, that there is in fact an effect that works very differently in different subpopulations. For example, if economic collapse increased the probability of political revolution under democratic regimes but had no effect (or even had a negative one) under repressive political regimes, in a dataset that lumps together both situations we would fail to find a statistically significant effect, although in reality the effect is 'real' and big enough substantively, but (unbeknownst to us) it works differently for different cases.

Since research in political science and especially in public policy and administration is often applied, providing information about the likely sizes of causal effects is even more important. Because results from research do and should assist decision-making, information about the likely effect size of policy interventions, institutional changes, and so on is vital, and the researchers should not consider the analysis of data complete once they have rejected or failed to reject a hypothesis that the treatment effect is exactly zero (which is what statistical tests for significance and p-values essentially do).

Two, with access to arbitrarily many observations, any effect or difference can attain statistical significance. Mathematically, statistical significance is a function of the number of observations. With an increasing number of observations a statistical hypothesis test will declare decreasingly small effects and differences significant. At the limit, any effect, however small, can gain statistical significance. Consider an analysis that estimates that having a secondary eduction decreases the probability of voting for an extreme right party by 0.005 percent. With enough observations, it is possible to discover that the difference eduction makes is distinguishable from zero, hence 'significant', but under what circumstances could we consider it important?

Three, even if a statistical test finds that an effect is unlikely to be due to chance alone, there is still *some* probability left that in fact there is no real relationship between the variables (this would be an example of the Type I error, or a false positive, see again Table 7.2). More precisely, using the conventional level of statistical significance (5 percent), we accept being wrong (mistaking randomness for a real effect) one time in twenty. This chance can be acceptable or not given the application of the analysis – if it is a question of life or death, a much higher standard would certainly be called for. But more importantly, the one in twenty chance is estimated under the assumption that we run a single test. But in reality, researchers could run hundreds and even thousands of different statistical tests before deciding which one to report. The different tests can involve different subsets of the population, different functional forms of the supposed relationship, and so on. Obviously, when one runs twenty tests each having a one-in-twenty chance of being wrong and subsequently reports only one of these tests, the test statistic cannot be taken at face value. An adjustment is called for, but it is quite hard to formulate precisely how and when the calculation of statistical significance should be adjusted to reflect the multiple tests being conducted before one arrives at the final analysis and decides which results to report and which to shelve.

Four, the calculation of statistical significance requires a number of technical assumptions about the distributions of the variables (normal or other), their variances, and the exact nature of the relationship between the variables (linear or other). If these assumptions are violated, the results of the tests could be misleading. In general, with more observations the influence of these assumptions gets smaller and it becomes possible to check some of them. But the point remains.

In sum, there are good reasons to be cautious in using statistical significance to decide when an observed difference in two conditional probabilities is big enough to be important and, more generally, when a relationship between two variables is systematic and real rather than illusory. Several recommendations can be made in order to address the problems described above. First, it is always advisable to focus on, present, and discuss the substantive size of the effects. Statistical significance is only part of a package of considerations one should have in mind to decide whether an effect is important or not. Second, one should discuss the range of values (intervals) estimating the strength of the hypothesized relationship that is compatible with the observed data rather than focus on a single piece of information such as significance or a point estimate of the average effect. Third, the reported uncertainty associated with the estimated effects should honestly reflect the data exploration (number of different tests) conducted before the results are presented in a strict hypothesis-testing template.

Linearity and beyond

We mentioned that two variables can be linked in a variety of ways. For example, the link can be linear, so that each additional percent rise in unemployment is associated with, say, a 2.5 percent drop in presidential approval, no matter whether unemployment goes from 1 to 2 percent or from 80 to 81 percent. Often, linearity would not be a good approximation of how the cause affects the outcome. Non-linearity means that the size of the effect of the explanatory variable differs for different values of the explanatory variable, for different expected values of the outcome variable, and/or for different combinations of values of the covariates included in the model. For example, the effect of a change in unemployment from 10 to 11 percent might have a much more dramatic effect on presidential approval than a change from 1 to 2 percent. The effect could also be different if the president's approval ratings are high compared to when the approval ratings are already very low (so that only the hard core supporters whose opinions would not be sensitive to unemployment news still approve of the president). And the effect of unemployment could be different depending on a covariate – for instance, whether the country is at war or not (this last non-linearity arising from an interaction effect).

How to account for non-linearities in the statistical models is a data analysis problem and as such falls outside the scope of this text. However, it is important to be aware of this issue as it has implications for research design as well. First, the form of relationship to be expected between a hypothesized cause and effect should be addressed during theory development, and ideally hypotheses should specify not only the likely direction and plausible size of the expected effect but also the form of the association – linear, quadratic, increasing, decreasing, step functions, or something else. Second, in general, we need more observations to obtain good estimates of a non-linear than of a linear relationship. It is easy to grasp why. If we are sure that the relationship is linear, observations that fall within any range of the explanatory variable and any range of the outcome variable would be equally relevant for estimating the effect (which after all is the same everywhere). But if the effect is non-linear, we need more data to estimate the relationship in its different parts. Moreover, we need observations that cover the whole range of possible variation of the variables. If the effect of unemployment on presidential approval is much stronger when approval is near the 50 percent mark than when it is below 20 percent, no amount of observations of approval ratings above 20 percent is going to help us much in estimating what effect unemployment has when presidents have already lost the sympathy of most people. (In a linear world, we could extrapolate even if the data did not fall within this range). In short, selection bias is even more of a problem when the hypothesized relationships are non-linear, and we should get observations along the entire range of variation for the explanatory and outcome variables, and for different combinations of the covariates as well.

Limited outcomes

The issue of non-linearity is closely related to the type of variables we study. Non-linearities *might* arise when all our variables are continuous and can take any values (positive, negative, zero). But they are *bound* to arise when the outcome can take only a range of specific values, such as binary, categorical, count, or other variables with limited variation. For example, statistical models of count data (say, the number of months an international negotiation lasts) are non-linear by design. There is a range of statistical tools that are appropriate for different types of variables, but we cannot go into the details of how to analyse and model them. We should note, however, that the level of measurement (see Chapter 4) is intimately related to the type and form of relationships one should expect to encounter in the data. And, to repeat, these complications call for more, and more spread out, data.

The Design of Large-N Observational Research

So far we have outlined the logic of large-N analysis, explained the problems of inferring causation from association, identified several strategies for casual inference, and outlined how the estimation of causal effects works. With this background, we are ready to focus on the more specific issues of research design. In observational studies, the crucial design decisions the researcher makes are which (and how many) cases and which variables to observe. Additional concerns related to the unit of analysis, the measurement of variables, and so on are mostly derivative of these two basic issues.

The main lessons for research design have already been apparent in the discussion so far. First, even if you are interested only in a single, possibly causal, relationship between one explanatory variable and one outcome, you have to consider a broader network of relationships in order to identify potential confounders, mediators, moderators, or instrumental variables to successfully identify the main effect you care about. Second, even if you are interested in a small set of cases (or even a single one), often you would need to broaden the set of observations so that you have the right type of cases to identify the causal effect of interest. Even if all you care about is the effect of education on political participation in the Netherlands in the 2000s, you might need to collect information on other variables, such as wealth and unemployment, and on other contexts (such as different countries and/or time periods) to have any chance of answering the original question.

Variable selection

Let's first consider in detail the question of which variables to include (meaning, to observe, measure, and employ in the analysis). A useful way to organize the process of variable selection is to draw the causal graphs (see Chapter 6) of the process you study. This would make clear not only the relationships you expect to hold and the assumptions you make but also the variables that you *should*, the variables that you *might*, and the variables that you *should not* include in the research.

Table 8.7 summarizes the general advice that can be offered with respect to the three main strategies for causal inference (natural experiments are subsumed under instrumental variables). Clearly, at the very least, the main explanatory variable of interest and the outcome variables should always be included in the study. Typically, in contemporary political science researchers would include several 'explanatory' (also called independent) variables in their statistical models and give all of them causal interpretations. This practice is too optimistic. As evident from the discussion so far, and even more so from what follows, it is hard enough to identify credibly a causal effect even of one single variable at a time. Trying to do that for several variables in the same statistical model requires heroic, and rarely justified, assumptions. It is more productive to focus on the effect of a single potential causal factor and tailor the research design to identify the effect of this one particular variable, rather than aim for more and achieve nothing. The reflex to include more and more variables often arises from confusing predictive and causal models and goals.

Table 8.7 *A guide to selecting which variables to include*

Type of variable	Causal strategy		
	Instruments	*Mediation*	*Conditioning*
Main explanatory variable (MEV)	*Should*	*Should*	*Should*
Outcome variable	*Should*	*Should*	*Should*
Instrumental variable	*Should*	*Should not*	*Should not*
Mediating variable	*Should not*	*Should*	*Should not*
Confounding variable	*May*	*May*	*Should*
Other cause of the outcome	*May*	*May*	*May*
Other effect of MEV	*May*	*May*	*May*
Effect of the outcome	*Should not*	*Should not*	*Should not*
Shared effect of MEV and outcome	*Should not*	*Should not*	*Should not*
Shares one cause with the MEV and another with outcome	*Should not*	*Should not*	*Should not*
Estimated causal effect	ETT	LATE	ATE (in general)

For strategies that rely on conditioning or on mediation to identify a causal effect, one should never *condition* on instrumental variables. But for an identification strategy built around an instrumental variable, one should, of course, measure and include an instrument in the analysis. However, instead of including the instrument as a covariate in a one-step regression, the analysis would proceed in two steps: first, the main explanatory variable is regressed on the instrument and, then, the outcome variable is regressed on the predictions from the first stage regression.

Similarly, one should not *condition* on a mediating variable or on *its* proxies and effects, because that would take away the causal effect of interest. A different way to express the same idea is to say that post-treatment variables should not be controlled for. However, if we are following a causal mediation analysis strategy, we will include the mediating variable. But the analysis would proceed differently from a one-stage regression in order to tease out the mediated effect, which is assumed to be uncontaminated by confounders (Imai et al., 2011).

Confounding variables should always be included for strategies that rely on conditioning to identify a causal effect. Moreover, *all* potential confounding variables need to be measured and entered into the analysis. Although instrumental variable and mediation approaches do not, strictly speaking, require the inclusion of confounders (if their assumptions hold), one would usually enter confounding variables in the equation as there is little harm and a potential benefit in doing so. This refers to confounders of the link between the main explanatory variable and the outcome. Confounders of the relationship between an instrument and the outcome should always be included in an instrumental variable approach. Similarly, a confounder of the link between a mediator and the outcome should also be included.

Should you include other alternative causes of the outcome that act independently from the main explanatory variable? Such variables are not confounders, so they do not *need* to be measured. However, including them brings no bias and they can help estimate the main causal effect we are after, because they would account for part of the unexplained variance. But we have to be careful not to induce collider bias in the system of all included variables.

We may also include other effects of the main explanatory variable. That would create no bias, and if such proxies are not affected by a confounder that we cannot measure, they can be useful. However, we have to be careful that such effects are not jointly produced by the main explanatory variable *and* by the outcome of interest, as conditioning on such a variable will induce collider bias.

In general, it is *never* a good idea to include in the analysis – hence it is not worth the trouble to collect information on – variables that are *effects* of the outcome. Something else to avoid is conditioning on a variable that shares one cause with the main explanatory variable and another with the outcome. If such a variable is not directly affecting the main explanatory variable and the outcome, including it will create collider bias. If it is, including it will still create collider bias, but excluding it will allow for bias due to confounding.

There are additional scenarios we can imagine about even more complex links between the variables in the system. However, without some formalization the discussion will get rather hard to follow. The best approach on which to base decisions about whether some variable should or may be included in the analysis, beyond the cases discussed here, is to draw a causal diagram that represents all assumed links in the system and then to systematically analyse the graph to see whether including or excluding a certain variable will create bias in identifying the main causal relationship we care about or not. The rules and algorithms for such analysis are given, for example, in Pearl (2009b).

The decisions about which variables may, should, and should not be included are rather tricky but still follow a certain logic once we know whether the variable is an instrument, a moderator, a confounder, and so on. In practice, we do not. All we can observe in a dataset is the *associations* between variables and, in the same way that an association cannot without assumptions support causation, associations or their lack cannot determine whether a variable is an instrument or a

confounder, for example. We can observe that rainfall is highly correlated with crop yields and that it is not correlated with civil war (which,
if taken at face value, would imply that it is a valid instrument), but
we do not know whether the lack of association between rainfall and
civil war is due to (1) lack of a causal connection between the two or
(2) a more complex story in which the direct effect of rainfall is can-
celled by some other variable in the data we happen to observe. Because
data alone can never reveal the system of relationships between variables we observe, our *assumptions* play an unavoidable role in deciding
which variables to observe, measure, and include in the analysis. Such
assumptions should be transparent, based on existing knowledge, and
whenever possible should be checked against data. And we can always
examine whether we reach different conclusions based on different sets
of assumptions and, more generally, how sensitive our inferences about
the main causal effect are to different assumptions.

The discussion so far considered the choice of variables to include for
one particular analysis at a time. It clarified what should and what should
not enter a single, self-contained line of causal inquiry. But in practice
we can, of course, combine different lines of inquiry to tackle the same
question. We can complement an instrumental variable approach with
an analysis explicitly controlling for confounder effects (conditioning).
And we can run a number of models including different sets of potential
confounders. If the results based on alternative strategies point in the
same direction, that would increase our confidence that the effects we
discover are real rather than statistical artefacts.

Furthermore, even when we cannot avoid all potential biases due to
the omission of some variable that should be controlled for or the inclusion of some variable the status of which we cannot ascertain, in many
cases we can at least gauge the likely direction and size of the bias. An
educated guess about its likely size and direction can help us judge how
the main results would change if the bias were to exist. In some cases,
a causal effect we find could actually only be strengthened if we could
avoid a certain bias. In others, the effect of the potential bias, even if
real, would probably be comparatively small to reverse the significance
or direction of the main findings. In sum, attack the research problem
with different causal identification strategies, each of which should follow the variable selection guidance offered above; explore the sensitivity
of the results to different assumptions about what influences what in the
system of variables; and gauge the likely impact of bias due to variables
that cannot be measured or that we do not know the status of.

Case selection

Having clarified the selection of variables, we move to the second major
issue of research design in observational large-N studies, which is case

selection. To rephrase the definition from Chapter 5, in the context of large-N research a case is a collection of observations on variables for a single unit (which can be an individual, a country, a time period, and so on). Case selection is about which and how many of these units to observe and include in the analysis.

Case selection answers two concerns. The first one is about the *internal* validity of the causal conclusions for the set of actual cases observed. The second is about the external validity of the conclusions, or their generalizability beyond the cases being observed to some large population. To recap, external validity refers to the credibility of the results for the target population, and we could speculate about the potential generalizability of the findings beyond the target population to the broader population as well.

Which observations?
There are several routes we can follow to make causal inferences about a target population from the analysis of a sample. The first and most convincing one would be to select the sample randomly from the target population. With enough numbers (see below) a random selection ensures that the sample will resemble as closely as possible the population. By implication, the causal relationships we find in the sample will be expected to hold in the target population as well. Generalization beyond the target population is always based on assumptions only. A useful demarcation line between the target and the potential population can be drawn if we ask: is it possible that a particular unit could have been selected and observed in the study? If yes, the unit is part of the target population and, provided that a random sample was drawn, the conclusions from the analysis should hold for it. If not, we can only speculate if they would do. To give another simple example, if we select randomly to study 900 Dutch citizens above the age of 18 from the Dutch census (or a random sample based on the census), we can be pretty sure that the results of the research would generalize to the population of Dutch individuals over 18. Whether the results would be valid for Germans, for South Africans, or for Dutch people 20 years from now, is a matter that cannot be resolved by the sample data.

In addition to, or in combination with, random sampling we can make sure that the sample resembles the population by explicitly selecting the same proportion of, say, males and females in the sample as there is in the population. The problem with this strategy is that we can never be completely certain in advance what the relevant variables are. Ideally, the sample should not be biased with regard to the outcome variable, main explanatory variable, confounders, mediators, moderators, and so on, but we have already explained why identifying all these variables in advance is extremely hard.

At the same time, for many of the same reasons that random *assignment* is not possible, random *sample selection* is often infeasible as well.

Social science researchers have to work in situations where little control over sample selection is possible or in situations where the only observations available are what are often referred to as convenience samples. For some research problems and in some settings this is not necessarily a problem. For example, much of the empirical research in psychology, social psychology, and cognitive science is done on convenience samples of college students. But as long as one is ready to assume that the processes being studied work in largely the same ways for all people, irrespective of age, socio-economic status, or cultural background, the results could well be relevant for a larger population than the observed students.

In other settings, however, working with convenience samples could severely bias the results of observational causal analysis, often rendering them completely untrustworthy. Moreover, the bias can work differently depending on whether the selection rule is related only to the values of the outcome, to the values of the outcome and the main explanatory variable simultaneously, or to some other relevant variable, such as a moderator.

Let us first consider selection bias arising from a sample selection rule related to the values of the outcome variable. For example, this would be the case if we select for study only politicians who win elections, only agencies that are subjects of a scandal, only conflicts that escalate to wars, and only international organizations that survive over time. Selection on the outcome (selection on the dependent variable) will always lead to bias in the estimate of the main causal effect we are interested in. The amount of bias is bound by the size of the effect and grows with the correlation between the outcome variable and the selection rule. The direction of the bias is opposite to the effect of the main explanatory variable: if the effect is positive, the bias will be negative, and vice versa. This means that in a sample biased by selection correlated with the outcome variable, the effects will be underestimated and biased towards zero. In other words, it will be more difficult to find an effect, even if one exists (Type II error).

But if the selection rule is related to the outcome *and* to the main explanatory variable, the effect of the bias will be different. For example, if the selection rule that determines which cases we observe and which we do not is correlated with the values of both the main explanatory variable and the outcome (so cases where these variables take certain values are more likely to be included for analysis), we have a case of collider bias as described above.

Selection bias is closely related to the problems resulting from conditioning on the wrong variables, which we have already discussed. The selection rule can be seen just as a shared effect of the main explanatory variable and the outcome. Conditioning on such a variable would induce associations where none exist. By implication, selecting cases based on such a rule would lead us to believe that there is a causal effect even if there is none (in the target population).

Imagine, for example, that we are interested in the effect of international trade on the political cooperation between states (the level of analysis being a pair of countries) and the hypothesis we want to test is that countries that trade with each other are more likely to develop stronger political ties. Assume for the moment that we have solved the potential problems of reversed causality and omitted variables. But the only observations we can get are for country-pairs that trade a lot (perhaps because they are the only ones that keep records) or that have high political cooperation (perhaps because they are the only ones willing to disclose trade records). Now, even if in the population no causal relationship exists whatsoever between trade and political cooperation, in the sample that we can observe an association will arise purely as an artefact of the case selection mechanism. (The same problem would occur if the selection rule is not itself a direct shared effect of the main explanatory variable and the outcome but is correlated with such a variable.)

Barbara Geddes (1990) makes a somewhat different argument against selection on the outcome (dependent) variable. In the example she uses, one initially looks only at cases that share an outcome (say, steep economic development) and if they all happen to share another factor (say, high level of labour repression) we would be fooled into thinking that the two are causally related. Of course, it could turn out that cases with low level of economic development have a similarly high level of labour repression or that countries with low labour repression can also achieve high economic growth.

Case selection where the rule determining which cases we observe is related to a moderating variable that sits on the path between the main explanatory variable and the outcome is another case selection mechanism that creates bias. The bias will tend to mask a possible effect. It is easy to see why – by selecting on the moderator we condition on the mechanism through which the explanatory variable and the outcome are related. For example, consider a study that identifies a negative causal effect of university education on tolerance for nepotism (an individual-level attitude). The causal mechanism is as follows: university provides people with a wider network of social contacts which weakens the need to rely on family ties for career advancement and, as a result, peoples' approval of this practice. If people with a wide social network are more likely to be part of the sample we observe, we will find a much weaker relationship between university eduction and tolerance to nepotism in the sample than the real one that exists in the population. Conditioning the sample selection on a mediating variable (partly) takes away the causal effect.

A selection rule related to the main explanatory variable creates no bias provided that the effect is linear. If the effect works differently depending on the values of the explanatory variable, the estimated effect in the sample would not characterize well the effect in the population. Similarly, a selection rule correlated with a confounder creates no bias, but if the main causal effect works differently for different values of the confounder, the estimate of the effect in the sample would not generalize to the effect in the population.

To sum up, random selection of units to observe, when possible to conduct and when many potential cases are available, is the best approach for large-N explanatory research. When random selection is not an option, purposeful selection of cases should avoid selecting on the outcome variable and on mediating variables and their proxies. As King, Keohane, and Verba (1994) point out, at the very least enough variation in the outcome variable should be retained, if it is not possible to avoid a selection based on its values. Selecting on the basis of the values of the main explanatory variable is admissible, assuming linear effects.

In the practice of political science research, the difficulty in following this advice is that we often do not have measures of the explanatory and other relevant variables *before* we conduct the research. Especially for research projects motivated by empirical puzzles, there might not be available data on which to base purposeful selection of cases. What can help in such situations is to divide the research project into several stages in which first some rough indicators of the variables of interest are created and measured and then, on the basis of this preliminary data, cases for further study are selected.

It is also important to emphasize that the possibility of selection bias should be recognized and, if possible, avoided. But, as with other kinds of biases, sometimes it would be possible to adjust or gauge the causal effect estimates even in the presence of selection bias. Furthermore, we can explicitly try to model the probability of a case being observed in much the same way we model the main causal relationship of interest and use that selection model as an intermediate step in the analysis (Heckman, 1979).

How many cases?

There can be no single answer to the question how many cases should a large-N observational design have. In general, the more, the better, but there are diminishing returns to each additional observation after some point.

First, more observations allow for more precise estimation of causal effects, if these are credibly identified, in the presence of statistical noise. Noise can arise from poor measurement (see below) or random variability of the outcome. This remaining variability is random only in the sense that its causes are unrelated to the observed variables. Moreover, if the outcome variable is distributed in a skewed (non-linear) way – if it has few really extreme values and these extreme values are of theoretical interest – we would need even more observations to make sure that they happen to be included in the sample.

Second, more observations provide an opportunity (more degrees of freedom, in statistical parlance) for more conditioning, *provided* we can actually measure the additional suspected confounders for all observations.

Third, we need more observations to detect smaller causal effects. This issue is related to the notion of statistical power introduced in Chapter 7. As with experimental designs, power calculations can (and should) be made to determine in advance how many observations would be needed to detect effects of sizes that can be reasonably expected and in data that has certain variability.

Including more cases comes at a double price. First, there is the effort necessary to collect the data for the additional observations. This point is readily recognized. Second, additional observations will often increase the heterogeneity of the sample (how fundamentally comparable the cases are), and this can do more harm than the benefit of having more observations for the statistical analysis. This point is not commonly understood, although there is nothing particularly difficult about it. Large-N designs rely on comparisons, and when the compared units become too dissimilar, there is not much that can be learned in the process of analysis. There is existing research showing that in the typical data that the social sciences use the bias introduced by having a bigger but more heterogeneous sample will often outweigh the gained precision of the estimates derived from the analysis of the enlarged sample data (Rosenbaum, 2005).

There is a further warning against trying to increase the number of cases at all cost. The collected data should cover reasonably well all the potential combinations of variables. For example, if the outcome variable is electoral turnout and the explanatory variables are political campaign spending and the competitiveness of the election, the observations should include a range of combinations of the latter two: low spending and high competitiveness, low spending and low competitiveness, and so on. Otherwise, we can be misled into thinking that an estimate calculated from a very specific combination of values of these variables can be extrapolated to combinations that have not been observed in the actual data at all! Statistical models would be only too happy to provide output even from data with limited variation and will give no warning that the numbers might not be very trustworthy when applied to a situation (combination of variables) not observed in the data. These projections will be driven almost entirely by the assumptions of the particular statistical model used for estimation (for example, linearity of the effects) and very little by the actual data. Hence, they would not by very trustworthy.

Matching, when applied as a data-preprocessing procedure, can help to avoid this problem. We already introduced matching as a method for conditioning earlier in this chapter. But matching can also be used to trim the available data to exclude observations with combinations of values that have no good counterfactuals (similar cases for comparison). Because matching creates comparable pairs (or groups) of observations before estimating the causal effect, it can identify and exclude observations that bring no real informational value.

Assume we want to know the effect of attending college on earnings after graduation and that we consider intelligence a possible confounder. Matching will group observations on their intelligence scores *before* deriving the average causal effect of college attendance. But imagine that within the group of extremely intelligent people, there is no individual who did *not* attend college. In other words, for the extremely intelligent people, there is no good counterfactual. Standard conditioning via multiple regression will still make use of these high-intelligence cases. A matching approach will remove them because the information they bring about what would happen to an individual of particular intelligence if he/she attended college or not is very limited. Removing these cases will limit the inferred causal effect only to individuals of low and average intelligence, but this is only fair – we have not observed anyone with high intelligence who did not attend college so we do not know what the effect of college on earnings for this particular subset of people would be. While having more limited scope of application, the causal effect estimated after matching will be, in this hypothetical example, more valid and reliable for the remaining set of cases.

It might appear counterintuitive at first that we would want to remove observations to increase the trustworthiness of causal inferences, but the rationale is simple: more observations are helpful only if they bring relevant information. What is relevant information depends on the purpose of the study (predictive models would have different criteria from causal ones). There is inevitably a trade-off involved between having more but less comparable and having fewer but more comparable observations.

Levels of analysis and observation

Another important research design choice is the level of observation. As explained above, different levels of observation are possible to define in political science research, and they can also be combined. Choosing the right level of observation will often provide solutions to seemingly intractable research questions. Consider that we are interested in the impact of the electoral system (majoritarian versus proportional) on corruption in a country. Inconveniently, the electoral system is one and the same at the national level in the set of potential observations and does not change over time. How can we examine the effect of the electoral system if it does not vary? Well, perhaps the electoral system does vary at the subnational level. By refocusing the study from the country as the unit of analysis to the subnational region, we can gain leverage to answer the original question.

In political science, aggregate data are more readily available than individual-level data. Institutional, economic, social, and political indicators are often only accessible at the country or local level, although in principle some of these variables might be aggregations from data originally collected at the individual level (such as educational level or wealth). Aggregates such as a national average rather than individual-level data might also be available for privacy reasons. And even if in principle the individual-level data are available, it might be necessary to use the aggregate since the other (say, institutional) variables do not vary across large sets of individuals.

Analysing aggregated data, however, is tricky because of the so-called problem of ecological inference. Simply put, the problem is that inference at the individual and at the aggregate level might differ even if based on the same underlying data. The most famous manifestation of this problem is Simpson's paradox. An illustration of the paradox in the context of political science is provided by the following example. While in the US richer *individuals* tend on average to vote for the Republican Party, richer *states* tend to exhibit higher voting shares for the Democratic Party (see Gelman et al., 2007; Gelman, 2009). Looking at the aggregate state-level data one would conclude that wealth is positively related to voting for the Democrats, while looking at the individual-level data exactly the opposite conclusion will be reached! The paradox arises because the absolute level of support for the Republican party is higher in poorer states for all levels of individual income.

The lesson of all this is that research designs using aggregate data need to be extra careful in advancing inferences about individual-level relationships. When possible, multilevel models should be used to describe the variation at each level of aggregation. When the individual-level data are not available, partial identification of individual-level relationships might be possible (King, 1997; King, Rosen, & Tanner, 2007). But, in general, the limits to individual-level inference from aggregate data should be acknowledged.

Measurement error and missing data

In large-N studies, we routinely encounter missing data for at least some of the variables and the related problem of measurement error. Chapter 5 explained that when measurement error is completely nonsystematic (random), causal inference will be inefficient, but the causal estimates would not be, on average, biased (King, Keohane, & Verba 1994). Conversely, if the measurement error is correlated with the values of the outcome variable or the values of the main explanatory variable of interest or with the values of an important confounder, the causal inference would be biased. Measurement error can be considered as another source of selection bias, as the consequences are rather similar. When measurement error is random, it can lead to a Type II error (false negative). When it is systematically related with the relevant variables of interest, it can bias the inferences in any direction (for a sophisticated approach of handling measurement error and missing data, see Blackwell, Honaker, & King 2015).

The problem of missing data in large-N research is rather similar. When data are missing completely at random, the price is inefficiency of the estimation, so that more data would be needed to gain the same statistical power. But when data are missing due to systematic factors that are also related to the data-generating process of interest, the causal inferences from the data would be biased. Missing data in observational research can result from problems such as nonresponse to all or some of the items in public opinion surveys but also from the fact that it is not possible at all to gather information about certain cases (for example, in totalitarian states or communities in a state of violent conflict). In most of these cases the mechanisms generating the missing data would not be random but correlated with the phenomena of interest, for example political knowledge in the case of surveys.

When data are missing systematically, we have a case of selection bias. If unaccounted for, this would not only affect the external validity of the results (assuming the case selection is taken randomly from a target population) but also the internal validity of the causal inference. Again, the error could be in any direction depending on how the missing data are correlated with the variables in the model. When missing data is a significant feature of the data the research project works with, we can try to model and predict which cases are likely to have missing data (for example, which individuals would refuse to answer a survey question). Then, we can adjust for this information in the estimation of the main relationship we are interested in, for example, by increasing the weight of the observations that *have* responded to the survey and that share the predictors of nonresponse identified in the previous step. See Little and Rubin (1989) and Blackwell, Honaker, & King (2015) for details about how to deal with missing data at the data analysis stage. From a research design perspective, remember that both measurement error and missing data, even when completely random, pose a requirement for collecting more data to reach the same level of statistical power; that their negative effects can be attenuated by collecting information and adjusting for variables related to the missing units; and that, in principle, causal inference with non-randomly missing data and measurement error is suspect.

Uses of Large-N Research

Now that we have a good idea about the logic and strategies of large-N analysis, we can go back a step and ask what it is good for. In political science, large-N analysis is usually deployed to *test* theories rather than *build* them, although outside of it inductive causal discovery (machine learning) is an active and promising field of research. Statistical analysis is in fact better geared for *prediction* and forecasting than for *causal* analysis, but in this chapter we focused on the latter, because it is currently considered a more legitimate goal for scientific research than the former. And the use of statistics for description and measurement was dealt with in Chapter 5.

Altogether, large-N designs are better suited to uncovering *general* relationships between *variables*. Causation inferred by large-N analysis may not be able to account for the outcome in any one particular case and still be valid for the population of cases as a whole. This is still a legitimate causal inference but, as explained in Chapter 6, the nuance in the meaning of causality is important and should be kept in mind when evaluating and communicating large-N research results. Large-N research is also better at tracing the effects of causes rather than the causes of effects (prospective versus retrospective causal questions).

Further Reading

Currently, the best single-volume introduction to large-N causal inference in observational studies is probably Morgan and Winship (2007), which is accessible yet rigorous and comprehensive. The texts of Judea Pearl (among others, 2009a, 2013) are more technical but essential for mastering causal inference using the causal diagram formalism. Rosenbaum (2002) examines observational designs from a statistician's point of view. David Freedman has perhaps done more than anyone to point out the dangers of using standard regression for causal inference (for example, Freedman 2009).

The presentation of large-N strategies and designs for causal inference in this chapter is heavily based on the work of Judea Pearl. Related, but slightly different, taxonomies are presented in Keele, Tingley, and Yamamoto (2015) and Glynn and Gerring (2013).

On natural experiments in the social sciences, see the book by Dunning (2012). Sekhon and Titiunik's (2012) article elucidates the complexities of counterfactual comparisons involved in natural experiment designs. Angirst and Pischke (2009) has an excellent, if technical, discussion of instrumental variables.

Keele and Minozzi (2013) provide a demonstration of the use of different causal strategies to identify and bound a causal effect in the context of a political science example. Manski (2007) is the text to go to to understand why and how to estimate bounds for causal effects with observational data.

On causal mediation analysis, see Keele, Tingley, & Yamamoto (2015) and Imai et al. (2011), which presents an accessible overview, and the references therein. There is an enormous literature on matching; for an entry point to the scholarship, see Ho et al. (2007).

On the selection of variables to adjust for, see the recent article by Ding and Miratrix (2015) and the subsequent comment by Pearl (2015).

From the innumerable options of books on statistical modelling, Gelman and Hill (2007) and Shalizi forthcoming are recommended.

Chapter 9

Comparative Designs

Comparison is at the heart of all political science research, if not all knowledge. The power of experimental and large-N observational research to uncover causal effects also comes from making comparisons – it is only that these comparisons are often embedded in complex statistical models. In this chapter we focus on comparative research when only a small number of observations are available. These designs require a separate treatment, because they face challenges of a different scale, although not altogether of a different type, from large-N observational research.

To address the usual problems of inferring causation from observation, small-N comparative research cannot rely exclusively on strategies such as randomization and conditioning nor on the law of large numbers, because, by definition the available observations are too few and their diversity is limited. Thus, comparative designs complement cross-case inference with within-case evidence for each case they study.

In essence, small-N comparative designs are *hybrids*. They have no unique approach to causation on their own but combine the strategies of large-N designs with the approach of within-case analysis.

Comparative research in political science typically has different goals from those of experimental or statistical research. First, it is often used to inductively derive theories (theory generation) rather than evaluate existing ones (theory testing). Second, even when its objectives are explicitly explanatory, it is more focused on retrospectively *accounting for* the outcomes of particular cases rather than prospectively estimating average causal effects.

After outlining the logic and rationale of small-N comparative research, this chapter moves on to discuss issues of research design proper. As with other observational research, the crucial design choices relate to the selection of variables and cases to observe, so these two aspects get the most attention. The popular most similar and most different system designs are presented in detail and their strengths and limitations for different research goals are outlined.

There is close affinity between comparative research and using necessary and sufficient conditions for theory building and data analysis. Therefore, the chapter illustrates the use of Boolean algebra for necessary and sufficient conditions analysis, and proceeds to introduce qualitative comparative analysis (QCA) as a distinct measurement and data-analytic approach to observational research.

The Logic of Small-N Comparative Research

People use comparisons to analyse situations, form conclusions, defend positions, and make decisions all the time. A child already knows the power of comparisons when pointing to the toys of her playmates and screaming to get the same. A teen needs no lessons in research design when building a case for going on vacation without his family by highlighting the liberty enjoyed by (a selection of) his peers. A policy maker at a big government agency or a small provincial town hall intuitively looks at what her colleagues at other organizations are doing to solve similar issues. It is altogether quite hard to imagine what human reasoning and argumentation would be like without the aid of comparisons. But the fact that making comparisons is so ingrained in the way we think doesn't mean that we are very good at it. Picking the right selection of comparison cases to reach a conclusion in the most efficient way possible or making the appropriate inferences from a set of cases that happen to be available does not come all that naturally to most of us. The logic of comparative inquiry is not really hard to learn, but it needs to be spelled out and respected.

Moreover, the logic is not fundamentally different from the one underlying experimental and large-N observational research for causal inference. The understanding of causality is still counterfactual. To decide if something makes a causal difference to an outcome, we have to approximate a counterfactual situation in which only the hypothesized factor differs and everything else remains the same. The ideas about how to achieve that are also the same – narrow down the range of possibly relevant factors, test specific hypotheses, rule out alternative explanations, explore the internal validity of the conclusions, consider the external validity and possible generalization of the insights. But because of its built-in limitations, small-N comparative designs for explanatory research need to put the emphasis on different aspects of the logic of inquiry from its experimental and large-N counterparts.

For one, by definition, small-N comparisons cannot rely on the law of large numbers to reduce measurement error and filter non-systematic random noise from data by piling up observations. This has two immediate implications. First, measurement validity becomes an even more pressing problem, and one that needs to be addressed through different means from those available to large-N studies. Second, small-N comparisons are just not suitable for the study of very weak and heterogeneous causal relationships.

On a related note, the small number of cases available for analysis limits the complexity of the causal identification strategies that can be used. Approaches that rely on conditioning via partialing out of confounding effects, instrumental variables, or mediation (see Chapter 8) require a rather specific and complex set of conditions that the cases should satisfy in order to be effective. So while in principle these strategies are applicable, the conditions would be hard to fulfil with the few potential cases comparative research usually has at its disposal for study. This leaves *conditioning via blocking or balancing* as the viable strategy for causal inference. In practice, the most similar systems design (see below) is employed to implement the conditioning strategy. To put it in the simplest terms possible, small-N comparative research for theory testing works by isolating the supposed causal relationship from other possible competing influences. Keep everything the same, but let your main explanatory variable of interest vary across the cases.

But theory testing is not the only and perhaps not the most prominent goal of comparative research. Small-N comparisons are often used to generate or sharpen new theoretical ideas as well. (And, of course, they have value even when purely descriptive.) To simplify, there are two typical scenarios for small-N comparative research. The first starts with a theoretically motivated research question and asks: what is the impact of variable X (for example, type of government) on outcome Y (for example, poverty reduction)? Then, from all available cases the researcher selects a small set (in some cases, as few as two) that satisfy the conditions of a conditioning (via blocking or balancing) approach to causal inference, conducts the data collection and analysis, and either does, or fails to, disconfirm the hypothesis that sparked the initial research question. The second scenario starts not with a hypothesis but with a set of cases and asks: what can we learn, *given* the cases we have? The combinations of variables represented in the cases would limit the inferences that could be made about the possible causal relationships between individual variables. The output of such research would necessarily be new theoretical *hypotheses*, which one may then proceed to *test* via different means and strategies.

You have probably guessed already that the first scenario follows deductive logic (start with theory, get data to evaluate hypotheses), while the second follows inductive logic (start with data, use it to generate theory). Much has been made of the question whether comparative research can be deductive in nature at all. Without going into the philosophical subtleties, to the extent that *any* empirical research can be deductive, small-N comparative studies can be as well. But it remains critical to keep in mind the different goals and corresponding design strategies of deductive and inductive research. When to choose one rather than the other is an important question to which we shall return at the end of the chapter.

The discussion so far touches upon only one side of comparative research: *cross-case inference*, either deductive or inductive. But there is another side to add, and that is *within-case analysis*. Within-case analysis will be dealt with at length in Chapter 10, but let us already note that it provides causal explanations not by studying cross-case patterns, but by evaluating competing hypotheses against numerous pieces of evidence (data) all concerning a single case. That is why small-N comparative research is ultimately *a hybrid*, borrowing from the unique strengths of both cross- and within-case research.

There are several reasons to combine cross-case evidence with detailed studies of the individual cases. As mentioned above, measurement error is a big threat to comparative work, and in-depth case analysis can improve the validity and reliability of measurement and operationalization. In addition, within-case evidence can uncover the causal mechanisms through which causal relationships operate. Such evidence can extend and complement the covariational patterns between variables that cross-case evidence provides. Lastly, questions about alternative explanations that cannot be addressed at the stage of cross-case comparisons can be further scrutinized during the in-depth within-case stage.

The use of within-case analysis matches well the goal of *accounting for* the particular outcomes of the cases, as a particular mode of explanatory analysis (see Chapter 6). And often comparativists seek just that – being able to account fully for the particular outcomes that occurred in each case they study (say, political revolutions during the 2000s in Ukraine and Georgia, but not in Belarus and Armenia). For them, being able to discover one causal factor that is systematically but weakly related to the onset of a revolution would just not do. The estimation of partial average causal effects is less important than building comprehensive explanatory accounts of outcomes, and then for each case being studied. It is in the interplay of these detailed explanatory accounts and the cross-case patterns emerging when they are juxtaposed to each other where the real power of small-N comparative research lies.

Because of the use of detailed case data extending beyond the collection of a small set of quantified variables per case, comparative work is often affiliated, and sometimes even confused with, qualitative research. The quantitative/qualitative distinction is not a terribly useful one, and we generally avoid it in this text as it refers to aspects of the collected data and not to the logic of inference and research design. But, yes, small-N comparisons are much more likely to use qualitative data than large-N research. However, there is a trade-off involved, because the denser and more contextualized the qualitative data becomes, the more difficult the comparisons between cases. It is one of the challenges of comparative research to balance the desire for rich empirical data for each case with the need for comparability of concepts, variables, and observations across cases.

Having cleared the ground, we are ready to discuss the details of particular comparative designs. But you might have noted that one rather obvious and fundamental question has not been addressed yet: what number of cases is too small for large-N studies, and how many cases are too many for small-N comparisons? Truth be told, there is no definite and carefully policed border between small- and large-N designs. In principle, there is nothing to prevent you from running a statistical regression on five cases (although the utility of doing so is dubious at best) or from conducting a comparison of 60 cases studied in depth. Unlike problems such as *how many cases do I need to detect a likely causal effect of size Z?* (see Chapter 7) or *what attributes should my two cases have so that I can isolate the possible effect of variable X?* (see below), which have very precise answers, the size question does not.

The boundary between small- and large-N research is fuzzy and contingent on the state of the art in the scientific field; on the assumed network of relevant causal relationships; and, last but not least, on the analytical capacity of the researcher and his or her readers. While the techniques used to analyse the data might change with the number of cases from informal discussion to Boolean minimization (see below) to statistical methods, the principles of research design do not. Yet, as explained above, the *emphasis* on different approaches to causal inference does shift. In practice, to benefit from the advantages related to reduced (random) measurement error and non-systematic noise that come with a large number of cases, one needs at least several dozen and, preferably, several hundred cases. At the same time, most of us do not have the capacity to handle (produce and consume) non-formalized comparisons of more than a dozen rich, in-depth, within-case studies. Between a dozen and a few dozen cases is a grey zone, a no man's land where all kinds of strategies and designs are being tried out, individually and in combination (see Chapter 11).

The Design of Small-N Comparative Research

The design of small-N comparative research primarily concerns the selection of cases to study and the selection of variables to observe. It is presumed that the research question has already been chosen and sharpened (see Chapter 2); that the goal and type of research is clear (Chapters 2 and 3); and that theory has identified the hypothesized relationships (Chapters 3) between the relevant concepts, which have been properly operationalized (Chapter 4).

Most similar systems design I

The first comparative design to present in detail is the so-called most similar systems design (MSS). The MSS design may take two forms, which are appropriate for different types of research questions and goals.

The first MSS design type works by focusing on one major hypothesized causal relationship (or a small set of these) and making sure that there is variation in the main explanatory variable, while the values of all other possibly relevant variables remain constant across the selected cases. Surely, you recognize the logic of the blocking conditioning strategy discussed at length in Chapter 8. Importantly, in this version of the design the researcher is not aware and does not care about the outcomes realized in the cases *before* the research is actually done. That is, the selection of cases takes into account only the values of the (hypothesized) explanatory variables, and not the values of the outcome variables.

Table 9.1 has a basic representation of the design. The researcher is interested in the possible (hypothesized) causal influence of the main explanatory variable on the outcome. For simplicity, assume that all variables are binary (1/0, presence/absence, true/false, and so on). The question marks for the values of the outcome variable signify that we neither know nor care about them *during the design stage*. It is crucial that there is variation in the main explanatory variable. And the potential influence of possible confounders must be blocked. It doesn't matter whether all cases have 1s or 0s as values on these additional variables but only that the values are the same (kept constant across the cases). It is not only confounders that need to be controlled for but other variables that can produce the outcome as well, even if they are not hypothesized to influence the main explanatory variable. This is because with only a couple of cases, the researcher cannot expect that the effect of such alternative causal factors will cancel out, as it would in a large sample of cases (see again Chapter 8 for why this *can* be expected to happen in large-N designs). Mediating variables and effects of the outcome should not be controlled for (as was the case for large-N designs; see again Table 8.7).

A very important, and often overlooked, point is that the variables on which the cases should be as similar as possible are not just any characteristics of the countries, counties, or time-periods being compared. It is the variables that are potential confounders or alternative causal factors that should be kept constant (or just very similar) across the cases. Hence, two countries can be very much alike in geographical location, relief, and climate. But if the outcome of interest is the party system

Table 9.1 *Most similar systems design (I)*

Variable	Case 1	Case 2
Main explanatory variable	1	0
Possible confounding variable I	1	1
Possible confounding variable II	0	0
Other possibly causally relevant variable	1	1
Outcome	?	?

and the two countries differ in their electoral systems, the design cannot be credibly described as an MSS one, because geographic location, relief, and climate might be similar but are probably unrelated to the party system, while the electoral system, which differs, is. So if we want to test the influence of, say, party financing rules on party systems, it is electoral systems that should be kept constant across the cases. No amount of similarities on other variables can compensate for a crucial difference on a relevant factor. We draw on existing theories, previous knowledge, and other people's empirical findings to identify potentially relevant factors.

In principle, this version of MSS design can be used for deductive theory testing with a focus on one or a small number of hypotheses. Once the data are collected, the researcher gets to know the outcomes realized in the cases. If the outcomes of the two cases turn out to be the same, it would be quite impossible for the main variable to be causally determining the outcome, since it differs across the two cases by design. At the very least, the researcher can conclude that this variable cannot be a sufficient condition for producing change in the outcome (think about the reason why this is the case). If the outcomes of the two cases turn out to be the same, the hypothesis that the main variable is causally important can be retained.

In its simplest form outlined above, this design is very weak. Even small measurement errors and/or random variability can lead to the wrong conclusions. Also, there is nothing to rule out reversed causality. Furthermore, the design cannot accommodate heterogeneous effects (effects that work differently in different contexts defined by the values of the other variables) or complex relationships in which the main explanatory variable interacts with other variables to produce the outcome.

The latter two limitations can be relaxed to some extent by adding more cases and extending the simple set-up outlined above. For example, suppose our theory states that the possible causal impact of variable X on Y is conditioned on variable Z, so that the effect is positive if Z is present and negative if it is absent. The design summarized in Table 9.2 would allow us to test these hypotheses.

One can add more cases for each theoretically relevant combination of variables to address the threats of measurement error and random variation. And, of course, the variables can be measured on a finer scale than binary (which would demand yet further cases to estimate the hypothesized causal relationship). As we keep adding cases, at some point this strategy would become indistinguishable from the 'conditioning by matching' approach to causal inference of large-N research.

In practice, in comparative work, instead of adding yet more cases researchers prefer to dig deeper into the small set of cases themselves. Issues of measurement, confounding, and sequence (reversed causation)

Table 9.2   *A slightly more complex most similar systems design*

Variable	Case 1	Case 2	Case 3	Case 4
Main explanatory variable (X)	1	0	1	0
Possible moderating variable (Z)	0	0	1	1
Possible confounding variable	1	1	1	1
Other possibly causally relevant variable	1	1	1	1
Outcome	?	?	?	?

are addressed by process tracing and a series of within-case analyses with a focus on the causal mechanisms behind the hypotheses rather than their implications for cross-case patterns of covariation.

While the primary goal of this mode of MSS remains theory testing, as detailed data are collected in the course of research one can often generate new alternative hypotheses, if it is discovered that the initial hypotheses are not corroborated or that the outcomes cannot be accounted for fully by existing theory.

The Martin–Vanberg model of parliamentary control of government

Let's illustrate how the MSS design works with a real example from political science research. One of the most important questions for democratic governance is the power of legislatures to control and scrutinize the actions of the executive branch (the government) in the European parliamentary democracies. Lanny Martin and Georg Vanberg have developed a powerful theory about this issue that puts major emphasis on the role of parliaments in solving conflicts between government partners in coalition governments. To simplify greatly (do read the original exposition of the theory in Martin & Vanberg, 2004, 2011), their main hypothesis is that the extent of parliamentary involvement in legislative affairs is related to the potential coalition conflict within the cabinet. The proposed causal mechanism is that the parliamentary groups of the governing parties scrutinize and correct the 'policy drift' of individual ministers from the policies agreed upon by the coalition.

The Martin–Vanberg model has been extensively tested with large-N research, and its hypotheses have been largely corroborated by the aggregate patterns of covariation between the size of the coalition conflict and the amount of parliamentary involvement in legislative decision making. While such large-N aggregate evidence is important to establish the credibility of the theory, it still leaves open the question whether the cross-case patterns are produced by the exact causal mechanisms proposed by the model.

To address the gap, Nora Dörrenbächer and colleagues (2015) designed a small-N comparative study in which they traced parliamentary involvement during the incorporation of one European Union directive into the national legal systems in four countries: Germany, Austria, the Netherlands, and France. (Although decided in Brussels, EU directives still need to be 'transposed' into national law by every member state.) The four countries are rather similar when it comes to the administrative capacity of their parliaments, executive–legislative relations, and political systems. Furthermore, because the countries have to adapt the same common piece of EU legislation, this keeps the topic, salience, and technicality of the issues involved the same across the cases. Crucially, what differs is the extent of coalition conflict, as the governments in the four countries included a single-party one (hence, no coalition conflict), a minority one, and two two-party coalitions with a varying degree of ideological distance between the parters.

Based on this MSS design, the authors compare the outcome of interest – the extent of parliamentary influence in law making – across the cases and trace in detail the legislative processes in the four countries. The results of the study show that, overall, the predictions of the Martin–Vanberg model about the covariation between coalition conflict and parliamentary involvement largely hold. But the causal mechanisms through which this occurs turn out to be more complex that the theory purports. For example, anticipation of parliamentary control by government ministers, inter-party divisions, and bicameral institutions all play much bigger roles than the theory anticipates. In conclusion, the small-N comparative study increases our confidence in the relevance of the theory but also generates new ideas about how to extend it.

Most similar systems design II

While the approach just discussed is essentially deductive, there is a different variation of the MSS design that is based on inductive logic. It can be traced back to the 'method of agreement' that the British philosopher and political economist John Stuart Mill outlined as far back as 1843 in his treatise *A System of Logic* (1843). In this version, *both* the values of the control and outcome variables are taken into account during the case selection phase. The researcher picks cases that are as similar as possible but differ in the outcome of interest. Such a situation would certainly qualify as an empirical research puzzle (see the second part of Chapter 2). The task is to discover a difference between the cases that can account for the difference in outcomes. Clearly, the approach is bottom-up, hypothesis-generating, rather than testing. An illustration of the design is provided in Table 9.3.

The logic embedded in the design is that no variable shared by the cases can be responsible for the different outcomes, so we have to find

Table 9.3   *Most similar systems design (II)*

Variable	Case 1	Case 2
Main explanatory variable	?	?
Other possibly causally relevant variable I	0	0
Other possibly causally relevant variable II	1	1
Outcome	1	0

a variable that is not shared. Clearly, this leaves open the possibility that we discover a difference between the cases that is real but causally *irrelevant* to the outcome, or one that it is part of a more complex causal ensemble that remains hidden.

The inductive MSS design is a rather weak one that cannot satisfactorily address issues of multiple causation, random variation, reversed causality, and complex interactive causal effects on its own. Nevertheless, as a first step in coming up with new plausible hypotheses, it serves its purpose. And within-case analysis can alleviate, though not completely compensate for, some of the deficiencies.

Institutions and health care policy
An example of the application of most similar systems comparative design with different outcomes comes from Ellen Immergut's (1990) classic study of health care policy making in Europe. The main research question is why some countries have been able to introduce national health insurance programs and impose strict government regulation of the medical profession, while others have not been so successful. The three countries under investigation – Switzerland, France, and Sweden – exhibit significant variation in this outcome of interest. While in Sweden, and to a lesser extent in France, a national health system with medical doctors as salaried employees has been established, in Switzerland the role of government has remained limited to national health insurance programs. Importantly, the interests and the organizational power of the medical profession in the three countries has been rather similar. As a result, these generally important factors for explaining change and persistence in health care policy *cannot* account for the variation in outcomes across the three countries. Instead, Immergut discovers that the institutional setting of health care policy making, and more specifically the number of access points where interest groups could have halted reforms, differs radically in the three countries. Hence, she concludes that the variation in institutional veto points can be held responsible for the variation in health policy reform outcomes. As explained above,

such an inductively generated finding had best be regarded as a hypothesis that can be tested against additional evidence (see also Immergut, 1992).

Aka, Mill's Method of Difference.

Most different systems design

The most different systems design (MDS) is based on the mirror image of the idea that no factor *shared* between the cases can explain a *difference* in outcomes, namely that no factor *not shared* between the cases can explain *a constancy* of outcomes. If the cases are as different as possible on all relevant dimensions but happen to experience the same outcomes, then we should search for the commonality that the cases share.

Table 9.4 shows an example implementing this design, which is also inductive and, as a consequence, more appropriate for generating ideas and new hypotheses rather than testing. It is subject to the same limitations as the inductive MSS design discussed above. Complex causal relationships in which variables interact to produce the outcome, reversed causality, and random variation can all wreak havoc on the conclusions of a simple MDS design. Making the design more complex by adding more cases, and more categories of cases reflecting different combinations of variables can help to some extent, but it is often impracticable or impossible due to lack of cases. Process tracing and within-case analysis are then used to compensate for the deficiencies of the small-N cross-case comparisons.

Table 9.4   *Most different systems design*

Variable	Case 1	Case 2
Main explanatory variable	?	?
Other possibly causally relevant variable I	0	1
Other possibly causally relevant variable II	1	0
Outcome	1	1

Note that the cases can be considered most different only if they are different on theoretically relevant dimensions for the research question at hand. What the relevant dimensions (variables) are depends also on what we already know about the subject of inquiry. Hence, the similarity or dissimilarity of cases is not absolute, but context-specific. The implication is that two cases can be part of an MSS in one project but of an MDS in another. Sweden and Finland can be considered most similar for many questions of economics, politics, and geography but could be part of a most different design when it comes to linguistics (Swedish is an Indo-European, while Finnish is a Finno-Ugric language).

Is there a deductive MDS design? While it is logically possible that we identify one similarity in an otherwise very diverse set of cases and then analyse any outcomes the similarity might be responsible for, in practice such an approach is not often used.

Development policy in Alabama and Jamaica
Gayle (1988) presents an example of the application of most different systems design for the study of development policy. The author compares Jamaica with the US state of Alabama. These two cases are clearly very different when it comes to institutional structures, level of economic development, and societal context, but they have pursued comparable policies for economic development. Beyond the dissimilarities, the author identifies state policy toward private enterprise and public–private sector interactions as the crucial similarities that can account for the similarity in policy outcomes.

Beyond the most simple designs

So far the MSS and MDS designs have been presented in isolation and illustrated with very simple set-ups having only a couple of cases. These are also called 'paired' or 'focused' comparisons. It is only natural to try and combine the strengths of the two approaches and add more complexity to the case-selection logic. Such extensions can be theory-motivated, so we purposefully search for relevant combinations of variables to be represented in the set of cases we study. Alternatively, we can ask, given the set of cases we have available, what can be learned about the causal structure producing the data? As we keep adding cases and complexity, informal analysis will no longer do as a method for analysing the implications of the data, so we have to turn to something more formal.

Qualitative Comparative Analysis

An approach called qualitative comparative analysis (QCA), developed and popularized by Charles Ragin (1987, 2000, 2008), presents one framework for the design and study of small- and medium-N comparisons. QCA generalizes the ideas and simple designs based on paired comparisons discussed so far in the chapter. It exists in several flavours – crisp-set QCA, which works with binary variables only; multivariate QCA; and fuzzy-set QCA, which can accommodate more nuanced levels of measurement. While a comprehensive presentation of QCA is beyond the scope of this text, this section will present a short overview of its basics, an intuition about how the data analysis works, and an example of its application to a political science question. In fact, QCA is only one approach to conducting small- and medium-N comparative research; set theory and the methodology of necessary and sufficient conditions that underpins QCA are more general and can be implemented in different approaches as well (see the sections on 'Extensions' and 'Further Reading' at the end of this chapter). But since for now QCA is the most popular of the approaches, it is practical to introduce these more general ideas in the context of its application.

QCA works with set relations rather than covariational patterns. The underlying concept of causality shared by QCA and other comparative approaches, such as comparative historical research, is one of conjunctural or combinatorial causation. Political and social outcomes can result from different processes (in technical terms, this is called equifinality). Moreover, these different processes cannot be represented as the additive influences of individual variables acting independently but only as the combined impact of various conjunctions of causal conditions. In short, causal complexity is assumed to result from conjunctural causation plus equifinality. Such complexity is better captured by set relations than by the regression framework of large-N analyses, which works mostly with linear additive effects. The interest in causal combinations goes hand in hand with attention to the *context* within which variables (conditions) operate.

Vaisey (2014) gives us another way to appreciate the different approaches of large-N designs discussed in the previous chapter and QCA which will be presented shortly. While large-N analysis starts with the assumption that there are no systematic relationships in the data and we only add some with positive evidence, QCA starts with the assumption of complexity and we search for relationships to remove. To simplify even further, for the comparativist everything matters unless there is evidence that it doesn't, while for the quantitative researcher it is the opposite: nothing matters unless there is evidence that it does.

Necessary and sufficient conditions

Set relations are conveniently expressed with the language of necessary and sufficient (N&S) conditions, so let us first review the basics of N&S causation. For a condition to be causally *necessary* for an outcome, the outcome must not occur in the absence of the condition. For example, oxygen is causally necessary for fire because in the absence of oxygen, there can be no fire. For a condition to be causally *sufficient* for an outcome, the outcome must always occur when the condition is present. For example, touching fire is sufficient to cause pain (under a very large range of circumstances).

N&S causation is in principle deterministic, but the determinism can be relaxed by allowing that a condition is 'almost always' necessary or sufficient to produce an outcome (see below). Note that N&S conditions are fully compatible with a counterfactual understanding of causality (Chapter 6).

The language of N&S conditions is appealing for causal analysis in political science, especially when we are interested in explaining (accounting for) particular political phenomena or events, as many comparative research projects do. The appeal has several sources, but the main one is that N&S conditions can handle multiple causality in a natural way. That is, when multiple causal paths can produce an outcome, these paths can be effectively summarized as combinations of N&S conditions. For example, there are multiple paths from a totalitarian regime towards a democracy. Simplifying, democracy can appear from (A) a strong protest movement imposing peacefully its wants on (B) a strong but divided government; from a violent and victorious fight of (C) the repressed population against (D) a militarily weak regime, or from (E) imposition from outside by a foreign power. Each of these three paths can be expressed as a combination of N&S conditions: A*B; C*D; E. The usual convention in N&S analysis is that the symbol * stands for logical 'AND', and the symbol + stands for logical 'OR'. Hence, we can summarize all three causal paths together in the expression:

$$A*B + C*D + E \rightarrow \text{Transition to democracy}$$

Each of the five conditions in the 'recipe' above is considered causally important. The first four are *insufficient but non-redundant parts of unnecessary but sufficient conditions* of the outcome, or INUS conditions for short (Mackie, 1974, p. 62). Condition 'E' is actually sufficient on its own, but such cases where a single factor is sufficient to produce an outcome would be quite rare in actual political science research.

How do we infer such patterns from the raw data we collect? How do we distil the rich and often messy information from original empirical cases into succinct expressions like the one above? To illustrate the procedure, we will start with a very simple case and add a small measure of complexity later. The illustration is only supposed to give us a taste of how the method works and shed light on its implications for research design – the selection of variables and cases to observe. To really learn the mechanics of analysing such data, you can consult one of the many excellent guides referenced in the 'Further Reading' section of this chapter.

Boolean minimization: a simple example

To start, assume that we are interested in explaining why some democracies are stable and survive the perils of time, while others perish or revert back to the totalitarian or authoritarian regimes they emerged from. To keep things tangible, imagine that from our reading of the literature and initial study of the cases we have decided to focus on the potential influence of only two conditions – whether the society is homogeneous or divided along ethnic or religious lines, and whether the society is wealthy or not. The remaining task is to ascertain whether any of these factors in isolation or the two in combination can account for the patterns of democratic stability observed in a particular region of the world over a specific period of time. Imagine that within the region and time period we study there are a total of six observations (I to VI), and the configurations of variables (conditions) they represent are summarized in Table 9.5. Each line of the table lists the values of the potential explanatory factors as well as the observed outcome: we have one instance of a failed democracy and five stable ones.

What can we say about the co-occurrence of homogeneous societies, economic wealth, and stable democracy on the basis of the hypothetical observations summarized in Table 9.5? For such a small data matrix, some might be able to grasp the conclusion immediately, but for even slightly more complex situations an intermediate analytical step would be needed. This intermediate step is the construction of the so-called 'truth table'. The truth table lists for each theoretically possible combination of variables (conditions) the occurrence of each of the possible outcomes. Table 9.6 shows the truth table constructed from the data in Table 9.5. Since we have two conditions, there are four lines in the table corresponding to each possible combination of conditions. Columns 3 and 4 list the number of observed cases for the two possible values of the outcome – 'Stable democracy' (1) or its absence (0); the last column shows the total number of cases and their corresponding indicator in Table 9.5.

Once we have constructed the truth table, we can express each line in the form: H*E→D (the top line) and ~H*~E→~D (the bottom line; the symbol 'tilde' (~) stands for negation, or the absence of a condition).

Table 9.5   *Summary of cases*

Case	Hom. society (H)	Econ. wealth (E)	Stable democracy (D)
I	yes (1)	yes (1)	yes (1)
II	no (0)	yes (1)	yes (1)
III	no (0)	yes (1)	yes (1)
IV	yes (1)	no (0)	yes (1)
V	yes (1)	no (0)	yes (1)
VI	no (0)	no (0)	no (0)

Table 9.6 *Truth table based on the cases presented in Table 9.5*

Hom. society (H)	Econ. wealth (E)	Outcome=1	Outcome=0	Total cases
yes (1)	yes (1)	1	0	1 (I)
yes (1)	no (0)	2	0	2 (IV,V)
no (0)	yes (1)	2	0	2 (II,III)
no (0)	no (0)	0	1	1 (VI)

For the next step, we have to decide whether we want to model the *presence* of stable democracy or its *absence*. Since N&S causality is not symmetric, different results can be obtained depending on this choice. Let us first focus on explaining the presence of stable democracy (Outcome = 1), so we take into account only the top three rows of Table 9.6, which exhibit this outcome. These three paths to stable democracy can be summarized in a single expression:

$$H*E + H*\sim E + \sim H*E \rightarrow D$$

In words, the expression says that stable democracy is observed when there is a homogeneous and wealthy society, or when there is a homogeneous and non-wealthy society, or when there is a divided and wealthy society. So far, it does not seem that we have gone much further from where we started from with the raw data from Table 9.5. But we haven't finished yet. Crucially, the expression above can be *simplified*. Note, for example, that a homogeneous society is related to a stable democracy when society is wealthy (case I) and when it is not (cases IV and V). Therefore, wealth is unlikely to be important for democracy when society is homogeneous. The simplified path is: $H \rightarrow D$. Similarly, a wealthy society experiences stable democracy when it is homogeneous (case I) and when it is divided (cases II and III), which implies that for a wealthy society it does not matter whether it is homogeneous or not when it comes to the stability of democracy. This leads to the simplified path: $E \rightarrow D$. Putting everything together we have:

$$H + E \rightarrow D$$

In words, a stable democracy is observed when a society is homogeneous or when it is wealthy. Each of the two conditions is unnecessary but sufficient (as either of the two can produce the outcome) and the expression as a whole is a necessary condition for the outcome to occur. We have managed to distil the information contained in the six cases into a single, succinct statement (sometimes also called a 'causal recipe') which entails a simple causal model of the presence of democratic stability. And what about its absence? Since there is only one line in the truth table that contains the outcome 'absence of stable democracy' (the bottom line), the answer is straightforward:

$$\sim H * \sim E \rightarrow \sim D$$

The combination of a divided *and* a poor society is associated with the absence of stable democracy. The two conditions together are sufficient to produce the outcome, but individually they are not. It is in the confluence of the two that democracies break down. (Note that this conclusion in its symbolic and verbal forms is not the mirror image of the one about democratic stability. That is why causality is not symmetric when expressed with N&S conditions.)

There are different algorithms with which the simplification of truth tables – formally referred to as 'Boolean minimization' – can be accomplished, and the minimization can be performed using computer programs and packages for data analysis (*fsQCA*, *TOSMANA*, the *qca* package for *R*). The most popular algorithm is the *Quine–McCluskey algorithm*, but alternatives are available and some of these might be more or less appropriate depending on the precise research task (see Baumgartner, 2015, for details). For the simple cases discussed in this chapter, all minimization algorithms will produce the same result. Boolean minimization is one procedure of the larger field of Boolean algebra, which is a branch of mathematics and mathematical logic working with truth values (true/false, 0/1) instead of numbers.

A slightly more complex example: the curse of dimensionality, logical remainders, and inconsistency

The previous example was deliberately designed to be as simple as possible. Not only were the cases few in number, but they covered all logically possible combinations of conditions and there was a straightforward pattern to be uncovered. In reality, things will be more messy than that, and it is important to get a sense of the types of complications that would be most often encountered in the practice of QCA. The next example to discuss adds only a couple more cases (G and H) and one more condition ('Predatory neighbour-state') to the data, but the complexity increases quite a lot, as we shall see.

Table 9.7 summarizes the new set of cases along the three hypothesized causal conditions and the outcome. The values for the first six cases have been preserved from the previous example. In the two new cases, there is one case of a stable democracy (VII) and one case of a failed one (VIII).

The truth table constructed on the basis of these data is presented in Table 9.8. The first thing to note is that, although we have added only one new condition, the truth table has twice as many rows. This is

Table 9.7 *Summary of cases: a more complicated example*

Case	Hom. society (H)	Econ. wealth (E)	Pred. neighbour (P)	Stable democracy (D)
I	yes (1)	yes (1)	no (0)	yes (1)
II	no (0)	yes (1)	no (0)	yes (1)
III	no (0)	yes (1)	yes (1)	yes (1)
IV	yes (1)	no (0)	yes (1)	yes (1)
V	yes (1)	no (0)	yes (1)	yes (1)
VI	no (0)	no (0)	no (0)	no (0)
VII	yes (1)	yes (1)	yes (1)	no (0)
VIII	no (0)	no (0)	no (0)	yes (1)

because with every additional (binary) condition the number of possible combinations among all conditions doubles. The growth is exponential, which means that even with a relatively small number of causal conditions the truth table will get very large. The problem is known as combinatorial explosion and is related to the 'curse of dimensionality'. For example, with eight conditions, the number of possible combinations – hence, the number of rows in the truth table – is already 256 (in general, for n binary conditions the number of combinations is 2^n).

The second complication visible in Table 9.8 is that for two of the logically possible combinations of conditions, we have no observed cases. There is no case that has a divided and poor society and a predatory neighbour (line 4), and no case that has a homogeneous and poor society and no predatory neighbour (line 6). Maybe cases like that just do not exist, or maybe we have not been able to collect data on such cases – whatever the reason, the fact remains that we cannot code the realized outcomes for these combinations of conditions since they have not been observed.

Missing combinations are called 'logical remainders', and the problem they pose is known as 'limited diversity'. In real research, such situations occur quite often. And the higher the number of conditions, the higher the chance that some combinations would not be covered by observations.

There are several different ways we can deal with missing rows (logical remainders) in the truth table. First, we can try to reason theoretically what would happen in such a case if it were to be observed. For example, the existence of a predatory neighbour-state is supposed to decrease the chance of democracy survival, because such states would

Table 9.8   *Truth table based on the cases in Table 9.7*

Hom. society (H)	Econ. wealth (E)	Pred. neighbour (P)	Outcome=1	Outcome=0	Total
yes (1)	yes (1)	yes (1)	0	1	1 (VII)
yes (1)	no (0)	yes (1)	2	0	2 (IV)
no (0)	yes (1)	yes (1)	1	0	1 (III)
no (0)	no (0)	yes (1)	?	?	0
yes (1)	yes (1)	no (0)	1	0	1 (I)
yes (1)	no (0)	no (0)	?	?	0
no (0)	yes (1)	no (0)	1	0	1 (II)
no (0)	no (0)	no (0)	1	1	2 (VI)

try to install authoritarian puppet regimes. But the second line in the truth table shows that when society is homogeneous and poor, *even* when there is a predatory neighbour, democracy survives (cases IV and V). The only way in which the unobserved situation in line six differs from cases D and E is that there is no predatory neighbour. But since the effect of the presence of this condition on democracy survival is supposed to be negative, its absence is unlikely to turn a case into a democratic failure. So we can substitute the unobserved outcome for the missing combination with 'Stable democracy' (1) and continue the analysis with this assumption. In this example, the assumption seems warranted on theoretical grounds and in view of the patterns in the observed cases, but in reality it would often be difficult to form strong and reasonable assumptions about what the outcome *would have been*. And with many missing observations, chances are at least some of these would turn out to be wrong.

A second approach to handle missing combinations is to make the assumption(s) about the unobserved outcomes that would lead to the most parsimonious (simplified) expression summarizing the data in terms of N&S conditions. In a 'best case scenario' strategy, the analyst looks at what is the most succinct data summary that can be achieved given the observed cases and the most advantageous assumptions that can be made about the unobserved combinations.

The third approach is the opposite of the 'best case scenario'. It asks what inferences can be made from the data if we do not use any of the missing combinations at all. The resulting solution would typically be more complex that the parsimonious one. In practice, researchers would report results based on all three approaches and discuss how sensitive the results are to the different assumptions about the unobserved combinations. Baumgartner (2015) forcefully argues, however, that only maximally parsimonious solution formulas can represent causal structures. Hence, if one is interested in causal analysis (rather than data description, for example), only the parsimonious solutions should be used as only they can reveal the true causal variables. When the purposes of the analysis are not causal, intermediate and complex solutions might be appropriate.

But before we illustrate what the results from the analysis of the data in Table 9.7 would be under different assumptions about the outcomes of the two missing combinations, we have to consider one additional complication – and one that is even more consequential – hidden in the table. The six cases in the previous example were all neatly distributed in the different outcome categories, so that no cases having the same combination of conditions exhibited different outcomes. But now, for the combination 'divided and poor society with a predatory neighbour', we have one case in which democracy was stable (VIII) and one in which it was not (VI). When there are no contradictory cases per combination of conditions (row of the truth table), 'consistency' is perfect. When the cases are evenly distributed among the categories of the outcome, consistency is at its lowest (for a binary outcome variable, the lowest possible consistency value would be 0.5). Lack of consistency is a real problem, and there is no single solution that can make it disappear.

One approach to remedy the situation is to discover another variable (condition) that can resolve the controversy. On the basis of a most similar systems design with different outcomes logic, one can try to identify a difference in the contradictory cases that is related to the difference in outcomes. Then all other cases would have to be scored on this new condition as well. Sometimes, this approach can help resolve the contradiction. But, as we already know, every new condition increases twice the number of rows of the truth table, and the chance that there will be new unobserved combinations explodes.

If many observations per row of the truth table are available and only very few cases exhibit an outcome different from the rest of the row (combination), we can set a threshold for the consistency value above which a combination is coded as fitting in only one of the outcome categories. If, say, nine out of ten of all observations with the same combination of conditions exhibit 'Stable democracy' while only one has experienced democratic breakdown, we can decide to ignore this one case and code the outcome unambiguously as '1'. Essentially, this one discordant observation is treated like random noise or measurement error and ignored. Of course, to apply this approach we have to have a reasonably high number of cases per combination and they have to be distributed in a very lopsided way. When this is not the case, we can resolve the contradictory combinations, similarly to the 'best and worst case scenario' approach discussed above, by coding them in ways that would be most advantageous for the analysis or by deciding not to use them in the analysis at all.

Having introduced the problems of limited diversity and inconsistency, let us see what can be inferred from the data in Table 9.8 despite these complications. The complex solution for the presence of the outcome 'Stable democracy' (1) is:

$$E * {\sim}P + {\sim}H * E + H * P * {\sim}E \rightarrow D$$

There are three paths that cover in total five out of the six cases of 'Stable democracy': a wealthy society with no predatory neighbour, a wealthy and divided society, and a homogeneous and poor society with predatory neighbour. If we look back at the raw data in Table 9.7, we can see that the first path covers cases I and II, the second path II and III, and the third one IV and V. Note that VIII (which has the same outcome) is not covered as it is part of a contradiction (compare with VI) and the logical remainders are not used. If we code the missing combinations on the basis of theoretical considerations – line four from the truth table as a '0' (democratic breakdown) and line six as a '1', there are two possible solutions that account similarly well for the data:

$$(1)\ E * {\sim}H + H * {\sim}E + H * {\sim}P \rightarrow D$$
$$(2)\ E * {\sim}H + H * {\sim}E + E * {\sim}P \rightarrow D$$

Case I can be covered either as a combination of 'Homogeneous society' with a lack of 'Predatory neighbour-state', or as a combination of a 'Wealthy society' with a lack of 'Predatory neighbour-state': both paths are consistent with the data. If we let the simplifying algorithm score the missing combinations in a way that would produce the most parsimonious solution possible, we get a total of six solutions that account equally well for the data, but none is really simpler that the ones already identified by the theoretically resolved logical remainders.

Turning towards the modelling of the absence of stable democracy, the complex and parsimonious solutions are the same, and both cover one of the two observed outcomes:

$$H * E * P \rightarrow {\sim}D$$

If we score the logical remainders on theoretical grounds as above, the expression is slightly more complex:

$$H * E * P + {\sim}H * {\sim}E * P \rightarrow {\sim}D$$

There are two paths to democratic breakdown: the combination of a homogeneous and wealthy society with a predatory neighbour and the combination of a divided and poor society with a predatory neighbour. Since the condition 'Predatory neighbour-state' appears in both paths, we can factor it out:

$$P*(H*E + \sim H*\sim E) \rightarrow \sim D$$

The interpretation remains substantively the same, but it is expressed slightly differently: the combination of a predatory state with either a homogeneous and wealthy or divided and poor society brings democratic breakdown. The factorization makes it easy to see that 'Predatory neighbour-state' is a necessary condition for the outcome to occur since there is no path that does not have it. Yet, it is not sufficient as it needs to be coupled with either of two types of societies so as to produce the demise of democracy.

In QCA, once the formal expressions are derived, their implications for the individual cases would be explored further and the logic of the mechanisms they propose would be probed with additional case-level data. For our purposes, the two hypothetical examples discussed above already provide sufficient insight into how the data-analytic part of QCA proceeds, and we can focus again squarely on the questions of research design.

Case and variable selection in QCA

For the relatively simpler scenarios of stand-alone most similar and most different system designs, case and variable selection were discussed earlier in this chapter. But we still have to deal with these issues in the context of QCA and other more complex forms of comparative research designs. In some situations the question about case selection in QCA does not arise at all, because the researcher works with all available cases (which are by definition not too many). Nevertheless, when the opportunity to purposefully select cases exists, we have to have some guidelines about how to choose. In general, the researcher should aim to include a set of cases that varies both with respect to the hypothesized causal conditions (variables) and with respect to the outcome of interest. At the same time, cases should remain similar in terms of possible alternative explanatory conditions or contextual variables that can moderate how the main effects work.

From a purely logical point of view, when only cases in which the outcome of interest occurred are selected, we can still examine whether a certain hypothesized cause is a necessary condition for the outcome. If in some of the cases the purported cause was absent while the outcome occurred, we would know that there can be no relation of necessity. But we cannot say anything about sufficiency, and the necessity relationship can turn out to be trivial (see Braumoeller & Goertz, 2000). Conversely, if we only select cases in which the hypothesized cause is present, we can establish whether the causal condition is sufficient for the outcome to occur (if we observe no cases in which the outcome is absent), but we can say nothing about necessity. Hence, to address both, we need variation in both the outcome and the hypothesized explanatory variable.

In a simulation study, Thomas Plümper and colleagues (2010) show that case selection in qualitative research leads to most reliable causal inferences when it maximizes the variation in the main explanatory variable of interest, simultaneously minimizing variation of the confounding factors and ignoring all information about the outcome variable.

While we are on the topic of case selection, it is worth reminding that what constitutes a *case* in the first place can be tricky to establish. In the QCA view, cases are specific configurations of aspects and features (Ragin, 2000, p. 5), not collections of distinct, analytically separable attributes. For example, the same country observed during different periods can sometimes be considered as providing several 'cases', if the respective 'configuration of aspects and features' change. It is in this sense that historical analysis, even when focused on a single country, can sometimes be considered a small-N comparison from the point of view of research design.

It is hard to say which variables should be included in QCA when the goals of research are explanatory. Obviously, all hypothesized causal conditions and outcomes of interest should be observed, measured, and included in the data analysis, but it is not quite clear what to do with potential confounders, mediators, and other types of possibly relevant variables. If such variables are entered in the analysis and a complex or intermediate solution from the minimization is derived, the results can frequently suggest that they are part of the causal recipes, while in reality they are not. When the most parsimonious solution is derived, the danger is that the causal recipes omit a true confounder, if relevant combinations of conditions are missing from the truth table. Altogether, the best a researcher can do is ensure that a potential confounder is measured and that all possible combinations of the main explanatory variables and the confounder being present or absent are actually observed. In this case, the confounder should be entered in the data analysis and the results would suggest which variable is in fact related to the outcome (if any).

Extensions and alternatives

In the examples discussed in this chapter all variables (conditions) were measured (scored) in dichotomous (binary) terms – zero/one, presence/absence, in/out. Of course, in many circumstances a more nuanced measurement scale would be appropriate to capture more fine-grained distinctions between the cases. QCA can accommodate categorical variables with more than two categories (multivalue qualitative comparative analysis, or mvQCA) and fuzzy-set membership values (fsQCA). *Crisp sets* allow only for full membership in a set (1) or non-membership (0). All examples we discussed in this chapter used crisp sets only. *Fuzzy sets* allow for various degrees of membership in a set: a case can be fully in (1), fully out (0), neither in nor out (0.5), and various levels in between (for example, more in than out, 0.75). Analysis using fuzzy sets is more flexible and can provide more valid measurement when the diversity of cases cannot be described well with simple binary oppositions. fsQCA operates along the same principles as crisp-set QCA presented above, searching for relationships of (quasi-)necessity and sufficiency in the data, so all major points from the discussion remain.

Another related technique is coincidence analysis (Baumgartner & Epple, 2014), which also attempts to identify N&S conditions but uses a different search algorithm from that of standard QCA. In addition to the alternative technique for Boolean minimization, the other main difference is that in the framework of coincidence analysis *any* measured variable (condition) can be treated as an outcome. The search for N&S relationships can be performed with respect to all measured conditions. As a consequence, coincidence analysis might be more successful in uncovering complex causal structures in data. In addition, it provides a tool for the detection of *causal chains* among the variables included in the analysis (Baumgartner, 2013).

QCA *in practice: women's representation in parliament*
Krook's (2010) study of women's representation in parliament provides an example of the application of QCA to research problems of interest to political science. The author aims to explain the variation in the extent to which women are represented in national parliaments. Several causal conditions (variables) are employed in the analysis: the type of electoral system, the presence of electoral quotas for women, the existence of a strong autonomous women's movement, women's status (operationalized through the welfare state model), and the strength of left parties in the country. For one of the analyses focused on Europe, the data comprise 22 cases (countries). Initially, the QCA solution suggests five rather complex causal paths to high women's representation on the basis of the observed cases only. When logical remainders are incorporated, four different paths to representation emerge, but each path is now rather simplified. According to one of the solution formulas, high representation results from (1) high women's status, or (2) proportional electoral systems and autonomous women's movements, or (3) quotas and strong new left parties, or (4) non-proportional electoral systems and strong new left parties. The article also analyses separately the occurrence of low representation and replicates the study with a different set of variables for a different world region (Africa). The result is

a conclusion about the multitude of paths that can lead to high women's representation in the state legislatures that strikes a balance between empirical detail and explanatory parsimony.

Limits of Small-N Comparative Research

Despite the popularity of comparative research and the increasing use of QCA in particular, there are important theoretical as well as practical limits to what cross-case analysis of a small number of observations can achieve when it comes to causal analysis and explanation.

The biggest challenge is susceptibility to measurement error and random variability. As by definition the number of cases is too small to filter out noise and average out random measurement errors, comparative designs face a challenge. Fuzzy-set QCA in particular has been criticized for parameter sensitivity (the inferences being very sensitive to small measurement errors and model specification changes), confirmation bias (identifying randomly generated conditions as causally important, and sufficient in particular), and failures to uncover the causal structure in the data more generally (Hug, 2013; Krogslund & Michel, 2014). Recent methodological efforts are targeted to address these problems, for example, by developing appropriate sensitivity tests for fsQCA (Eliason & Stryker, 2009).

Since often comparative analysis is performed on a set of available cases (and in most of the cases for very good reasons, for example, because these cases constitute the entire population) rather than probability samples, the generalizability of the analytical insights is dubious. This is less of a problem for researchers who are interested in retrospectively accounting for the cases at hand rather than generalizing, but the limitation should be kept in mind when the inferences are projected beyond the context they were generated from.

Lastly, the cross-case analysis stage of comparative research is weak in distinguishing association from causation (Seawright, 2005). The directionality of causal paths, causal mechanisms, and the refutation of alternative explanations all need to be addressed in a subsequent stage of within-case analysis. It is not that this is a challenge unique to small-N comparisons or QCA – as we discussed at length in previous chapters, these are issues relevant to all research designs with explanatory goals – but the toolbox of large-N approaches to address these issues is often unavailable to comparativists. Therefore, the importance of connecting cross-case patterns to within-case analysis looms large. Comparative scholars must seek more intimate knowledge of all their cases than quantitative researchers can afford to have. Otherwise, small-N comparisons appear to be nothing more than degenerate forms of large-N designs (which they are not).

The tone of the discussion and the focus on the limits of small-N comparative research for *causal analysis* might create an overly negative impression of the merits of comparative work in general. That would be wrong. Comparative research is a fundamental part of political science in all its substantive subfields. Like travel, comparative research is fatal to prejudice and narrow-mindedness. It shows that much of what we take for granted in our local context is in fact contingent, unique, or just an aberration. (For someone living in Western Europe, for example, the reality of an open, liberal, democratic polity might appear the natural state of affairs, but as soon as one moves away from this relatively small geographic region, or looks back in time, it will be obvious how rare, special, and fragile liberal democratic polities are.) Comparisons can show that basic human practices, such as raising a child, selecting a leader, or negotiating a deal can be organized in vastly different ways, often with vastly different social and political results. They open the mind to the amazing variety of institutional forms, moral standards, and cultural practices that societies across the world have developed.

But comparisons do more than relativize our own experiences and ideas. They can reveal that seemingly trivial differences in otherwise similar social and political settings can lead to dramatically divergent national political and policy outcomes. And they can suggest shared patterns beyond the idiosyncrasies of particular cases, commonalities that bring 'most different' cases together. After all, the need for just and efficient collective decisions, which underpins all political and governance concerns, is shared by all humans, so there must be a common theme to the human experience.

Comparisons remain indispensable for the generation of new ideas, research questions, theoretical concepts, and insight. But what this chapter made clear is that the observation of a small number of available cases has important limitations when in comes to delivering precise and reasonably certain answers about causal effects and retrospective explanations. The analysis of small-N comparative data can inspire new hypotheses or narrow down the field of potential explanations, but it cannot, in general, support prediction or the prospective evaluation of policy interventions. These limitations should be kept in mind when small-N informal comparisons are used to support policy advice, propose cross-national institutional transplants, or advocate radical social reforms.

Further Reading

There is no shortage of books on comparative designs and methods in political science. Some classics include Merritt and Rokkan (1966), Guy Peters (1998), Lijphart (1971), and Przeworski and Teune (1970) (but beware of the outdated part on most similar and most different designs in the last one). The interviews with prominent comparativists collected in Munck and Snyder (2007) sometimes provide more illuminating insights on the conduct of comparative research in political science than books on methodology do.

Goertz and Mahoney (2012) is an engaging exploration of the differences and commonalities between the quantitative and qualitative research traditions in the social sciences. This is the theme of a never-ending discussion, and many useful perspectives are collected in the contributions in the symposium in *Comparative Political Studies* (2013, 46 (2)), the special issue of *Political Analysis* (2006, 14 (3)), and Brady and Collier (2004); see as well King, Keohane, and Verba (1994).

The design and methodology of small-N comparisons are closely affiliated to the agenda of comparative historical analysis (see Mahoney & Rueschemeyer, 2003). Methodological challenges of comparative work in the context of public policy studies are discussed in depth in Engeli and Allison (2014).

Goertz (2006) has an excellent discussion of necessary and sufficient conditions, but mostly in the context of concept formation. See also his article with Bear Braumoeller (2000).

The main developer and proponent of QCA over the years has been Charles Ragin, and his books are a natural starting point to learn more about the method (1987, 2000, 2008). Other recent textbooks on QCA and other set-theoretic methods for comparative analysis include Caramani (2009), Rihoux and Ragin (2008), and Schneider and Wagemann (2012). The COMPASS website (http://www.compasss.org) is a treasure trove of resources about QCA, including best practice guides (for example, Schneider & Wagemann, 2010), working papers, bibliographies, and links to software.

QCA is also a subject of great controversy. Some good entry points into the debates about the merits, limits, and future of QCA include the symposiums in APSA's *Qualitative and Multi-Method Research* (Spring 2014), *Sociological Methodology* (2014, 44 (1)), and *Political Research Quarterly* (2013, 66 (1)).

Chapter 10

n = 1

Single-Case Study Designs

Single-case studies are surrounded by more confusion than any other type of research design in political science. Much of the confusion arises from misunderstanding the label 'case study'. In a sense, all research projects are case studies. A public opinion survey of 1,500 randomly selected Americans is a case study of American public opinion. A laboratory experiment of altruism with 30 participants from one German town is a case study on altruism in contemporary Germany. A comparison of the East German, Polish, and Romanian political upheavals in 1989 is a case study of regime change in Eastern Europe.

What distinguishes the single-case designs discussed in this chapter from other research is the type of evidence used to derive inferences and explanations. Instead of looking across units, single-case studies examine multiple pieces of evidence about a single unit. The analysis is *within* rather than *across* cases. Instead of measuring few variables for many cases, we make many observations related to a single case. Within-case explanatory analysis does not only focus on the relationship between one outcome variable and one main explanatory variable, but explores the alternative predictions and mechanisms of competing theories/explanations about a multitude of observable aspects related to a single case. Much like detective work, explanatory case study research investigates the congruence between a wide range of evidence with a small number of hypotheses that compete to account for it.

Single-case studies can provide valuable contributions to science, but the connection between the empirical case and existing theories needs to be even stronger than in the context of comparative, quantitative, or experimental research. Case studies can be useful either when we have very few theoretical ideas about the research topic or when we have very strong and well-established theories. In the former case, we can use purely descriptive or exploratory case studies for theory generation, or plausibility probes and 'most likely case' designs for preliminary tests and illustrations of new theoretical models. In the latter, we can use 'crucial case' or 'least likely case' designs to undermine or delimit the scope of existing well-established theories. And, last but not least, we use case studies when we want to, well, explain cases.

In practice, the process of scientific explanation for single cases much more closely resembles logical *abduction* than either pure induction nor deduction, so this chapter clarifies the nature of abductive reasoning.

285

Then it goes on to introduce Bayesian inference as a way to systematically evaluate competitive explanations on the basis of observational data.

What Is a Case?

Case study research is about the intensive study of a single case. This definition is close to the one offered in the influential text of John Gerring (2007, pp. 20 and 37) but excludes the study of 'a small number of units' (which would be a small-N comparative design in the terminology adopted in this text) from its scope and does not require that the research purpose is to understand a larger class of similar units (the purpose could well be only understanding the particular case being studied). Unlike the experimental, large-N, and small-N comparative designs discussed so far, single-case designs are based on the analysis of rich data about a single case rather than on cross-case comparisons. When single-case designs are used for *explanatory* research (and this is only one of their possible uses, as we shall shortly see), their power derives not from comparisons across cases, but from within-case analysis.

This definition of case study research raises the question, '*What is a case?*' The somewhat surprising answer is that it depends. More specifically, it depends on the research question, on the analytical framework (concepts and theories, assumptions and hypotheses), and on the intended domain of generalization of the inferences. At a certain level of abstraction, all (empirical) research is a case study of something. A monumental three-volume history of the Roman empire is nothing but a case study of the Roman empire; a Eurobarometer public opinion survey, which typically has more than 35,000 respondents, is nothing but a case study of European public opinion at a specific point in time; a statistical analysis of the causal link between political stability and economic development is nothing but a case study of this relationship, even if it includes all countries in the world. And the year-long observation and documentation of all aspects of life in a small American town by a whole team of social scientists is nothing but a case study of a town in a particular year. While this meaning of the term 'case study' is certainly legitimate, it is too broad for our purposes in the current chapter. By the term 'single-case studies', we agree to refer to analysis that makes *exclusive* use of within-case evidence only. Even this narrower definition leaves some doubt, but a few examples can help clarify what would and what would not be covered by it.

Imagine that we are interested in explaining why the Dutch health care sector was radically reformed in 2006 by the introduction of a new system of health insurance and strengthening market-based competition in the sector. This reform episode constitutes our (single) case. If we were to answer the question '*What were the main causal factors behind the reform?*' there are two principal paths we can take. The first path is comparison across cases. The comparison can be with other countries, but it can also be with other reform or near-reform episodes in the same country. Both of these strategies would count as cross-case comparative designs. The comparison over time would *not* be considered a single-case study, because it is the reform or near-reform episodes that constitute the case and not the country as such. For example, if our main hypothesis is that the major causal factor behind the reform was health care spending pressure on the national budget, then each year (or some slightly longer period) becomes a separate case even when it still concerns the same country, and the evidence for or against the hypothesis would be provided by the strength of covariation between budget pressure and the incidence of reform (after all necessary adjustments, as discussed at length in Chapters 8 and 9).

But there is a second path to approaching the original question that relies exclusively on within-case evidence. Along this path, we would examine in detail how the different hypotheses we have identified fare against multiple pieces of information about the particular reform episode that constitutes our case. For example, we would examine whether the budget pressure created by health care costs was discussed in Parliament as a motivation for the reform, whether it featured prominently in internal cabinet budget negotiations, whether the individual health care provision units struggled under the existing budget allocation, and so on. If the alternative hypothesis is that the reform was produced by a change in the preferences of the medical profession, we would examine what evidence there is that these preferences changed indeed and whether this can be considered enough to push through the reform. This chapter will have more to say about what kind of within-case evidence should be sought and how strong can inferences based on such evidence be, but for now just note that the data analysed according to this approach are not about a small number of variables across several or many cases but about a larger number of variables (observations of different aspects of the case) within a single case.

For another example, consider we want to explain the decision of Britain to intervene militarily against the Islamic State (ISIS) in 2014. A cross-case approach will compare the United Kingdom to other countries or perhaps the 2014 intervention decision to other historical episodes when the UK has had the possibility of intervening or not. A within-case analysis will examine each hypothesis (expectation) against evidence related to the 2014 decision only. For instance, the hypothesis that pressure from Levantine communities living in Britain led to the intervention would be checked against evidence that there were wide-spread public demonstrations or lobbying by these communities in favour of the intervention.

These two short examples help clarify the distinction between cross-case and within-case approaches to explanation, but there is almost always some doubt about what exactly constitutes the case and where its temporal boundaries in particular lie. With reference to the example above, can we set unambiguously the beginning of the health care reform episode and clearly delineate it from the previous episode of stability (or near-reform)? Probably not to everyone's satisfaction, especially if the relevant variables change only gradually. This problem is often encountered in historical case studies that focus on a single country but over an extended period of time, so that it is unclear whether for analytical purposes the study is based on one or several cases.

Let us not forget that despite all its idiosyncrasies, in the social-scientific context *a case* always remains *a case of* some broader phenomenon, as the term itself implies. We might or might not be interested in the broader phenomenon of which our case is a case, but the fact remains that if we cannot place our case into a more general reference class, scientific research would not be possible. This is because within-case analysis relies on causal relationships and mechanisms established for this general class of phenomena and applied to the particular case. In the absence of a general reference class, we would know no relevant relationships and mechanisms to use in the explanation of our case. For example, we only know that natural resource endowment is a probable cause for the lack of democratization in Azerbaijan because the political system of this country is an instance of the class of non-democratic political systems, its economy is an instance of an economy based on the extraction of natural resources, and a link between the two has been proposed on theoretical grounds in the academic literature on the 'resource curse'. Yet, in a case study, we might only use within-case evidence to support or refute this hypothesis for the specific case of Azerbaijan by focusing on the causal processes and mechanisms on which the hypothesis relies (for example, seeking evidence that potential dissenting voices in Azeri society are 'bought off' with the revenues from oil).

To sum up, what is considered a 'case' is context-dependent, and the case itself remains but an instance of a broader class of phenomena. What distinguishes single-case designs from other approaches is the reliance on within-case observations that go deeper and wider than quantitative scores on a small number of variables rather than on cross-case comparisons.

Uses of Single-Case Designs

Theory application and abductive explanation

Naturally, single-case designs are often used when one is interested in accounting for (explaining in full) the particular outcome(s) of an individual case. To some, that would actually be the only legitimate use of the term 'explanation' and the only legitimate approach to establishing causality for *individual* cases. With reference to the broad types of research goals introduced in Chapter 2, this would fall under 'theory application', but in practice the research process would not be as deductive as the label suggests. Rather, it would be based on the evaluation of competing hypotheses, which in turn would be linked to broader theories. But the hypotheses themselves would also be inspired by empirical clues about of the case itself. In a process that resembles logical abduction, discovered as a separate mode of inference by the American philosopher Charles Sanders Peirce (for a collection of his writings, see Peirce, 1955), hypotheses are created and discarded when they meet incompatible evidence until one hypothesis remains that cannot be refuted and is elevated, for the time being, as the most plausible explanation. In the words of the famous detective Sherlock Holmes, 'when you have excluded the impossible, whatever remains, however improbable, must be the truth' (Sir Arthur Conan Doyle, *The Adventures of Sherlock Holmes*, 1892, p. 315).

Single-case studies invite the explanation of individual cases, but is this a goal pertinent to science as such? Isn't science, the social and political varieties included, about the general and not about the particular, about regularities and not about individuals, about relationships between concepts and not about the idiosyncrasies of cases? One can have different opinions on the matter. On the one hand, generalities that cannot account for particular processes and events would appear to be nothing more than sterile scholasticism. What's the use of political science, if it cannot explain the 1789 French Revolution? What are theories of international relations good for, if they cannot make the conflict between Israel and Palestine comprehensible? On the other hand, not all cases are as important as the French Revolution or the Israeli-Palestinian conflict, and there is no obvious way to draw the line between the ones that are and the rest. Explaining the process of coalition formation in a French village would probably not excite too many people outside the village, *unless* the case study offers some broader insights as well.

A case might have substantive as well as scientific relevance. Substantive relevance is about the real-world societal importance of the case. Such importance may stem from the relevance of the case for broad groups of people or society and the economy at large. Alternatively, it can stem from the high importance of the case for a smaller group of people who are willing to commission or conduct research into the case. It would be rather far-fetched to say that *all* individual case studies fall by definition outside the scope of political science. At the same time, not all single-case studies deserve to be published in the scientific journals of the discipline as their *general* substantive relevance might be low.

In short, a researcher is free to be interested in any and every case and apply whatever theories and approaches to derive inferences as seems fit. However, he or she cannot assume that the broader academic community would also be interested in this case. The routine application of existing theories and methods to explain particular cases is what true science enables and supports, but not all such routine applications will be intriguing to people beyond those directly affected by the case. Whether such projects qualify as science, only as applied (versus fundamental) science, or not at all is a matter of definition, which is not too interesting for our purposes. Whatever its scientific status, the explanation of individual cases is a skill students of political science should have which justifies our attention to the topic in this text.

Sometimes, irrespective of its societal relevance, a single case might have scientific (theoretical) implications as well. Case studies can be used to test existing theories and to generate new theoretical ideas and hypotheses. For these two research goals they have certain advantages and disadvantages vis-à-vis other larger-N approaches that we are going to discuss shortly. Theoretical relevance cannot be assumed, however, but must be demonstrated, and the selection of a case to study needs to be performed with an eye to the intended theoretical contribution. In other words, if scientific relevance is the goal, the substantive importance of the case cannot be the leading motivation for case selection. Of course, in some happy circumstances a case would have both societal and scientific relevance.

Theory testing: outcomes and mechanisms

In principle, single-case studies can be used for theory testing, although in practice their utility for this purpose is limited. There are two main motivations for such an exercise: first, to test whether the hypothesized effect of one set of variables on another obtains in a particular case; second, to examine whether the effects are realized according to the hypothesized causal mechanisms. The first strategy – theory testing focused on causal effects – has very limited potential, especially when there is great heterogeneity in the population and the hypothesized effects are weak. There is not much point in testing a weak causal relationship relevant for a heterogeneous population with a single-case study design because the result of the investigation, whatever it may be, would have very little import. At most, it can show that a relationship is *possible* or that its *absence* is possible – inferences that *might* be valuable, but only rarely so. Sometimes just documenting the existence of a particular case can have profound theoretical consequences – imagine the implications of a case study of a 150-year old man, a society without language, an elected female political leader in a conservative Islamic state, or free press in an autocratic regime. As a direct consequence of the mere fact of their existence, such cases would undermine and even overturn established theoretical relationships and intuitions. But their discovery would be, by definition, a rare event.

Note that the power of such case studies is inversely proportional to how well established the theory they relate to is. If the theory is widely accepted and deeply ingrained in the existing body of knowledge, even a single discordant case can be truly consequential. The classic example is Arend Lijphart's case study of politics in the Netherlands (1968), which demonstrated that democracy is possible even when dividing lines in society are deep and reinforce each other, against the orthodox theory of the day. But the more porous, contested, and riddled with exceptions a theory already is, the less of an impact a single-case study can have. Sliding down this scale we would reach a point where no sound theories and guiding hypotheses exist at all for the phenomenon of interest, and at that point single-case study designs gain relevance again, but now as theory-generating rather than theory-testing exercises.

Still in a theory-testing context, single-case studies can also be used with a focus on causal mechanisms rather than on outcomes. Often, comparative and large-N studies establish a systematic relationship between variables and purport a causal mechanism that connects them, but do not bring evidence that the mechanism operates in reality. Single-case studies provide possibilities to analyse a case at a much higher resolution and at much greater depth, so that not only the covariation between variables but also the detailed causal mechanisms that connect them are made visible. For example, large-N studies of political decision-making can establish systematic relationships between, say, preference heterogeneity of the actors and the duration of international negotiations, but leave the question how and why exactly the relationship obtains open. With a single-case study or a small collection of within-case analyses, one can go beyond the covariational pattern and show *how* the two variables are connected, detailing for instance the rate at which actors' positions are brought closer together, the number of negotiation rounds, the bargaining strategies used, and the timing of the compromises being made. There is no fundamental reason why experimental and large-N observational studies cannot be focused on causal mechanisms rather than outcomes, but in practice they rarely are. As a result, within-case designs can fill such research gaps. In more general terms, single-case studies can investigate the proposed causal paths, the imagined explanatory logic, or the analytical story that theoretically is supposed to connect a set of variables that have been shown to covary in expected ways.

Exploration, theory generation, and description

As valuable as theory-testing activities are, most practitioners of case study research in political science would not see theory testing as the primary objective of their work. Instead, even when the motivation for case study research is explicitly set to be a contribution to a broader theoretical field of knowledge rather than interest in the case as such, the research goal is likely to be exploratory. Exploratory research is a fuzzy concept that covers a range from 'pure' description to 'enhanced' analytical description (exploration in a narrower sense of the word) to inductive theory generation and the formulation of explanatory hypotheses. The difference with previously discussed uses for single-case designs is that the output of the research is 'softer' and can be best characterized as 'insight' or a novel idea rather than a 'hard' inference about a clearly and previously stated hypothesis or a 'definitive' explanation of a case. The status of the conclusions of such studies would be more speculative, which does *not* automatically mean that they are less valuable.

When a research field lacks a dominant theory or when the theory is not able to explain well large and important classes of cases, exploratory theory-generating case studies can certainly bring added value. In this design the researcher focuses on a puzzling or aberrant case (so the values of both the main explanatory and the outcome variables are known), or if theory is non-existent, on a typical case. The quest is to derive inductively from the case information about possible causal ideas that can account for the particular case but also become the building blocks of new theories or the scaffolding for extensions of existing ones.

The theory of coalition cabinet formation is one that would appear to be in need of such extensions at the moment (see Andeweg, De Winter, & Dumont, 2011; Crombez, 1996; Laver & Schofield, 1990). While the main theoretical expectation that minimum-winning coalitions between the parties that are closest together in ideological space should form is supported in general, exceptions abound – oversized coalitions and those between ideologically distant partners are a regular feature of the real world of politics. Single-case studies of coalition formation of such anomalous cases can propose explanations of why this is the case. As it happens, it is easy to propose new idiosyncratic explanations of why particular cases do not fit the theory based on the intensive study of aberrant coalitions, but it is much harder to generate new hypotheses that find *general support* in the wider population of cases and that fit with the *overall logic* of the theory.

Next to hypothesis generation, 'enhanced' descriptions (or 'explorations' in the narrow sense) are a form of case study research that collects comprehensive and detailed information about a case in a manner that is generally informed by theory but without the goal of *explaining* the case or making a contribution to theory. A case study like that can be seen as a stepping stone towards explanatory research or as preparatory work for further, more structured within- or cross-case analyses. Data collection and observation in these designs are driven to comparable degrees by theory and by case evidence. The researcher seeks information about particular variables previously identified by theories but also pursues promising leads suggested by the case evidence itself.

'Pure' descriptions, in contrast, explicitly abandon connections to theory and hypotheses and only aim to assemble as detailed as possible, uncontaminated by theory, information about the case. As we explained in Chapter 2, completely *atheoretical* description is not possible, as perception is always mediated by the available analytical concepts, but this type of case study research consciously tries to minimize the influence of theory and stay true to the case.

Whether in their pure or enhanced forms, descriptive case studies have important roles to fulfil in the scientific process. First, description is important in its own right. Second, descriptive case studies act like reservoirs from which insight is generated, hypotheses are formed, and theories are constructed (not necessarily by the same researchers or even researchers from the same generations as the ones who did the case studies). Some of the most famous social-scientific case studies, which are best considered descriptive in goals, have for decades provided inspiration, impetus, and a testing ground for further research. In sociology, such case research is exemplified by the Middleton studies (Lynd & Lynd, 1929, 1937), which detailed all aspects of life in a small American town. In political science, the rich information assembled for the Cuban Missile Crisis episode has provided analytical material for innumerable studies of decision-making and international relations (for a great collection of such essays, see Allison & Zelikow, 1999). For the study of organizations and institutions, Selznick's (1949) study of the Tennessee Valley Authority has comparable paradigmatic status. In cultural anthropology, the Human Relations Area Files collect rich case information on world cultures that has been widely used for cross-cultural studies (see Ford, 1970).

Descriptive case studies can be valuable teaching resources as well (Flyvbjerg, 2001). By putting together all kinds of rich information about particular cases, the assembled material can be used for didactic purposes with great effect as the students can sharpen analytical skills, get a sense of the often messy real world of data analysis, and build explanations from the case information. The case-based teaching method is especially popular in law and business administration, but also in some areas with relevance for political science as well, such as the study of group decision-making (see, for example, Raiffa, 1982).

At this point, after all the careful separation between explanatory and descriptive goals, you might be wondering what was the big deal about separating the two, especially since both are said to have intrinsic value. The answer was given in Chapters 2 and 6, but is worth repeating one more time. Descriptive and exploratory (theory building) research are legitimate and often useful, but only truly causal arguments that have survived rigorous testing should be used to direct action (for example, provide policy recommendations and advice), assign responsibility (for example, blame for particular events), and reveal the deeper structure of social reality beyond perceptions and apparent correlations.

Single-case studies are quite a versatile tool. Summarizing the discussion so far, they can be used with descriptive, theory-generating (with two varieties depending on whether a theory is only complemented or created from scratch), or theory-testing (with two varieties focused on outcomes and mechanisms) goals. The latter two goals are explanatory in nature, as is the goal of accounting for a particular case (theory application).

In the context of theory application, a case is selected on the grounds that it is important to somebody who is willing to conduct or commission research into the case. When the substantive relevance of the case is broad, the findings can still be found on the pages of academic journals and books and considered (applied) science. In the context of theory testing, case selection depends on the state of theory in the field. If a dominant theory exists, a least likely case can be selected. On failure in the empirical test, the domain of application of the theory will be delimited, on success it will be expanded. If you show an established theory failing a most likely case, that would be even more consequential, but nobody will be thrilled to see an established theory succeed in a most likely case. If a theory is new, most likely cases and plausibility probes illustrating that the theory *could* be relevant are to be selected. For theory generation, selecting aberrant cases provides a good strategy, if theory, even if not entirely satisfactory, exists; and selecting typical cases is a good option when one really starts from scratch. When case studies are descriptive, case selection can be motivated by either of these reasons, but those studies that have often long-lasting impact are either descriptions of cases that are typical of a population (for example, Middleton) or that are highly unusual for some reason (for example, the dramatic, high-stakes Cuban Missile Crisis).

Selecting Evidence to Observe

Cross-case research works by observing and comparing a small number of well-defined variables across a larger set of cases. Within-case research observes and analyses a larger number of variables and aspects of a single case. Still, even the most-detailed and meticulously researched single-case studies cannot document *all* variables and aspects. As a result, choices need to be made about what to observe and what evidence to collect. And, you will not be surprised to read, these choices are guided by research design considerations.

For the remaining part of this section, the discussion will be restricted to explanatory case studies. To understand the logic of design choices, remember that within-case evidence is always evaluated in light of several competing expectations or, more formally stated, hypotheses. The evidence we seek must increase our confidence in one of these hypotheses and refute or make much less likely other alternative explanations.

Clearly, not *any* evidence will do for these purposes. And some pieces of evidence will be much more efficient in discriminating between the hypotheses than others.

In the context of case studies, we make *observations* of various *aspects* of a case. It is somewhat awkward to refer to these case aspects as *variables*, although in reality these are analytically very similar (compare with Bennett, 2015, p. 7). Some or all observations we collect will become *evidence*, when considered in light of theory and explanatory hypotheses. In the methodological literature, relevant observations are sometimes called 'causal-process observations' (for example, Collier, Brady, & Seawright, 2010), but we will do better to avoid the term, because it wrongly if unintentionally suggests that causal processes and mechanisms can be directly observed (we will discuss why this is wrong shortly) (see also Blatter & Haverland, 2012).

The many observations we collect about aspects of a single case are not *comparable* the way many observations on a single aspect of many case are. Hence, single-case study observations are not quantifiable and do not fit a standard rectangular data matrix with rows for observations and columns for variables. This has led John Gerring to conclude that single-case studies are essentially qualitative in nature (2007). In this specific sense, indeed they are. But note that evidence about any aspect of a single case can be expressed in numbers (for example, the president had five advisors, or the president had 23 percent public approval), as well as qualitatively (the president's house was white). The point is that one cannot compare the number of advisors to the percentage of public approval in the same way one could compare the number of advisors of the presidents of two different countries.

A popular scheme to classify the types of evidence and their implications for the evaluation of competing hypothesized explanations of single cases is organized along the two dimensions of *certitude* and *uniqueness*. The scheme can be traced back to Van Evera (1997) and has been adapted by Bennett (2010), Collier (2011), Mahoney (2012), and Rohlfing (2014). Certitude or certainty refers to the likelihood that the evidence will be there *if* the hypothesis is true. High certitude means that the hypothesis is very unlikely to hold if the piece of evidence is not available, and vice versa. Uniqueness refers to the likelihood that the evidence will be there if the hypothesis is not true. High uniqueness means that, if the evidence is found, it could have been produced under only one hypothesis and not others. Low uniqueness means that the evidence could have been left by several of the competing hypotheses.

By juxtaposing certitude and uniqueness, we end up with a two-by-two matrix with four cells, each exemplifying a type of evidence in the context of single-case designs (see Table 10.1).

Evidence that is low in uniqueness and low in certitude is like a 'straw in the wind'. Its presence cannot differentiate between competing

Table 10.1   *Types of evidence and their implications*

		Certitude	
		High	*Low*
Uniqueness	High	*Doubly decisive*	*Smoking gun*
	Low	*Hoop*	*Straw-in-the-wind*

hypotheses, and its absence cannot imply that any of the hypotheses are disconfirmed. Evidence that is high in certitude but low in uniqueness is a 'hoop'. Finding the evidence is necessary to keep the hypothesis afloat but is not enough to disconfirm alternative hypotheses. Highly unique evidence that is low in certitude is a 'smoking gun'. Finding it is sufficient to take alternative hypotheses out of the race, but not finding it is no reason to abandon a hypothesis. Finally, evidence that is high on both dimensions is 'doubly decisive' because its presence disconfirms all alternative hypotheses but one (the one for which the certitude is high).

Ingo Rohlfing (2014) makes a further distinction between unique and *contradictory* evidence. The presence of some evidence might be a unique implication of one hypothesis but unrelated to another (so that the evidence is not mutually exclusive to the hypotheses). An even stronger form of evidence would be one that is not only unique, but its presence directly contradicts other hypotheses.

When choosing where to focus evidence-collecting efforts in case study research, it is important to keep this classification in mind. Clues that are highly unique to one hypothesis, contradictory to the rest, and have high certitude of being present if the one hypothesis is true are certainly nice to obtain, but in most real research that would be asking for too much. When certitude is low ('smoking gun'), finding the evidence will also be a cause for celebration, but it is less clear what to conclude from not finding it – it could be that the hypothesis is wrong or that we are only not lucky enough to find the evidence. 'Hoop' types of evidence are not very useful, unless we are interested in disconfirming a hypothesis – passing through the 'hoops' is not very informative but failing is (see also, below, the section on Bayesian analysis).

What this discussion makes very explicit is that to marshal data-collecting efforts in case study research efficiently, we need to consider *ahead of time* the implications of finding or not finding a particular piece of evidence for the competing hypotheses we consider. In turn, this necessitates that we elaborate these hypotheses and tease out their empirical implications in as much detail as possible, so that we identify what would be unique, contradictory, or trivial evidence for their support and what would be the chances that the evidence would be available under each hypothesis. Now it should be even clearer why case study research is so intimately related to theories, even when the goals are firmly set in the empirical ground (to account for a particular case or generate inductively a new theory).

The discussion of the implications of different types of evidence provides a bridge to the counterfactual understanding of causality as well. We concluded in Chapter 6 that counterfactual causality is a relevant notion for different types of research designs, be they experimental or observational, large- or small-N, cross- or within-case. In cross-case studies, statistical and comparative alike, the counterfactual is approximated by combining information from the pool of available cases. In within-case studies, the counterfactual is evaluated in light of each new piece of evidence. If our favoured hypothesis is *not* true, how likely is it to find this particular piece of evidence? Conversely, if it is true, how likely is it *not* to find it? The inherent counterfactual nature of such reasoning, which lies at the heart of (explanatory) case study research, is undeniable (Fearon, 1991).

Conducting Case Study Research

As single-case study research can be used in so many contexts and with so many different goals in mind, it is hard to present just one view of how it is to be conducted. To make matters worse, different academic disciplines and subdisciplines have distinct styles and traditions of doing case studies research – it is not easy to see the commonalities among the 'thick description' interpretative case studies of political anthropology, the process-oriented case studies of historical political sociology, the analytic narratives of rational choice political economy, and the in-depth descriptions of policy change in public administration, to name but a few. This section of the text will outline process tracing – one of the styles, or modes, of performing case study research that is currently most popular in political science – in order to provide a sense of how the study works, so that the design choices discussed above are put in the context of data collection and analysis.

Process tracing

Especially in the subfields of international relations and historical (political) sociology, process tracing has become the preferred style for single-case study research to the extent that much of the recent methodological literature on case studies should be sought under this label.

Analytical foundations

Andrew Bennett and Jeffrey Checkel define process tracing as 'the use of evidence from within a case to make inferences about causal explanations of that case' (2015, p. 4), which corresponds rather closely to our definition of a case study. But what is defining about process tracing as *a mode* of doing case study research is the focus on causal mechanisms. The processes to be traced are *causal* processes which is not much different from saying 'causal mechanisms' or 'causal chains'. According to David Waldner, 'the core idea of process tracing is concatenation' (Waldner, 2012, p. 68). Concatenation is a difficult word for a simple concept: to link together; the underlying idea being that in process tracing the researcher uncovers a tight sequence of events that are linked together as if in a chain.

But there is more to process tracing than just the enumeration of events preceding the outcome of interest. To be causally relevant, the sequence of events must be held together by one or more causal mechanisms that strongly imply the links between the individual events. These mechanisms need to be explicitly identified and discussed by the researcher rather than left to the imagination of the reader. And they need to be based on something more than just co-occurrence of events, the same way that cross-case correlation does not suffice to imply causation. But causal mechanisms are not directly observable, according to, among others, Mahoney (2001) and Bennett and Checkel (2015) (see Hedström & Ylikoski, 2010, for a dissenting opinion).

The question is, then, how do we know about mechanisms if not from observing the case itself? The answer is that knowledge of relevant causal mechanisms comes from the body of existing scholarship. It comes from all the experimental, statistical, comparative, and other work that has established causal relationships between sets of variables; from the accumulated theory about the research topic narrowly defined; and from insights borrowed from other related disciplines.

This is a crucial point for understanding the links between different styles, designs, and methods of doing research, so let us dwell on it a little longer. Single-case studies, whether in the process-tracing mode or not, rely on existing knowledge, established via other research methods more suitable for theory *testing*, to provide the causal links between the individual events from which the case explanations are built. Prior research establishes what the possible building blocks of causal explanations are and how they can be linked together, and process tracing uses and combines these building blocks to account for individual cases and events.

Sometimes, it might appear that mere *observation* of two events unfolding in time is enough to establish their causal connection. If we observe that a bus runs over a cat, we conclude with certainty that the bus caused the poor cat's death – no knowledge of previously established mechanisms seems to be necessary. But this is only seemingly so. In fact, we only perceive the causal connection between the two events because experience and research has established that contact between a speeding heavy vehicle and a fluffy animal is sufficient to bring about the latter's death. In the social and political realms, few causal connections would be so apparent that mere observation would be enough to prove their causal relevance. By and large, in the social sciences knowledge about general causal relationships is uncertain and contested. Yet, it is the only knowledge from which explanations of individual cases can be constructed.

A further difficulty in perceiving the link between general relationships (as established by experimental and large-N observational research) and specific explanations of individual cases is that the former are about facts (states of affairs, variables) while the latter are usually about events and personalities. How do we make the transition from abstract relationships between variables, such as economic hardship and geopolitical strategy, to links between specific events, such as the speech of the last leader of the Soviet Union Mikhail Gorbachev at the UN on 7 December 1988 and the fall of the Berlin Wall on 9 November 1989 (Evangelista, 2015)? Again, mechanisms come to the rescue as they connect the variables and the events (Waldner, 2015). Because a plausible theoretical mechanism, established and tested through a variety of methods, connects economic decline with diminishing capability to project military power abroad, events such as Gorbachev's speech and the subsequent demise of the Berlin wall can be perceived as individual links bound in a causal chain. In their turn, the events recounted by process tracing become evidence supporting or contradicting explanatory hypotheses based on these mechanisms.

The practice of process tracing

How does process tracing work in practice? How does one go about identifying evidence and collecting data? Process tracing can work at different levels of analysis (individuals, organizations, states, and so on) and with different types of data collection methods (archival research, document analysis, various types of more or less structured interviews, participant observation, and so on). But whatever the form, data collection is intensive and often the researcher works in close proximity to the subjects of the research, who remain in their own natural surroundings, be that a village in Afghanistan or a ministry in Paris, and sometimes for long periods of time. In the words of Jason Lyall (2015, p. 204), 'many of the methodologies best suited for process tracing ... mandate an often-substantial investment in field research'.

One typical direction in which process tracing research goes is the investigation of actors' motivations and information. Although many aggregate-level theories and empirical studies rely on individual-level mechanisms, in large-N research it is not always possible to verify the incentives that the various actors face, the information they have, and the beliefs they hold. Process tracing case studies can probe these assumptions and elicit a more realistic picture of what the actors want, what ideas they have, and what capabilities they posses to achieve their goals. One way to do so is through interviews. Another is to examine written sources – speeches, minutes from meetings, and so on. Evidence from verbal and written sources can answer questions about actors' motivations and ideas directly: as when a politician reveals in an interview to the researcher that the position she supported in public was only her second best option, but she had to vote for it due to a deal with a fellow legislator. But transcripts and records can provide evidence indirectly as well: as when a researcher elucidates the implicit cognitive frames in an actors' discourse, or when subjects are faced with an endorsement experiment (see Blair, Imai, & Lyall, 2014).

Another typical direction for process tracing research is recovering in as much detail as possible the institutional context and reconstructing the chronology of events leading to an outcome of interest. For example, if the outcome is the enactment of a major piece of legislation, data will be collected on the authors of the draft legislation within and outside the government administration; the intellectual source of the policy ideas embedded in the draft; public opinion; suggestions made during public consultations and government coordination meetings; the formal rules and informal standards of appropriate behaviour in the institutions dealing with the proposal, including but not restricted to agenda-setting rights, voting thresholds, amendment powers, opportunities for linking unrelated proposals in packages, and others; amendments made during the decision-making process with the nature, source, and motivation of these amendments; debates and arguments made in the legislatures; opinions of advisory committees, pronouncements in the media, any public rallies, interest group support, or other forms of advocacy; intra-party discussions; votes in legislative committees responsible for the proposal; and expressed support or opposition of individual legislators. Such material would provide but the raw information, some of which would serve as evidence for or against the various hypotheses competing to explain the legislative decision.

When the outcome of interest is a broader social process, such as the expansion of suffrage in the United Kingdom in the first half of the twentieth century, or a bigger event, such as the start of World War I, the focus of process tracing expands accordingly to cover more general and more abstract processes and events as well. The minor details of some institutional provision can still be shown to play a decisive causal role, but attention will be devoted to aggregate phenomena, such as shifts in womens' labour participation or the strategic nature of alliances in Europe, as well. In short, process tracing incorporates individual events and general facts, mediates between structure and agency, and shifts between the abstract and the concrete when building explanatory accounts.

Taxing economic elites in South America

At this point, let's look into a real-world example of the application of process tracing methods and case study design. Tasha Fairfied (2013) investigates the general question of how policy makers in developing countries can tax economic elites. Because the economically powerful will resist attempts by the state to impose direct taxation of their assets, this is a knotty problem for governments, especially in democracies with great degrees of economic inequality, such as many of the Latin American states. Fairfield's article presents four cases (two tax reform attempt episodes in Chile, one in Argentina, and one in Bolivia), but most of the explanatory power comes from the within-case analysis of each case and not from cross-case comparisons.

Let's zoom in on the 2005 reform episode in Chile. According to the author, it achieved a success by eliminating a tax benefit for the rich (p. 48). Two factors appear causally relevant. First, the issue of economic inequality became central to the ongoing presidential election campaign; the electoral *salience* and the *timing* raised the political costs for defending the unpopular tax break for the rich. Second, the *type of vertical equity appeal* made by the supporters of the reform in the public debate on the issue made it very difficult for the economic elites and their powerful political allies to resist the reform (p. 49).

Most of the evidence that the author brings to support these two related claims comes from interviews with high-ranking politicians and policy makers. She employs the interviews to clarify the strategies that the political actors considered, their subjective evaluations of the situation, and the incentives they faced. She uses an explicitly counterfactual reasoning to draw inferences from the evidence, for example in the following passage (pp. 55–56):

> These observations suggest that right votes to eliminate [the tax break for the rich] would have been highly unlikely without some new, distinct political dynamic.

Furthermore, the evidence is classified in terms of its certitude and uniqueness (see Table 10.1 above). For example, the fact that right-wing politicians (generally opposing extending taxation to the rich) explicitly stated in newspapers and interviews with the researcher that they supported this instance of reform so as not to lose the looming presidential elections is considered a 'smoking gun' for the impact of the equity appeal, as 'the evidence would be extremely surprising if the null hypothesis [of no effect] were correct' (p. 56). Fairfield also considers and finds no support for alternative explanations, such as the relative institutional stability of Chilean democracy.

The other three case studies that Fairfield presents operate methodologically along similar lines and, taken together, create a powerful account of how legitimating appeals, political strategy, and tax program design features interact to make taxing the rich in developing democratic countries possible. Among process tracing studies, this one is exemplary for paying close attention to issues of research design and causal inference and for explicating how evidence is collected and used to reach the conclusions. Such rigour can help avoid the many traps one can fall into when doing and reporting process tracing work.

Improving process tracing

It is easy to commit two mistakes in doing process tracing (or other modes of case study research). The first one is to bring ever more context into the explanatory account, no matter whether it is truly causally relevant or not. The second is to construct narratives that are nothing more than 'just so' stories. There are plenty of recommendations one can follow to avoid these traps. The most important one is probably the advice to always consider alternative explanations (Bennett & Checkel, 2015, make the point, but it actually follows directly from the concept of causality discussed in Chapter 6 of this text). This already presumes that the study has clearly identified a leading and alternative explanations, as it should.

When a hypothesis is generated inductively from the case material, beware of the dangers of inductive generalization: test the hypothesis against new evidence that has not been available in its creation and explore its logic to derive further observable implications.

Purposefully seek for evidence that would *contradict* the favoured hypothesis. Moreover, try to identify evidence that is independently generated and different in kind. It is nice to have a lot of evidence about a suspect's motives, but it is even better to have some about the motive and some linking the suspect with the weapon used in the crime.

Remember that absence of evidence is not evidence of absence. Some evidence might be unavailable because actors have an incentive to hide it or because it is easily perishable. Therefore, do not rush to dismiss hypotheses just because there is no positive evidence in their favour, if this evidence has low certitude in the first place. Interviewees and other primary sources can not only fail to disclose evidence but can purposefully provide misleading clues as well.

Sources always need to be considered in terms of their possible biases. The possibility that they may give socially desirable, false, incomplete, or manipulated information should always be entertained. Even when evidence (written political statements, for example) is produced not for the researcher but in a real-life setting, it can rarely be taken at face value. More often than not, it will be strategic. Evidence is always contextual, and part of the job of process tracing is to interpret the evidence in light of its context and then reason what it implies for possible explanations.

Process tracing and Bayesian analysis

If there is one underlying theme behind the recommendations above, it is that the researcher should be open to re-evaluating all hypotheses in light of the evidence that becomes available in the process of research. This view is rather close to the philosophy of Bayesian analysis, which is a formalized method for inference combining prior information and new evidence. Bayesian analysis is by no means confined to process tracing. In fact, it is primarily a method for *statistical* inference, but its underlying logic and procedures can be applied to the analysis of individual cases and the explanation of unique events as well; something that would be extremely hard or, for many, even beyond the reach of 'classic' frequent-ist understanding of probability and statistical methods.

Bayesian analysis is being increasingly introduced in the context of process tracing (Abell, 2009; Beach & Pedersen, 2013; Bennett & Checkel, 2015; Humphreys & Jacobs, 2015; Rohlfing, 2012). While a full exposition of Bayesian philosophy and methodology is beyond the scope of this text, the fundamental idea is easy to understand.

We start with prior beliefs about the likelihood of two or more hypotheses competing to explain the same outcome being true. These beliefs are based on prior knowledge, theory, common sense, or even intuition. When new evidence (*E*) becomes available, we update the probability that each *hypothesis* (*H*) is true *given the evidence* in view of (1) the prior probability of the hypothesis Pr(*H*), (2) the likelihood of the evidence given that the probability is true Pr(*E*|*H*), (3) the prior probability that the hypothesis is false *Pr*(¬*H*), and (4) the probability of the evidence given that the hypothesis is false Pr(*E*|¬*H*). Bayes' Theorem gives us the correct way to combine these pieces of information to derive a posterior (after observing the evidence) belief about the likelihood that the hypothesis is true:

$$\Pr(H|E) = \frac{\Pr(E|H)\Pr(H)}{\Pr(E|H)\Pr(H) + \Pr(E|\neg H)\Pr(\neg H)}$$

Intuitively, the updated posterior probability increases with the prob-ability of observing the evidence when the hypothesis is true and falls with the probability of observing the evidence when the hypothesis is false. But further formal analysis using Bayesian methods can do much more than capture this basic intuition.

In fact, the four general types of evidence discussed earlier in this chapter can be conveniently expressed in Bayesian terms. A 'hoop' piece of evidence is one with relatively high probability of being observed when the hypothesis is true Pr(*E*|*H*) *and* when the hypothesis is false Pr(*E*|¬*H*). A 'smoking gun' has a low probability of being observed when the hypothesis is true Pr(*E*|*H*) but close to zero probability of being observed when the hypothesis is false Pr(*E*|¬*H*) (Bennett & Checkel,

2015). That is why a 'smoking gun' type of evidence can be so efficient in narrowing down the field of competing hypotheses, *if only* we are lucky enough to find one. Remember that a *failed* 'hoop' test can be equally informative, however. The probabilities that enter into Bayes' Theorem can be assigned numbers so that the posterior likelihood can be estimated precisely and the relative likelihood of competing hypotheses can be compared. We can also quantify the diagnostic power of different pieces of evidence based on how much they change the relative posterior probabilities of different hypotheses (Humphreys & Jacobs, 2015; Rohlfing, 2012).

Another advantage of the formalization of the analysis that a Bayesian approach enforces is that some counterintuitive insights come to the fore. For example, it turns out that finding a piece of evidence consistent with one hypothesis can actually decrease its posterior likelihood. In short, the reason is that the same piece of evidence might also be consistent with *and much less likely to be observed* under a competing hypothesis, so that the posterior of the competing hypothesis rises much more sharply than the posterior of the alternatives (Bennett & Checkel, 2015).

All in all, a Bayesian approach to process tracing and case studies more generally seems to hold great promise, but as of now there are few applications that take advantage of the formalization. Theoretical developments that would allow for the simultaneous evaluation of various, possibly interrelated pieces of evidence against a set of hypotheses in a Bayesian framework (for example, adapting work on Bayesian networks) would be welcome. At the very least, even if one does not go as far as quantifying prior probabilities and evidence likelihoods, thinking in terms of updating beliefs over competing hypotheses in light of evidence, which is the heart of a Bayesian approach, disciplines the researcher's mind and helps avoid the common problems listed in the previous part of the text.

Limitations of Single-Case Designs

Like all types of research designs, single-case studies have a number of limitations. These limitations are readily recognized and extensively discussed in the literature.

The most important one is the dubious possibility of generalization beyond the case being studied. Because there is, by definition, only one case under investigation and because this case would often be selected for its substantive rather than methodological importance, generalization (external validity) is not ensured, unless one assumes absolute homogeneity of the population of cases and deterministic causal links. Few scholars would be willing to make these assumptions. As a result, the problem of (lacking) generalization looms large.

In some situations, however, this is not a deal-breaker, because generalization might not be a goal of the research. Generalization is nice, but not always essential. For example, when we are interested in explaining why Nigeria was not able to contain the Boko Haram insurgency in the period 2009–2014, the lack of generalization of our results to other insurgencies or other time periods is not necessarily problematic. Yet, it should be acknowledged. Beware of making frivolous or taking seriously claims that arguments developed in a single-case study can be generalized to other cases. There is no guarantee that the arguments would travel in time, space, and social context. Even worse, we would have no estimate of the *uncertainty* about whether they would do.

That being said, individual case studies can lead indirectly to generalization by being embedded in a larger theoretical body of literature. When single cases test or extend theories, uncover new causal mechanisms, and suggest novel concepts, they contribute to general arguments that might prove useful for the explanations of other cases.

A second limitation of explanatory case study designs is that they have to rely on existing theory to provide the building blocks of individual explanations. If these building blocks are missing and if prior knowledge fails to suggest strong causal links between them, it is very hard to connect various pieces of within-case material into compelling explanations. For process tracing to work, 'Events [need to be] linked to each other by an invincible fatality', or at least with a very high probability. But as Voltaire, who penned the above quote, himself recognized back in 1764 (1924),

> present events are not the children of all past events: they have their direct lines; but a thousand little collateral lines do not serve them at all.

The problem is that case studies need a lot of prior knowledge to sort out which lines are direct (causal) and which are collateral.

While the two limitations discussed above are well known, the limited range of tools available to social and political scientists for case study work is less often recognized. To appreciate this point, consider how the work of a political scientist differs from the related professions of journalist, police investigator, judge, medical doctor, and clinical psychologist. These professions share two rather important things with the researcher doing case studies. First, they all need to evaluate explanations of *individual* cases – diagnose diseases for concrete individuals, convict or acquit particular people, identify suspects for specific crimes. Second, they all rely on empirical evidence – medical symptoms, clues from crime scenes, testimonies in the courtroom – to reach conclusions about the truth of competing explanations; crucially, the evidence is almost always incomplete and uncertain. In short, all these professions have to provide retrospective, backward-looking, causes-of-effects, origin-type explanations of particular events.

There are interesting parallels with how the political scientist, the journalist, the detective, and the medical doctor make inferences from evidence to causal hypotheses, and even more interesting contrasts, but what is most relevant for our discussion is how different the tools they have at their disposal are. The journalist benefits from privileged access to the people of the day, leaks from whistle-blowers and other anonymous sources, and even from the ethically questionable practice of undercover reporting. Police detectives have wide-ranging investigative powers, for example to search and interrogate, in addition to significant capabilities to conduct and commission highly technical analyses, not to mention their special prerogatives for surveillance and covert interception of communications. Testimonies in the courtroom are delivered under oath, and for perjury (lying under oath) you can end up in prison. When examining patients, medical doctors usually benefit from the fact that patients have all the incentives in the world to reveal all the evidence they have about their symptoms and other relevant private information. Moreover, because doctors are bound by the Hippocratic Oath and legal standards, patients can share information with confidence that it will not be abused. And, of course, doctors can request highly specialized tests to acquire targeted evidence that can confirm or rule out a certain hypothesis.

Political scientists have none of that. Even when compared to historians, who have access to archives and memoirs, they are acutely disadvantaged. Potential interviewees often do not have the incentives to truthfully share information (too often even to meet the researcher), and there is not much that the scientist can do about it. (Still, some smart techniques for eliciting information, such as endorsement experiments, that do not require testimony under oath, covert surveillance, or waterboarding are being developed; see Blair, Imai, & Lyall 2014.) Similarly, the political scientist rarely has privileged access to persons and locations of interest or resources for expensive, highly technical tests probing for specific evidence. The fact that many of the research questions of interest are (nearly) contemporary does not make matters easier, as many potentially crucial pieces of data about actors' motivations, available information, and actions – exactly the evidence case studies target – would still be classified. To sum up, in addition to the problems of generalization and inductive 'just so' stories, the political scientist doing single-case studies is significantly handicapped due to the limited set of professional tools available for data collection.

These difficulties are very real in their impact. They obstruct the accumulation of academic scholarship and the utility of scientific results. While proposed 'explanations' proliferate, understanding and reliable knowledge lag far behind. A good case in point is the study of the end of the Cold War. *After the fact*, a small academic industry has been engaged in building explanations of this event (see Evangelista, 2015, for an overview), but very few academics had the insight to predict the fragility of the Communist world *before* its actual disintegration.

It would be unfair, however, to suggest that shortcomings like these are peculiar to political science or the social sciences more generally. In fact, the challenges of retrospectively explaining individual cases and events are logical rather than methodological in nature. The uncertainty of causal inference for individual cases will never completely go away, although one can get more or less close to a valid explanation. Just consider that, despite the practitioners' special powers and privileged access to all kinds of evidence, inference in police investigations, the courts, and in health is far from immune from mistakes. Criminal, judicial, and medical hypotheses about individual cases that have been accepted and acted upon are routinely proven wrong, often with tragic consequences. And debates have still not settled issues such as Hitler's motivation to invade the Soviet Union on 22 June 1941, despite more than 70 years of historical research. Simply put, causal inference is difficult, and there is always a kernel of uncertainty remaining, even in the best of circumstances. This is not a cause for despair. It invites humility, but at the same time it vindicates the case study researcher in political science.

One way to engage some of the difficulties of within-case analysis is, of course, to combine it with cross-case inference. In this chapter we deliberately avoided the topic of combining research designs in order to focus squarely on the logic of within-case analysis, but, in practice, there is a lot to be gained from mixing and nesting research approaches. The next chapter will explain how.

Further Reading

The second decade of the twenty-first century has seen a renewed methodological interest in case studies, and several major new books have appeared that redefine the state of the art. Van Evera (1997) remains a classic and the original source of the oft-used typology of evidence. Despite its popularity, Yin (various editions, 1984–2008) offers less coherent and in-depth treatment than the rest of the works mentioned here. Rohlfing (2012) is an excellent contemporary source on case study research and design that deals with many of the issues raised in this chapter in more depth. Blatter and Haverland (2012) is another state of the art text on single and small-N case research that covers various issues of design. (Note that its taxonomy of explanation types is richer than the one used in this text, as the book makes a distinction between causal-process observation and congruence analysis, the latter being closer to the concept of process tracing.)

Bennett and Checkel (2015) is a major new effort to present both the analytical foundations and the more practical issues involved in conducting process tracing. The chapters in the volume provide plenty of examples of real-world applications of the techniques as well as a synthesis of 'good practices' to follow. The book also contains a concise introduction to Bayesian analysis and a discussion of its relevance to process tracing. Beach and Pedersen (2013) is another comprehensive textbook.

George and Bennett (2005) is an earlier treatment that focuses on case studies in the context of theory development in particular. Gerring (2007) is another useful general overview of the nature and uses of case studies. Note that Gerring's general social-scientific methodology textbook (2012b) is relatively short on case studies and process tracing (causal-process observation) for causal inference.

Collier (2011) is a good article-length introduction to process tracing and also an excellent didactic resource. Waldner (2012) is another excellent, if more critical, introduction and one that articulates more explicitly the underlying philosophy of science issues. The symposium in *European Political Science* (2013, Volume 12) offers an additional perspective on this increasingly popular technique.

See Brady and Collier (2004) on contrasts between cross-case inference (or what they call data-set observations) and process tracing (causal-process observations). Beck (2006) offers a critical take from the point of view of the quantitative researcher. Waldner (2015) tries to connect process tracing reasoning to the more general approach to causation embodied in the causal diagrams discussed in Chapters 6 and 8.

Analytic narratives are another mode of conceptualizing the role of (historical) case studies rooted in rational choice institutionalism. For applications, see the collection of studies in Bates, Grief, and Levi (1998) and Morris, Oppenheimer, and Soltan (2004). For a more recent statement on the possible connections between process tracing and game theory, see Kuehn (2013).

'Sequence elaboration' in the context of historical case studies is discussed in Mahoney, Kimball, and Koivu (2009). Katz (2015) focuses on the use of field notes from participant observation case studies for causal reasoning.

McGrayne (2012) is a popular and entertaining history of Bayesian analysis written with the general reader in mind. Stone (2013) is a beginner's tutorial. For advanced textbooks on applying statistical Bayesian data analysis, see Gelman et al. (2013) or Kruschke (2014). For a discussion of Bayesian philosophy and epistemology, start with the corresponding entry in the online *Stanford Encyclopedia of Philosophy*. Dawid (2002) is a great, concise introduction to Bayesian analysis in the context of legal criminal cases, which also reviews the common fallacies an intuitive approach to the evaluation of evidence falls into.

Applications of Bayes' Theorem to police investigation are discussed in Blair and Rossmo (2010) and to criminal profiling in Baumgartner, Ferrari, and Palermo (2008). Broemeling (2007) discusses the theorem's potential for medical diagnosis. Neapolitan (2004) is a (rather demanding) textbook on Bayesian networks.

Chapter 11

Mixed and Nested Designs

The previous chapters considered research designs as separate self-contained modules: a randomized experiment, a large-N instrumental variable strategy, a most similar systems case comparison, a most likely case single-case analysis, and so on. This chapter discuses how individual modules can be combined in the practice of political science research. Combining different designs and approaches can alleviate the relative weaknesses of each individual one and can amplify their respective strengths.

Designs can be combined to attack the same problem (for example, causal inference) from different starting points (for example, cross-case comparisons and within-case analysis). Or they can be combined sequentially for different steps of the research process. Case studies can be used to develop and validate measures that can later be used in quantitative designs. Alternatively, they can be employed to shed light on the causal mechanisms behind statistical associations discovered in large-N analyses. In-depth study of 'deviant cases' (cases that are not explained well by a statistical model) is another strategy for combining case studies with other research approaches.

While mixing and nesting individual research approaches can be done in the context of single research projects, it arises more often as a result of different researchers complementing and responding to each other's work. That is why the chapter presents the progress of one important political science research programs over the course of several decades in order to illustrate how empirical research and theory development, theory-generating comparisons and theory-testing quantitative and within-case analyses combine to move scientific agendas forward. The dialectical nature of the research process is exemplified by a short presentation of the 'management of common-pool resources' research program of Elinor Ostrom and colleagues.

A Pragmatic Approach to Political Science Research

Throughout the chapters, we have adopted a very pragmatic approach to political science research. We have recognized that every research design has relative strengths and weaknesses for different research goals and in different contexts. We have steered clear of the major ideologically charged debates between quantitative and qualitative research and the various *-isms* that characterize the academic study of politics and governance. No design is superior in absolute terms, but this does not mean that 'anything goes'. The multitude of research designs discussed in the text so far are all, by and large, compatible, as long as one is willing to accept a minimum of common epistemological ground (primarily, a rejection of determinism, a denial of radical subjectivity, and a broadly counterfactual understanding of causation).

Within a pragmatic paradigm, the opportunity to mix and combine individual research designs based on different strategies – experimental and observational, large- and small-N, cross- and within-case – is compelling (see Morgan, 2007, for an in-depth discussion of the links between pragmatism and mixed-methods research). According to Louis Mario Small (2011),'the pragmatist researcher is first and foremost concerned with an empirical puzzle, solving it through whatever means appear useful in the process.' Then why not take advantage of the relative strengths and capabilities of individual strategies to achieve a result that compensates for their relative weaknesses? Not only that; combination could even be *synergetic*, so that the end result is bigger than the sum of its parts.

To unlock the potential of combining research designs, we need to consider *how* exactly they can complement and reinforce each other. These strategies for mixing and nesting are not 'rocket science', but they do require some explication. Before that, however, let's clarify *when* to combine.

The modular self-contained research designs introduced so far can work on their own. For small-scale research projects, for example undergraduate student research papers, they would almost always be sufficiently informative. They can, and do, also work on their own for much grander projects as well. It is not that we *have to* mix and nest different research approaches (although some research funding agencies increasingly demand this).

Combining research designs can be conceptualized at three levels at least. First, it can be a part of a single project resulting in a single research article. Second, it can be embedded into bigger, composite projects with several work packages; the output being typically a scholarly book or a series of papers. Third, it can operate at the level of the research field as a whole, with researchers choosing individual projects to challenge, extend and complement previous work with different methods and designs. At the third, most abstract level, mixing and nesting research designs provides a way to think about the evolution of *research programmes* (Lakatos, 1970).

Actually, the previous chapters have already covered a lot of ground related to the benefits and mechanics of combining research methods and designs. The need for combining theoretical and empirical research, which some regard as the application of mixed methods as well (for example, Dunning, 2007), has permeated practically every chapter of this text and does not need a special mention. Chapter 5 emphasized the need for measurement cross-validation. Chapter 8 discussed how various large-N strategies for causal inference – time-series and cross-sectional, instrumental variable and conditioning based – can be fruitfully combined to answer the same underlying research question. *Multilevel analysis* briefly mentioned in Chapter 8 is also similar in spirit to mixed designs. The difference is that the method of analysis remains the same, while the *level* of analysis changes. In the remaining sections of the current chapter we will focus on combining methods that span the boundaries of large-N, small-N, and single-case designs. Chapter 9 defined small-N comparative studies as hybrids, meaning that they combine cross-case and within-case evidence by definition. As we will shortly see, that would make small-N case studies examples of nested designs in particular, where the cases studied at the different phases of the research are the same. The discussion in Chapter 10 has already emphasized that case selection of single-case studies needs to be done in view of how the case relates to existing theoretical and empirical literature. Thus, *indirectly*, we learnt about combinations of single-case studies and other research designs that are especially powerful. The remaining task of the current chapter is only to complement and systematize all these insights dispersed among the preceding pages.

Mixing and Nesting

There are various ways to combine research approaches. First, we can distinguish between research that collects different types of data (*mixed data collection*) and research that uses different methods to analyse the same type of data (*mixed data analysis*) (Small, 2011). Our attention will be focused on the first, the data-collecting variety, as it is more relevant for research *design*. Developments in mixed data-analysis techniques, especially ones that try to cross the qualitative-quantitative divide, are exciting (see, for example, Abbott, 1995; Franzosi, 2004; Singer, Ryff, Carr, & Magee, 1998) but too technical to be presented here.

Mixed designs can be *nested* or not. When they are nested, the same cases are analysed at each stage of the research process. For example, in a nested design, if the first stage is a large-N survey of individuals and the second stage is in-depth interviews with a smaller number of people, the people sampled for the second stage must be part of the large-N survey as well. Similarly, if the first stage is a case study of a country, the second stage of a cross-country regression analysis would need to include that country. For non-nested designs, there is no requirement for the same cases to feature at all stages of the research. For example, one sample from a population can be used for the large-N survey and another sample (from the same population) for the subsequent in-depth interviews. The choice between a nested and non-nested design is usually driven by practical considerations. In many circumstances, it is not possible (and for good reasons) to identify the individual respondents of a survey so that one can go back and conduct further interviews with them. Some techniques of combining research designs require that the same cases are included at each stage (see below), but for others this is not a necessity, provided that one is willing to assume a relatively homogeneous population of people, organizations, states, or whatever else constitutes the level of analysis.

Combining methods of data collection can be done at the same time (concurrently) or one after another (sequentially). The first option can be used when the exact timing of data collection does not matter and when the stages are not closely interrelated. When the results from the first-stage analysis are used to select cases for further study, for instance, concurrent data collection clearly cannot work. Sequencing research designs can take many forms, depending on the goal and motivation of mixing.

Uses of Mixed Research Designs

Triangulation and cross-validation

One major goal of combining research designs can be triangulation (Ragin, 1987). Triangulation means that the same problem is approached with different methods. If they lead to the same result, then we can be more confident that the result is valid. Triangulation is often used for measurement issues. Say we are interested in the question of which societal issues people in Spain find most important. We can administer a standardized questionnaire to measure people's priorities in which the respondents choose an issue from a predefined set, and we can have unstructured interviews in person in which the interviewees talk freely about which issues they consider important. If both measurement approaches lead to the same result, we would have increased our confidence in the validity of the measures. For another example, a leader's effectiveness can be measured by interviewing the leader, observing his actions, and collecting formal performance records (Jick, 1979).

Triangulation can be performed using different varieties of the same method (for example, different scales for measuring public opinion), but it is stronger when totally different methods are used. The combination of methods can be implemented either sequentially or concurrently as the timing does not matter. Triangulation can also be used at the stage of data analysis where different techniques are used to explore the same data.

In contemporary political analysis, a good example of where triangulation of measures is possible and often advisable is the estimation of the ideological preferences of political parties. As discussed in Chapter 5, there are several, rather different methods for deriving party preferences – some based on expert opinions, others on the analysis of party manifestos, yet others based on observed behaviour such as voting. In any empirical application where party preferences and other political attitudes feaure in the analysis, triangulation of the measure from the stand points of the different measurement methods can be very informative. If the methods agree, our confidence in the validity of the measure would greatly increase. If the methods disagree, the analysis can be rerun with the different measures to see how the conclusions change depending on which measure is used. In sum, triangulation as a type of mixing methods can be very useful for the validation of measurement.

In the examples above, triangulation involved the measurement of the *entire* set of cases using different methods. This is not always possible or even necessary. Often, measurement validity can be improved by triangulating or cross-validating only a subset of the cases. A survey item can be shown to provide a valid measure of a public attitude by interviewing in depth only a small subset of the total survey sample and demonstrating that the two measures agree for the cases in the subsample.

This can be especially useful when one proposes a novel measurement method or technique. For example, for her study of interest group politics in the European Union, Heike Klüver developed a new measure for interest group preferences (policy positions) based on automated text analysis (Klüver, 2009). The measure was to be used for coding a large number of cases. To demonstrate the validity of the new measure, for one case of consultation on a single piece of legislation by multiple interest groups, the author measured interest groups' policy positions using more traditional content analysis and through interviews as well. As the measures derived using different methods agreed, our confidence that the new method derives valid measures of interest group positions for the remaining cases greatly increased.

Validating theoretical and methodological assumptions

The combination of different data collection methods and research designs can be performed for purposes other than measurement validation. One can use in-depth case studies to validate assumptions made in theory development and in the process of designing large-N research strategies. In the context of theory development and model building, many assumptions need to be made about, say, the preferences and incentives of actors, and the actors' interpretation of the institutional setting. As explained in Chapter 10, in-depth case studies can probe these assumptions and generate more appropriate ones.

Importantly, case studies can also be used to validate methodological assumptions that underpin large-N strategies for causal inference. In-depth study of a small number of cases can examine whether the process of 'treatment' assignment (the distribution of the main explanatory variable) works according to the researcher's expectations, for example whether it can be assumed to be random. Case studies can also be used to check whether the subjects *comply* with their 'treatment' assignment. For example, consider a study that examines the impact of information on political attitudes and uses a randomized delivery of messages through the internet to some of the people in the sample. A small number of follow-up interviews can be conducted in order to check whether the subjects who were sent the message actually read and understood it and whether the subjects who did not receive the message did read it nonetheless (which is possible, for example, because they heard about it from their peers). Such assumptions play an important role in the identification of causal effects via cross-case comparisons, and any information testing their validity can be very valuable. Rohlfing (2008) also advocates the use of within-case analysis (as a complement to standard quantitative tests) to investigate misspecification of statistical models of cross-case variation.

Exploring and validating causal mechanisms

The previously discussed uses of mixing designs help validate measures, theories, and strategies estimating causal effects. As already mentioned in Chapter 10, a single-case study or a small combination of these, can be employed to explore or validate causal mechanisms as well. If the first stage of the research finds evidence for some average causal effect via a large-N observational design, a second stage can look deeper into one or a few cases either to illustrate and validate the mechanisms that link the purported causes and effects, if these mechanisms are known, or to discover and explore them, if they are not. We have already introduced an example of such an application in Chapter 9 (Dörrenbächer, Mastenbroek, & Toshkov 2015).

A related use of mixed-methods research is to interpret and make sense of results from large sample surveys with follow-up in-depth interviews. The stories behind patterns of responses found in the entire data can be reconstructed by individual people in interviews or focus groups, making the correlations between the different attitudes and opinions being measured comprehensible to the researcher.

Mixed-methods research can also be employed to *search* for causal mechanisms in qualitative mode after a quantitative stage has discovered association between variables. Weller and Barnes (2014, p. 7) call this type of research design 'pathway analysis', which has two goals: '[T]o (1) gain insight into the mechanisms that connect some explanatory variable (X1) to some outcome (Y) in specific cases and (2) use the insights from these cases to generate hypotheses about mechanisms in the unstudied population of cases that feature the X1/Y relationship.'

Building theories before testing theories

In the examples above, the small-N in-depth qualitative phase followed up the large-N quantitative one with the aim to clarify mechanisms or increase validity. Mixing research design can work in the opposite direction as well, with ideas developed by in-depth case studies being tested subsequently in larger-N modules.

As discussed at length in the chapter on single-case studies, when no good theories and plausible explanations are available, the intense study of a small number of cases, even as few as one, can help generate hypotheses and ideas that can be subsequently developed further and then tested. If we are interested in the reasons why young citizens of Western Europe join the ranks of radical Islamic fighters in the Middle East, it could be that we do not have a good initial hypothesis to test or that the most obvious hypothesis – for example, that religious extremism at home is the sole reason for violent radicalization – can be easily dismissed with the available facts. Then it might be a fruitful strategy to assemble rich data on the personal background and life histories of a small number of radicalized youths and use this rich information to propose new hypotheses or, even better, develop an integrated theory of radicalization. Importantly, these hypotheses would need to be tested on a new, and larger, set of cases. Since the initial in-depth work would have narrowed down the potentially important variables, the large-N testing phase would not need to be as comprehensive when it comes to data collection about any single case as the initial, theory-generating phase. If the hypotheses do not hold in the large sample, a new phase of in-depth research can be conducted, and so on. The process is iterated until a robust, satisfactory answer to the original research question is discovered.

Testing explanations with cross-case and within-case evidence

Mixing research methods can be done not only for different purposes within the same research project but for the same purpose as well. Namely, a combination of cross- and within-case analysis can be deployed to test a causal argument via different means. Although large-N analysis is by its nature probabilistic, hence, it cannot be expected to account for each and every case, in some contexts it makes a lot of sense to confront the same causal question with evidence from comparisons across cases and within-case (process tracing) evidence about a subset of these cases. This strategy should appear familiar because it is essentially the strategy of small-N comparative designs. The difference is, however, that the within-case studies can be performed only on a subset of the total sample used for cross-case inference. In the case of small-N comparative designs, as defined in Chapter 9, in principle all cases that are compared are also studied in depth.

One good reason to attack a causal question with quantitative comparisons and process tracing case studies in the framework of a single project is when the power of the statistical tests is too low to differentiate between competing hypotheses. Consider the following example. The research question concerns the diffusion of policy innovations in Europe, with a focus on one particular policy area, say, the spread of bans on smoking in bars and restaurants during the 2000s (see Toshkov, 2013, for a study of this question). Theory and data limit the number of potential cases (countries) to less than 30. After we collect data on the timing of adoption of smoking bans in the individual countries, we can examine the pattern of adoption and ask whether it suggests policy diffusion, meaning interdependent policy choices across countries, or independent adoption, in which each country examines and legislates on the issue on its own without looking at the experiences of others. In principle, in a large sample, the distribution of policy adoptions under the two hypotheses would look rather different. In practice, however, with a sample as small as 30, the two competing hypotheses would generate almost exactly the same observable pattern of policy adoptions over time. That is, a statistical analysis of the data would have very little power to distinguish between the two hypotheses of diffusion and independent adoption. Simply put, the patterns would look awfully similar, even to a formal statistical analysis, making it impossible for us to decide which of the hypotheses is more likely to have generated the data. Here is where within-case analysis of a smaller number of cases can help.

Process tracing the adoption of smoking bans in a couple of countries can bring or fail to find direct evidence of whether policy learning and other diffusion mechanisms played a role. For example, the case studies can seek evidence that national officials were aware of the experience of other countries, that they had purposefully examined this experience, that the national policy discourse was affected by foreign policy frames presenting the issue in a certain light, and that the normative appeal of a smoking ban was raised as a function of previous adoptions in other states. The bottom line is that within-case evidence for a few cases can complement a cross-case analysis, especially when the power of the latter is limited, due to, among other possible reasons, a relatively small number of available cases. If the two phases of the research point in the same direction, then our conclusions, for instance that the smoking bans diffused in Europe during the 2000s, would be strengthened.

It is more tricky to decide what the implications are when the two phases of research point in opposite directions – for example, when the cross-case analysis suggests policy diffusion while the case studies can find no evidence of it. Since causal arguments in political science are almost never deterministic, the two sets of inferences *can* be compatible – the intensively studied case might be one for which the general causal pattern does not hold, although the pattern remains relevant for the sample as a whole. But if we too easily accept this logic, then the rationale for mixing cross-case and within-case evidence is undermined. So the possibility that only one set of inferences is correct should also be entertained. The judgement about which one to trust should be made in view of the likelihood of finding within-case evidence, the statistical power of the cross-case analysis, and other considerations, but, in any case, the uncertainty about any conclusions from the analysis would increase when different methods lead to opposite inferences. This discussion naturally leads us to the next problem to consider: when designing mixed and nested research projects, which cases should we select in order to make the most of the combination?

Selecting Cases in Mixed and Nested Designs

Case selection when combining large-N and single-case designs

Let us first consider a scenario where we have a relatively satisfactory large-N model which uncovers a strong relationship between one (or a set of) explanatory variables and an outcome, but a few outliers do not conform to the general relationship. Figure 11.1 illustrates a scenario like that. It plots a hypothetical dataset of 54 cases along two dimensions – *GDP*

Figure 11.1   *A hypothetical example of a strong relationship between GDP per capita and government effectiveness, with outliers*

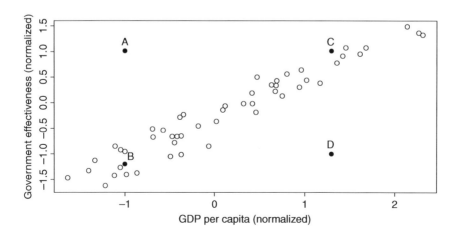

per capita (the main explanatory variable) on the x-axis and *government effectiveness* (the outcome of interest) on the y-axis. Each dot represents a country. The two variables appear very strongly positively related, and the relationship is very tight – there is not much residual random variation. To make the example more believable, imagine that the figure plots the residual relationship between the two variables after other relevant variables have been taken into account and appropriate transformations of the variables have been made. Despite the extremely strong relationship, there are a couple of outliers: point 'A', which has way too high government effectiveness given the general pattern and its GDP per capita level, and point 'D', which has way too low government effectiveness given the general pattern and its high level of GDP per capita.

Although the explanatory power of such a strong pattern as the one depicted in Figure 11.1 would be rather compelling on its own, we might still want to achieve an even more comprehensive explanation of our cases, and we might have the resources for a small number of additional in-depth analyses. Which cases to select for further study? Well, it seems natural to focus on the outliers as they are the ones that cannot be accounted for by the general pattern. Lieberman (2005) makes the case that we should conduct a focused comparison in which the outlier is studied next to a similar case that is 'on the regression line', meaning that it fits the general pattern well. In our hypothetical example, we could compare the outlier 'A' to case 'B', or the outlier 'D' to case 'C' as each pair has the same value on the main explanatory variable (GDP per capita) but very different values on the outcome variable. Essentially, the in-depth study would look for differences between 'A' and 'B', and between 'D' and 'C' that can account for the different levels of government effectiveness these cases have. The logic of this case selection strategy is the same as the one of most similar systems design with different outcomes discussed in Chapter 9. As we pointed out then, this strategy of small-N comparisons can be useful to generate new hypotheses. And, of course, these new hypotheses can and should be tested against a larger set of cases.

An alternative case selection strategy would be to compare the outlier 'A' to case 'C', and the outlier 'D' to case 'B'. That would imply that the cases share the outcome, but differ in the levels of GDP per capita. It is the logic of most different systems design with shared outcomes. Again, as noted in Chapter 9, this strategy can also suggest new explanatory ideas, but its potential is weaker than the one of a most similar design with shared outcomes in this type of nested analysis. The reason is that the explanation of the good government levels of cases 'C' and 'B' are already known from the statistical model: it is their respective levels of GDP per capita. Obviously, these cannot be the right explanations for cases 'A' and 'D', so the comparison cases ('A' with 'C', and 'B' with 'D') cannot share the same explanation, which is required by the logic of most different systems with same outcomes design.

The discussion above presupposes that the large-N part of the research had discovered a strong pattern and built a convincing explanation with only a small number of cases that do not fit. When the large-N analysis is altogether unsatisfactory, the situation is the same as if we have no prior theory. Under that scenario, a *typical* case can be selected for in-depth study, so that any hypotheses generated from its investigation would have a higher a priori likelihood of being relevant for the entire sample (see also Lieberman, 2005).

Note that these recommendations for case selection in nested designs (see also Rohlfing, 2008) differ from the ones in the highly-cited article, by Lieberman (2005). Evan Lieberman suggests that, if robust and satisfactory results appear from a statistical model, 'on-the-regression-line' cases (meaning, cases that fit well in the model) for in-depth study should be selected randomly or deliberately in order to 'test the robustness of the findings' (p. 442). Alternatively, if the statistical model is not robust and satisfactory, a comparison of deliberately selected cases on and off the regression line (the latter would be outliers) should be done (see p. 437 for an overview). In practice, however, there would never be a statistical model that fits the data so well that the only thing left for the researcher is to test its robustness (in our terminology, that would be to validate the model's assumptions) with a case study. Therefore, one is better off using the comparison between well-fitting cases and the outliers to extend the theory, as our discussion above suggests. Alternatively, when the statistical model does not produce a good explanation, there is little point in focusing on 'on-the-regression-line' cases, since the overall model – hence, the underlying theory – is not good at all. Perhaps the differences between the case selection strategies advocated in this chapter and the ones suggested in Lieberman (2005) arise from differences in the evaluation of how good a model needs to be to qualify as 'robust and satisfactory'. For example, the model depicted in Figure 11.1 is already extremely good, despite the few outliers, according to what one encounters in the practice of political science research, but maybe in Lieberman's understanding that would be an unsatisfactory model that needs to be improved with a focused comparison.

Weller and Barnes (2014) provide recommendations for case selection when one is interested in discovering with case studies casual mechanisms underlying a previously established association between variables. Their argument is quite involved, but in short, the strategy is to take into account the degree to which cases are expected to feature the relationship of interest and the expected variation in case characteristics.

Case selection when combining small-N and single case designs

The preceding section focused on the case selection when combining large-N statistical designs with within-case analysis. Small-N comparisons based on set-theoretical relations rather than statistical techniques such as regression analysis can also be complemented by within-case analysis. Indeed, as Chapter 9 argued, small-N comparisons *should* be complemented with in-depth study of the cases. When the number of cases is greater, however, it might not be possible to study closely all cases, so some selection of where to focus the research efforts needs to be made.

Schneider and Rohlfing (2013) discuss the question of combining qualitative comparative analysis (QCA) and process tracing at length. The authors distinguish between process tracing within-case analysis conducted prior to and after the cross-case QCA. The rationales for doing pre-QCA case studies are familiar – to generate and explore possible hypotheses and to validate measurement and model assumptions. In the context of QCA, these tasks are related to the delineation of the population, the choice and calibration of causal conditions (variables), and the examination of contradictory truth table rows (Schneider & Rohlfing, 2013, p. 561) (see Chapter 9 for a reminder of what these activities entail). The rationales for doing post-QCA case studies are also parallel to the ones already introduced above – to verify and explore causal mechanisms linking cases and outcome or to extend, amend, and improve the theoretical model tested in the QCA stage. The two uses of post-QCA process tracing within-case research necessitate different case selection strategies.

Case selection when mixing QCA and within-case studies depends on whether the focus is on relationships of necessity or sufficiency. When the analysis is focused on *necessity* and we want to validate causal mechanisms, the advice of Schneider and Rohlfing (2013, pp. 566–567) is to select at least one case per term of the relevant causal recipe, and these cases had better not have joint membership in the different terms of the recipe. A simple example can clarify the idea. If the causal recipe '*wealth* OR *democracy*' is (almost) necessary for the outcome *government effectiveness of a state*, we would want to select for further in-depth analysis one state that is wealthy and one state that is democratic, and preferably the wealthy state should not be democratic and vice versa (otherwise, the cases would be overdetermined and it would be hard to disentangle the causal impact of the two conditions). If we are interested not in verifying the causal mechanism but in extending the causal model, for example by improving the consistency of the causal recipes, we should focus on a deviant case instead. A deviant case in this context would be one that is not a member of any of the causal terms part of the causal recipe for necessity but still exhibits the outcome. Considering the example above, a case that is neither wealthy nor democratic but still has an effective government would be deviant. In-depth study of such cases can suggest additional causal factors to be considered which can increase the consistency of the causal formula for necessity. For example, process tracing of one state can discover that a poor and undemocratic state might achieve government effectiveness if religion plays a large role in state and society. The updated causal recipe '*wealth* OR *democracy* OR *religion*' can be tested against the full set of cases to see how much consistency would improve.

Turning to the analysis of sufficiency, if we are interested in validating causal mechanisms, the principle of case selection is the same as with the analysis of necessity: choose a typical case for each term that is sufficient for the outcome, and the case had better have unique membership in that term. Things are more complicated when the purpose of post-QCA process tracing is to improve and extend the model by resolving deviant cases (that is, cases that do not conform to the sufficiency relationship). Cases that have the causal condition (formally, when they are members of the relevant set) but lack the outcome are deviant with respect to sufficiency. In-depth study of such a deviant case can suggest a relevant causal condition that has been omitted by the recipe for sufficiency, and by adding this condition the consistency of the recipe will improve. Schneider and Rohlfing (2013, 2014) extend these insights to the combination of fuzzy-set QCA and process tracing.

Case selection for composite projects

It often happens that a researcher or a research team has the resources for several research modules that can be connected into an overarching project. For example, the scale of projects supported by many national and European Union science funding agencies makes such complex, composite designs possible and desirable. Each individual research module can be self-sufficient and based on any of the designs discussed in the previous chapters to ensure the internal validity of the findings. But then several of these can be conducted in different contexts. What is a good rationale for case selection at the composite project level?

While case selection at the level of the individual research module should be guided by the considerations discussed at length so far in the text – controlling for alternative explanations, providing leverage for causal identification, and so on – the selection of research modules can be made with an exploratory goal in mind. That is, the selection of research modules can explore how the relationships identified in the individual modules vary across contexts. In political science, the relevant contexts are often institutional, socio-economic, and cultural. Prior knowledge and theory would indicate what the possibly relevant contextual variables are. Then case selection of the research modules can ensure that there is variation in these contextual variables. For example, if individual country-level projects examine the relationship between public opinion and public policy (policy responsiveness), the selection of countries for study might ensure that there is variation in the electoral system, since this is considered an important moderator of the link between the preferences of the people and policy change.

If the relationship studied by individual modules is novel and tentative, the variation in contexts can be kept small in order to probe tentatively the generalizability of the results. If the relationship is well established, case selection at the project level can ensure that the contexts are widely different in order to probe the boundaries of the results. In essence, this logic resembles the logic of selecting and combining single-case studies for theory-relevant research. The difference is that the module project can be based on any of the designs introduced so far and not only on within-case analysis.

Policy implementation in the EU   Luetgert and Dannwolf (2009) is an example of the application of a mixed nested design for the study of policy implementation in the European Union. The authors aim to explain the variation in performance of the member states of the European Union in implementing the common supranational laws and policies. First, they conduct a large-N analysis of implementation performance at the level of individual laws which covers 1192 cases (laws) across nine different countries. This stage of the analysis includes explanatory factors such as the type of law, the national institutional setting, and the preferences of the domestic implementing actors. Second, the authors identify outliers from the fit of the large-N statistical model. These are cases that the model does not predict well. Many of these outliers turn out to be cases that have been extensively studied previously by qualitative, case-study-based methods. This suggests that the existing literature on the topic might have suffered from selection bias due to focusing on atypical cases. But the insights from the individual case-study-based research suggest further causal factors, for example government change during the implementation process, that can complement and further improve the large-N model. Altogether, by taking into account the findings from a large-N statistical analysis and from single-case studies, the article nicely integrates and moves forward the state of the art in this research field.

Mixing Methods at the Level of Research Programs

Mixing research methods and designs can be employed in individual projects or in large composite projects. It can be done by the same researcher or by a team, working simultaneously or in sequence. When we expand the idea of mixing methods and designs to include related research projects done in sequence by different researchers, we reach nothing less than the notion of a research program. A research program

is an idea introduced by Imre Lakatos (1970) that refers to the evolution
of scientific theories in particular scientific (sub)fields, with the evolution
being driven by a dialectic between theoretical and empirical research.
A research program is held together by a common research goal and
question, and the research done in the framework has enough methodological common ground to allow the researchers to speak to each other.
In political science, the evolution of research programs showcases how
various research designs contribute to the accumulation of knowledge
and how they motivate new research puzzles and questions.

An inspiring case in point is provided by the research program studying the management and distribution of public (common-pool) resources
associated primarily with the name of Elinor Ostrom. Initially, research
was motivated by a problem that was simultaneously an issue of great
societal concern and a theoretical puzzle: communal water management
in the American state of California. Water is a scarce resource in most
of the state, but after years of in-depth, intensive research in the field,
Ostrom noted that while some communities managed to use water in
sustainable ways, others overused and eventually depleted the common
resource. The initial stage of descriptive, qualitative, ethnographic type
of work was followed by a more structured comparison of communal
management practices along the lines of a most similar systems design
with different outcomes. Essentially Ostrom asked what made some of
the otherwise similar communities successful while others were not. The
general conclusion was that success had to do with communal institutions for the management of common resources, related to the monitoring and enforcement of user rights, the settlement of conflicts, and more
(Ostrom, 1965; Ostrom & Ostrom, 1972; Blomquist, 1992).

Building on these insights, a stage of active theory development followed. Ostrom and research collaborators connected their research to
broader economic theories of market failures (Hardin, 1968), made
a conceptual innovation by introducing the notion of 'common-pool
good' as a specific type of public good, and used game theory to tease
out the implications of their theoretical ideas about institutions (see
E. Ostrom, Gardner, & Walker, 1994; E. Ostrom, 1995). Even laboratory experiments were used to test the micro-foundations of the theory
(for an overview, see Poteete, Janssen, & Ostrom, 2010).

Getting a solid theoretical base, the research program vastly expanded
its empirical scope as well. Projects using the common-pool resources
framework were deployed to study the communal management of public goods from the forests of Switzerland to inshore fisheries in Nova
Scotia. The empirical research confirmed the general usefulness of
the framework, but it also brought new insights into what made some
self-organizing communal institutions successful and resilient. While
not conducted in strict theory-testing mode, the empirical case studies
explored the limits of the framework by applying it to very different

economic and cultural contexts. The research program also expanded to the related problem of institutional change.

On the basis of empirical and theoretical research spanning several decades, Ostrom and her collaborators were able to synthesize a small number of conclusions about what can make sustainable management of common-pool resources by self-organized communities possible. These conclusions have informed the design of contemporary governance institutions from the global to the communal level (see Dietz, Ostrom, & Stern, 2003). Moreover, they have been integrated into the fundamental management theories in economics and public policy. This research program has received wide recognition and earned Ostrom the Nobel Prize in Economics in 2009.

The story of the common-pool resources management research program nicely illustrates how various research designs and approaches – from descriptive ethnographic work to deductive theory development to comparative case studies and beyond – become useful and appropriate at different phases of the evolution of our shared knowledge about the motivating problem (see also Poteete, Janssen, & Ostrom 2010). It is through the mix and combination of designs and approaches that the scientific field evolves. The discussion also makes it clear that even small-scale individual projects can make a scientific contribution, if they are well embedded in existing literature and choose a design appropriate for the state of the art in the field.

Critiques of Combining Research Methods and Designs

Mixing methods and designs has many possible applications and *can* be synergetic. But it is not a silver-bullet solution to all problems of research design and causal inference. Not all ways of doing political science research are compatible to a sufficient extent that they can be combined (Harrits, 2011). Some specific ways of mixing designs, such as nesting, require rather strong assumptions in order to be effective (Rohlfing, 2008), and, more generally, it is not always clear whether the benefits of methodological specialization outweigh the added value of mixing methods in the context of individual research projects (Ahmed & Sil, 2012).

Harrits (2011) makes the point that research approaches are not always comparable ontologically and epistemologically, citing the different assumptions that underlie the work of Lieberman (2005) and Bourdieu (1973). In stronger terms, some research paradigms can be *incommensurable* (Kuhn, 1962). Bridging between positivist and interpretive methodologies in particular is taking the idea of mixing too far. The fundamental differences, especially with regard to the question of whether mechanistic explanation or only hermeneutic understanding is possible in the social world, are just too large to allow fruitful collaboration across the divide. As Haverland and Yanow (2012) point out, scholars working in these two traditions have a hard time even communicating with each other, as the meanings of their basic epistemological concepts are so different.

Even when mixing methods and designs is possible and desirable, it is not always clear that it should be done by the same researcher in the context of individual research projects. In contemporary social science, learning particular methods and techniques for data collection and analysis and keeping this knowledge up to date is so demanding that narrow methodological specialization is almost inevitable. Few people can master to the same extent the skills necessary for competent statistical analysis and, say, interview-based data collection for process tracing case studies. The added value from producing a state of the art analysis based on one methodology can well be greater than the one derived from two flawed analyses based on a mixed design (Ahmed & Sil, 2012). This calls for collaboration between scholars specializing in different methodologies in the context of bigger projects and research programs.

A more specific critique of nested designs in the spirit of Lieberman (2005) is offered by Rohlfing (2008), who underlines that the selection of case studies for the second stage depends on the results of the first-stage statistical model and the identification of what are well-explained cases and outliers, typical and deviant cases. But the latter judgements are always relative to the model being correctly specified in terms of included variables, assumed functional forms of the relationships, and so on. When the model is misspecified, either by including too many variables or by omitting relevant variables, what appears to be an outlier may in fact be a typical case *if* we had the correct model, and vice versa. Overall, this undermines the rationale of case selection in nested designs, because rarely would one claim to have a completely correct specification of a statistical model in the practice of political science research. Furthermore, the combination of quantitative and qualitative methods can lead to conceptual stretching and slippage (Ahram, 2013).

Further Reading

There is a lot of interest in the topic of mixed-methods research in many parts of the social sciences (there is even a dedicated academic outlet, the *Journal of Mixed Method Research*), but political science appears relatively less enthusiastic about their *methodological* virtues, though *in practice* research in politics and governance often combines different methods and designs.

Teddlie and Tashakkori (2009) and Cresswell and Plano Clark (2007) are two general social science introductory texts on mixed methods.

Their terminology and classifications, however, may not be very easy to follow for political scientists. Axinn and Pearce (2006) focuses on collecting mixed data.

Weller and Barnes (2014) is a major recent effort to synthesize advice on doing mixed-methods research with a focus on studying casual mechanisms. It is written at a more advanced level, but its concepts are more compatible with the social-scientific terminology and concerns endorsed in the current text. Glynn and Ichino (2014) proposes a new way of formally incorporating qualitative information into a standard large-N statistical framework, which seems very promising but is not well established yet in the discipline. For another proposed framework for integration of cross-case and within-case data in a Bayesian context, see Humphreys and Jacobs (2015).

Dirk Berg-Schlosser (2012) is a recent book on 'mixed methods in comparative politics', but it is focused more on using *different* methods to analyse problems in the subfield of comparative politics rather than on *mixing* methods in an integrated framework. In fact, the book is a good source on the application of qualitative comparative analysis.

Burch and Heinrich (2015) is a comprehensive introduction to the application of mixed methods for policy research and program evaluation, which has developed a somewhat different tradition and language of talking about mixed research from other subfields of political science. Wolf (2010) reviews applications in comparative public policy research.

Chapter 12

Communicating Research

We have identified an interesting and important research question, developed theory and concepts, decided on a goal and matching research strategy, and we have selected cases and the variables to observe. The preceding chapters should have prepared you well for all these tasks. Imagine now that the research is complete: the data have been gathered and meticulously analysed, the inferences have been made, and the conclusions have been drawn. What now?

This final chapter focuses on the communication of scientific research results and the social context of political science research. We discuss how to present scientific results, but in a way that is fair both to their strengths and to their limitations. The chapter provides some practical tips about structuring research reports, writing in academic style, and effectively communicating the often nuanced research findings.

This is also the place where we discuss the ethics of doing research in political science. First, the chapter presents good practices for data archiving and sharing that serve the core values of scientific research: transparency, accumulation, cooperation, and falsifiability. Next, it draws attention to the ways in which empirical research in the social sciences can negatively affect the identities of research subjects and, more generally, how results from academic research feed back into the social world. The chapter considers the rules of scientific conduct related to practical matters such as disclosing funding and associations with political parties, advocacy groups, and other sponsors, and how to cite interviewees who cannot be directly identified.

Students of politics and governance have a particular responsibility to uphold because their research is often directly used to advocate for or against social and institutional change. The chapter points to the perils of hard-nosed social engineering and the duty of researchers to communicate the inherent uncertainty, unpredictability, and unintended consequences of virtually all interventions in politics, policy, and society.

Finally, the concluding section reminds the reader about the limitations of social science while summarizing the ways in which proper research design can help us better understand, and perhaps manage, our world.

The Outputs of the Research Process

Political science is a social activity and depends on effective communication of scientific plans and results. Results from research projects in political science most often take the form of written documents. But other types of research output are increasingly popular. For example, instead of narratives or tables of statistics, descriptive research can be communicated with the help of interactive data visualizations. The researcher collects and makes the data available, identifies relevant dimensions and possible comparisons of interest, and prepares the initial settings of the visualization. But the user has a lot of flexibility in how to interact with the visualization and the underlying data, for example, by choosing which cases to highlight, what kind of comparisons to put forward, which time periods to zoom in on, or which associations between variables to explore. The design and development of interactive data visualizations is one exciting and relatively novel way in which political science insight can be communicated to wider audiences, and it is one that is bound to have a prominent role to play in the future.

Another type of research output that is getting increasingly important in political science is predictive models. For now, these are focused predominantly on predicting results from elections, but there are models that try to predict the onset of conflicts as well, and others. Voting advice applications are another product that utilizes insight from political science theories for a more practical purpose; in this case to compare people's preferences to the profiles of political parties and assist informed electoral choice.

The making of all kinds of country rankings on topics ranging from human development to government effectiveness to corruption is another form of research output that is not confined to a book or a research paper (see Chapter 5).

Despite all these new and, in the case of country rankings, not so new developments, however, writing remains the primary mode through which research is communicated. Even online data visualizations, predictive models, and rankings need to be documented and explained, which again requires writing. Therefore, students and practitioners of political science need to master writing as one of their major tools of trade.

Alas, becoming a proficient writer is easier wished for than accomplished. Good and effective writing does not come all that naturally. It requires years of learning and practice, and there are no universal formulas and laws to follow (well, grammar rules are pretty widely and rigorously enforced).

There are several books that offer excellent advice on writing style that every aspiring political scientist should take to heart. (My personal recommendations are the recent volume by Steven Pinker, 2014; the very short and useful book by Alastair Fowler, 2006; and the collection of masterpieces of scientific writing put together by Richard Dawkins, 2008.) One can also learn by closely studying and imitating the style of good political science writers such as Charles Tilly, Jon Elster, or Robert Goodin. In the pages to follow I will offer some of my own views on what makes communicating findings from political science research projects special, and some tips on organizing research papers and proposals.

Styles of academic writing

First, let us focus on the right rhetorical posture to take. Scientific writing and argumentation is quite unlike political or legal rhetoric. In a political debate or in court you try to convince others that you are right and your opponent is wrong. In science, you write as if you have to present the position of your adversary, making the best case he or she could, but no better. No rhetorical tricks, no emotional appeals, no omissions that strengthen the position, no selective use of evidence. You write as if you critically examined all possible flaws in the argument and could not find any, so you reluctantly have to accept it for the time being. It is a rather unnatural attitude to adopt. After all, you want your argument to be persuasive, accepted, and influential. But here is the trick. In science, the influential arguments will be the ones that survive the scrutiny of your peers, and you have to be your most critical reader of all. Being open about the limitations and uncertainties of your work is always better than trying to hide them with rhetorical gimmicks, obscure language, or methodological sophistry.

Second, academic writing works best when it is expressed in simple and direct language. There is a common misconception that to feel sufficiently 'scientific', research reports must use long and winding sentences with complex structure and language sprinkled heavily with jargon. None of that is necessary. Using short, to-the-point sentences and arguments expressed with common words wherever possible will not make you look like a simpleton. It will just make it more likely that the research findings and ideas you want to communicate will reach their intended audience. Sometimes, jargon is unavoidable in scientific writing. But scientific terms should be clearly defined, especially when they can be confused with a common word that has a different meaning in everyday usage (see Chapter 4).

Academic writing is also often embodied in indirect language, for no good reason. The passive voice has its uses, but it is overused in scientific papers, sometimes to create an illusion of impartiality, often to hide lack of specificity. Verbs are regularly made into nouns, such as 'exclusion' from 'exclude' or 'comprehension' from 'comprehend' (the dreaded 'zombie nouns' of Helen Sword and Steven Pinker, 2014). Vivid language and bold metaphors are avoided for fear of sounding naive and unschooled in the canons of the academic style. If you think that, due to the complexity of its subject matter, scientific writing must be difficult, hard to follow, and dull, read carefully the best examples of writing in the natural, life, and social sciences (for example, from the collection put together by Richard Dawkins, 2008) and stand corrected.

Crafting effective sentences and paragraphs is necessary not only for communicating research results but also for expressing clearly and persuasively ideas and proposals for research. In addition to attention to style, good writing requires sound structure. When it comes to structure, there are in fact some pretty standard templates you can build on and adapt for your particular purposes.

Structuring research proposals

In Box 12.1, you can see a sample research proposal structure. This example works best for empirical explanatory theory-testing research designs. But in fact a similar template is what many research funding agencies and university departments demand, irrespective of the research goal. Special projects, such as literature reviews, deductive theory development, normative and philosophical work, and research in the interpretivist tradition might need significantly different formats.

The research proposal starts with a brief elaboration of the necessary background to introduce the research question. As explained in Chapter 2, the research question itself needs to be carefully selected and sharpened until it conveys in an effective and succinct way the main intention of the proposed research project. This part of the proposal also specifies the research goal, which, as explained in Chapter 2, requires more than a simple division between descriptive and explanatory objectives. The appropriateness of the selected research goal needs to be justified in terms of its theoretical and/or societal relevance. Even when the question is motivated primarily by its substantive importance, we have to clarify how it relates to an existing body of literature.

The next section of the proposal outlines the theoretical propositions that inform the project. The content and scope of this part can differ a lot depending on the actual research goal. The section is most straightforward for theory-testing projects and most difficult to complete for descriptive and theory-generating ones, since they are less theory-driven. Nevertheless, even in the latter cases it is useful to reflect on the broader theoretical background of the proposal, which is present in all cases.

The next section briefly reviews the main concepts of the study. As explained in Chapter 4, the concepts need to be defined in a precise and unambiguous way.

What follows is to clarify, along general lines, the main research strategy on which the proposal will be based: experimental or observational, large- or small-N, cross- or within-case, or any mixture of these. Once

Box 12.1　*A sample structure of a research proposal*

- Background
- Research question
    Type of research question and research goal
    Scientific and/or societal relevance
- Overview of the theoretical propositions
- Conceptualization of the main concepts in brief
- Type of research strategy
- Research design
    Defining the population of interest
    Sample selection: method and size
    Variables to observe/evidence to collect
        Operationalizations
        Data sources
- Expected output
    Expected scientific contribution
    Expected societal contribution
    Dissemination plan
- Practical issues
    Time-plan
    Budget and other necessary resources
    Other practical considerations
- Ethical issues

the broad outlines of the research strategy are clear, we need to explain the details of the design. The content and scope of this section again differ per type of research but inevitably require us to address the definition of the relevant population that is the intended domain of generalization (even for single-case study proposals); the sample and case selection methods (including power analysis where appropriate); and the type of observations to be made, variables to be measured, and evidence to collect. A discussion of operationalization and possible data sources is usually required at this step as well.

Having presented the research design proper, the proposal needs to specify the type of expected output, which as mentioned above is usually but not necessarily a research article or paper. If possible, a dissemination plan should be devised (including, for example, ideas for conference presentations, academic publications, policy briefs, and blog posts) for the research findings, which requires again a reflection on the intended scientific and societal contribution.

The proposal is not complete without a consideration of the time needed to complete the project, the necessary financial and other resources, and, last but not least, the ethical issues possibly raised by the project. Sometimes this would require a plan for getting all the necessary permissions for conducting the research.

Clearly, the preparation of a research proposal takes a lot of work. It fact, it might need more creative input and work than the subsequent steps of data collection and analysis themselves. It is also important to realize that the amount of work that goes into preparing each of the sections is not always proportional to the amount of space they take on the page. For example, the selection of the research question would often take a large proportion of the preparation time but only occupy a couple of paragraphs in the proposal. Naturally, much of the work done for the proposal finds its way into the final research product as well.

Structuring research reports

The structure of typical research reports resembles to some extent, but also differs in important ways from, the structure of research proposals.

Box 12.2 presents a sample template of the structure of a research report. Again, the template works best for empirical explanatory theory-testing research, but, again, it is often demanded or employed for descriptive, exploratory, and theory-generating projects as well. In the latter cases, it often proves a Procrustean bed for reporting research that is not motivated by the testing of previously defined hypotheses.

The first part of the report – the Introduction – is relatively standardized in terms of scope and straightforward to write (note that although it comes first, it is often written last once all other parts are complete). What often proves difficult in practice is the separation between the next two sections – the Literature Review and the Theory – as their scope overlaps to a great extent in projects that do not develop original theory. Yet, there is a difference, and it is one that should be strictly enforced. While the literature review provides a summary of what is already known about the research question and the topic, the theoretical section elaborates on the theoretical background of the hypothesized answers (including concepts, causal mechanisms, and possibly a model).

The research design section in research reports briefly reviews the logic of the general research strategy, as well as the operational choices about variables and case selection. If necessary, details about the data collection stage are also provided. The next section(s) present(s) the actual findings from the research. Currently, to keep the main text of the report short, many technical details, extensions, and additional results are relegated to a Supplementary Materials section at the end of the report.

Box 12.2   *A sample structure of a research paper*

- Introduction
    Background and motivation
    Research question
    Very brief statement about the approach
    Very brief statement about the results
- Literature review (what do we already know?)
- Theory (not the same as the previous item!)
    Main concepts
    Describing the logic of the argument
    Implications and hypotheses
    Causal mechanisms
    A model summarizing the theory (e.g. in a causal diagram)
- Research design
    General research strategy
    Defining the population of interest
    Sample selection: method and size
    Operationalizations and data sources of the variables (possibly in an appendix)
- Results from the analyses
- Conclusions
    Summary of findings
        The answer to the research question!
    Broader implications
        Scientific
        Practical and normative
    What remains to be studied?
- References
- Supplementary materials (technical details on the derivation of the theoretical model, details on data collection, research design issues, descriptive summaries, complementary analyses, etc.)

The concluding section varies in form and content but at the very least summarizes the fidings, including the proposed answer to the original research question, draws the broader implications of the study, outlines its limitations, and possibly suggests directions for future research.

The structure outlined above works well for research projects that proceed linearly from a question to hypotheses to data analysis and conclusions. But in reality projects rarely if ever work in this fashion. As explained, a lot of research has descriptive, predictive, or exploratory goals that do not require a hypothesis-testing logic. But when reporting the research findings is made to fit a hypothetico-deductive template, the result is a mistaken characterization of the actual research process. It is not uncommon to see even inductive case-focused within-case analysis presented as if it were conceived as a hypothesis-testing exercise. Researchers need to be much more open in reporting their results in a way and in a structure that are fair to the actual goals and logic of their projects, be they purely descriptive, inductive, or abductive. Otherwise, the failure is not only one of style; it is one of substance, as the reader is led to have more confidence in the results than they deserve. This last point brings us to the ethics of research.

The Ethics of Political Science Research

Political science is a social activity and one that interferes directly and indirectly with people's lives, so it is naturally subject to ethical rules, standards, and concerns. The ethics of political science research has two main dimensions – one internal and one external. The internal one is about the integrity of the research work and concerns issues such as fraud, selective and biased used of evidence, and plagiarism. The external dimension of research ethics is about the relationship of the researcher with the outside world and concerns issues such as seeking the consent of research subjects, the boundaries of legitimate interference in real-world political affairs, and more general questions about the role of political science in society.

Research integrity

Let us first discuss the internal ethical dimension or research integrity, broadly defined. Integrity refers to the correspondence between the actions of researchers and the values of the research community. The values of the political science research community include transparency, impartiality, collegiality, and professionalism, but above all a commitment to truth.

Transparency and sharing data

It goes without saying that political scientists have an obligation to be truthful in the conduct and reporting of their research. They should not actively make up or edit data to fit their favoured ideas and hypotheses. And they should not passively omit to report or fail to look for evidence that could disconfirm their conclusions. In fact, outright fraud related to fabricating data or research experiences is very rare in the field. One likely case was disclosed in 2015 and led to the retraction of an already published article from a scientific journal (LaCour & Green, 2014). But it is reassuring that the possible misconduct was discovered relatively fast by other scientists trying to replicate the original work (Broockman et al., 2015). This, coupled with the lack of other cases of fraud over the last few decades, suggests that the scientific process has reasonably well-functioning safeguards protecting the field from data fabrication and other types of gross misconduct. Of course, the absence of evidence for fraud is not evidence for its absence, but it is noteworthy.

There are rather strong norms in the field of political science, and ones that are getting ever more widely accepted, for disclosing and sharing research data, once the research is complete and open to scrutiny. This practice of making research data open and available to others not only protects against data fabrication (because it is, in fact, rather difficult to make up data that look convincingly real), but it also allows for faster and more reliable knowledge accumulation as scientists are able to replicate, extend, and critique the work of others. Several academic journals in political science require that data used for publications is made freely available once the research article is published. Such policies benefit the community of scholars and the field as a whole. (Of course, due credit should be given to the researchers who have collected the original data, as this often comes at considerable cost and effort.) There are many (online) services that collect, catalogue, host, and distribute data relevant for political science. Some excellent ones include GESIS (Leibniz Institute for the Social Sciences) Data Archive for the Social Sciences (http://www.gesis.org), ICPSR (Interuniversity Consortium for Political and Social Research) (http://www.icpsr. umich.edu/icpsrweb/ICPSR/), and Harvard Dataverse (https:// dataverse.harvard.edu/).

Archiving and sharing data is more complicated when it comes to qualitative, ethnographic research based on interviews and participant observation. Often, data are provided by the research subjects under conditions of anonymity. And even when this is not the case, making the original data available might have negative consequences both for the researchers and for their respondents. Political science by definition deals with questions of power, repression, and freedoms. Ethnographic work in particular often documents the overt and subversive ways in which marginalized groups and individuals resist and evade the state and its enforcement apparatus. Obviously sharing too much detail from the 'participant observation' of such actions can endanger the research subjects and can create trouble for the researcher as well. At the same time, to answer normative demands for transparency and replicability, researchers must be able to keep a record in some form of the data being collected and of the process of data collection as well. These conflicting demands create a dilemma that is not easily resolved, and the social sciences are still searching for the right procedures to achieve the appropriate balance.

For a case in point, consider the controversy surrounding the failure of sociologist Alice Goffman to produce her field notes from her intensive, participant observation type of study of young black men caught up in the criminal justice system. The field notes and the original data were requested in order for the author to answer the critics who questioned her methodology and interpretations. At the same time, these data could directly harm her research subjects who often live running from the law. Furthermore, the published book suggested that the original data could contain evidence leading to a felony charge for the researcher herself (see, for details, the story on the case by Marc Parry in the *Chronicle of Higher Education* from 12 June 2015 http://chronicle.com/article/Conflict-Over-Sociologists/230883/).

Protecting the anonymity of respondents is necessary in large-N surveys and censuses as well, which may conflict with the requirement for data transparency and availability. In effect, this means that often survey and census data are not revealed in full or at the lowest level of aggregation at which the data have been collected to avoid inadvertently identifying respondents. So in large datasets, anonymity is achieved through data-analytic means.

Opportunistic data analysis

While outright data fabrication is rare in political science, there are more subtle ways in which the researcher can influence the findings during the data analysis stage. Taken together, these certainly create a much bigger potential problem than fraud. They may take many forms, from unintended errors in data coding and transformation, to tweaking the statistical models until they produce the desired results, to selective reporting of research findings.

Making data open and shareable can help with the first problem of unintended errors. Furthermore, some academic journals require that the authors deposit not only their data but their data-analytic scripts as well (the list of commands with which the data have been prepared and analysed).

Opportunistic data analysis, or tweaking the analysis until it returns favourable results, is a much harder problem to detect and correct. As explained in Chapters 7–9, all research and data analysis is built around a complex set of assumptions. By manipulating these assumptions, researchers can often get different sets of results, some of which will fit much better with their favoured ideas and hypotheses. By deleting outliers from the data, adjusting the statistical details, and 'controlling' for different sets of covariates in the models, different inferences can be made to appear from the data. When the researcher has an incentive to report only some of these, the scientific field as a whole has a problem. What can help is exploring the sensitivity of research results to various assumptions and making sure that the findings are reasonably robust to different model specifications and substantive assumptions.

Another recent development that is proposed to address this problem is the so-called preregistration of research proposals. The idea is that the researcher submits to an independent study register a detailed plan for data collection and analysis, which not only specifies (as in standard research proposals) what type of data would be collected and how, but also what type of analysis would be conducted, what variables would be included in the statistical model, what effects and interactions would be tested, and so on. To protect the originality of the research, the plan can be made publicly available only after the research is conducted, but it is still submitted beforehand. The preregistered plan would significantly limit the discretion of the researcher to tweak the analysis to get favourable results and would also help with the 'file-drawer' problem as well (see below).

For now, preregistration is a novel idea that is gaining some ground in political science. In the future, it could become a standard practice, especially for experimental hypothesis-testing type of research. But it is harder to see how the idea would apply to more exploratory, theory-generating, and even theory-testing *observational* research. (For more information on preregistration, see the symposium on the topic in *Political Analysis*, 2013, Issue 1. You can preregister a research plan at the Harvard Dataverse web portal.)

Again, the problem of opportunistic data analysis is even trickier to address in qualitative research, as in its context it is much harder to define what even counts as an observation in the first place. Furthermore, the researcher is the only one who would have intimate knowledge of the case and, as a result, more leeway in what information to highlight and what to ignore. While in large-N research other scientists can analyse the original dataset in different ways and explore the robustness of any inferences drawn from it, in qualitative research the findings hinge to a much greater extent on the integrity of the researcher, as replication of the data collection process is often impossible.

Selective reporting and the 'file-drawer' problem
The next problem – selective reporting and publication of results – is perhaps the most serious, and one for which the blame must be shared between individual researchers and the scientific publication outlets. The problem concerns the tendency of positive findings about causal effects to be more easily published in academic journals and books, while negative ('null') findings of no effects are left unreported or unpublished (this is known as the 'file-drawer problem'). To some extent this is natural. To gain publicity and readership, journals and researchers want to focus on what is new, exciting, and promising rather than 'null' results and failed replications of old findings. But positive, novel, and surprising research results routinely turn out to be exaggerated, fragile, or just wrong. Yet, they would already have their place in the scientific literature, while the failed attempts at replications would not. Taken together,

this implies that much of what is considered the state of the art in a field can be untrustworthy.

It is unclear to what extent the problem affects contemporary political science, but related disciplines such as psychology and social psychology are in the midst of a replication crisis as many of what were considered seminal studies in these fields have turned out to be quite difficult to replicate. The problem is compounded by a tendency to rely exclusively on a criterion of statistical significance to decide which effects are 'real' and worth publishing. As we explained in Chapter 8, statistical significance is only one consideration among others when the validity and importance of causal claims is decided. In many situations, for example when a very large number of observations is available and uncontroversial effects are tested, statistical significance is largely irrelevant. In other situations, for example underpowered studies of small causal effects, it would actually lead to a preponderance of wrong inferences in the literature as a whole (Gelman, 2009).

To address the 'file-drawer' problem and the issue of the 'statistical significance filter', replications and the reporting of negative results should be encouraged, and what is accepted as an established causal relationship should be subject to higher standards than one that passed a statistical test. All the preceding chapters should have prepared you well to appreciate this last point. Careful research design can also ensure that the empirical research findings will be valuable, whichever direction they happen to point to.

Plagiarism
Another dimension of research integrity is avoiding plagiarism, and giving credit to other researchers where credit is due. While originality is of course valued in political science, there is a strong norm against appropriating the work of others and presenting it as your own. This refers to ideas, but also to sentences and even phrases. Acknowledging the work of others is a hallmark of the scientific process, and cases of plagiarism cut to its very heart. Details on how and when to cite might appear tedious and pedantic, but they ensure that previous work is acknowledged, and through that, rewarded. This goes for referencing in academic reports and student papers, but also when it comes to using the work of other researchers for articles in the media and policy advice.

Disclosing funding and vested interests
Impartiality and independence are other core values of academic political science. There is an informal contract between society and academia in which society funds, directly or not, scientists and their research and, in their turn, academic scientists have the freedom and the obligation to produce research in an impartial and independent manner, not tainted by partisan, ideological, or economic interests. At the same time, research

is often funded by private organizations and non-governmental public organizations with particular missions as well. When this is the case, researchers should disclose any funding or support they have received through financial grants, privileged access to information, and so on.

Political science and the broader society

All the potential problems discussed so far refer mostly to the work of individual researchers and their interactions in the profession. But political science engages with the larger society as well, and this creates additional ethical challenges. There are explicit ethical standards when it comes to research involving human subjects, even if these have been drafted primarily with other scientific disciplines, such as medicine or psychology, in mind. In many countries and universities, research involving humans must gain prior approval from ethics boards and committees. This is especially relevant for experimental research, but also for participant observation type of studies and, indeed, any research project that deals directly with people.

Seeking consent and avoiding deception

In general, when research is performed on human subjects, their prior informed consent should be sought. Informed consent means that the individuals have been informed about the research they would be part of and have agreed to that. There are different forms that obtaining consent can take (signing a form, answering a question, reading a statement, and so on), but it is the principle that is important. People should not be subject to research they have not agreed to. That much is clear, but in practice it is very difficult to delineate exactly how much people should know about the research. Often, alerting the participants to the nature of the study would affect the results. For example, if people know that they are participating in an experiment on altruism, they might exhibit more pro-social behaviour than otherwise. If families know that they are part of a study of education policy, they might be more diligent in sending their kids to school for the duration of the project. There is no standard recipe that can be given for when and how much of the nature and aims of the research to disclose, but the principle is that unless withholding information would compromise the integrity of the research project, participants should have the right to know.

Seeking consent from all participants in a study seems quite impractical for the massive field and social-network based experiments involving tens of thousands and more subjects that are being conducted in the social sciences nowadays. The rules and standards of what to do in these cases are still being debated and developed.

The possibility of deception is a related issue. Sometimes it might be necessary for the research project not only to withhold certain information from the participants, but to actively deceive them about the nature of the study. For example, an accomplice of the researcher can pose as a regular participant in the context of a lab experiment. Again, there can be no sharp line when and how much deception is admissible, but in any case the advice and approval of ethics commissions should be sought in such situations.

Protecting participants

Researchers have a responsibility to protect participants in their research from any harm or other negative effects that can arise due to their involvement in the project. Scientists should take appropriate measures not to disclose the identity of their subjects, for example by careless handling of data and communications. We already mentioned that this can be a tricky requirement to uphold when working with subjects outside the law. But failing it might have even more dire consequences when research is done in places subject to violence, state repression, or international conflict. Researchers should have the sense and sensibilities to avoid actions that would endanger their respondents in such circumstances, even if that would be detrimental to their projects. At the same time, this is not a call for political science to disengage entirely from research in violence-prone areas, as they constitute an important part of its subject matter.

Interference in society

But the practical effects and moral implications of political science research are not confined to those directly participating in the research projects. Research has the potential to affect entire communities and even society at large, and this requires another level of ethical reflection.

Take, for example, the randomized controlled trials evaluating social policies that we discussed in Chapter 7. To many, the mere idea of randomly selecting people who would receive some benefits and, even more importantly, withholding benefits from others is morally questionable. Moreover, if the participants in the study themselves realize that their neighbours are getting some benefit while they are excluded, this can lead to backlash and protest against the research project altogether. Is it ethical for some families to receive free bed nets against malaria that might save their children from death, while others are denied this privilege for the sake of a credible causal identification strategy?

As scientists, we might be aware of the positive long-term effect of randomized experiments for understanding whether, when, and how public policies work, but this might be a difficult point to explain to the participants in the research who are denied some benefit for seemingly no good reason *right now*. (And it might be even more tricky to gain the approval of public officials for such actions.) There are mechanisms to compensate financially or otherwise participants who happen to fall in the 'wrong' group in experimental studies, but the ethical dilemma remains. And in some cases it might actually be illegal to deliver a public policy in a way that is discriminatory, even if the discrimination is temporary and done for the benefit of science.

When researchers interfere with the social and political worlds, the potential for damage looms large, and such interventions should always be planned and conducted with great care. Political scientists aim to understand how citizens evaluate politicians and policies, how politicians respond to citizens' demands, how bureaucrats handle partisan pressures, and so on. All these are processes that happen in the real world and affect the lives of millions. When we interfere with them, for example, by sending emails that pretend to come from ordinary citizens to politicians in order to see to whom the politicians would respond, we might be changing the very social context we are trying to study. Sometimes the change can be positive, but it cannot be assumed to be so.

A case from 2014 illustrates both the potential harm that can be done, as well as the scale of controversy in which political science research can get entangled. The case concerns a study of electoral behaviour in the US state of Montana. The team of researchers from Stanford University and Dartmouth College sent messages to more than 100,000 voters ahead of the election for the state Supreme Court in which they informed the voters about the ideological standings of the election candidates in reference to well-known national political figures. The messages also had the official insignia of the state.

When the experiment became known, a burst of outrage followed in the media, the political science academic community, and other parts of society. Many people, including fellow political scientists, considered that by attributing ideological positions to formally apolitical figures and by contacting such a big proportion of the electorate (Montana is a small state, and turnout for this type of election is typically low), the researchers could have significantly altered the election outcome. Moreover, the public felt that it had been deceived about the true nature of the messages due to the presence of a picture of the official state seal. A debate ensued about whether political scientists have the right to affect election outcomes, even if inadvertently, in the course of their research, and about the appropriate institutions to sanction and approve such research. This debate still continues and goes to the heart of the broader issue about the role of political science in society.

The Role of Political Science

Even if we imagine that all approvals from the relevant ethics commissions have been received and the informed consent of the public has been obtained, is it ever legitimate for political scientists to affect real-world social and political processes of great significance, such as elections or international negotiations? If yes, what are the boundaries? If no, what is the relevance of political science research?

In the introductory chapter we defined positive research as a type of research that relies on relatively sharp lines between facts and values and between research and social action. We proceeded to discuss at length the various ways in which positive political science can work, the types of questions it can address, and the limitations its designs are subject to. The underlying philosophy of this approach is that the relevance of political science is in its rigour and impartiality; that the source of its power is a commitment to method and design.

It is easy to confuse impartiality with disinterest and disengagement. That would be wrong. Political science research should feed into real-world debates and discussions (see also Stoker, Peters, & Pierre, 2015), and the most effective way to do so is to rigorously pursue the discovery and confirmation of facts and generalizations about the way the social and political worlds operate. Political science research should be engaged with fundamental theoretical and methodological research, but also with applied developments, such as predictive models, voting advice applications, data visualizations, and survey technology. It should contribute to media commentary and to policy consultations. It should disseminate its research results to politicians, to policy makers, and to society when it is invited to do so and, even more importantly, when it is deliberately ignored.

If there is one message about the nature of explanatory research in political science that has emerged from the previous chapters, it is that it is always difficult. This teaches humility about making strong predictions about the effects of proposed social interventions, international negotiations, institutional transplants, or public policy programs. Often, we just do not know on the basis of available data and methods. With the data and methodological tools we have, we do not know the precise effects of early education on success later in life, of the death penalty on crime, of economic cutbacks on growth, of development aid on prosperity. Well, we know to *some* extent, and we can exclude certain effects as implausible, but for all these societal problems and more, large uncertainties remain.

It is in fact one of the responsibilities of scientists to signal, explain, and communicate the inherent uncertainty of many descriptive, predictive, and causal claims about political science and public policy phenomena and relationships. This is not pedantic, but prudent.

Unlike economists, who also regularly offer policy advice to governments, political scientists have no excuse for ignoring the political context of public policy making. For all its merits, policy advice coming from economists often ignores the political context of its propositions, which means that the effects of the proposed actions can have vastly different consequences from those intended (Acemoglu & Robinson,

2013). Political scientists should know not only what public policies might be desirable but also which are likely to be feasible. By integrating insight into both desirability and feasibility, they can make valuable contributions to public debates.

In sum, political science research can and should contribute to societal progress and political advancement, but by constructive engagement with existing institutions. This is in line with the broadly positivist outlook adopted in these chapters, but it would fall short of the demands of more radical research traditions in political science. Improving marginally the effectiveness of public policies or the methods of citizen engagement in governance is just not enough for adherents to social action research, critical theory, phronesis, and related approaches. They call for nothing short of a revolutionary new way of organizing politics and society. Persuading politicians and policy makers is too slow and ineffective; what they call for is direct action and intervention. Under the positivist view in which these chapters are rooted, political scientists have more modest goals, if not less difficult, and methods that can ultimately prove more effective. But what all approaches – positivist and interpretivist, experimental and observational, quantitative and qualitative – share is a commitment to integrity, a call for critical thinking, and an invitation for research.

References

Abadie, A., & Gardeazabal, J. (2003). The Economic Costs of Conflict: A Case Study of the Basque Country. *American Economic Review*, 93 (1), 113–132.

Abadie, A., Diamond, A., & Hainmueller, J. (2015). Comparative Politics and the Synthetic Control Method. *American Journal of Political Science*, 59 (2), 495–510.

Abbott, A. (1995). Sequence Analysis: New Methods for Old Ideas. *Annual Review of Sociology*, 1, 93–113.

Abell, P. (2009). A Case for Cases: Comparative Narratives in Sociological Explanation. *Sociological Methods & Research*, 38 (1), 38–70.

Acemoglu, D., & Robinson, J. A. (2013). *Economics versus Politics: Pitfalls of Policy Advice*. NBER Working Paper (18921).

Achen, C. (1982). *Interpreting and Using Regression*. Thousand Oaks: Sage.

Adcock, R., & Collier, D. (2001). Measurement Validity: A Shared Standard for Qualitative and Quantitative Research. *American Political Science Review*, 95 (3), 529–546.

Adler, E. (1997). Seizing the Middle Ground: Constructivism in World Politics. *European Journal of International Relations*, 3 (3), 319–363.

Ahlquist, J. S., & Breunig, C. (2012). Model-Based Clustering and Typologies in the Social Sciences. *Political Analysis*, 20 (1), 92–112.

Ahmed, A., & Sil, R. (2012). When Multi-Method Research Subverts Methodological Pluralism or, Why We Still Need Single-Method Research. *Perspectives on Politics*, 10 (4), 935–953.

Ahram, A. I. (2013). Concepts and Measurement in Multimethod Research. *Political Research Quarterly*, 66 (2), 280–291.

Aldenderfer, M. S., & Blashfield, R. K. (1985). *Cluster Analysis*. Thousand Oaks: Sage.

Allison, G., & Zelikow, P. (1999). *Essence of Decision: Explaining the Cuban Missile Crisis*. Second edition. New York: Addison-Wesley Longman.

Almeida, P. D. (2003). Opportunity Organizations and Threat-Induced Contention: Protest Waves in Authoritarian Settings. *American Journal of Sociology*, 109 (2), 345–400.

Andersen, L. B., Jorgensen, T. B., Kjeldsen, A. M., Pedersen, L. H., & Vrangbaek, K. (2013). Public Values and Public Service Motivation: Conceptual and Empirical Relationships. *American Review of Public Administration*, 43 (3), 292–311.

Anderson, C. J., Blais, A., Bowler, S., & Listhaug, O. (2005). *Losers Consent: Elections and Democratic Legitimacy*. Oxford: Oxford University Press.

Andeweg, R., De Winter, L., & Dumont, P. (2011). *Puzzles of Government Formation: Coalition Theory and Deviant Cases*. New York: Routledge.

Angrist, J. D., & Pischke, J.-S. (2009). *Mostly Harmless Econometrics*. Princeton: Princeton University Press.

345

Angrist, J. D., Imbens, G. W., & Rubin, D. B. (1996). Identification of Causal Effects Using Instrumental Variables. *Journal of the American Statistical Association*, 91 (434), 444–455.

Armitage, P. (2003). Fisher, Bradford Hill, and Randomization. *International Journal of Epidemiology*, 32 (6), 925–928.

Arrow, K. (1951). *Social Choice and Individual Values*. New Haven: Yale University Press.

Axelrod, R. (1984). *The Evolution of Cooperation*. New York: Basic Books.

Axinn, W., & Pearce, L. (2006). *Mixed Method Data Collection Strategies*. New York: Cambridge University Press.

Bakker, R., de Vries, C., Edwards, E., Hooghe, L., Jolly, S., Marks, G., Polk, J., Rovny, J., Steenbergen, M., & Vachudova, M. A. (2015). Measuring Party Positions in Europe: The Chapel Hill Expert Survey Trend File, 1999–2010, *Party Politics*, 21 (1), 143–152.

Balashov, Y., & Rosenberg, A. (2002). *Philosophy of Science: Contemporary Readings*. New York: Routledge.

Banerjee, A. V., & Duflo, E. (2009). The Experimental Approach to Development Economics. *Annual Review of Economics*, 1, 151–178.

Bass, F. M. (1969). A New Product Growth for Model Consumer Durables. *Management Science*, 15 (5), 215–227.

Bates, R., Grief, A., & Levi, M. (1998). *Analytic Narratives*. Princeton: Princeton University Press.

Bateson, W., & Mendel, G. (2009). *Mendel's Principles of Heredity: A Defence, with a Translation of Mendel's Original Papers on Hybridisation*. Cambridge: Cambridge University Press.

Baumgartner, F., Christian, B., Christoffer, G.-P., Bryan, D. J., Peter, B. M., Michiel, N., & Stefaan, W. (2009). Punctuated Equilibrium in Comparative Perspective. *American Journal of Political Science*, 53 (3), 603–620.

Baumgartner, K., Ferrari, S., & Palermo, G. (2008). Constructing Bayesian Networks for Criminal Profiling from Limited Data. *Knowledge-Based Systems*, 21 (7), 563–572.

Baumgartner, M. (2013). Detecting Causal Chains in Small-n Data. *Field Methods*, 25 (1), 3–24.

Baumgartner, M. (2015). Parsimony and Causality. *Quality & Quantity*, 49 (2), 839–856.

Baumgartner, M., & Epple, R. (2014). A Coincidence Analysis of a Causal Chain: The Swiss Minaret Vote. *Sociological Methods & Research*, 43 (2), 280–312.

Beach, D., & Pedersen, R. (2013). *Process-Tracing Methods: Foundations and Guidelines*. Ann Arbor: University of Michigan Press.

Becher, M., & Donnelly, M. (2013). Economic Performance, Individual Evaluations, and the Vote: Investigating the Causal Mechanism. *Journal of Politics*, 75 (4), 968–979.

Beck, N. (2006). Is Causal-Process Observation an Oxymoron? *Political Analysis*, 14 (3), 347–352.

Behaghel, L., Crépon, B., Gurgand, M., & Le Barbanchon, T. (2009). Sample Attrition Bias in Randomized Experiments: A Tale of Two Surveys. *IZA Discussion Papers* (4162).

Bennett, A. (2010). Process Tracing and Causal Inference. In H. E. Brady & D. Collier (Eds.), *Rethinking Social Inquiry: Diverse Tools, Shared Standards* (pp. 207–219). Lanham: Rowman and Littlefield.

Bennett, A. (2015). Disciplining our Conjectures: Systematizing Process Tracing with Bayesian Analysis. In A. Bennett & J. Checkel (Eds.), *Process Tracing: from Metaphor to Analytic Tool* (pp. 276–298). New York: Cambridge University Press.

Bennett, A., & Checkel, J. (2015). *Process Tracing: From Metaphor to Analytic Tool.* New York: Cambridge University Press.

Benoit, K. (2007). Electoral Laws as Political Consequences: Explaining the Origins and Change of Electoral Institutions. *Annual Review of Political Science*, 10 (1), 363–390.

Benoit, K., & Laver, M. (2006). *Party Policy in Modern Democracies.* London: Routledge.

Berg-Schlosser, D. (2012). *Mixed Methods in Comparative Politics: Principles and Applications.* Basingstoke: Palgrave Macmillan.

Berger, P., & Luckman, T. (1966). *The Social Construction of Reality.* New York: Anchor Books.

Berkhout, J., & Lowery, D. (2008). Counting Organized Interests in the European Union: A Comparison of Data Sources. *Journal of European Public Policy*, 15 (4), 489–513.

Berry, W. (1993). *Understanding Regression Assumptions.* Thousand Oaks: Sage.

Bevir, M. (2000). *Interpretive Political Science.* Thousand Oaks: Sage.

Bevir, M., & Kedar, A. (2008). Concept Formation in Political Science: An Anti-naturalist Critique of Qualitative Methodology. *Perspectives on Politics*, 6 (3), 503–517.

Blackwell, M., Honaker, J., & King, G. (2015). A Unified Approach to Measurement Error and Missing Data: Overview and Applications. *Sociological Methods and Research*, 1–39.

Blair, G., Imai, K., & Lyall, J. (2014). Comparing and Combining List and Endorsement Experiments: Evidence from Afghanistan. *American Journal of Political Science*, 58 (4), 1043–1063.

Blair, J. P., & Rossmo, D. K. (2010). Evidence in Context: Bayes' Theorem and Investigations. *Police Quarterly*, 13 (2), 123–135.

Blatter, J., & Haverland, M. (2012). *Designing Case Studies: Explanatory Approaches in Small-N Research.* Basingstoke: Palgrave Macmillan.

Blomquist, W. (1992). *Dividing the Waters: Governing Groundwater in Southern California.* ICS Press Institute for Contemporary Studies.

Bond, R. M., Fariss, C. J., Jones, J. J., Kramer, A. I., Marlow, C., Settle, J. E., & Fowler, J. H. (2012). A 61-Million-Person Experiment in Social Influence and Political Mobilization. *Nature*, 489 (7415), 295–298.

Bourdieu, P. (1973). Cultural Reproduction and Social Reproduction. In R. K. Brown (Ed.), *Knowledge, Education and Cultural Change* (pp. 71–112). London: Tavistock.

Box, J. F. (1978). *R.A. Fisher: The Life of a Scientist.* New York: Wiley.

Brady, H. E., & Collier, D. (2004). *Rethinking Social Inquiry: Diverse Tools, Shared Standards.* Oxford: Rowman and Littlefield.

Braumoeller, B. F., & Goertz, G. (2000). The Methodology of Necessary Conditions. *American Journal of Political Science*, 44 (4), 844–858.

Broemeling, L. (2007). *Bayesian Biostatistics and Diagnostic Medicine.* Boca Raton: Chapman and Hall/CRC.

Bronner, S. E. (2011). *Critical Theory: A Very Short Introduction*. New York: Oxford University Press.

Broockman, D., Kalla, J., & Aronow, P. (2015). Irregularities in LaCour (2014). Unpublished paper.

Brown, S. (1980). *Political Subjectivity: Applications of Q Methodology in Political Science*. New Haven: Yale Univeresity Press.

Brown, S. (2003). *Scurvy: How a Surgeon, a Mariner, and a Gentleman Solved the Greatest Medical Mystery of the Age of Sail*. New York: Thomas Dunne Books (St. Martins Press).

Buchanan, M. (2000). *Ubiquity*. London: Phoenix.

Budge, I., Klingermann, H.-D., Volkens, A., Bara, J., & Tanenbaum, E. (2001). *Mapping Policy Preferences: Estimates for Parties, Electors, and Governments 1945–1998*. Oxford: Oxford University Press.

Burch, P., & Heinrich, C. (2015). *Mixed Methods for Policy Research and Program Evaluation*. Thousand Oaks: Sage.

Burkhart, R. E., & Lewis-Beck, M. S. (1994). Comparative Democracy: The Economic Development Thesis. *American Political Science Review*, 88 (4), 903–910.

Canon, D. T. (1999). Electoral Systems and the Representation of Minority Interests in Legislatures. *Legislative Studies Quarterly*, 24 (3), 331–385.

Cao, X. (2010). Networks as Channels of Policy Diffusion: Explaining Worldwide Changes in Capital Taxation, 1998–2006. *International Studies Quarterly*, 54 (3), 823–854.

Caramani, D. (2009). *Introduction to the Comparative Method with Boolean Algebra*. Thousand Oaks: Sage.

Carey, S. (1985). *Conceptual Change in Childhood*. Cambridge: MIT Press.

Carroll, R., & Cox, G. W. (2007). The Logic of Gamson's Law: Pre-election Coalitions and Portfolio Allocations. *American Journal of Political Science*, 51 (2), 300–313.

Carroll, S. (2012). *The Particle at the End of the Universe: The Hunt for the Higgs and the Discovery of a New World*. New York: Dutton.

Cartwright, N. (2007). *Hunting Causes and Using Them: Approaches in Philosophy and Economics*. Cambridge: Cambridge University Press.

Casal Bertoa, F., & Spirova, M. (2013). Get a Subsidy or Perish! Public Funding and Party Survival in Eastern Europe. *The Legal Regulation of Political Parties Working Paper* (29).

Cederman, L.-E. (1997). *Emergent Actors in World Politics: How States and Nations Develop and Dissolve*. Princeton: Princeton University Press.

Cederman, L.-E. (2003). Modeling the Size of Wars: From Billiard Balls to Sandpiles. *American Political Science Review*, 97 (1), 135–150.

Chalmers, A. F. (1999). *What Is This Thing Called Science?* Maidenhead: Open University Press.

Chapman, L. J., & Chapman, J. P. (1969). Illusory Correlation as an Obstacle to the Use of Valid Psychodiagnostic Signs. *Journal of Abnormal Psychology*, 74 (3), 271–280.

Charmaz, K. (2006). *Constructing Grounded Theory*. London: Sage.

Clark, W. R., & Golder, M. (2015). Big Data, Causal Inference, and Formal Theory: Contradictory Trends in Political Science? *PS: Political Science & Politics*, 48 (1), 65–70.

Clarke, K. A., & Primo, D. M. (2007). Modernizing Political Science: A Model-Based Approach. *Perspectives on Politics*, 5 (4), 741–753.

Clinton, J., Jackman, S., & Rivers, D. (2004). The Statistical Analysis of Roll Call Data. *American Political Science Review*, 98 (2), 355–370.

Clinton, J. D., & Jackman, S. (2009). To Simulate or NOMINATE? *Legislative Studies Quarterly*, 34 (4), 593–621.

Cochran, W. (1977). *Sampling Techniques*. Third edition. New York: Wiley.

Coffe, H. (2005). Do Individual Factors Explain the Different Success of the Two Belgian Extreme Right Parties. *Acta Politica*, 40 (1), 74–93.

Cohen, J., & Dupas, P. (2010). Free Distribution or Cost-Sharing? Evidence from a Randomized Malaria Prevention Experiment. *Quarterly Journal of Economics*, 125 (1), 1–45.

Collier, D. (2011). Understanding Process Tracing. *PS: Political Science & Politics*, 44 (4), 823–830.

Collier, D., & Levitsky, S. (1997). Democracy with Adjectives: Conceptual Innovation in Comparative Research. *World Politics*, 49 (3), 430–451.

Collier, D., Brady, H. E., & Seawright, J. (2010). Sources of Leverage in Causal Inference: Toward an Alternative View of Methodology. In H. E. Brady & D. Collier (Eds.), *Rethinking Social Inquiry: Diverse Tools, Shared Standards* (pp. 161–99). Lanham: Rowman and Littlefield.

Collier, D., LaPorte, J., & Seawright, J. (2012). Putting Typologies to Work: Concept Formation, Measurement, and Analytic Rigor. *Political Research Quarterly*, 65 (1), 217–232.

Colomer, J. M. (2005). It's Parties That Choose Electoral Systems (or, Duverger's Laws Upside Down). *Political Studies*, 53 (1), 1–21.

Cook, T., & Campbell, D. (1979). *Quasi-Experimentation: Design & Analysis Issues for Field Settings*. Houghton Mifflin.

Cooper, T. L. (2001). *Handbook of Administrative Ethics*. Second edition. New York: Marcel Dekker.

Cox, D. R., & Reid, N. (2000). *The Theory of the Design of Experiments*. New York: Chapman & Hall.

Cox, D. R., & Wermuth, N. (2004). Causality: A Statistical View. *International Statistical Review*, 72 (3), 285–305.

Cox, G. W. (1997). *Making Votes Count*. Cambridge: Cambridge University Press.

Cresswell, J. W., & Plano Clark, V. L. (2007). *Designing and Conducting Mixed Methods Research*. Thousand Oaks: Sage.

Crombez, C. (1996). Minority Governments, Minimal Winning Coalitions and Surplus Majorities in Parliamentary Systems. *European Journal of Political Research*, 29 (1), 1–29.

Crutch, S. J., & Warrington, E. K. (2005). Abstract and Concrete Concepts Have Structurally Different Representational Frameworks. Brain, 128 (3), pp. 615–627.

Cusack, T., Iversen, T., & Soskice, D. (2010). Coevolution of Capitalism and Political Representation: The Choice of Electoral Systems. *American Political Science Review*, 104 (2), 393–403.

Darwin, C. (1876). *Variation in Animals and Plants under Domestication. Volume 1*. Second edition. New York: D. Appleton and Co.

Dawid, A. P. (2000). Causal Inference without Counterfactuals. *Journal of the American Statistical Association*, 95 (450), 407–424.

Dawid, A. P. (2002). Bayes's Theorem and Weighing Evidence by Juries. *Proceedings of the British Academy*, 113, 71–90.

Dawkins, R. (2008). *The Oxford Book of Modern Science Writing*. Oxford University Press.

de Ayala, R. J. (2009). *The Theory and Practice of Item Response Theory*. New York: Guildford.

De Landa, M. (2000). *A Thousand Years of Nonlinear History*. New York: Swerve.

De Marchi, S. (2005). *Computational and Mathematical Modeling in the Social Sciences*. New York: Cambridge University Press.

Diamond, L. (1999). *Developing Democracy: Toward Consolidation*. Baltimore: Johns Hopkins University Press.

Diesing, P. (1966). Objectivism vs. Subjectivism in the Social Sciences. *Philosophy of Science*, 33 (1/2), 124–133.

Dietz, T., Ostrom, E., & Stern, P. C. (2003). The Struggle to Govern the Commons. *Science*, 302 (5652), 1907–1912.

Ding, P., & Miratrix, L. W. (2015). To Adjust or Not to Adjust? Sensitivity Analysis of M-Bias and Butterfly-Bias. *Journal of Causal Inference*, 3 (1), 41–57.

Dixit, A., Skeath, S., & Reiley, D. (2009). *Games of Strategy*. Third edition. New York: W. W. Norton.

Dobel, J. P. (1999). *Public Integrity*. Baltimore: The Johns Hopkins University Press.

Doherty, D., Gerber, A. S., & Green, D. P. (2006). Personal Income and Attitudes toward Redistribution: A Study of Lottery Winners. *Political Psychology*, 27 (3), 441–458.

Donnelly, J. (2000). *Realism and International Relations*. Cambridge: Cambridge University Press.

Dörrenbächer, N., Mastenbroek, E., & Toshkov, D. (2015). National Parliaments and Transposition of EU Law: A Matter of Coalition Conflict? *JCMS: Journal of Common Market Studies*, 53(5), 1010–1026

Downs, A. (1957). *An Economic Theory of Democracy*. New York: Harper & Row.

Doyle, A. C. (1892). *The Adventures of Sherlock Holmes*. London: George Newnes Ltd.

Doyle, M. W., & Sambanis, N. (2000). International Peacebuilding: A Theoretical and Quantitative Analysis. *American Political Science Review*, 94 (4), 779–801.

Doyle, M. W., & Sambanis, N. (2006). *Making War and Building Peace: United Nations Peace Operations*. Princeton: Princeton University Press.

Druckman, J. N., Green, D., Kuklinski, J., & Lupia, A. (2011). *Cambridge Handbook of Experimental Political Science*. Cambridge: Cambridge University Press.

Dryzek, J. S., Honig, B., & Phillips, A. (2008). *The Oxford Handbook of Political Theory*. Oxford: Oxford University Press.

Duflo, E., Glennerster, R., & Kremer, M. (2006). Using Randomization in Development Economics Research: A Toolkit. *NBER Technical Working Paper Series* (333).

Duncan, O. D. (1984). *Notes on Social Measurement*. New York: Russell Sage Foundation.

Dunning, T. (2007). The Role of Iteration in Multi-Method Research. *Qualitative Methods*, 5 (1), 22–24.

Dunning, T. (2012). *Natural Experiments in the Social Sciences: A Design-Based Approach.* New York: Cambridge University Press.

Duverger, M. (1954). *Political Parties: Their Organization and Activity in the Modern State.* New York: Wiley.

Easton, D. (1965). *A Systems Analysis of Political Life.* New York: Wiley.

Eliason, S. R., & Stryker, R. (2009). Goodness-of-Fit Tests and Descriptive Measures in Fuzzy-Set Analysis. *Sociological Methods & Research*, 38 (1), 102–146.

Elster, J. (2007). *Explaining Social Behavior: More Nuts and Bolts for the Social Sciences.* Cambridge: Cambridge University Press.

Engeli, I., & Allison, C. (2014). *Comparative Policy Studies: Conceptual and Methodological Challenges.* Basingstoke: Palgrave Macmillan.

Epstein, D., & O'Halloran, S. (1999). *Delegating Powers: A Transaction Cost Politics Approach to Policy Making under Separate Powers.* Cambridge: Cambridge University Press.

Evangelista, M. (2015). Explaining the Cold War's End: Process Tracing All the Way Down? In A. Bennett & J. Checkel (Eds.), *Process Tracing: From Metaphor to Analytic Tool* (pp. 153–185). New York: Cambridge University Press.

Fabian, J. (2002). *Time and the Other: How Anthropology Makes Its Object.* New York: Columbia University Press.

Fairfield, T. (2013). Going Where the Money Is: Strategies for Taxing Economic Elites in Unequal Democracies. *World Development*, 47 (0), 42–57.

Fama, E. F., & French, K. R. (2010). Luck versus Skill in the Cross Section of Mutual Fund Returns. *Journal of Finance*, 65 (5), 1915–1947.

Fearon, J. D. (1991). Counterfactuals and Hypothesis Testing in Political Science. *World Politics*, 43 (2), 169–195.

Feddersen, T. J. (2004). Rational Choice Theory and the Paradox of Not Voting. *Journal of Economic Perspectives*, 18 (1), 99–112.

Fisher, R. A. (1925). *Statistical Methods for Research Workers.* Edinburgh: Oliver and Boyd.

Fisher, R. A. (1935). *The Design of Experiments.* Edinburgh: Oliver and Boyd.

Flyvbjerg, B. (2001). *Making Social Science Matter: Why Social Inquiry Fails and How It Can Succeed Again.* New York: Cambridge University Press.

Flyvbjerg, B. (2004). A Perestroikan Straw Man Answers Back: David Laitin and Phronetic Political Science. *Politics & Society*, 32 (3), 389–416.

Flyvbjerg, B., Landman, T., & Schram, S. (2012). *Real Social Science: Applied Phronesis.* Cambridge: Cambridge University Press.

Ford, C. S. (1970). *Human Relations Area Files: 1949–1969. A Twenty-Year Report.* New Haven: Human Relations Area Files.

Fowler, J. H. (2006). Connecting the Congress: A Study of Cosponsorship Networks. *Political Analysis*, 14 (4), 456–487.

Franzosi, R. (2004). *From Words to Numbers: Narrative, Data, and Social Science.* Cambridge: Cambridge University Press.

Freedman, D. A. (2006). Statistical Models for Causation: What Inferential Leverage Do They Provide? *Evaluation Review*, 30 (6), 691–713.

Freedman, D. A. (2009). *Statistical Models: Theory and Practice.* New York: Cambridge University Press.

Friedman, J. (1996). *The Rational Choice Controversy: Economic Models of Politics Reconsidered*. New Haven and London: Yale University Press.

Friedman, M. (1953). *Essays in Positive Economics*. Chicago: University of Chicago Press.

Frisch, S. A., Harris, D. B., Kelly, S. Q., & Parker, D. C. (2012). *Doing Archival Research in Political Science*. London: Cambria Press.

Fukuyama, F. (2013). What Is Governance? *Governance*, 26 (3), 347–368.

Gamson, W. (1961). A Theory of Coalition Formation. *American Sociological Review*, 26 (3), 373–382.

Gartzke, E., & Weisiger, A. (2013). Permanent Friends? Dynamic Difference and the Democratic Peace. *International Studies Quarterly*, 57 (1), 171–185.

Gayle, D. J. (1988). Applying Most Different Systems Designs: Comparing Development Policy in Alabama and Jamaica. *Comparative Political Studies*, 21 (2), 257–280.

Geddes, B. (1990). How the Cases You Choose Affect the Answers You Get: Selection Bias in Comparative Politics. *Political Analysis*, 2 (1), 131–150.

Geertz, C. (1973). *The Interpretation of Cultures*. New York: Basic Books.

Gelman, A. (2009). *Red State, Blue State, Rich State, Poor State: Why Americans Vote the Way They Do*. Princeton: Princeton University Press.

Gelman, A., & Hill, J. (2007). *Data Analysis Using Regressson and Multilevel/Hierarchical Models*. Cambridge: Cambridge University Press.

Gelman, A., Shor, B., Bafumi, J., & Park, D. (2007). Rich State, Poor State, Red State, Blue State: What's the Matter with Connecticut? *Quarterly Journal of Political Science*, 2 (4), 345–367.

Gelman, A., Carlin, J., Stern, H., Dunson, D., Vehtari, A., & Rubin, D. B. (2013). *Bayesian Data Analysis*. Third edition. Boca Raton: Chapman and Hall/CRC.

George, A. L., & Bennett, A. (2005). *Case Studies and Theory Development in the Social Sciences*. Cambridge: MIT Press.

Gerber, A., & Green, D. (2012). *Field Experiments: Design, Analysis, and Interpretation*. New York: W. W. Norton.

Gerring, J. (2007). *Case Study Research: Principles and Practices*. Cambridge: Cambridge University Press.

Gerring, J. (2012a). Mere Description. *British Journal of Political Science*, 42 (4), 721–746.

Gerring, J. (2012b). *Social Science Methodology: A Unified Framework*. Second edition. Cambridge Universtiy Press.

Gerring, J., & Yesnowitz, J. (2006). A Normative Turn in Political Science? *Polity*, 38 (1), 101–133.

Giannetti, D., & Laver, M. (2005). Policy Positions and Jobs in the Government. *European Journal of Political Research*, 44 (1), 91–120.

Giddens, A. (2000). *Runaway World*. New York: Routledge.

Gine, X., & Mansouri, G. (2011). Together We Will: Experimental Evidence on Female Voting Behavior in Pakistan. *World Bank Policy Research Working Paper* (5892).

Glennan, S. (2002). Rethinking Mechanistic Explanation. *Philosophy of Science*, 69 (3), 342–353.

Glymour, B. (1998). Contrastive, Non-Probabilistic Statistical Explanations. *Philosophy of Science*, 65 (3), 448–471.

Glymour, M. M. (2006). Using Causal Diagrams to Understand Common Problems in Social Epidemiology. In J. M. Oakes & J. S. Kaufman (Eds.), *Methods in social epidemiology*. San Francisco: Jossey Bass.

Glynn, A. N., & Gerring, J. (2013). Strategies of Research Design with Confounding: A Graphical Description. Unpublished paper.

Glynn, A. N., & Ichino, N. (2014). Using Qualitative Information to Improve Causal Inference. *American Journal of Political Science*, 59 (4), 1055–1071.

Godwin, M. L., & Schroedel, J. R. (2000). Policy Diffusion and Strategies for Promoting Policy Change: Evidence from California Local Gun Control Ordinances. *Policy Studies Journal*, 28 (4), 760–776.

Goertz, G. (2006). *Social Science Concepts: A User's Guide*. Princeton: Princeton University Press.

Goertz, G., & Mahoney, J. (2012). *A Tale of Two Cultures: Qualitative and Quantitative Research in the Social Sciences*. Princeton: Princeton University Press.

Gonzalez, R. (2009). *Data Analysis for Experimental Design*. New York and London: The Guilford Press.

Goodin, R. E., & Tilly, C. (2006). *The Oxford Handbook of Contextual Political Analysis*. New York: Oxford Univerisity Press.

Granato, J., & Scioli, F. (2004). Puzzles, Proverbs, and Omega Matrices: The Scientific and Social Significance of Empirical Implications of Theoretical Models (EITM). *Perspectives on Politics*, 2 (2), 313–323.

Granger, C. W. J., & Newbold, P. (1974). Spurious Regressions in Econometrics. *Journal of Econometrics*, 2 (2), 111–120.

Gray, V., & Lowery, D. (2000). *The Population Ecology of Interest Representation*. Michigan: Michigan University Press.

Green, D., & Shapiro, I. (1996). *Pathologies of Rational Choice Theory: A Critique of Applications in Political Science*. New Haven and London: Yale University Press.

Greenwood, D. J., & Levin, M. (1998). *Introduction to Action Research: Social Research for Social Change*. Thousand Oaks: Sage.

Grofman, B. (2001). Introduction: The Joy of Puzzle Solving. In B. Grofman (Ed.), *Political Science as Puzzle Solving* (pp. 1–12). Ann Arbor: University of Michigan Press.

Guimera, R., & Sales-Pardo, M. (2011). Justice Blocks and Predictability of U.S. Supreme Court Votes. *PLOS One*, 6 (11), e27188.

Guinier, L. (1994). *The Tyranny of the Majority: Fundamental Fairness in Representative Democracy*. New York: Free Press.

Häge, F. M. (2013). Coalition Building and Consensus in the Council of the European Union. *British Journal of Political Science*, 43, 481–504.

Hammersley, M. (2007). The Issue of Quality in Qualitative Research. *International Journal of Research & Method in Education*, 30 (3), 287–305.

Hammond, K. (1996). *Human Judgment and Social Policy: Irreducible Uncertainty, Inevitable Error, Unavoidable Injustice*. New York: Oxford University Press.

Hardin, G. (1968). The Tragedy of the Commons. *Science*, 162 (3859), 1243–1248.

Harford, T. (2014). *The Undercover Economist Strikes Back*. New York: Riverhead Books.

Harrits, G. S. (2011). More than Method? A Discussion of Paradigm Differences within Mixed Methods Research. *Journal of Mixed Methods Research*, 5 (2), 150–166.

Haverland, M., & Yanow, D. (2012). A Hitchhiker's Guide to the Public Administration Research Universe: Surviving Conversations on Methodologies and Methods. *Public Administration Review*, 72 (3), 401–408.

Heckman, J. J. (1979). Sample Selection Bias as a Specification Error. *Econometrica*, 47 (1), 153–161.

Hedström, P. (2005). *Dissecting the Social: On the Principles of Analytical Sociology*. New York: Cambridge University Press.

Hedström, P., & Ylikoski, P. (2010). Causal Mechanisms in the Social Sciences. *Annual Review of Sociology*, 36, 49–67.

Hellman, J. S., Jones, G., & Kaufmann, D. (2000). Seize the State, Seize the day: State Capture, Corruption and Influence in Transition. *World Bank Policy Research Working Paper* (2444).

Hempel, C. G. (1965). *Aspects of Scientific Explanation and Other Essays in the Philosophy of Science*. New York: The Free Press.

Herndon, T., Ash, M., & Pollin, R. (2013). Does High Public Debt Consistently Stifle Economic Growth? A Critique of Reinhart and Rogoff. *Political Economy Research Institute Working Paper* (322).

Hill, M. R. (1993). *Archival Strategies and Techniques*. Thousand Oaks: Sage.

Hindmoor, A., & Taylor, B. (2015). *Rational Choice*. Ninth edition. Basingstoke: Palgrave.

Hirschmann, A. O. (1970). *Exit, Voice, and Loyalty*. Cambridge: Harvard University Press.

Ho, D. E., Imai, K., King, G., & Stuart, E. A. (2007). Matching as Nonparametric Preprocessing for Reducing Model Dependence in Parametric Causal Inference. *Political Analysis*, 15 (3), 199–236.

Hoerl, C., McCormack, T., & Beck, S. R. (2011). *Understanding Counterfactuals, Understanding Causation: Issues in Philosophy and Psychology*. New York: Oxford University Press.

Holland, P. (1986). Statistics and Causal Inference. *Journal of the American Statistical Association*, 81 (396), 945–960.

Hooghe, L., & Marks, G. (2005). Calculation, Community and Cues: Public Opinion on European Integration. *European Union Politics*, 6 (4), 419–443.

Hooghe, L., Bakker, R., Brigevich, A., De Vries, C., Edwards, E., Marks, G., Rovny, J. A. N., Steenbergen, M., & Vachudova, M. (2010). Reliability and Validity of Measuring Party Positions: The Chapel Hill Expert Surveys of 2002 and 2006. *European Journal of Political Research*, 49 (5), 687–703.

Horiuchi, Y., Imai, K., & Taniguchi, N. (2007). Designing and Analyzing Randomized Experiments: Application to a Japanese Election Survey Experiment. *American Journal of Political Science*, 51 (3), 669–687.

Hough, S. (2010). *Predicting the Unpredictable: The Tumultuous Science of Earthquake Prediction*. Princeton: Princeton University Press.

Hug, S. (2013). Qualitative Comparative Analysis: How Inductive Use and Measurement Error Lead to Problematic Inference. *Political Analysis*, 21 (2), 252–265.

Hume, D. (2000). *A Treatise of Human Nature*. New York: Oxford University Press.

Humphreys, M., & Jacobs, A. (2015). Mixing Methods: A Bayesian Approach. Unpublished Manuscript.

Humphreys, M., Sachs, J. D., & Stigliz, J. (Eds.). (2007). *Escaping the Resource Curse*. New York: Columbia University Press.

Illari, P., & Russo, F. (2014). *Causality: Philosophical Theory Meets Scientific Practice*. New York: Oxford University Press.

Imai, K. (2005). Do Get-Out-the-Vote Calls Reduce Turnout? The Importance of Statistical Methods for Field Experiments. *American Political Science Review*, 99 (2), 283–300.

Imai, K., & Yamamoto, T. (2013). Identification and Sensitivity Analysis for Multiple Causal Mechanisms: Revisiting Evidence from Framing Experiments. *Political Analysis*, 21 (2), 141–171.

Imai, K., King, G., & Nall, C. (2009). The Essential Role of Pair Matching in Cluster-Randomized Experiments, with Application to the Mexican Universal Health Insurance Evaluation. *Statistical Science*, 24 (1), 29–72.

Imai, K., Tingley, D., & Yamamoto, T. (2013). Experimental Designs for Identifying Causal Mechanisms. *Journal of the Royal Statistical Society: Series A (Statistics in Society)*, 176, 5–51.

Imai, K., Keele, L., Tingley, D., & Yamamoto, T. (2011). Unpacking the Black Box of Causality: Learning about Causal Mechanisms from Experimental and Observational Studies. *American Political Science Review*, 105 (4), 765–789.

Imbens, G. (2011). Experimental Design for Unit and Cluster Randomized Trials. *International Initiative for Impact Evaluation Paper*.

Imbens, G., & Pizer, W. (2000). The Analysis of Randomized Experiments with Missing Data. *Resources for the Future Discussion Paper* (00–19).

Immergut, E. (1992). *The Political Construction of Interest*. Cambridge and New York: Cambridge University Press.

Immergut, E. M. (1990). Institutions, Veto Points, and Policy Results: A Comparative Analysis of Health Care. *Journal of Public Policy*, 10 (4), 391–416.

Jablonski, R. S., & Oliver, S. (2013). The Political Economy of Plunder: Economic Opportunity and Modern Piracy. *Journal of Conflict Resolution*, 57 (4), 682–708.

Jaccard, J., & Jacoby, J. (2010). *Theory Construction and Model-Building Skills: A Practical Guide for Social Scientists*. New York: The Guilford Press.

Jackman, S. (2009). Estimating Ideal Points: The 110th US Senate. Unpublished paper.

Jang, J., & Hitchcock, D. B. (2012). Model-Based Cluster Analysis of Democracies. *Journal of Data Science*, 10 (2), 321–343.

Jelec, A. (2014). *Are Abstract Concepts Like Dinosaur Feathers? Conceptual Metaphor Theory and the Conceptualisation Strategies in Gesture of Blind and Visually Impaired Children*. Poznan: Wydawnictwo Naukowe UAM.

Jick, T. D. (1979). Mixing Qualitative and Quantitative Methods: Triangulation in Action. *Administrative Science Quarterly*, 24 (4), 602–611.

Johnson, S. (2006). *The Ghost Map: The Story of London's Most Terrifying Epidemic – and How It Changed Science, Cities, and the Modern World*. New York: Riverhead Books.

Jones, B., & Baumgartner, F. (2005). *The Politics of Attention: How Government Prioritizes Problems*. Chicago: University of Chicago Press.

Kahan, D. M., Peters, E., Dawson, E., & Slovic, P. (2013). Motivated Numeracy and Enlightened Self-Government. *Yale Law School, Public Law Working Paper* (307), 1–35.

Kahneman, D. (2011). *Thinking, Fast and Slow*. New York: Farrar, Straus and Giroux.

Kahneman, D., & Tversky, A. (1979). Prospect Theory: An Analysis of Decision under Risk. *Econometrica*, 47 (2), 263.

Kahneman, D., & Tversky, A. (2000). *Choices, Values and Frames*. New York: Cambridge University Press.

Kahneman, D., Slovic, P., & Tversky, A. (1982). *Judgment under Uncertainty: Heuristics and Biases*. Cambridge: Cambridge University Press.

Kapiszewski, D., MacLean, L. M., & Read, B. L. (2015). *Field Research in Political Science: Practices and Principles*. New York: Cambridge University Press.

Karp, J. A., & Banducci, S. A. (2008). Political Efficacy and Participation in Twenty-Seven Democracies: How Electoral Systems Shape Political Behaviour. *British Journal of Political Science*, 38, 311–334.

Katz, J. (2015). Situational Evidence: Strategies for Causal Reasoning from Observational Field Notes. *Sociological Methods & Research*, 44 (1), 108–144.

Katznelson, I., & Milner, H. (2003). *Political Science: State of the Discipline (Centennial Edition)*. New York: W. W. Norton.

Keele, L., & Minozzi, W. (2013). How Much Is Minnesota Like Wisconsin? Assumptions and Counterfactuals in Causal Inference with Observational Data. *Political Analysis,* 21 (2), 193–216.

Keele, L., Tingley, D., & Yamamoto, T. (2015). Identifying Mechanisms behind Policy Interventions via Causal Mediation Analysis. *Journal of Policy Analysis and Management*, 34 (4), 937–963.

Kerkhoff, T. (2011). Organizational Reform and Changing Ethics in Public Administration: A Case Study on 18th Century Dutch Tax Collecting. *Journal of Public Administration Research and Theory*, 21 (1), 117– 135.

Kerkhoff, T. (2013). Changing Perceptions of Corruption in the Netherlands: From Early Modern Pluralism to Modern Coherence. *Journal of Modern European History*, 11 (1), 88–108.

Kerkhoff, T., Kroeze, R., & Wagenaar, P. (2013). Corruption and the Rise of Modern Politics in Europe in the Eighteenth and Nineteenth Centuries: A Comparison between France, the Netherlands, Germany and England. Introduction. *Journal of Modern European History*, 11 (1), 19–30.

Kern, H. L., & Hainmueller, J. (2009). Opium for the Masses: How Foreign Media Can Stabilize Authoritarian Regimes. *Political Analysis,* 17 (4), 377–399.

Kiel, D., & Elliott, E. (1996). *Chaos Theory in the Social Sciences: Foundations and Applications*. Ann Arbor: Univeristy of Michigan Press.

King, G. (1997). *A Solution to the Ecological Inference Problem: Reconstructing Individual Behavior from Aggregate Data*. Princeton: Princeton University Press.

King, G., Keohane, R. O., & Verba, S. (1994). *Designing Social Inquiry: Scientific Inference in Qualitative Research*. Princeton: Princeton University Press.

King, G., Rosen, O., & Tanner, M. A. (2007). *Ecological Inference: New Methodological Strategies*. Cambridge: Cambridge University Press.

Kish, L. (1995). *Survey Sampling. Wiley Classics Library Edition*. Hoboken: Wiley.

Kittel, B., Luhan, W., & Morton, R. B. (2012). *Experimental Political Science: Principles and Practices*. Basingstoke: Palgrave Macmillan.

Klüver, H. (2009). Measuring Interest Group Influence Using Quantitative Text Analysis. *European Union Politics*, 10 (4), 535–549.

Krebs, V. E. (2002). Mapping Networks of Terrorist Cells. *Connections*, 24 (3), 43–52.

Kreuzer, M. (2010). Historical Knowledge and Quantitative Analysis: The Case of the Origins of Proportional Representation. *American Political Science Review*, 104 (2), 369–392.

Kriner, D., & Shen, F. (2014). Responding to War on Capitol Hill: Battlefield Casualties, Congressional Response, and Public Support for the War in Iraq. *American Journal of Political Science*, 58 (1), 157–174.

Krogslund, C., & Michel, K. (2014). A Larger-N, Fewer Variables Problem? The Counterintuitive Sensitivity of QCA. *Qualitative & Multi-Method Research*, 12 (1), 25–33.

Krook, M. L. (2010). Women's Representation in Parliament: A Qualitative Comparative Analysis. *Political Studies*, 58 (5), 886–908.

Kruschke, J. (2014). *Doing Bayesian Data Analysis: A Tutorial with R, JAGS, and Stan*. Second edition. New York: Academic Press.

Kuehn, D. (2013). Combining Game Theory Models and Process Tracing: Potential and Limits. *European Political Science*, 12 (1), 52–63.

Kuhn, T. (1962). *The Structure of Scientific Revolutions*. Chicago: University of Chicago Press.

Laakso, M., & Taagepera, R. (1979). Effective Number of Parties: A Measure with Application to West Europe. *Comparative Political Studies*, 12 (1), 3–27.

LaCour, M. J., & Green, D. P. (2014). When Contact Changes Minds: An Experiment on Transmission of Support for Gay Equality. *Science*, 346 (6215), 1366–1369.

Lacy, D., & Niou, E. M. S. (2004). A Theory of Economic Sanctions and Issue Linkage: The Roles of Preferences, Information, and Threats. *Journal of Politics*, 66 (1), 25–42.

Lakatos, I. (1970). Falsification and the Methodology of Scientific Research Programmes. In I. Lakatos & A. Musgrave (Eds.), *Criticism and the Growth of Knowledge* (pp. 91–195). Cambridge: Cambridge University Press.

Lakatos, I., & Musgrave, A. (1970). *Criticism and the Growth of Knowledge*. Cambridge: Cambridge University Press.

Lakoff, G. (1987). *Women, Fire, and Dangerous Things: What Categories Reveal about the Mind*. Chicago: University of Chicago Press.

Lasswell, H. D. (1936). *Politics: Who Gets What, When, How*. New York: Whittlesey House.

Laurence, S., & Margolis, E. (1999). Concepts and Cognitive Science. In E. Margolis & S. Laurence (Eds.), *Concepts: Core Readings* (pp. 3–81). Cambridge: MIT Press.

Laver, M. (2014). Measuring Policy Positions in Political Space. *Annual Review of Political Science*, 17 (1), 207–223.

Laver, M., & Schofield, N. (1990). *Multiparty Government: The Politics of Coalition in Europe*. Ann Arbor: University of Michigan Press.

Laver, M., Benoit, K., & Garry, J. (2003). Extracting Policy Positions from Political Texts Using Words as Data. *American Political Science Review*, 97 (2), 311–331.

Lazer, D., Rubineau, B., Chetkovich, C., Katz, N., & Neblo, M. (2010). The Coevolution of Networks and Political Attitudes. *Political Communication*, 27 (3), 248–274.

Lehnert, M., Miller, B., & Wonka, A. (2007). Increasing the Relevance of Research Questions. Considerations on Theoretical and Social Relevance. In T. Gschwend & F. Schimmelfennig (Eds.), *Research Design in Political Science: How to Practice What They Preach* (pp. 21–40). Basingstoke: Palgrave Macmillan.

Leopold, D., & Stears, M. (2008). *Political Theory: Methods and Approaches*. New York: Oxford University Press.

Lewis, D. (1973). Causation. *Journal of Philosophy*, 70 (17), 556–567.

Lewis, D. (1986). Causal Explanation. In *Philosophical Papers. Volume* 2 (pp. 214–240). Oxford: Oxford University Press.

Lewis, D. E. (2007). Testing Pendleton's Premise: Do Political Appointees Make Worse Bureaucrats? *Journal of Politics*, 69 (4), 1073–1088.

Lieberman, E. S. (2005). Nested Analysis as a Mixed-Method Strategy for Comparative Research. *American Political Science Review*, 99 (3), 435–452.

Lijphart, A. (1968). *The Politics of Accommodation: Pluralism and Democracy in the Netherlands*. Berkeley: University of California Press.

Lijphart, A. (1971). Comparative Politics and the Comparative Method. *American Political Science Review*, 65 (3), 682–693.

Lijphart, A. (1994). Democracies – Forms, Performance, and Constitutional Engineering. *European Journal of Political Research*, 25 (1), 1–17.

Lipsey, M. (1990). *Design Sensitivity: Statistical Power for Experimental Research*. London: Sage.

List, C., Elsholtz, C., & Seeley, T. D. (2009). Independence and Interdependence in Collective Decision Making: An Agent-Based Model of Nest-Site Choice by Honeybee Swarms. *Philosophical Transactions of the Royal Society B: Biological Sciences*, 364 (1518), 755–762.

Little, D. (1991). *Varieties of Social Explanation: An Introduction to the Philosophy of Social Science*. Boulder: Westview Press.

Little, R. J. A., & Rubin, D. B. (1989). The Analysis of Social Science Data with Missing Values. *Sociological Methods & Research*, 18 (2–3), 292–326.

Lohr, S. (2009). *Sampling: Design and Analysis*. Second edition. Boston: Brooks-Cole.

Lowe, W., Benoit, K., Mikhaylov, S., & Laver, M. (2011). Scaling Policy Preferences from Coded Political Texts. *Legislative Studies Quarterly*, 36 (1), 123–155.

Lowery, D., & Brasher, H. (2004). *Organized Interests and American Government*. New York: McGraw Hill.

Luetgert, B., & Dannwolf, T. (2009). Mixing Methods: A Nested Analysis of EU Member State Transposition Patterns. *European Union Politics*, 10 (3), 307–334.

Lumley, T. (2010). *Complex Surveys: A Guide to Analysis Using R*. Hoboken: Wiley.

Lyall, J. (2015). Process Tracing, Causal Inference, and Civil War. In A. Bennett & J. Checkel (Eds.), *Process Tracing: From Metaphor to Analytic Tool* (pp. 186–208). New York: Cambridge University Press.

Lynd, R. S., & Lynd, H. M. (1929). *Middletown: A Study in American Culture.* San Diego: Harcourt, Brace & World.

Lynd, R. S., & Lynd, H. M. (1937). *Middletown in Transition: A Study in Cultural Conflicts.* Harcourt, Brace & Co.

McCarty, N., & Meirowitz, A. (2014). *Political Game Theory: An Introduction.* New York: Cambridge University Press.

MacDonald, P. K. (2003). Useful Fiction or Miracle Maker: The Competing Epistemological Foundations of Rational Choice Theory. *American Political Science Review*, 97 (4), 551–565.

McGrayne, S. B. (2012). *The Theory That Would Not Die: How Bayes' Rule Cracked the Enigma Code, Hunted Down Russian Submarines, and Emerged Triumphant from Two Centuries of Controversy.* New Heaven: Yale University Press.

Mackie, J. L. (1965). Causes and Conditions. *American Philosophical Quarterly*, 12 (1), 245–265.

Mackie, J. L. (1974). *The Cement of the Universe.* Oxford: Oxford University Press.

Mahoney, J. (2001). Beyond Correlational Analysis: Recent Innovations in Theory and Method. *Sociological Forum*, 16 (3), 575–593.

Mahoney, J. (2012). The Logic of Process Tracing Tests in the Social Sciences. *Sociological Methods & Research*, 41 (2), 570–597.

Mahoney, J., & Rueschemeyer, D. (2003). *Comparative Historical Analysis in the Social Sciences.* Cambridge: Cambridge University Press.

Mahoney, J., Kimball, E., & Koivu, K. L. (2009). The Logic of Historical Explanation in the Social Sciences. *Comparative Political Studies*, 42 (1), 114–146.

Manski, C. (2007). *Identification for Prediction and Decision.* Cambridge: Harvard University Press.

Manski, C., & Pepper, J. (2011). Deterrence and the Death Penalty: Partial Identification Analysis Using Repeated Cross Sections. *NBER Working Paper* (17455), 1–41.

Mantzavinos, C. (2009). *Philosophy of the Social Sciences: Philosophical Theory and Scientific Practice.* Cambridge: Cambridge University Press.

Margolis, E., & Laurence, S. (1999). *Concepts: Core Readings.* Cambridge: MIT Press.

Margolis, E., & Laurence, S. (2007). *Creations of the Mind: Theories of Artifacts and Their Representation.* Oxford: Oxford University Press.

Marradi, A. (1990). Classification, Typology, Taxonomy. *Quality & Quantity*, 24 (2), 129–157.

Martin, L. W., & Vanberg, G. (2004). Policing the Bargain: Coalition Government and Parliamentary Scrutiny. *American Journal of Political Science*, 48 (1), 13–27.

Martin, L. W., & Vanberg, G. (2011). *Parliaments and Coalitions: The Role of Legislative Institutions in Multiparty Governance.* New York: Oxford University Press.

Marx, K. (1990). *Capital: Critique of Political Economy.* London: Penguin Books.

Merritt, R. L., & Rokkan, S. (1966). *Comparing Nations, The Use of Quantitative Data in Cross-National Research.* New Haven: Yale University Press.

Merton, R. (1967). *On Theoretical Sociology.* New York: The Free Press.

Miguel, E., Satyanath, S., & Sergenti, E. (2004). Economic Shocks and Civil Conflict: An Instrumental Variables Approach. *Journal of Political Economy*, 112 (4), 725–753.

Mill, J. S. (1843). *A System of Logic*. London: John W. Parker.

Monroe, B. L., Pan, J., Roberts, M. E., Sen, M., & Sinclair, B. (2015). No! Formal Theory, Causal Inference, and Big Data Are Not Contradictory Trends in Political Science. *PS: Political Science & Politics*, 48 (1), 71–74.

Moore, W. H. (2000). The Repression of Dissent: A Substitution Model of Government Coercion. *Journal of Conflict Resolution*, 44 (1), 107–127.

Morgan, D. L. (2007). Paradigms Lost and Pragmatism Regained: Methodological Implications of Combining Qualitative and Quantitative Methods. *Journal of Mixed Methods Research*, 1 (1), 48–76.

Morgan, M. (2011). *Classics of Moral and Political Theory*. Fifth edition. Indianapolis: Hackett Publishing.

Morgan, S., & Winship, C. (2007). *Counterfactuals and Causal Inference: Methods and Principles for Social Research*. Cambridge: Cambridge University Press.

Morris, I. L., Oppenheimer, J. A., & Soltan, K. E. (2004). *Politics from Anarchy to Democracy: Rational Choice in Political Science*. Stanford: Stanford University Press.

Morton, R. B., & Williams, K. (2010). *Experimental Political Science and the Study of Causality: From Nature to the Lab*. Cambridge: Cambridge University Press.

Mudde, C. (2007). *Populist Radical Right Parties in Europe*. Cambridge: Cambridge University Press.

Mullins, W. A. (1972). On the Concept of Ideology in Political Science. *American Political Science Review*, 66 (2), 498–510.

Munck, G. L., & Snyder, R. (2007). *Passion, Craft, and Method in Comparative Politics*. New York: John Hopkins University Press.

Muralidharan, K., & Prakash, N. (2013). *Cycling to School: Increasing Secondary School Enrollment for Girls in India*. NBER Working Paper (19305).

Murphy, G. (2004). *The Big Book of Concepts*. Boston: MIT Press.

Neapolitan, R. E. (2004). *Learning Bayesian Networks*. Upper Saddle River: Prentice Hall.

Nooruddin, I. (2011). *Coalition Politics and Economic Development: Credibility and the Strength of Weak Governments*. Cambridge: Cambridge University Press.

Nye, J. (2004). *Soft Power: The Means to Success in World Politics*. New York: Public Affairs.

Nyhan, B., & Reifler, J. (2010). When Corrections Fail: The Persistence of Political Misperceptions. *Political Behavior*, 32 (2), 303–330.

Omnes, R. (1999). *Understanding Quantum Mechanics*. Princeton: Princeton University Press.

Oreskes, N. (2003). *Plate Tectonics: An Insider's History of the Modern Theory of the Earth*. Boulder: Westview Press.

Osborne, M. (2003). *An Introduction to Game Theory*. Oxford: Oxford University Press.

Ostrom, E. (1965). *Public Entrepreneurship: A Case Study in Ground Water Basin Management*. Los Angeles: University of California.

Ostrom, E. (1990). *Governing the Commons: The Evolution of Institutions for Collective Action*. Cambridge: Cambridge University Press.

Ostrom, E. (1995). *Understanding Institutional Diversity*. Princeton: Princeton University Press.

Ostrom, E. (1999). Coping with Tragedies of the Commons. *Annual Review of Political Science*, 2 (1), 493–535.

Ostrom, E., Gardner, R., & Walker, J. (1994). *Rules, Games, and Common-Pool Resources*. Ann Arbor: University of Michigan Press.

Ostrom, V., & Ostrom, E. (1972). Legal and Political Conditions of Water Resource Development. *Land Economics*, 48 (1), 1–14.

Pearl, J. (2000). *Causality: Models, Reasoning, and Inference*. New York: Cambridge University Press.

Pearl, J. (2009a). Causal Inference in Statistics: An Overview. *Statistics Surveys*, 3, 96–146.

Pearl, J. (2009b). *Causality*. Second edition. New York: Cambridge University Press.

Pearl, J. (2013). Linear Models: A Useful Microscope for Causal Analysis. *Journal of Causal Inference*, 1 (1), 155–170.

Pearl, J. (2015). Comment on Ding and Miratrix: To Adjust or Not to Adjust? *Journal of Causal Inference*, 3 (1), 59–60.

Pearson, K. (1911). *Grammar of Science*. Third edition. London: A. and C. Black.

Pearson, K. (1920). Notes on the History of Correlation. *Biometrika*, 13 (1), 24–45.

Peirce, C. S. (1955). *Philosophical Writings of Peirce*. Ed. Justus Buchler. New York: Dover.

Peters, B. Guy (1998). *Comparative Politics: Theory and Method*. New York: NYU Press.

Peterson, E. (2015). The Rich Are Different: The Effect of Wealth on Partisanship. *Political Behavior*, 1–22.

Pinker, S. (2014). *The Sense of Style: The Thinking Person's Guide to Writing in the 21st Century*. London: Allen Lane.

Plümper, T., Troeger, V., & Neumayer, E. (2010). Case Selection and Causal Inference in Qualitative Research. Unpublished paper.

Poole, K. T. (2005). *Spatial Models of Parliamentary Voting*. New York: Cambridge University Press.

Poole, K. T., & Rosenthal, H. (1997). *Congress: A Political-Economic History of Roll Call Voting*. New York: Oxford University Press.

Popper, K. (1959). *The Logic of Scientific Discovery*. London: Hutchinson & Co.

Poteete, A. R., Janssen, M. A., & Ostrom, E. (2010). *Working Together: Collective Action, the Commons, and Multiple Methods in Practice*. Princeton: Princeton University Press.

Powdthavee, N., & Oswald, A. J. (2014). Does Money Make People Right-Wing and Inegalitarian? A Longitudinal Study of Lottery Winners. *Warwick University Economics Working Paper* (1039).

Powell, R. (1999). *In the Shadow of Power: States and Strategies in International Politics*. Princeton: Princeton University Press.

Przeworski, A. (2010). *Democracy and the Limits of Self-Government*. Cambridge: Cambridge University Press.

Przeworski, A., & Teune, H. (1970). *The Logic of Comparative Social Inquiry*. New York: Wiley-Interscience.

Putnam, H. (2002). *The Collapse of the Fact/Value Dichotomy and Other Essays*. Cambridge: Harvard University Press.

Putnam, R. (2000). *Bowling Alone: The Collapse and Revival of American Community*. New York: Simon and Schuster.

Quattrone, G., & Tversky, A. (1984). Causal versus Diagnostic Contingencies: On Self-Deception and on the Voter's Illusion. *Journal of Personality and Social Psychology*, 46 (2), 237–248.

Quine, W. V. O. (1951). Two Dogmas of Empiricism. *The Philosophical Review*, 60 (1), 22–43.

Raadschelders, J. C. N. (2000). *Handbook of Administrative History*. New Brunswick: Transaction Publishers.

Ragin, C. C. (1987). *The Comparative Method: Moving beyond Qualitative and Quantitative Strategies*. Berkeley: California University Press.

Ragin, C. C. (2000). *Fuzzy Set Social Science*. Chicago: University of Chicago Press.

Ragin, C. C. (2008). *Redesigning Social Inquiry: Fuzzy Sets and Beyond*. Chicago: University of Chicago Press.

Ragin, C. C., & Becker, H. S. (1992). *What is a Case? Exploring the Foundations of Social Inquiry*. Cambridge: Cambridge University Press.

Raiffa, H. (1982). *The Art and Science of Negotiation*. Cambridge: Harvard University Press.

Rawlings, L. B., & Rubio, G. M. (2005). Evaluating the Impact of Conditional Cash Transfer Programs. *World Bank Research Observer*, 20 (1), 29– 55.

Rawls, J. (1971). *Theory of Justice*. Cambridge: Harvard University Press.

Reilly, B. (2001). *Democracy in Divided Societies: Electoral Engineering for Conflict Management*. Cambridge: Cambridge University Press.

Reinhart, C. M., & Rogoff, K. S. (2010). Growth in a Time of Debt. *American Economic Review*, 100 (2), 573–578.

Reynolds, C. (1987). Flocks, Herds, and Schools: A Distributed Behavioral Model. *Computer Graphics*, 21 (4), 25–34.

Riggs, F. (1975). The Definition of Concepts. In G. Sartori, F. Riggs, & H. Teune (Eds.), *Tower of Babel: On the Definition and Analysis of Concepts in the Social Sciences* (pp. 39–76). Pittsburgh: International Studies Association.

Rihoux, B., & Ragin, C. C. (2008). *Configurational Comparative Methods: Qualitative Comparative Analysis (QCA) and Related Techniques*. Thousand Oaks: Sage.

Rohlfing, I. (2008). What You See and What You Get: Pitfalls and Principles of Nested Analysis in Comparative Research. *Comparative Political Studies*, 41 (11), 1492–1514.

Rohlfing, I. (2012). *Case Studies and Causal Inference: An Integrative Framework*. Basingstoke: Palgrave Macmillan.

Rohlfing, I. (2014). Comparative Hypothesis Testing via Process Tracing. *Sociological Methods & Research*, 43 (4), 606–642.

Rosch, E. (1973). Natural Categories. *Cognitive Psychology*, 4 (3), 328–350.

Rosch, E., & Mervis, C. B. (1975). Family Resemblances: Studies in the Internal Structure of Categories. *Cognitive Psychology*, 7 (4), 573–605.

Rosenbaum, P. R. (2002). *Observational Studies*. Second edition. New York: Springer-Verlag.

Rosenbaum, P. R. (2005). Heterogeneity and Causality. *The American Statistician*, 59 (2), 147–152.

Rosenberg, A. (2000). *Philosophy of Science: A Contemporary Introduction*. New York: Routledge.

Rubin, D. B. (1974). Estimating Causal Effects of Treatments in Randomized and Nonrandomized Studies. *Journal of Educational Psychology*, 66 (5), 688–701.

Rubin, D. B. (2005). Causal Inference Using Potential Outcomes. *Journal of the American Statistical Association*, 100 (469), 322–331.

Rueschemeyer, D. (2009). *Usable Theory: Analytic Tools for Social and Political Research*. Princeton: Princeton University Press.

Rummel, R. J. (1970). *Applied Factor Analysis*. Evanston: Northwestern University Press.

Russell, B. (1948). *Human Knowledge*. New York: Simon and Schuster.

Salmon, W. (1984). *Scientific Explanation and the Causal Structure of the World*. Princeton: Princeton University Press.

Salmon, W. (1998). *Causality and Explanation*. New York: Oxford University Press.

Salsburg, D. (2001). *The Lady Tasting Tea: How Statistics Revolutionized Science in the Twentieth Century*. New York: Henry Holt.

Sarsons, H. (2015). Rainfall and Conflict: A Cautionary Tale. *Journal of Development Economics*, 115, 62–72.

Sartori, G. (1970). Concept Misformation in Comparative Politics. *American Political Science Review*, 64 (4), 1033–1053.

Sartori, G. (1975). The Tower of Babel. In G. Sartori, F. Riggs, & H. Teune (Eds.), *Tower of Babel: On the Definition and Analysis of Concepts in the Social Sciences* (pp. 7–38). Pittsburgh: International Studies Association.

Sauermann, J., & Kaiser, A. (2010). Taking Others into Account: Self-Interest and Fairness in Majority Decision Making. *American Journal of Political Science*, 54 (3), 667–685.

Savun, B., & Tirone, D. C. (2012). Exogenous Shocks, Foreign Aid, and Civil War. *International Organization*, 66 (3), 363–393.

Schatz, E. (2013). *Political Ethnography: What Immersion Contributes to the Study of Power*. Chicago: University of Chicago Press.

Schelling, T. (1969). Models of Segregation. *American Economic Review*, 59 (2), 488–493.

Schelling, T. (1971). Dynamic Models of Segregation. *Journal of Mathematical Sociology*, 1 (2), 143–186.

Schelling, T. (2006). *Micromotives and Macrobehavior*. New York: W. W. Norton.

Schneider, C. Q., & Rohlfing, I. (2013). Combining QCA and Process Tracing in Set-Theoretic Multi-Method Research. *Sociological Methods & Research*, 42 (4), 559–597.

Schneider, C. Q., & Rohlfing, I. (2014). Case Studies Nested in Fuzzy-Set QCA on Sufficiency. Formalizing Case Selection and Causal Inference. *Sociological Methods & Research*, 0049124114532446.

Schneider, C. Q., & Wagemann, C. (2010). Standards of Good Practice in Qualitative Comparative Analysis (QCA) and Fuzzy-Sets. *Comparative Sociology*, 9 (3), 397–418.

Schneider, C. Q., & Wagemann, C. (2012). *Set-Theoretic Methods for the Social Sciences: A Guide to Qualitative Comparative Analysis*. Cambridge: Cambridge University Press.

Schorlemmer, D., Wiemer, S., & Wyss, M. (2005). Variations in Earthquake-Size Distribution across Different Stress Regimes. *Nature*, 437 (7058), 539–542.

Schram, S., & Caterino, B. (2006). *Making Political Science Matter: Debating Knowledge, Research and Method*. New York: New York University Press.

Schuck, A. R. T., & de Vreese, C. H. (2006). Between Risk and Opportunity – News Framing and Its Effects on Public Support for EU Enlargement. *European Journal of Communication*, 21 (1), 5–32.

Schwartz-Shea, P., & Yanow, D. (2012). *Interpretive Research Design: Concepts and Processes*. New York: Routledge.

Scott Long, J. (1997). *Regression Models for Categorical and Limited Dependent Variables*. Thousand Oaks: Sage.

Scriven, M. (1959). Explanation and Prediction in Evolutionary Theory. *Science*, 30, 477–482.

Seawright, J. (2005). Qualitative Comparative Analysis vis-à-vis Regression. *Studies in Comparative International Development*, 40 (1), 3–26.

Sekhon, J., & Titiunik, R. (2012). When Natural Experiments Are Neither Natural Nor Experiments. *American Political Science Review*, 106 (1), 35–57.

Selznick, P. (1949). *TVA and the Grass Roots: A Study in the Sociology of Formal Organization*. Berkeley: University of California Press.

Shadish, W. R., Cook, T. D., & Campbell, D. T. (2002). *Experimental and Quasi-Experimental Designs for Generalized Causal Inference*. Boston: Houghton Mifflin.

Shalizi, C. (n.d.) Advanced Data Analysis from an Elementary Point of View. Unpublished Manuscript.

Sharma, S. (1996). *Applied Multivalued Techniques*. New York: Wiley.

Shepsle, K. A. (2010). *Analyzing Politics: Rationality, Behavior, and Institutions*. Second edition. New York: W. W. Norton.

Shoemaker, P., Tankard, J., & Lasorsa, D. (2004). *How to Build Social Science Theories*. Thousand Oaks: Sage.

Shuker, K. (2000). A Sense of Disaster. In A. Grayson (Ed.), *Equinox: The Earth* (pp. 177–212). Basingstoke and Oxford: Channel 4 Books.

Sigelman, C. K., Sigelman, L., Walkosz, B. J., & Nitz, M. (1995). Black Candidates, White Voters: Understanding Racial Bias in Political Perceptions. *American Journal of Political Science*, 39 (1), 243–265.

Sinclair, B., McConnell, M., & Green, D. P. (2012). Detecting Spillover Effects: Design and Analysis of Multilevel Experiments. *American Journal of Political Science*, 56 (4), 1055–1069.

Singer, B., Ryff, C. D., Carr, D., & Magee, W. J. (1998). Linking Life Histories and Mental Health: A Person-Centered Strategy. *Sociological Methodology*, 28 (1), 1–51.

Skemer, D. (1991). Drifting Disciplines, Enduring Records: Political Science and the Use of Archives. *The American Archivist*, 54 (3), 356–368.

Sloman, S. (2005). *Causal Models: How People Think about the World and Its Alternatives*. New York: Oxford University Press.

Small, M. L. (2011). How to Conduct a Mixed Methods Study: Recent Trends in a Rapidly Growing Literature. *Sociology*, 37 (1), 57.

Soroka, S., & Wlezien, C. (2010). *Degrees of Democracy: Politics, Public Opinion, and Policy*. Cambridge: Cambridge University Press.

Steenbergen, M. R., & Marks, G. (2007). Evaluating Expert Judgments. *European Journal of Political Research*, 46 (3), 347–366.

Steunenberg, B. (1994). Decision Making under Different Institutional Arrangements: Legislation by the European Community. *Journal of Institutional and Theoretical Economics (JITE)/Zeitschrift für die gesamte Staatswissenschaft*, 642–669.

Steunenberg, B., Schmidtchen, D., & Koboldt, C. (1999). Strategic Power in the European Union: Evaluating the Distribution of Power in Policy Games. *Journal of Theoretical Politics*, 11 (3), 339–366.

Stinchcombe, A. (1968). *Constructing Social Theories*. Chicago: Chicago University Press.

Stoker, G., Guy Peters, B., & Pierre, J. (eds.) (2015). The Relevance of Political Science. Basingstoke: Palgrave Macmillan.

Stone, J. (2013). *Bayes' Rule: A Tutorial Introduction to Bayesian Analysis*. Sheffield: Sebtel Press.

Taagepera, R. (2008). *Making Social Sciences More Scientific: The Need for Predictive Models*. New York: Oxford University Press.

Teddlie, C., & Tashakkori, A. (2009). *Foundations of Mixed Methods Research*. Thousand Oaks: Sage.

Tetlock, P. E. (2006). *Expert Political Judgment: How Good Is It? How Can We Know?* Princeton: Princeton University Press.

Teune, H. (1975). On the Analysis of Concepts. In G. Sartori, F. Riggs, & H. Teune (Eds.), *Tower of Babel: On the Definition and Analysis of Concepts in the Social Sciences* (pp. 77–94). Pittsburgh: International Studies Association.

Thomson, R. (2011). *Resolving Controversy in the European Union*. Cambridge: Cambridge University Press.

Thomson, R., Stokman, F., Achen, C., & König, T. (2006). *The European Union Decides*. Cambridge: Cambridge University Press.

Thorbjørnsrud, K. (2015). Mediatization of Public Bureaucracies: Administrative versus Political Loyalty. *Scandinavian Political Studies*, 38 (2), 179–197.

Tilly, C. (1975). *The Formation of National States in Western Europe*. Princeton: Princeton University Press.

Tilly, C. (2003). Inequality, Democratization, and De-democratization. *Sociological Theory*, 21 (1), 37–43.

Tomz, M. (2007). Domestic Audience Costs in International Relations: An Experimental Approach. *International Organization*, 61 (4), 821–840.

Toonen, T. A. J., Dijkstra, G. S. A., & Van Der Meer, F. (2006). Modernization and Reform of Dutch Waterboards: Resilience or Change? *Journal of Institutional Economics*, 2 (2), 181–201.

Toshkov, D. (2013). Policy-Making beyond Political Ideology: The Adoption of Smoking Bans in Europe. *Public Administration*, 91 (2), 448–468.

Toshkov, D. (2014). The Dynamic Relationship between Asylum Applications and Recognition Rates in Europe (1987–2010). *European Union Politics*, 15 (2), 192–214.

Toulmin, S. (1961). *Foresight and Understanding: An Enquiry into the Aims of Science*. Bloomington: Indiana University Press.

Treier, S., & Jackman, S. (2002). Beyond Factor Analysis: Modern Tools for Social Measurement. Paper presented at the *Annual Meeting of the Western Political Science Association* paper.

Tsebelis, G. (1990). Are Sanctions Effective? A Game-Theoretic Analysis. *Journal of Conflict Resolution*, 34 (1), 3–28.

Tversky, B., & Marsh, E. J. (2000). Biased Retellings of Events Yield Biased Memories. *Cognitive Psychology*, 40 (1), 1–38.

Vaisey, S. (2014). Comment: QCA Works When Used with Care. *Sociological Methodology*, 44 (1), 108–112.

Valliant, R., Dever, J., & Kreuter, F. (2013). *Practical Tools for Designing and Weighting Survey Samples*. New York: Springer-Verlag.

Van Evera, S. (1997). *Guide to Methods for Students of Political Science*. Ithaca: Cornell University Press.

Vayda, A., & Walters, B. (2011). *Causal Explanation for Social Scientists: A Reader*. Lanham: AltaMira Press.

Voltaire (1924). *The Philosophical Dictionary*. Selected and Translated by H.I. Woolf. New York: Knopf.

Waldner, D. (2012). Process Tracing and Causal Mechanisms. In H. Kincaid (Ed.), *The Oxford Handbook of Philosophy of Social Science* (pp. 65–84). New York: Oxford University Press.

Waldner, D. (2015). What Makes Process Tracing Good? Causal Mechanisms, Causal Inference, and the Completeness Standard in Comparative Politics. In A. Bennett & J. Checkel (Eds.), *Process Tracing: From Metaphor to Analytic Tool* (pp. 126–152). New York: Cambridge University Press.

Wallerstein, I. (2004). *World-Systems Analysis: An Introduction*. Durham: Duke University Press.

Wang, J., Conder, J. A., Blitzer, D. N., & Shinkareva, S. V. (2010). Neural Representation of Abstract and Concrete Concepts: A Meta-analysis of Neuroimaging Studies. *Human Brain Mapping*, 31 (10), 1459–1468.

Ward, M. D., Stovel, K., & Sacks, A. (2011). Network Analysis and Political Science. *Annual Review of Political Science*, 14 (1), 245–264.

Wason, P. C. (1960). On the Failure to Eliminate Hypotheses in a Conceptual Task. *Quarterly Journal of Experimental Psychology*, 12 (3), 129–140.

Weber, M. (1947). *The Theory of Social and Economic Organization*. Translated by A. M. Henderson and T. Parsons. London: Collier Macmillan Publishers.

Wedeen, L. (2010). Reflections on Ethnographic Work in Political Science. *Annual Review of Political Science*, 13 (1), 255–272.

Weller, N., & Barnes, J. (2014). *Finding Pathways: Mixed-Method Research for Studying Causal Mechanisms*. Cambridge: Cambridge University Press.

Weston, A. (2008). *A Rulebook for Arguments*. Indianapolis: Hackett.

Whang, T. (2010). Empirical Implications of Signaling Models: Estimation of Belief Updating in International Crisis Bargaining. *Political Analysis*, 18 (3), 381–402.

Wildavsky, A. (1979). *Speaking Truth to Power: The Art and Craft of Policy Analysis*. Boston: Little, Brown and Co.

Wlezien, C. (1995). The Public as Thermostat: Dynamics of Preferences for Spending. *American Journal of Political Science*, 39 (4), 981–1000.

Wolf, F. (2010). Enlightened Eclecticism or Hazardous Hotchpotch? Mixed Methods and Triangulation Strategies in Comparative Public Policy Research. *Journal of Mixed Methods Research*, 4 (2), 144–167.

Wolff, J. (2011). *Ethics and Public Policy: A Philosophical Inquiry.* Abington and New York: Routledge.

Wonka, A., Baumgartner, F. R., Mahoney, C., & Berkhout, J. (2010). Measuring the Size and Scope of the EU Interest Group Population. *European Union Politics*, 11 (3), 463–476.

Woodward, J. (2003). *Making Things Happen: A Theory of Causal Explanation.* New York: Oxford University Press.

Yin, R. K. (2008). *Case Study Research: Design and Methods.* Fourth edition. Thousand Oaks: Sage.

Zwane, A. P., Zinman, J., Van Dusen, E., Pariente, W., Null, C., Miguel, E., Kremer, M., Karlan, D. S., Hornbeck, R., Giné, X., Duflo, E., Devoto, F., Crepon, B., & Banerjee, A. (2011). Being Surveyed Can Change Later Behavior and Related Parameter Estimates. *Proceedings of the National Academy of Sciences,* 108 (5), 1821–1826.

Index